DIVERSITY IN CONTEMPORARY AMERICAN POLITICS AND GOVERNMENT

Edited by

DAVID A. DULIO

ERIN E. O'BRIEN

JOHN S. KLEMANSKI

PEARSON
Longman

New York   San Francisco   Boston
London   Toronto   Sydney   Tokyo   Singapore   Madrid
Mexico City   Munich   Paris   Cape Town   Hong Kong   Montreal

Editor-in-Chief: Eric Stano
Assistant Editor: Donna Garnier
Executive Marketing Manager: Ann Stypuloski
Production Coordinator: Scarlett Lindsay
Project Coordination and Electronic Page Makeup: Lorraine Patsco
Senior Cover Design Manager: Nancy Danahy
Cover Designer: Nancy Sacks
Cover Illustration/Photo: Stockbyte/Getty Images Inc.
Photo Researcher: Rebecca Karamehmedovic
Senior Manufacturing Buyer: Roy L. Pickering, Jr.
Printer and Binder: RR Donnelley & Sons Company / Crawfordsville
Cover Printer: RR Donnelley & Sons Company / Crawfordsville

For permission to use copyrighted material, grateful acknowledgment is made to the copyright holders on page 346, which is hereby made part of this copyright page.

Library of Congress Cataloging-in-Publication Data

Dulio, David A.
  Diversity in contemporary American politics and government / David A.
Dulio, Erin E. O'Brien, John S. Klemanski.
      p. cm.
  Includes bibliographical references and index.
  ISBN-13: 978-0-205-55036-4 (alk. paper)
  ISBN-10: 0-205-55036-3 (alk. paper)
  1. Political participation--United States. 2. Equality--United States. 3.
Cultural pluralism--Political aspects--United States. 4. Political
culture--United States. 5. United States--Politics and government--1989-
I. O'Brien, Erin E. II. Klemanski, John S. III. Title.
  JK1764.D85 2009
  320.97308--dc22
                              2008039726

Copyright © 2009 by Pearson Education, Inc.

Visit us at www.pearsonhighered.com

ISBN-13: 978-0-205-55036-4
ISBN-10:   0-205-55036-3

2 3 4 5 6 7 8 9 10—DOC—11 10 09

For
Abby and Sophia
D.A.D.

For
my students
EO'B

In memory of my Mom, Mary Marshall, who taught me
tolerance, curiosity, and humor
J.S.K.

CONTENTS

Alternative Contents: Demographic Groupings   ix

Acknowledgments   xvii

About the Editors   xix

Introduction   1

Section 1: The Constitution and Contested Notions of Equality   7

READING 1: "Equal Rights Redux: The Three-State Solution," Jonathan Turley   9
READING 2: "Whatever Happened to the ERA?" Jane Mansbridge   12
READING 3: "Supreme Confusion," Terry Eastland   17
READING 4: "Unsound Constitution," George P. Fletcher   20

Section 2: Federalism: Governmental Competition or Cooperation?   27

READING 1: "When Government Fails—Katrina's Aftermath," *The Economist*   29
READING 2: "Judge Rejects Hazleton Law on Immigrants; A City Cannot Take Such a National Issue into Its Own Hands, He Says," David G. Savage and Nicole Gaouette   34
READING 3: "A Ban We Don't (Yet) Need," Charles Krauthammer   37
READING 4: "Welfare Policy Choices in the States: Does the Hard Line Follow the Color Line?" Joe Soss, Sanford F. Schram, Thomas P. Vartanian, and Erin E. O'Brien   39

Section 3: American Political Culture: Notions and Boundaries   48

READING 1: "What Is the American Dream?" Jennifer Hochschild   50
READING 2: "Poverty Weaves Through the Lives of Many Americans," Jean Hopfensperger   63
READING 3: "Racial Discrimination Still at Work," David Wessel   66
READING 4: "The End of Multiculturalism," Lawrence E. Harrison   69

Section 4: Public Opinion: Many Voices?   74

READING 1: "The Male Perspective," Roberta Sigel   76
READING 2: "Race, Income, and Perceptions of the U.S. Court System," Richard R.W. Brooks and Haekyung Jeon-Slaughter   84
READING 3: "Religion and Public Opinion about Same-Sex Marriage," Laura R. Olson, Wendy Cadge, and James T. Harrison   88
READING 4: "Support for Vouchers," Terry Moe   97

Section 5:   Political Participation: Definitions, Patterns, and Consequences   108

READING 1:   "American Democracy in an Age of Rising Inequality," American
Political Science Association Task Force   110

READING 2:   "The Double-Edged Sword of Women's Organizing: Poverty and
the Emergence of Racial and Class Differences in Women's Policy
Priorities," Erin E. O'Brien   119

READING 3:   "Mass Imprisonment and the Disappearing Voters," Marc Mauer   128

READING 4:   "Several Factors Contributed to 'Lost' Voters in Ohio," Michael
Powell and Peter Slevin   132

Section 6:   Political Parties: Who Gets Invited?   138

READING 1:   "Party Coalitions and Party Change," Marjorie Randon Hershey   139

READING 2:   "The American Debate: GOP Drops the Ball on Hispanic Vote,"
Dick Polman   150

READING 3:   "How Gay Republican Strategies Can Advance the Gay Equality
Movement," Richard Tafel   153

READING 4:   "Can Women Enter the 'Big Tents'? National Party Structures and
Presidential Nominations," Melissa Haussman   160

**Section 7:   Organized Interest Groups: What Are Interests and Who
Organizes Them?   169**

READING 1:   "EMILY's List: A Force for 20 Years," Margaret Talev   171

READING 2:   "Injecting a Woman's Voice: Conservative Women's Organizations,
Gender Consciousness, and the Expression of Women's Policy
Preferences," Ronnee Schreiber   173

READING 3:   "African-Americans, Latinos Seek to Build Coalition," Janita Poe   188

READING 4:   "Number of Black Lobbyists Shockingly Low," Jeffrey H.
Birnbaum   191

Section 8:   Media Sources and the Politics of Use and Representation   195

READING 1:   "Who's Talking Now: A Follow-Up Analysis of Guest
Appearances by Women on Sunday Morning Talk Shows,"
TheWhite House Project   197

READING 2:   "Correlational Framing: Media Portrayals of Race and Poverty,"
Martin Gilens   207

READING 3:   "American Women and Politics in the Media: A Review Essay,"
Stephanie Greco Larson   213

READING 4:   "The Access Divide," Karen Mossberger, Caroline J. Tolbert,
and Mary Stansbury with Ramona McNeal   217

Section 9:   Campaigns and Elections: Searching for Voters   228

READING 1:   "Looking for Voters in All the New Places: Hispanic Immigrants
             Are Settling in Unexpected Spots, and Pols Scramble to Enlist Their
             Support," Ari Pinkus   230
READING 2:   "The Man from New Mexico; The Candidates: Bill Richardson
             and the Latino Vote," *The Economist*   232
READING 3:   "The Rules for Female Candidates," Libby Copeland   235
READING 4:   "Who Voted?" Paul R. Abramson, John H. Aldrich, and
             David W. Rohde   238

Section 10: The Legislative Branch: How Representative Is It?   249

READING 1:   "Hill Demographic Goes Slightly More Female," Lois Romano   251
READING 2:   "The Representation of Black Interests in Congress," Carol Swain   253
READING 3:   "Representing Women's Interests in the U.S. House of
             Representatives," Debra L. Dodson   257
READING 4:   "In the Eye of the Overhaul Storm," Martin Kady II   268

Section 11: The Executive Branch: More Than a One-*Man* Show   275

READING 1:   "Is America Too Racist for Barack? Too Sexist for Hillary?"
             Benjamin Wallace-Wells   277
READING 2:   "Presidential Leadership: Governance from a Woman's
             Perspective," Lori Cox Han   281
READING 3:   "Bush Is Opening Doors with a Diverse Cabinet," Susan Page   292
READING 4:   "Political Appointees in the United States: Does Gender Make a
             Difference?" Julie Dolan   295

Section 12: The Courts: Symbolic and Substantive Representation   304

READING 1:   "Some Disappointed Nominee Won't Add Diversity to Court,"
             Dan Balz and Darryl Fears   306
READING 2:   "The First Latino Supreme Court Justice?" Kevin R. Johnson   309
READING 3:   "A Diversity of Minds, Not Biology," Cass R. Sunstein   312
READING 4:   "Representative Decision Making on the Federal Bench: Clinton's
             District Court Appointees," Jennifer A. Segal   314

**Section 13: Civil Rights and Civil Liberties: Protecting *Everyone's* Rights
             in a Democracy   323**

READING 1:   "An Ode to Justice Lewis F. Powell, Jr.: The Supreme Court
             Approves the Consideration of Race as a Factor in Admissions by
             Public Institutions of Higher Education," James E. Coleman, Jr.   325
READING 2:   "Wal-Mart Values," Liza Featherstone   328

READING 3: "Flying while Arab: Lessons from the Racial Profiling
              Controversy," David Harris   333
READING 4: "Similar Struggles: Gay Rights and Civil Rights," Eric Deggans   339

Photo Credits   **346**

ALTERNATIVE CONTENTS:
DEMOGRAPHIC GROUPINGS

I. Age

SECTION 8: Media Sources and the Politics of Use and Representation
+ "The Access Divide," Karen Mossberger, Caroline J. Tolbert, and Mary Stansbury with Ramona McNeal   217

SECTION 9: Campaigns and Elections: Searching for Voters
+ "Who Voted?" Paul R. Abramson, John H. Aldrich, and David W. Rohde   238

II. Considering the Concept of "Demographic Diversity" and U.S. American Politics

SECTION 1: The Constitution and Contested Notions of Equality
+ "Unsound Constitution," George P. Fletcher   20

SECTION 3: American Political Culture: Notions and Boundaries
+ "The End of Multiculturalism," Lawrence E. Harrison   69

SECTION 10: The Legislative Branch: How Representative Is It?
+ "In the Eye of the Overhaul Storm," Martin Kady II   268

SECTION 11: The Executive Branch: More Than a One-*Man* Show
+ "Is America Too Racist for Barack? Too Sexist for Hillary?" Benjamin Wallace-Wells   277
+ "Bush Is Opening Doors with a Diverse Cabinet," Susan Page   292

SECTION 12: The Courts: Symbolic and Substantive Representation
+ "Some Disappointed Nominee Won't Add Diversity to Court," Dan Balz and Darryl Fears   306
+ "A Diversity of Minds, Not Biology," Cass R. Sunstein   312
+ "Representative Decision Making on the Federal Bench: Clinton's District Court Appointees," Jennifer A. Segal   314

SECTION 13: Civil Rights and Civil Liberties: Protecting *Everyone's* Rights in a Democracy
+ "An Ode to Justice Lewis F. Powell, Jr.: The Supreme Court Approves the Consideration of Race as a Factor in Admissions by Public Institutions of Higher Education," James E. Coleman, Jr.   325

III. Gender

SECTION 1: The Constitution and Contested Notions of Equality
+ "Equal Rights Redux: The Three-State Solution," Jonathan Turley   9
+ "Whatever Happened to the ERA?," Jane Mansbridge   12

SECTION 3: American Political Culture: Notions and Boundaries
✦ "What Is the American Dream?," Jennifer Hochschild   50

SECTION 4: Public Opinion: Many Voices?
✦ "The Male Perspective," Roberta Sigel   76

SECTION 5: Political Participation: Definitions, Patterns, and Consequences
✦ "The Double-Edged Sword of Women's Organizing: Poverty and the Emergence of Racial and Class Differences in Women's Policy Priorities," Erin E. O'Brien   119

SECTION 6: Political Parties: Who Gets Invited?
✦ "Party Coalitions and Party Change," Marjorie Randon Hershey   139
✦ "Can Women Enter the 'Big Tents'? National Party Structures and Presidential Nominations," Melissa Haussman   160

SECTION 7: Organized Interest Groups: What Are Interests and Who Organizes Them?
✦ "EMILY's List: A Force for 20 Years," Margaret Talev   171
✦ "Injecting a Woman's Voice: Conservative Women's Organizations, Gender Consciousness, and the Expression of Women's Policy Preferences," Ronnee Schreiber   173

SECTION 8: Media Sources and The Politics of Use and Representation
✦ "Who's Talking Now: A Follow-Up Analysis of Guest Appearances by Women on Sunday Morning Talk Shows," The White House Project   197
✦ "American Women and Politics in the Media: A Review Essay," Stephanie Greco Larson   213

SECTION 9: Campaigns and Elections: Searching for Voters
✦ "The Rules for Female Candidates," Libby Copeland   235
✦ "Who Voted?" Paul R. Abramson, John H. Aldrich, and David W. Rohde   238

SECTION 10: The Legislative Branch: How Representative Is It?
✦ "Hill Demographic Goes Slightly More Female," Lois Romano   251
✦ "Representing Women's Interests in the U.S. House of Representatives," Debra L. Dodson   257
✦ "In the Eye of the Overhaul Storm," Martin Kady II   268

SECTION 11: The Executive Branch: More Than a One-*Man* Show
✦ "Is America Too Racist for Barack? Too Sexist for Hillary?" Benjamin Wallace-Wells   277
✦ "Presidential Leadership: Governance from a Woman's Perspective," Lori Cox Han   281
✦ "Political Appointees in the United States: Does Gender Make a Difference?" Julie Dolan   295

SECTION 12: The Courts: Symbolic and Substantive Representation

✦ "Some Disappointed Nominee Won't Add Diversity to Court,"
Dan Balz and Darryl Fears   306

✦ "Representative Decision Making on the Federal Bench: Clinton's
District Court Appointees," Jennifer A. Segal   314

SECTION 13: Civil Rights and Civil Liberties: Protecting *Everyone's* Rights in a
Democracy

✦ "Wal-Mart Values," Liza Featherstone   328

IV. Ethnicity

SECTION 2: Federalism: Governmental Competition or Cooperation?

✦ "Judge Rejects Hazleton Law on Immigrants; A City Cannot Take
Such a National Issue into Its Own Hands, He Says," David G. Savage
and Nicole Gaouette   34

✦ "Welfare Policy Choices in the States: Does the Hard Line Follow the Color
Line?" Joe Soss, Sanford Schram, Tom Vartanian, and Erin E. O'Brien   39

SECTION 3: American Political Culture: Notions and Boundaries

✦ "The End of Multiculturalism," Lawrence E. Harrison   69

SECTION 4: Public Opinion: Many Voices?

✦ "Race, Income, and Perceptions of the U.S. Court System,"
Richard R.W. Brooks and Haekyung Jeon-Slaughter   84

SECTION 6: Political Parties: Who Gets Invited?

✦ "Party Coalitions and Party Change," Marjorie Randon Hershey   139

✦ "The American Debate: GOP Drops the Ball on Hispanic
Vote," Dick Polman   150

SECTION 7: Organized Interest Groups: What Are Interests and Who
Organizes Them?

✦ "African-Americans, Latinos Seek to Build Coalition," Janita Poe   188

SECTION 8: Media Sources and the Politics of Use and Representation

✦ "The Access Divide," Karen Mossberger, Caroline J. Tolbert, and Mary
Stansbury with Ramona McNeal   217

SECTION 9: Campaigns and Elections: Searching for Voters

✦ "Looking for Voters in All the New Places: Hispanic Immigrants
Are Settling in Unexpected Spots, and Pols Scramble to Enlist Their
Support," Ari Pinkus   230

✦ "The Man from New Mexico; The Candidates: Bill Richardson and the
Latino Vote," *The Economist*   232

SECTION 12: The Courts: Symbolic and Substantive Representation

✦ "The First Latino Supreme Court Justice?" Kevin R. Johnson   309

SECTION 13: Civil Rights and Civil Liberties: Protecting *Everyone's* Rights in a Democracy
- ✦ "Flying while Arab: Lessons from the Racial Profiling Controversy," David Harris 333

V. Intersectionality

SECTION 4: Public Opinion: Many Voices?
- ✦ "The Male Perspective," Roberta Sigel 76
- ✦ "Race, Income, and Perceptions of the U.S. Court System," Richard R.W. Brooks and Haekyung Jeon-Slaughter 84
- ✦ "Support for Vouchers," Terry Moe 97

SECTION 5: Political Participation: Definitions, Patterns, and Consequences
- ✦ "American Democracy in an Age of Rising Inequality," American Political Science Association Task Force on Inequality and American Democracy 110
- ✦ "The Double-Edged Sword of Women's Organizing: Poverty and the Emergence of Racial and Class Differences in Women's Policy Priorities," Erin E. O'Brien 119

SECTION 6: Political Parties: Who Gets Invited?
- ✦ "How Gay Republican Strategies Can Advance the Gay Equality Movement," Richard Tafel 153

SECTION 7: Organized Interest Groups: What Are Interests and Who Organizes Them?
- ✦ "Injecting a Woman's Voice: Conservative Women's Organizations, Gender Consciousness, and the Expression of Women's Policy Preferences," Ronnee Schreiber 173

SECTION 9: Campaigns and Elections: Searching for Voters
- ✦ "Who Voted?" Paul R. Abramson, John H. Aldrich, and David W. Rohde 238

VI. Race

SECTION 1: The Constitution and Contested Notions of Equality
- ✦ "Supreme Confusion," Terry Eastland 17

SECTION 2: Federalism: Governmental Competition or Cooperation?
- ✦ "When Government Fails—Katrina's Aftermath," *The Economist* 29
- ✦ "Welfare Policy Choices in the States: Does the Hard Line Follow the Color Line?" Joe Soss, Sanford Schram, Tom Vartanian, and Erin E. O'Brien 39

SECTION 3: American Political Culture: Notions and Boundaries
- ✦ "What Is the American Dream?" Jennifer Hochschild 50
- ✦ "Racial Discrimination Still at Work," David Wessel 66
- ✦ "The End of Multiculturalism," Lawrence E. Harrison 69

SECTION 4: Public Opinion: Many Voices?

✦ "Race, Income, and Perceptions of the U.S. Court System,"
Richard R.W. Brooks and Haekyung Jeon-Slaughter   84

SECTION 5: Political Participation: Definitions, Patterns, and Consequences

✦ "American Democracy in an Age of Rising Inequality," American Political
Science Association Task Force on Inequality and American Democracy   110

✦ "The Double-Edged Sword of Women's Organizing: Poverty and the
Emergence of Racial and Class Differences in Women's Policy Priorities,"
Erin E. O'Brien   119

✦ "Mass Imprisonment and the Disappearing Voters," Marc Mauer   128

✦ "Several Factors Contributed to 'Lost' Voters in Ohio," Michael
Powell and Peter Slevin   132

SECTION 6: Political Parties: Who Gets Invited?

✦ "Party Coalitions and Party Change," Marjorie Randon Hershey   139

SECTION 7: Organized Interest Groups: What Are Interests and Who Organizes
Them?

✦ "African-Americans, Latinos Seek to Build Coalition," Janita Poe   188

✦ "Number of Black Lobbyists Shockingly Low," Jeffrey H. Birnbaum   191

SECTION 8: Media Sources and the Politics of Use and Representation

✦ "Correlational Framing: Media Portrayals of Race and Poverty,"
Martin Gilens   207

✦ "The Access Divide," Karen Mossberger, Caroline J. Tolbert, and
Mary Stansbury with Ramona McNeal   217

SECTION 9: Campaigns and Elections: Searching for Voters

✦ "Who Voted?" Paul R. Abramson, John H. Aldrich, and
David W. Rohde   238

SECTION 10: The Legislative Branch: How Representative Is It?

✦ "The Representation of Black Interests in Congress," Carol Swain   253

SECTION 11: The Executive Branch: More Than a One-*Man* Show

✦ "Is America Too Racist for Barack? Too Sexist for Hillary?" Benjamin
Wallace-Wells   277

SECTION 12: The Courts: Symbolic and Substantive Representation

✦ "Representative Decision Making on the Federal Bench: Clinton's
District Court Appointees," Jennifer A. Segal   314

SECTION 13: Civil Rights and Civil Liberties: Protecting *Everyone's* Rights in a
Democracy

✦ "An Ode to Justice Lewis F. Powell, Jr.: The Supreme Court Approves
the Consideration of Race as a Factor in Admissions by Public
Institutions of Higher Education," James E. Coleman, Jr.   325

✦ "Flying while Arab: Lessons from the Racial Profiling Controversy,"
David Harris   333

VII. Religion

SECTION 4: Public Opinion: Many Voices?
✦ "Religion and Public Opinion about Same-Sex Marriage,"
Laura R. Olson, Wendy Cadge, and James T. Harrison   88
✦ "Support for Vouchers," Terry Moe   97

SECTION 9: Campaigns and Elections: Searching for Voters
✦ "Who Voted?" Paul R. Abramson, John H. Aldrich,
and David W. Rohde   238

VIII. Sexual Orientation

SECTION 2: Federalism: Governmental Competition or Cooperation?
✦ "A Ban We Don't (Yet) Need," Charles Krauthammer   37

SECTION 4: Public Opinion: Many Voices?
✦ "Religion and Public Opinion about Same-Sex Marriage,"
Laura R. Olson, Wendy Cadge, and James T. Harrison   88

SECTION 6: Political Parties: Who Gets Invited?
✦ "Party Coalitions and Party Change," Marjorie Randon Hershey   139

SECTION 13: Civil Rights and Civil Liberties: Protecting *Everyone's*
Rights in a Democracy
✦ "Similar Struggles: Gay Rights and Civil Rights," Eric Deggans   339

IX. Social Class

SECTION 2: Federalism: Governmental Competition or Cooperation?
✦ "When Government Fails—Katrina's Aftermath," *The Economist*   29

SECTION 3: American Political Culture: Notions and Boundaries
✦ "What Is the American Dream?" Jennifer Hochschild   50
✦ "Poverty Weaves Through the Lives of Many Americans," Jean
Hopfensperger   63

SECTION 5: Political Participation: Definitions, Patterns, and Consequences
✦ "American Democracy in an Age of Rising Inequality," American Political
Science Association Task Force on Inequality and American Democracy   110
✦ "The Double-Edged Sword of Women's Organizing: Poverty and the
Emergence of Racial and Class Differences in Women's Policy Priorities,"
Erin E. O'Brien   119

✦ "Several Factors Contributed to 'Lost' Voters in Ohio," Michael Powell and Peter Slevin 132

Section 6: Political Parties: Who Gets Invited?
 ✦ "Party Coalitions and Party Change," Marjorie Randon Hershey 139

Section 8: Media Sources and the Politics of Use and Representation
 ✦ "The Access Divide," Karen Mossberger, Caroline J. Tolbert, and Mary Stansbury with Ramona McNeal 217

Section 9: Campaigns and Elections: Searching for Voters
 ✦ "Who Voted?" Paul R. Abramson, John H. Aldrich, and David W. Rohde 238

Section 13: Civil Rights and Civil Liberties: Protecting *Everyone's* Rights in a Democracy
 ✦ "Wal-Mart Values," Liza Featherstone 328

ACKNOWLEDGMENTS

This book began as a conversation between two of us on the way to a meeting in the fall of 2004, just before the presidential election. We were talking about the need to inject more content related to the diversity of the citizenry of the United States as it relates to our politics in our introductory courses. Each of us has taught many introduction to American politics courses over the years, and it was becoming obvious to us that a more explicit treatment of the importance of the differences between demographic groups of Americans was important.

As it turns out, professors and instructors at many other institutions across the United States have similar thoughts and ideas. There has been an increasing realization at universities and colleges across the nation that not only is diversity important, but that it plays a big part in a well-rounded liberal arts education. It was our goal to try and meet this new demand in a way that was both academically rigorous and accessible to students. We hope that as you read the pages that follow you will agree.

This book would not have been possible without the work and contributions of many individuals. At Oakland University, Professors Dulio and Klemanski would like to thank Provost Virinder Moudgil, Dean of the College of Arts and Sciences Ron Sudol, Associate Dean and former Chair of the Political Science Department Michelle Piskulich, and Chair of the Political Science Department Paul Kubicek for their leadership and support of not only this project but all of our scholarly endeavors. In addition, Michelle Piskulich and Julie Walters provided early guidance on the direction of many sections of the volume; and Beth Campbell, Mary Delaney, and Tim Neville helped identify possible articles. And very importantly, Karen Meyer and Katie Forzley provided invaluable research and administrative help copying, scanning, and formatting page after page of articles we included here.

At the University of Massachusetts Boston, Erin O'Brien would like to thank the Dean of the College of Liberal Arts Donna Kuizenga, the Chair of the Political Science Department Elizabeth Bussiere, and her colleagues in the Department of Political Science and the McCormack Graduate School of Policy Studies. Each of these individuals provide sound examples of how rigorous scholarship, social justice, and attention to diversity interact both empirically and in the classroom. O'Brien dedicates this volume to her students—past, present, and future. Their intellectual curiosity and willingness to engage tough issues inspires this volume and ensures that being a part of their collegiate experience is a luxury bar none.

In addition, Eric Stano and Donna Garnier were very helpful in the development not only of the final version of this book, but of the concept in general. They challenged us to refine our thinking in many places which ultimately led to a better product. In addition we would like to thank Wesley Hall for his great work obtaining the permissions for this book, Lorraine Patsco for her work as a typesetter, Scarlett Lindsay for her production help, Rebecca Karamehmedovic for researching the photos, as well as one of our Pearson book representatives Dorelle Less. Each of these individuals helped us produce a volume of which we are quite proud.

Of course, we could not have undertaken and finished this project without the help, love, and support of each of our families. For this we are eternally grateful.

ABOUT THE EDITORS

DAVID A. DULIO is Associate Professor of Political Science at Oakland University in Rochester, Michigan. He is the author of *The Mechanics of State Legislative Campaigns* (with John S. Klemanski, Wadsworth 2006), *Vital Signs: Perspectives on the Health of American Campaigning* (with Candice J. Nelson, Brookings Institution Press 2005), *For Better or Worse? How Political Consultants Are Changing Elections in the United States* (State University of New York Press 2004), and is the editor of *Crowded Airwaves: Campaign Advertising in Elections* (with James A. Thurber and Candice J. Nelson, Brookings Institutions Press 2000), and *Shades of Gray: Perspectives on Campaign Ethics* (with Candice J. Nelson and Stephen K. Medvic (Brookings Institutions Press 2002), in addition to many articles and book chapters on campaigns and elections. During 2002, Professor Dulio served as an American Political Science Association Congressional Fellow in the office of the U.S. House of Representatives Republican Conference headed by J.C. Watts, Jr. (R-Oklahoma).

ERIN E. O'BRIEN is Assistant Professor of Political Science and Faculty Affiliate in Public Policy at the University of Massachusetts Boston. Her book, *The Politics of Identity: Solidarity Building among America's Working Poor*, appears in Anne Schneider and Helen Ingram's public policy series, published by the State University of New York Press. O'Brien is also author of pieces appearing in journals such as *The American Journal of Political Science* and *Women & Politics*, as well as in books such as *Campaigns and Elections American Style* and *Race and the Politics of Welfare Reform*. She is former President of the Women's Caucus for Political Science South and teaches courses including The Politics of Poverty and Social Welfare Policy, Diversity and Public Policy, and Women and Politics.

JOHN S. KLEMANSKI is Professor of Political Science at Oakland University, in Rochester, Michigan. He is the author or co-author of over 20 articles and books, mostly on political campaigns and urban economic development politics and policy. His books include *The Mechanics of State Legislative Campaigns* (with David A. Dulio, Wadsworth 2006), *Power and City Governance* (with Alan DiGaetano, University of Minnesota Press 1999), and *The Urban Politics Dictionary* (with John W. Smith, ABC-CLIO 1990).

INTRODUCTION

"Is America Too Racist for Obama? Too Sexist for Hilary?"[1]

"Selling Plan B Pill Up to Pharmacies' Discretion"[2]

"Seniors Suffer and Endure in Sweltering CHA High-Rise"[3]

"Several Factors Contributed to 'Lost' Voters in Ohio"[4]

"Gay Marriage Ban Belongs to Legislators, Justices Say"[5]

Imagine you are reading the morning paper. At least two or three of the above headlines might make you want read further. This is because each of the headlines involve defining issues in U.S. politics; they are also issues that are interesting and, most often, the subject of considerable debate. They cover lightening-rod issues that capture the challenges and conflicts that define U.S. politics.

A closer examination of these headlines reveals something else: demographic diversity in the United States interweaves itself throughout each of them:

+ *Is America Too Racist for Obama? Too Sexist for Hilary?* This article speculates about the prospects of electing a black male or a white female as President of the United States. Regardless of what you think the answers to these questions are, answering them requires discussing race, ethnicity, gender, and presidential politics.

+ *Selling Plan B Pill Up to Pharmacies' Discretion.* Perhaps you believe pharmacists should be allowed to make their own choice as to whether or not they provide the controversial contraceptive "Plan B" based on the their personal beliefs. Perhaps you think that because Plan B has been approved for distribution by the Food and Drug Administration that pharmacists must unilaterally provide this reproductive option. Maybe you are unsure. One certainty, however, is that taking on this question means operating at the nexus of gender and public policy in the United States.

+ *Seniors Suffer and Endure in Sweltering CHA High-Rise.* If this headline leads you to read the accompanying article, you would learn of the disproportionate deaths Chicago's poor elderly suffered during the heat wave of 1995. Trying to keep history from repeating itself requires engaging local politics, federalism, and disaster relief management along with issues of age, social class, race, and ethnicity. Diversity and American politics again interact.

+ *Several Factors Contributed to "Lost" Voters in Ohio.* What is more important, and potentially more damning to the legitimacy of American democracy than allegations of voter fraud? Democrats, Republicans, Independents, and those of other political stripes can agree that voter fraud undermines democracy. Figuring out whether the 2004 election involved such fraud, however, is decidedly more tricky, and piecing together an answer means conversations involving race, ethnicity, social class, political participation, and election administration.

1

+ *Gay Marriage Ban Belongs to Legislators, Justices Say.* Opinions on this question run the gamut. You may vehemently disagree with the student who sits next to you, but each of you can agree that this issue involves sexual orientation as well as civil rights, civil liberties, public opinion, and the courts.

The pattern is clear: many of the defining issues in U.S. politics are deeply intertwined with demographic diversity. Whether it is political participation, the courts, the media, or some other facet of U.S. politics, demographic diversity is usually involved. Realizing this allows you as a student of politics to more fully engage American governance and political culture. Demographic diversity is surely not all that matters for U.S. politics but, as the above headlines and those that likely appear in today's paper surely attest, diversity continually influences American politics. *This is the thesis of this volume: Demographic diversity and American politics are intricately interwoven and affect political outcomes and policy processes.*

DEFINING DIVERSITY

Diversity, of course, can mean many things to different people. Given the thesis of this book, however, we define "diversity" as *the demographic differences within the American population.* Using this demographic definition, we focus most explicitly on the politics of race, ethnicity, gender, social class, and sexual orientation as these group cleavages have been most influential in American politics to date. However, we also take up group cleavages such as immigration status and age because of the ways in which they shape American political processes and outcomes.

For example, differences in race, ethnicity, and gender can produce different values, norms, and perspectives—and these differences can produce cleavages and conflict. In this book, you will encounter pieces that encourage you to think about issues such as the conflicts—and the politics involved in conflict resolution—that arise in a diverse society over who gets what, when, and how, as well as the importance of governmental power and authority in these issues. You will also encounter readings focusing on legal issues of discrimination and equal opportunity/access and equity, as well as stigmatization and privilege. You will also see the value of the contributions made by individuals and groups representing different races, genders, and ethnic groups, along with the increasing importance of "identity politics" in contemporary U.S. politics. Finally, there is the opportunity to examine different political events through a diversity lens that will assist the reader in engaging familiar issues from the (sometimes different) perspective of others. As this volume will show, it is possible to explore in detail—and in manifold applications—how the theme of diversity is a core aspect of American politics.

Once you have a better understanding of diversity and its role in contemporary American politics, we believe you also will realize its importance and relevance to you—and to modern life in the United States. The diversity of the U.S. population is a given and constantly evolving. For example, the year 2007 saw nonwhites become the majority of the population in over 30 percent of the most-populous counties in the United States and in one in ten of the total of over 3,100 counties.[6] In addition, Latinos surpassed African-Americans as the largest minority group in the United States according to the 2000 Census. Such changes affect everyone who seeks to live, work, and function as an informed citizen of the United States and the world.

DIVERSITY'S IMPORTANCE FOR AMERICAN POLITICS

The readings in each section highlight issues related to these demographic changes and the continuing reality of the diverse U.S. population. They do so for each major field of American politics. Collectively, the readings demonstrate the myriad ways that the diversity of our citizenry is intertwined with American politics, and present a variety of perspectives on these issues. For example, Section 2, on federalism, includes readings that demonstrate government's role in the response to Hurricane Katrina and the disproportionate impact felt by the poorest residents of New Orleans—themselves disproportionately black. Federalism is also shown to interact with gender politics; another reading, for example, shows how decisions on an issue as pressing as gender-based employment discrimination can turn on federalism. Readings on political culture consider the role of the American Dream, definitions of just what American political culture is, and quality of life standards in the United States from a diversity angle. One reading demonstrates how, for instance, poor and more affluent African-Americans view the American Dream. In another, Lawrence Harrison argues that Latino immigration are maintaining the culture of their countries of origin and this poses a threat to American virtues.

As these examples attest, highlighting the relationship between American politics and diversity does not promote a particular political party or ideology. Those of every political persuasion, for example, can agree that sexual orientation is a major cleavage in American politics that influences public opinion (gay adoption), campaigns and elections (referenda on gay marriage and/or domestic partnerships), or public policy (gay marriage law). The *answers* individuals craft to these questions may sometimes fall along party lines, but *making the connection* between demographic diversity and so many of the most pressing issues in American politics is not partisan. This volume seeks *not* to tell you what the answers to these questions are. Rather, we seek to help you draw the manifold connections between U.S. politics and American demographic diversity.

WHY DOES THIS MATTER TO YOU?

As a student of American politics, you are setting out on a journey to understand how politics operates and unfolds in the United States. That journey begins now, but a longer-term goal will be reached when you have the tools to thoughtfully engage politics long after you complete this course. Twenty years from now, you should be able to pick up a newspaper, understand what is happening around you, and ask critical questions about it. You should feel comfortable with your capability to not only engage politics, but to affect it. Understanding how diversity interacts with American politics is central to that process. If you want to truly understand why some issues (such as abortion, immigration, or gay marriage) are so deeply felt, if you want to see why opinions sometimes diverge so much on matters of politics and public policy, then you must be able to see the role that diversity is playing. American politics does not start and end with diversity, but neither can American politics be adequately understood or changed without applying the diversity lens this volume provides.

A diversity lens matters because it helps you ask pressing questions about the major issues of the day and helps you answer them. You will be able to see the role of diversity in shaping American politics as well as be able to thoughtfully discuss places where it is not as relevant. In short, with this lens, you gain more insight into politics and an increased ability from which to critique and engage it.

PLAN AND ORGANIZATION OF THE BOOK

The plan of the book is simple: to provide articles in each of the major subfields of American politics that are interesting, speak to major debates/issues in U.S. politics, and make the diversity overlay apparent. We have organized the volume into thirteen sections. Each section reflects a major field of U.S. politics. They include: the Constitution and Founding; Federalism; Political Culture; Public Opinion; Political Participation; Political Parties; Interest Groups; Mass Media; Campaigns and Elections; the Legislative Branch; the Executive Branch; the Courts; and Civil Rights and Liberties. If your class uses a standard American politics textbook, you may notice that these sections mirror the major chapters in that text.

Each section provides four readings on the relevant field that show how diversity informs that slice of American politics. The specific topic of each reading within a section often differs. Which group cleavage or mix of cleavages highlighted also regularly differs from reading to reading. All the readings, however, demonstrate how diversity informs one of the areas in U.S. politics.

We could have included only one type of article—just newspapers, just blog entries, or just scholarly pieces—but doing so would not illustrate the range of opinions or forms that political journalism and the systematic study of politics can take. Thus, we selected a wide range of pieces from several types of sources: newspapers, magazines, think tank reports, academic journal articles, and book chapters. In some instances, it is clear that the author or authors of a particular selection have an ideological slant. In others, there is no obvious normative component or ideological viewpoint to the particular piece because it is based on empirical evidence. In any case, when reading a particular selection that follows in any of the sections, you should always consider the source of the argument being made and whether or not there is an equally compelling argument from another perspective.

We also could have provided articles that only looked at gender. Or only looked at race. Or only looked at sexual orientation. But this would not reflect the volume's thesis. It is demographic diversity *in its whole* that plays such a central role in American politics. Singular attention to race or singular attention to social class are very appropriate, but appropriate in other venues.

The organization of this book lets you see the range of diversity applications. To this end, your instructor may or may not assign every reading in this volume. Regardless of your instructor's decision, the organization of this book allows you to see diversity in action.

GOALS OF THE VOLUME

Our primary goal with this volume is to help students recognize how American politics and demographic diversity interact, and then assist you in identifying the multiple impacts this interaction has across U.S. political processes. Other benefits include a more well-rounded understanding of politics. Reading the range of articles in this book provides information on defining issues of the day. You will learn more about the "nuts-and-bolts" of everyday political issues, such as affirmative action. While it is clear that diversity is at the heart of any affirmative action debate, you will also learn how this policy relates to university admissions.

Another goal of the volume is to expose you to the wide array of source materials where politics is discussed and debated. Including materials from original texts, magazines, book chapters, newspapers, and academic journals allows your instructor flexibility in selecting what pieces work best with your course. This range of materials lets you experience different styles of political writing and scholarship. Politics is not just reported or discussed in the newspaper, nor is it only studied in scholarly books or journal articles.

Our final goal involves your improved ability to think critically and to improve your analytical abilities. The contrasting perspectives and values contained in these readings will require you to think more carefully and deeply about an issue. What is the evidence for your views? Is your logic sound? Have you reached your conclusions on fundamental issues of the day through emotion, or are your views based on an understanding of the issues and a real attempt to sift through the evidence? If this volume helps you fall on the latter side of this question then the final goal of this volume has been met.

Notes

1. Benjamin Wallace-Wells. "Is America Too Racist for Barack? Too Sexist for Hillary?" *Washington Post*, November 12, 2006, p. B1

2. Anna Velasco. "Selling Plan B Pill Up to Pharmacies' Discretion," *Birmingham News* (Alabama), August 25, 2006, p. 8A.

3. Neil Steinberg. "Seniors Suffer and Endure in Sweltering CHA High-Rise," *Chicago Sun-Times*, July 17, 1995, p. 10.

4. Michael Powell and Peter Slevin. "Several Factors Contributed to 'Lost' Voters in Ohio," *Washington Post*, December 15, 2004, p. A01.

5. Sean Robinson. "Gay Marriage Ban Belongs to Legislators, Justices Say," *The News Tribune* (Tacoma, Washington), July 27, 2006, p. A1.

6. Sam Roberts, "Minorities Now Form Majority in One-Third of Most-Populous Counties," *New York Times*, August 9, 2007 (http://www.nytimes.com/2007/08/09/us/09census.html) [accessed August 9, 2007].

1

THE CONSTITUTION AND CONTESTED NOTIONS OF EQUALITY

Equality was a value espoused by the Framers of the Constitution; however, in practice, it has not been adhered to at numerous times in our history.

From one perspective, the U.S. Constitution has stood out as a model document for modern democracies ataround the world. As a founding set of principles, the Constitution is often thought of as one of the most eloquent descriptions of governing principles ever drafted. When considering the U.S. Constitution, many people first think about the Bill of Rights, equality, and the freedoms from governmental interference granted to us.

In addition, the Constitution also laid out the framework for the three branches of government and the power-sharing principles of separation of powers and checks and balances. It sought to resolve various political debates of the time (the competing sovereignty of national and state governments, large and small state representation in Congress, the "counting" of slaves for purposes of representation and taxation) while attempting to rectify the failures of the first attempt at providing a governing document for the new nation—the Articles of Confederation.

Interestingly, after the Framers at the Constitutional Convention had agreed on a draft, some advocated that key protections for individual freedom and liberty be added—the very principles that caused the colonists to break from Britain in the first place. Because of this, the final document that was ratified included ten Amendments to the Constitution—the Bill of Rights.

However, the document ratified in 1789 is not the same as the one we operate under today. While the Framers spoke of embracing the principle of equality—most notably in the Declaration of Independence with the phrase "all men are created equal"—they did not necessarily mean equality for all. In one sense they meant what they said; all rights were available only for men, but these men had to be white, land-owning men (those considered to be "citizens"). The Constitution ratified in 1789 did not, for example, grant slaves, free African-Americans, women, or 18- to 20-year-olds the right to vote. Those rights were provided later—through the 15th Amendment in 1870 for former slaves, the 19th Amendment in 1920 for women, and the 26th Amendment in 1971 for 18- to 20-year-olds. Indeed, "equality" as we know it in the more contemporary sense did not begin to emerge as an important value until after the Civil War—approximately 100 years after ratification of the original Constitution.

However, the Framers did rely on the idea that a diversity of political interests would help sustain the American democratic experiment. For example, many theorists of the time—including Rousseau and Montesquieu—assumed or argued that a democratic political system was possible only in small homogeneous areas (such as the Swiss cantons that Rousseau wrote about). The Framers articulated a different view. In The Federalist papers, for example, Madison argued that larger, diverse populations were more likely to support democracies. This diversity of competitive political interests would prevent a single person, group, or set of interests from taking power and protect the United States from tyranny.

In contemporary times, American politics as expressed through the Constitution interacts with diversity because we continue to struggle over the rights of political minorities on the Constitutional issues of equality, justice, and discrimination. These issues are addressed in the Bill of Rights, several other Amendments to the Constitution, and numerous federal statutes.

As a constitutional question, "diversity" has experienced varying acceptance and challenge over the years. In the period after the 1960s, programs such as affirmative action were promoted by the federal government, and saw expression through decisions in hiring, minority set-asides for government contracting purposes, and admissions decisions at universities. At that time, court cases reviewing such programs generally upheld diversity programs because they served a "compelling public interest."

More recently, the courts and the public have appeared to move away from this "compelling interest" in diversity. Issues of legal equality in a diverse society such as in the United States remain an important part of the political and constitutional landscape, as we engage in newer debates over gay rights and continue a long-standing debate regarding equal rights for women. In the readings that follow, the constitutional foundation for "equality" is explored, then through specific examples of the failed Equal Rights Amendment and recent court cases involving university admissions programs designed to promote diversity.

*A*fter over 25 years, the Equal Rights Amendment (ERA) has resurfaced as a political and constitutional issue. The ERA originally fell short by three states to be
ratified (although five states that had approved later rescinded their approval).
However, ratification of the 27th Amendment (regarding congressional votes on pay
raises) took over 200 years, and supporters of the ERA (now also called the "Women's
Equality Amendment") are advocating for a renewed push for ratification. Part of the
controversy over the ERA is over whether such an amendment is constitutionally
necessary. Some opponents of the ERA have argued that the 14th Amendment to the
U.S. Constitution protects all citizens and already "nationalizes" equal protection,
whether male or female. Therefore, they argue that a separate ERA is unnecessary.

In this selection, Jonathan Turley's article in the Los Angeles Times summarizes the
arguments for and against ratification. His argument addresses the wisdom of allowing the Amendment to be ratified by only the three states remaining states needed for
ratification (as judged by some), or whether the debate should start from the beginning and enjoy a full and contemporary discussion.

Equal Rights Redux: The Three-State Solution

Jonathan Turley

Last week, a quarter of a century after its demise, the Equal Rights Amendment suddenly reappeared on Capitol Hill. Like Jacob Marley's ghost, the ERA came to
Congress dragging a heavy load: the 35 states that voted to ratify the amendment
decades ago. By counting these past votes as still valid, its sponsors claim that they can
make the ERA part of the Constitution with passage in just three more states—rather
than the constitutionally mandated 38. This novel argument would not only deny the
right of current citizens to vote on the amendment, it would count states that later
rescinded their ratification votes.

The inevitable court challenge to this theory will focus on Article V of the
Constitution, which requires that any constitutional amendment be approved by two-
thirds of each house of Congress and three-fourths of the state legislatures. The article was designed to make it difficult for politicians to clutter the Constitution with
impulsive amendments designed to appease constituents. The vote of the two houses
and the states was meant to ensure that there was an overwhelming consensus before
the Constitution was changed.

Jonathan Turley, "Equal Rights Redux: The Three-State Solution," *Los Angeles Times*, April 8,
2007, p. M3. Reprinted by permission of the author. © 2007 Jonathan Turley.

Yet the article's language does not contain an explicit time limit for ratification. Nor is there any discussion of a time frame in the constitutional debates. On the face of it, there's nothing to say that if a state approved the ERA in the late 1970s, its approval is not still valid today (especially because the text of the amendment introduced last week is identical).

The Supreme Court and many scholars, however, have insisted that there is an implied time limit to guarantee that any amendment, in the words of the court, is ratified by a "sufficiently contemporaneous" vote. Congress has long honored this rule by setting a seven-year period for ratification. If a measure could not pass in seven years, it clearly was not a consensus matter worthy of adding to the Constitution.

In the past, proposed amendments have had little difficulty in obtaining a contemporaneous consensus. The first 10 amendments were enacted within 27 months, and only one amendment took more than four years.

In contrast, the ERA, first introduced in 1923, was not approved by Congress until March 22, 1972. At that point, Congress put a seven-year limitation on the ratification process. When the amendment failed to attract approval from the required 38 states within this time period, Congress extended the deadline three more years. In an extremely questionable move, Congress also prohibited states from reconsidering the amendment if they previously ratified it, to avoid states rescinding their approval. (Five states did vote to rescind their votes.)

Yet even with this extension and the bar on rescission, the ERA could not secure enough states by 1982, and the Supreme Court (and various ERA supporters) treated it as dead.

Supporters of the new ERA, now called the Women's Equality Amendment, are likely to base their case for a three-state strategy on the history of the 27th Amendment, which lays out the conditions for congressional pay raises. James Madison first proposed that this amendment be part of the original Bill of Rights, but it failed to meet the three-quarters requirement. Nevertheless, legislatures kept approving it through the years, and after a congressional pay raise scandal, five states spontaneously ratified the amendment in 1992—202 years after its original submission.

The ratifications were spread over two centuries, but because there had been no time limit placed on the process, members of Congress treated the new amendment (and their ability to raise their salaries) as an accomplished fact. Many academics objected to the amendment as untimely, but to no avail.

The most obvious problem with the three-state strategy is that it is presumptively unconstitutional. The Supreme Court held in 1921 that there must be "contemporaneous consensus" and that the votes of state legislatures be part of "succeeding steps in a single endeavor." A delay of decades is hardly a good showing of a "contemporaneous consensus," and the votes of three states cannot be successive steps to a process that the court and Congress treated as expired in 1982. Although the court has held that any time limits should be left to Congress, it has never stated that a proposed amendment can live eternally in constitutional amber, like some Jurassic fossil.

There are other constitutional problems. Congress twice limited the period for the ERA's ratification—first March 22, 1979, then June 30, 1982—and both deadlines expired. A retroactive extension made decades later would defeat the obvious intent of Congress and alter the conditions under which the states originally cast their ratification votes. There is also the not-so-small matter that five states rescinded their ratification, which Congress conveniently chose to ignore. The ERA failed in 1982 by eight, not three, states.

Then there are the five other "dormant" proposed constitutional amendments that share the ERA's status. There is the 218-year-old House reapportionment amendment, a 197-year-old amendment depriving people of citizenship for accepting titles of nobility, a 186-year-old amendment that would bar the prohibition of slavery by constitutional amendment, an 83-year-old child labor amendment and a 29-year-old amendment to make the District of Columbia a state.

All were passed by Congress, but their sponsors agreed to play by the rules and accepted defeat when time expired. Indeed, under the three-state logic of the ERA sponsors, the amendment making the District of Columbia a state would need only a few more states to be retroactively declared ratified.

Perhaps most important, this opportunistic new strategy would do great harm to our constitutional traditions and the amendment process. The framers wanted Americans in consensus by a supermajority before amending the Constitution. They clearly did not mean consensus of voters spread across decades. Indeed, I believe Madison would have objected to his own amendment passing 202 years later because it lacked a contemporaneous vote of Congress and the states.

Our country was a very different place when Congress approved the ERA in 1972. It was before *Roe v. Wade* and before the widespread enforcement of anti-discrimination laws. Because of statutory protections and cultural changes, women have made huge strides and currently count the speaker of the House, the leading Democratic candidate for president, the secretary of State and many other powerful leaders among their numbers.

The fact is that many Americans may no longer see the need for the ERA given the great advances of women since the 1970s. No doubt there are many others who disagree and would fight hard for ratification.

It is a fight that we should welcome. It is through that difficult process that a nation can reach consensus on issues that divide us. In the end, to sneak in an amendment through clever legal maneuvers does an injustice to both the cause and the country.

If the ERA is right for the nation, then we should ratify it in the right way. The sponsors should reject the three-state strategy and let the debate begin.

In this selection, Jane Mansbridge summarizes several different perspectives from legal scholars and feminist activists regarding the Equal Rights Amendment (ERA). This article traces the ups and downs of attempts to ratify the ERA, including the possibility of a renewed attempt in the twenty-first century. Interestingly, Mansbridge notes that not all feminists currently support ratification of the ERA, even if the ratification process is allowed to continue. The different views about the ERA and what it would likely bring provide a range of outcomes for the reader to consider.

This reading also raises some questions about the ratification process in general. In the past, there was a time limit for ratification of proposed amendments. The time limit for the ERA expired first in 1979, with Congress extending the deadline until 1982. By that final deadline, 35 of the required 38 states had ratified the ERA. As both this reading and the previous reading by Jonathan Turley point out, the so-called "Madison Amendment" (requiring congressional roll call votes for pay increases) took over 200 years for approval, thus establishing a potential precedent that no time limits should be imposed on any amendment ratification process. These articles suggest that, while everyone would likely support the abstract goal of "equal rights" for all citizens, the specific policy proposals that are formulated to achieve that goal may be vigorously contested.

Whatever Happened to the ERA?

JANE MANSBRIDGE

—Equality of rights under the law shall not be denied or abridged by the United States or by any State on account of sex.

Why We Lost the ERA, written in 1986, made the point that actors in a social movement are deeply influenced by their own contexts and incentives.[1]

* * * * *

The present chapter reveals that many of the dynamics identified in the movement from 1972 to 1982 still operate in the current social movement activity around the ERA.

This final chapter has . . . separate perspectives on the Equal Rights Amendment (ERA) from different corners of the legal and political universe. . . . It looks briefly at . . . separate "takes" on the ERA in 2001—those of (1) feminist constitutional lawyers Martha Fineman and Mary Becker; (2) state courts interpreting state ERAS since 1982; (3) women activists still trying to get their states to ratify the original amendment in unratified states such as Missouri; and (4) the National Organization for Women (NOW), which has crafted a Constitutional Equality Amendment that might or might not replace the original ERA. . . .

1

In 1990 Nancy Fraser and I invited three feminist legal theorists, along with a feminist practitioner teaching a legal clinic at Northwestern University, to give a panel at Northwestern on "Women, Public Policy, and the Law." After a set of presentations in

---

which the participants explained their stance toward the subject, I asked them all, "If you could simply push a button and put the ERA in the constitution right now, with no political struggle, would you do it?"

All three feminist constitutional scholars said no. The practitioner, surprised at the others' responses, produced a strong yes.

* * * * *

I recently telephoned Martha Fineman and Mary Becker, two of the constitutional lawyers on the panel we held at Northwestern, to see if they would hold today to their conclusion in 1990. Both said they would.

Martha Fineman would continue to oppose the ERA because of the trouble formal equality has brought in its wake.

* * * * *

. . . Fineman would propose something like the Common Benefit Clause of the Vermont Constitution. . . . It was under this clause that the Vermont judiciary legalized gay and lesbian marriage. Fineman points out that this clause was adopted as part of the Vermont Constitution in 1777, preceding the Fourteenth Amendment by nearly a century. . . . Interpreting the clause in the gay/lesbian marriage case, the Vermont Supreme Court stated that the clause was part of the "powerful movement for social equivalence unleashed by the Revolution," and commented that it "mirrors the confidence of [citizens] aggressively laying claim to the same rights as their peers."

Mary Becker reaches the same result as Martha Fineman—a repudiation of the ERA as worded when it went before the states between 1972 and 1982. But she has a different emphasis. Whereas Fineman focuses on caretaking labor and the right to work (an economic and structural analysis of the work/family conflict), Becker focuses on issues of custody and maintenance at divorce and on issues of affirmative action. . . . [4]

* * * * *

2

Meanwhile, in state courts all over the country, people have been using their state equal rights amendments to bring cases charging abridgement of rights on account of sex. . . . Texas is the most populous ERA state. It also has the largest judicial system of any state with an ERA in its constitution. Yet no one would claim that it was representative of all the other states. Among other things, in Texas, the words that constitute the state's ERA ("equality under the law shall not be denied or abridged because of sex, race, color, creed, or national origin"), adopted as an amendment to the state constitution in 1972, were not interpreted to require "strict scrutiny" until 1987.[7]

* * * * *

Of the 27 cases from 1972 to 1993 brought to the Texas Supreme Court under the state's ERA, men brought 16 and women 11. Of the seven claimants who prevailed, three were men and four women. The pattern is even more favorable to men in the 28 equal protection sex discrimination cases brought before the U.S. Supreme Court from 1971 to 1998. There men brought 18 of the cases and women 10. Of the 16 claimants who prevailed, nine were men and seven women. In both venues men have been more likely than women to bring cases. They have been about as likely or more likely to prevail.[10]

* * * * *

3

Meanwhile again, in yet a third corner of the universe—the unratified states—women activists are continuing to try to get their state legislature to ratify the 1972 ERA. . . .

The legal strategy these women are using is worth attention.

The roots of this strategy lie in a series of events, seemingly unrelated to the ERA, that in 1992 culminated in putting the Twenty-Seventh Amendment in the constitution. That amendment, originally proposed by James Madison in 1789, required Congress to take a roll-call vote whenever it approved a pay raise. The amendment garnered six state ratifications in the three years from 1789 to 1791, then none for eighty-nine years. In 1873 one more state ratified. Then 105 years passed. In 1978 one more state ratified. Then five more years passed. An extraordinary push from 1983 to 1992, in which thirty-two more states ratified, taking the amendment over the top, was begun and entrepreneured by Gregory Watson, a student at the University of Texas, who . . . is credited with influencing twenty-six state legislatures to ratify the Madison amendment.[12]

* * * * *

In December 1992 Richard Bernstein of the NYU Law School . . . pointed out that the controlling Supreme Court case, *Coleman v. Miller,* decided in 1939, had concluded that "the question of the efficacy of ratifications by state legislatures . . . should be regarded as a political question pertaining to the political departments, with the ultimate authority in the Congress in the exercise of its control over the promulgation of the adoption of the amendment."[14] . . .

* * * * *

The key breakthrough, however, came with a 1997 article in the *William and Mary Journal of Women and the Law* by three women graduates of the T. C. Williams School of Law in Richmond, Virginia.[15] . . . The three authors pointed out that the acceptance of the Madison amendment implies . . . that "there is no requirement of contemporaneous ratification."[16] . . . In short, Congress can legally repeal or extend a deadline at will. It can also accept a running total. Apparently, the only thing it cannot do is accept a rescission. So if the legislatures of three more states ratify the ERA, Congress can simply adopt it, as it did the Madison amendment.

4

Meanwhile, back at the offices of the National Organization for Women, we find yet a fourth take on the ERA.

In the years 1978 to 1982, when the struggle for the ERA had shifted to the last unratified states, NOW took considerable trouble to make the feminist message palatable to middle America. . . . The ERA issue appealed to women who had never been involved in any feminist cause. They took busses or carpooled to the state capital to lobby, organized coffee-and-cake district meetings with their representatives, sacrificed evenings when they would have been with their kids and families, wrote letters to the editor, and gave the first money they had ever given to a political cause. Every time they thought about the issue or talked about it with a neighbor, they got madder. They had experienced being second-class citizens all their lives, and with the ERA it came together for them. Women "weren't even in the constitution." And it was intolerable.

* * * * *

In this environment, where the ERA had to get votes in southern Illinois, rural Florida, and rural North Carolina (the most recalcitrant areas in the states where ratification was most likely), feminism had to have meaning to women whose political and lifestyle choices were neither cosmopolitan nor radical. Those women nevertheless supported the ERA because it spoke to them of the many ways they had been ignored, put aside, and counted as less all their lives. NOW, as the richest and most energetic feminist organization in America, threw itself into the ERA struggle. As a result, its membership soared from 55,000 in 1977 to 210,000 in 1982.

When the ERA deadline finally passed in 1982, however, the pent-up energy of all the other projects that had been put on the back burner for the ERA exploded and NOW activists turned to other things. The ERA never went off NOW's agenda, but it did not dominate as it had in the last few years of struggle before the deadline.

* * * * *

According to a NOW representative, NOW does not believe that the organization should continue to promote an ERA that embodies the meaning established when the amendment was originally introduced in 1972. The problem is not so much the wording of the original ERA as the understanding of it that prevailed during the 1972 legislative debate, which suggested that the amendment would not affect issues such as combat exemption, sex discrimination in insurance, taxation of single-sex schools, and abortion issues. Because that limited understanding would govern the attempted ratification of the remaining three states today, NOW objects to actions that would continue the ratification process by using the precedent of Madison to declare meaningless the time limit on the original ERA.[27]

Accordingly, NOW gives no support to the women in Missouri, Illinois, and elsewhere who are organizing to ratify the ERA.

* * * * *

At the moment the only people working for an ERA that might stand a chance of becoming part of the constitution of the U.S. in the next ten—or perhaps more—years are the lonely women in Missouri, Virginia, and Illinois, pouring their hours into organizing in the districts. If they begin to succeed, their actions will provoke a far fuller deliberation on this subject within the movement than has yet taken place. That will be good.

Notes

1. The Equal Rights Amendment was passed by the House of Representatives in 1971 (by a vote of 354 to 23) and the Senate in 1972 (by a vote of 84 to 8). Thirty of the required thirty-eight states ratified in 1972 and 1973, often with unanimous or nearly unanimous votes. . . . The struggle for the required last three states focused on Florida, Illinois, Nevada, and North

Carolina. None had ratified by 1982, the deadline for ratification. . . .

3. In 1971 Senator Birch Bayh proposed such a wording on the grounds that this wording would insure passage.

4. Mary Becker, "The Sixties Shift to Formal Equality and the Courts: An Argument for Pragmatism and Politics," *William and Mary Law Review* 40 (1998): 209–76.

7. This standard, routinely applied in cases dealing with race, requires that laws drawing distinctions on the basis of the characteristic in question will be held unconstitutional unless they further a "compelling" state objective that cannot be accomplished otherwise. . . . For expectations regarding interpretation at the time of ratification, see Jane Mansbridge, *Why We Lost the ERA* (Chicago: University of Chicago Press, 1986), pp. 250–51, nn. 25–26, and accompanying text.

9. Id., 1594.

10. Calculations from Becker 1998. See also Susan Gluck Mezey, *In Pursuit of Equality: Women, Public Policy, and the Federal Courts* (New York: St. Martin, 1992), 22.

12. Ruth Ann Strickland, "The Twenty-Seventh Amendment and Constitutional Change by Stealth," *P.S.: Political Science and Politics* 26 (1993) 716–22, 720.

13. Richard B. Bernstein, "The Sleeper Wakes: The History and Legacy of the Twenty-seventh Amendment," *Fordham Law Review* 61 (1992): 497–555, 539.

14. Chief Justice Hughes, joined by Stone and Reed, in 307 U.S. 433, 450 (1939), cited at id. 545.

15. Allison L. Held, Sheryl L. Herndon, and Danielle M. Stager, "The Equal Rights Amendment: Why the ERA Remains Legally Viable and Properly Before the States," *William and Mary Journal of Women and the Law* 3 (1997): 113–36.

16. Id., 121.

17. Id., 126.

24. Goodman, 2000.

27. Telephone communication from Twiss Butler of NOW to Karen Taylor, February 5, 2001. . . .

*B*y the late 1970s and early 1980s, majority social values and the changing politics of the Supreme Court began to revisit some programs originally designed to promote equality through increased diversity. A number of "reverse discrimination" court cases began to challenge such programs, and consequently brought limits to affirmative action and minority contracting practices. Two recent court cases involving policies and practices at the University of Michigan further raised issues of fairness and equality in college admissions practices. One case reviewed the admissions practices of the university's undergraduate programs (Gratz v. Bollinger) and the other reviewed the university's Law School admissions practices (Grutter v. Bollinger) (see the Courts Section 12 for details on these two cases).

This selection by Terry Eastland from the Weekly Standard covers the issues inherent in these decisions, making the argument that diversity is not a positive value in *higher education, but rather promotes an inequality of a different kind. Eastland argues that for the Constitution to uphold equality, it must be "color-blind" and reject diversity programs. His argument, and those of others, suggests affirmative action unfairly advantages those in particular demographic groups and improperly stigmatizes minority group members who arrive on some college campuses.*

Supreme Confusion

TERRY EASTLAND

In response to the Supreme Court's decisions in the Michigan race-preference cases, President Bush issued a statement. "I applaud the Supreme Court for recognizing the value of diversity on our nation's campuses," he said. "Diversity is one of America's greatest strengths. Today's decisions seek a careful balance between the goal of campus diversity and the fundamental principle of equal treatment under the law."

From the president's statement, you'd never know that in its briefs the administration hadn't even addressed the most important issue the Court resolved in the Michigan cases—whether "diversity" is a compelling interest that can justify race preferences, and therefore racial discrimination, in admitting students. Justice Department lawyers were prepared to take a principled stand against the notion that diversity is just such a compelling interest. But the administration decided not to do that. Silent on the diversity rationale, the administration may have contributed to the Court's decision declaring diversity a compelling interest—a decision the administration surely should not be applauding.

Twenty-five years ago, in the landmark *Bakke* case, the Supreme Court left unsettled the role race might play in admissions, though it did outlaw quotas. Writing only for himself, Justice Lewis Powell set forth the view that "educational diversity" is a compelling interest sufficient to support making race a "plus" factor in admissions. Selective schools quickly embraced the diversity rationale and used it to support race preferences. In recent years, however, lower court rulings had questioned and even repudiated diversity, and the High Court itself had issued a series of equal protection rulings that seemed to leave in doubt whether a majority of the justices would accept the rationale. Even so, when the race-based policies used by its undergraduate and law schools were challenged, the University of Michigan resolved to persuade the Court of the merits of diversity. It enlisted scores of allies and pressed the matter as hard as it could—and it won.

Declining to challenge the diversity rationale, the Bush administration argued in its brief only that the admissions policies at both the law school and the undergraduate

Terry Eastland, "Supreme Confusion," *The Weekly Standard*, July 7, 2003. Reprinted by permission of The Weekly Standard.

school weren't tailored narrowly enough—indeed that their use of race amounted to unconstitutional quotas. The administration's refusal to take issue with the diversity rationale (even as its brief effusively praised diversity as a concept) could not have escaped notice inside the Court. And it may well have influenced the Court's decision to endorse the rationale.

Writing for the Court in *Grutter v. Bollinger*, the law school case, Justice Sandra Day O'Connor announced "our conclusion" that a school's "interest in [assembling] a diverse student body" is indeed compelling. That conclusion was essentially an act of deference, as O'Connor put it, to "the law school's educational judgment that diversity is essential to its educational mission." The Court's deference extended to the law school's further judgment that it must enroll a "critical mass" of minority students—critical mass being something expressed in numbers—in order to achieve the educational benefits of diversity. O'Connor also accepted the law school's view that, notwithstanding the similar percentages of minorities admitted each year, it did not engage in racial balancing, which would be unconstitutional. And she accepted the law school's representations on the educational benefits of diversity—that having a "critical mass" of minorities helps break down racial stereotypes, enables students "to better understand persons of different races," and makes classroom discussion "livelier, more spirited, and simply more enlightening and interesting."

O'Connor's treatment of the diversity rationale was hardly searching. In a vigorous dissent, the justice the president has held up as a model for the kind of judges he'd appoint—Clarence Thomas—scored devastating points. The law school seeks to obtain the "educational benefits that flow from student body diversity," he wrote, pointing out that diversity is thus supposed to be the means to the educational benefits, not an end of itself. And yet the law school "apparently believes that only a racially mixed student body can lead" to those benefits. Thomas asked: "How, then, is the law school's interest in these allegedly unique educational 'benefits' not simply the forbidden interest in 'racial balancing' that the majority expressly rejects?" He drew the obvious conclusion—that the distinction between the two ideas is "purely sophistic." Thomas sharply observed that the O'Connor majority conceded the point by using the terms interchangeably: He invited readers to compare two passages in the Court's opinion. One refers to the law school's "compelling interest in attaining a diverse student body," the other to "the compelling interest in securing the educational benefits of a diverse student body."

Thomas also cited social science disputing the claimed educational benefits of diversity. And he emphasized that diversity not only works discrimination against applicants of nonfavored races but also constitutes "racial experimentation" upon "test subjects." Such experimentation is at odds with the moral imperative of treating people not as means to other ends, but as the individuals they are.

What would have happened had the administration articulated some of the same points in challenging the diversity rationale? Maybe O'Connor, a split-the-difference justice often looking for the middle ground, would have deferred to the government's view. Maybe she would not have embraced the diversity rationale as easily as she did, or even at all. Maybe she would have voted to decide both cases on narrow-tailoring grounds, leaving for another day the whole diversity issue. And then again, maybe not. Maybe she would have voted as she did and written the opinion she did. What is clear is that the administration failed to take the stand that was needed in the Michigan cases.

There is something good to say about the two decisions. Now that the Court has settled the diversity question (at least for the time being), future litigation over preferences will deal with "narrow tailoring." And on that issue, the Court's decision in the undergraduate case, *Gratz v. Bollinger,* may prove helpful in limiting race preferences in admissions.

In *Gratz,* Chief Justice William Rehnquist concluded that the automatic award of 20 points to minority applicants on account of their race was a violation of narrow tailoring. The admissions policy was interested only in the fact of a person's race, a constitutional violation. *Gratz* is a victory for equal treatment under the law, and its application could lead eventually to a different evaluation of even a preference scheme like the one upheld in *Grutter.*

Gratz points to a day that cannot come too soon in America—when people truly are treated as individuals, without regard to race or ethnicity. It's too bad, then, that the president's statement didn't make more of *Gratz,* which, after all, is the case in which the administration was on the winning side. The long-term goal of achieving a color-blind Constitution will require sounder judicial opinions, but also firmer leadership from the president.

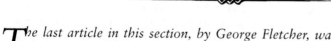

The last article in this section, by George Fletcher, was published in the New Republic *and continues to tackle the issue of equality as written in the Constitution and as interpreted by the Courts. Fletcher suggests that universal equality was far from a driving concern of the original Framers. Rather, he draws a sharp distinction between the focus of the U.S. Constitution as ratified in the 1700s, and the U.S. Constitution as understood following the Civil War. In "Unsound Constitution," Fletcher argues that, "The republic created in 1789 is long gone. It died with the 600,000 Americans killed in the Civil War." According to Fletcher, equality became a dominant Constitutional principle only after the bloodshed in the Civil War and that a real engagement and prioritization of equality was "absent from the original document." His analysis encourages readers to consider what value the Framers really placed on equality as well as consider how the public's views on the document are influenced by political events and historical context. Fletcher's article suggests that the original Constitution was clearly "time bound" and reflected the political and social values of the men who drafted it.*

Unsound Constitution

GEORGE P. FLETCHER

When the police stopped Timothy McVeigh seventy-five miles from the freshly exploded Alfred P. Murrah Federal Building in Oklahoma City, he was wearing a T-shirt with an apparently incriminating message on the front: "Sic semper tyrannis." The message on the back was just as provocative: "The tree of liberty must be refreshed from time to time with the blood of patriots and tyrants." An illustration of "the tree of liberty" dripped blood.

At the trial in Denver, which concluded with a guilty verdict last week, prosecutors presented the content of McVeigh's shirt as evidence that he was a madman capable of killing scores of innocent people. Prosecutor Joseph Hartzler, who presented the case against McVeigh, implied as much in his opening statement to the jury. Referring to the language of the shirt and similar political slogans, Hartzler said, "These documents are virtually a manifesto declaring McVeigh's intention." The jury obviously agreed, finding McVeigh guilty on all charges against him, including eight counts of first degree murder.

Surely the verdict was reasonable. The case against McVeigh established fairly strongly that he was the Oklahoma City bomber. But the underlying assumption in the case—that McVeigh's beliefs define him as an extremist—is not quite right. After all, are the words that McVeigh carried on his chest really so radical? "Sic semper tyrannis" was popular among revolutionary leaders long before John Wilkes Booth gave it an infamous sting. Thomas Jefferson's metaphor of "the tree of liberty" is no more outrageous than Patrick Henry's "Give me liberty or give me death" or New Hampshire's license plate motto, "Live free or die."

More important, McVeigh's belief that the Constitution should be interpreted exactly as it was written is surprisingly conventional. Not only is it in line with the conceptions held by many of the nation's founders, but it lives on today in the works of an influential minority of legal scholars and advocates. Although we generally teach lawyers to read the Constitution as judges have read it over time, many contemporary judges—Antonin Scalia, William Rehnquist, Robert Bork—hold that we should read the Constitution precisely as it is written. If these "originalists" are right, then McVeigh had a reason to think the Brady Bill's restrictions on gun ownership were a direct assault on the Second Amendment's right to bear arms. Similarly, McVeigh was employing—if perhaps stretching—originalist logic when he concluded that the federal raid on Waco violated the Branch Davidians' First Amendment guarantee of religious freedom.

Faced with a government that he believed had systematically violated the Constitution's core rights, McVeigh also had at least some reason to believe it was appropriate to take up arms. As Alexander Hamilton wrote in Federalist 28: "If the persons intrusted with supreme power become usurpers ... The citizens must rush tumultuously to arms, without concert, without system, without resource. . . ." Of

---

George P. Fletcher, "Unsound Constitution," *The New Republic*, June 23, 1997, pp. 14, 18. Reprinted by permission of the author. © 1997 George P. Fletcher.

course, the concept of "arms" may not have included Ryder trucks wired to explode next to federal buildings, but the idea of armed resistance against "usurpers" is rooted in the original understanding of the Constitution.

Let me be clear: this is not at all to say that McVeigh had any legitimate reason to kill 168 people, nor is it to say that originalist legal scholars are responsible for McVeigh and his terrorist ilk. But McVeigh's notion of the Constitution, a notion that in his deranged mind led to terrorism, is far more influential than we commonly assume. And it is fundamentally wrong.

With the shots "heard round the world," Americans rebelled against an oppressive foreign authority. Then, after a generation as semi-independent states, they entered into a compact as "the People" in order, as the Preamble to the Constitution reads, to "secure the Blessings of Liberty to ourselves and our Posterity." The purpose of the 1789 Constitution was to charter a government of limited powers that could never become a tyrannical overlord. To guard against government's tendency toward self-aggrandizement, the framers not only expressly delimited the powers of Congress but tried in the Bill of Rights to carve out certain areas of freedom—speech, press, assembly, religion, arms—that would remain beyond the federal government's reach. They would remain vested in "the People," who preceded and superseded the Constitution they established.

Of all the myths that support Timothy McVeigh's antigovernment reading of the Constitution, the greatest is the idea that the People are sovereign and superior to the Constitution. In this argument, the People—represented if necessary by McVeigh and alleged accomplice Terry Nichols—are superior to constituted government authority. They are in a position to judge whether the government has exceeded its authority. Sitting as jurors, they can nullify laws democratically enacted and properly applied. As freemen they must be prepared, as Hamilton argued, "to rush tumultuously to arms" as soon as "the persons intrusted with supreme power become usurpers."

This is exactly what some on the radical right are starting to do. The illegal stockpiling of weapons helped prompt the federal siege at Waco, which outraged McVeigh so deeply. And the Fully Informed Jury Association (FIJA), a small nationwide movement, has begun a major campaign in many western states to inform those called for jury duty of their power and supposed right to nullify the law as instructed to them by the trial judge. To many, the distribution of leaflets near courthouses urging juries not to apply democratically enacted law looks very much like obstruction of justice, if not overt sedition against the government. But the devout believers of FIJA see themselves as doing no more than engaging in civic education. They are joined in this campaign to exploit the jury's power to say no by outspoken members of the black left, who argue, as does George Washington University law professor Paul Butler, that justice for blacks requires jury nullification in certain cases in which African Americans are likely to be targeted. Right and left are able to cite on their behalf— accurately—academic writing that praises the jury's ultimate power to pass on the wisdom of laws it is supposed to apply.

If only eccentrics of the fringe believed in this exalted power of the People, we could dismiss them as mere and uninfluential anarchists. But these views are not foreign to the academy of constitutional law teachers, nor are they the exclusive province of the fringe. In *We the People*, an influential study of constitutional history, Yale professor Bruce Ackerman, a liberal, argues that the People retain the authority to legitimate illegal constitutional transformations, such as the adoption of the Constitution itself, which was illegal under the amendment provisions of the Articles of Confederation, and the transformation of Supreme Court jurisprudence after FDR's high-handed court-packing threat. The People can provide their imprimatur at the ballot box, as they did when they voted by a large majority for Roosevelt, or, implicitly, by adopting a practice of support and adherence to new laws. However they do it, the mythical People still function as the ultimate source of legitimacy. The power to say "yes" entails, of course, the power to say "no." And therefore it is but a short step from Ackerman's view to the right wing's faith in jury nullification as a legitimate response to unjust authority and the necessity of being armed to say "no" to the "usurpers."

Writing in the *Yale Law Journal* in 1991, Yale law professor Akhil Amar interpreted the First Amendment's "right of the people peaceably to assemble and to petition the Government for a redress of grievances" as "an express reservation of the collective right of We the People to assemble in a future convention and exercise our sovereign right to alter or abolish our government by a simple majority vote." The thought that a convention could abolish the federal government, including the Supreme Court, before the Court could rule on the convention's legality, goes to the heart of our constitutional confusion. We tolerate and encourage views about the constitutional power of the People that some receptive minds take to be an invitation to fight for the original republic.

Some might think that a clear distinction presents itself between fighting the British and taking up arms against a federal government that appears to be encroaching on our freedoms. As prosecutor Hartzler argued to the jury, " Our forefathers didn't fight British women and children. They fought other soldiers. They fought them face to face, hand to hand. They didn't plant bombs and run away wearing earplugs."

That is so, but, as McVeigh might well have seen it, the federal government had shown by its own example that the rules of engagement had changed. After all, women and children perished at Waco, too.

Still, there's a more fundamental problem with the originalist line of reasoning. The "original republic"—the one for which our "forefathers" fought "face to face, hand to hand"—exists only in the minds of academics and fundamentalist patriots. The republic created in 1789 is long gone. It died with the 600,000 Americans killed in the Civil War. That conflict decided once and forever that the People and the States do not have the power to govern their local lives apart from the nation as a whole. The People have no power either to secede as states or to abolish the national government.

The original republic died because it was grounded in a contradiction. It glorified the freedom of some and condoned the slavery of others. It valued persons "not free" at only three-fifths the Census value of those defined as free persons. It required free states to return runaway slaves to their owners. The flaw that spelled its demise was the failure of the framers to recognize the principle of human equality. Neither the word "equality" nor its practical equivalent appears in the document. (The "Privileges and Immunities" clause of Article IV could have become the near equivalent, but it became a dead letter instead.) Today, it would be unthinkable to adopt a constitution anyplace in the world without a commitment to equality. But in late-eighteenth-century America, equality was less important than the fear that a federal government might infringe our liberties.

The new Constitution—the one that shapes and guides the national government and disturbs the new patriots to their core—begins to take hold in the Gettysburg Address, in which Lincoln skips over the original Constitution and reconstitutes it according to the principles of equality articulated in the Declaration of Independence. This short speech functions as the Preamble to a new charter that crystallizes after the war in the Thirteenth, Fourteenth and Fifteenth Amendments. The Gettysburg Address signals the beginning of a new Constitution. The language is so familiar that we do not realize the implicit transformation:

> Four score and seven years ago our fathers brought forth on this continent, a new nation, conceived in liberty and dedicated to the proposition that all men are created equal . . . that we here highly resolve that these dead shall not have died in vain—that the nation, under God, shall have a new birth of freedom—and that government of the people, by the people, for the people, shall not perish from the earth.

Three changes signaled by Lincoln's words shake the foundation of our constitutional identity: the notion of organic nationhood—including the dead and the unborn—replaces the sovereignty of the (living) People. Equality, absent from the original document, comes front and center. And the United States evolves from an elitist republic into a democracy "of the people, by the people, for the people."

The reconstituting of "We the People" as the American nation defines the spirit of the new Constitution. The new nation, mentioned four times in Lincoln's 272 indelible words, is shaped by its past as well as its future. The entire focus of the Gettysburg Address is whether the nation "can long endure," whether the "nation might live." A nation born in a historic struggle will not hold itself hostage to those who say they speak in the here and now in the name of the People. Lincoln's nation could not be dismembered.

In contrast, those who wrote the 1789 Constitution had little sense of an American nation originating in the past and inhabiting the future; they wrote and argued as though they thought primarily of their moment, their generation, as unique. Those living then, and by extension any cohort who loved freedom as they did, could simply decide to dismantle the United States—it was merely a creation of the present. It was Jefferson, after all, who famously wrote that no constitution should be valid past nineteen years.

The recognition that the People are one group, an American nation, makes possible the sustained campaign to convert the elitist Constitution of 1789 into an egalitarian constitution of popular suffrage—that is, a constitution that bases democratic rule on the majority of all the people. Beginning with the Fifteenth Amendment, securing the right to vote for emancipated slaves, the United States begins to take democracy seriously. Of the ensuing twelve amendments to the Constitution, five are devoted to increasing the franchise and the role of the citizenry in running the country.

Nationhood, equality and democracy—these are the ideas that forge a new Constitution. But Lincoln was a good lawyer, and lawyers always seek to camouflage conceptual transformations as the continuous outgrowth of language used in the past. That's why he invoked government "by the people" to capture the new principle of democratic rule. But the significance of the People had changed. They no longer exist as the guarantors of the Constitution, the bestowers of legitimacy. States and individuals can no longer set themselves apart from the nation. The people exist exclusively as voters, as office holders and as beneficiaries of legislation.

The relevant concept in the new Constitution, then, is not "We the People" but "We the citizens of the nation"—and this transformation is apparent in the post–Civil War amendments. The Fourteenth Amendment, for example, gives us our first concept of national citizenship. "All persons born or naturalized in the United States, and subject to the jurisdiction thereof" are henceforth citizens. Prior to the Civil War, we allowed each state to define for itself who could become a citizen of the state and, on that basis, a citizen of the country. The new definition of who belongs to the polity marks a new beginning.

The Fourteenth Amendment further confirms the new sense of the United States as a national community with its clause prohibiting the states from "depriving any person of life, liberty, or property, without due process of law; or denying to any person within its jurisdiction the equal protection of the laws." These clauses account for the enormous expansion of judge-made constitutional law in the last fifty years, particularly in the field of criminal justice. Under these clauses of the new Constitution, virtually all the constitutional guarantees of the Bill of Rights apply, for the first time, to the states. Yet, as do all proper constitutions, the Fourteenth Amendment contains its own grant of legislative authority to Congress to implement its principles by appropriate legislation.

The Thirteenth Amendment also wreaks a radical transformation. On the surface, it merely abolishes slavery—expected in the wake of the war. But the Thirteenth Amendment also signals a new conception of constitutional power. The original Constitution limits only government power; the Thirteenth Amendment is the first direct intervention into the private affairs of citizens. The amendment invalidates a certain kind of private relationship—namely, involuntary servitude—and provides the legal hook for the first Civil Rights Acts, by recognizing that citizens—not just government—can deprive an individual of his or her constitutional rights. (This is the constitutional basis for the federal government's prosecuting and convicting Lemrick Nelson for violating the civil rights of Yankel Rosenbaum by fatally wounding him on a public thoroughfare.)

The most significant and, for fundamentalists, the most threatening aspect of the new Constitution is that it necessitates an activist federal government committed to preserving some semblance of equality—in other words, the government must intervene in the states and in private affairs to protect the disadvantaged. Early efforts in this direction—the income tax amendment, prohibition—represented significant moves to level the playing field and protect the weak. And, after the economic collapse of 1929, national government took its new role even more seriously with the New Deal.

This is the point at which the conflict with the original Constitution becomes acute. Some constitutional fundamentalists, like McVeigh, explicitly reject the new Constitution in their propaganda. They maintain that the original Constitution—everything that comes before the Thirteenth Amendment—is the only legitimate one, and they believe their task as freemen is to protect the People against the "usurpers" who would have the federal government exceed its minimalist origins.

So if the extremists can grasp this distinction, why is it foreign to the rest of us? Quite simply, because we do not teach this historical rupture—not in our grade schools, not in our law schools. We are all good lawyers and therefore, like Lincoln, we pretend that the second Constitution is simply the natural continuation of the founding document. According to the official story, we corrected the racist mistakes of 1789 and got the Constitution on the right track. "We the People" are still in power. Our constitutional situation would be much clearer if we marked the discontinuity in our history by calling the first Constitution the "founding republic" and the second, say, the "egalitarian republic." This new terminology would acknowledge that our constitutional history is close to that of France, with its multiple constitutions, including some legal institutions such as the Declaration of the Rights of Man and the Code civil that date back as far as the late eighteenth century.

The sentencing of Timothy McVeigh and the ensuing trial of Terry Nichols will presumably play out without any serious attention to the defendants' constitutional beliefs. But there was more at stake in this trial than the terrorism of one or two men. The basic question is whether we as a legal and intellectual community will face up to the truth about the false view of the Constitution that we have nurtured for generations. We have propagated myths about the binding force of the 1789 Constitution that some people, unfortunately, take too zealously. We have planted the ideas that have grown crooked in the minds of some. On the basis of the evidence presented at the trial, the jury reached a well founded verdict on McVeigh's guilt. Yet we should be filled with horror that this heinous crime was committed with motives derived from the basic teachings of the republic.

DISCUSSION QUESTIONS

1. Why did it take so long for former slaves, African-Americans, other individuals of color, women, and young adults to achieve the right to vote in the United States? Did initially excluding these groups violate the Constitution?

2. Is an Equal Rights Amendment (ERA) necessary? Why or why not? Aren't women assigned the same rights as men in the current language of the Constitution? Are women still discriminated against in hiring, wages, credit approval, or other areas? If so, is such discrimination within the authority of government to solve?

3. Should ERA ratification be achieved through approval of only three more states, or should the process begin all over again? What are the arguments for imposing a "contemporary consensus" time limit, and what are the arguments for allowing an unlimited amount of time for state approval?

4. Is there a "compelling public interest in diversity" to support programs that favor disadvantaged groups in our society? Why or why not? What sorts of higher education admissions policies do you think best adhere to the compelling interest standard?

5. George Fletcher's article makes a distinction between the original focus of the Constitution, and the later emphasis (beginning in the 1860s) on "equality." What parts of the Constitution have been used to promote equality—and do these parts (and their inclusion in the Constitution) support Fletcher's argument?

Additional Resources

http://www.equalrightsamendment.org/
This web site, sponsored by the nonprofit Alice Paul Institute and the National Council of Women's Organizations, promotes ratification of the Equal Rights Amendment through information and recommendations on various political strategies that focus on the states that have not yet ratified the ERA.

http://www.usconstitution.net/
Provides information about the Constitution (and a comparison with the Articles of Confederation), the Electoral College, and the demographic backgrounds of the Framers.

http://www.aei.org/
The American Enterprise Institute supports research on a wide variety of public policy issues, including "Legal and Constitutional Studies" (as part of their "Political and Social Studies" division).

http://www.landmarkcases.org/
This site provides a forum to discuss and analyze various landmark U.S. Supreme Court cases related to diversity issues. Among the cases discussed include *Dred Scott v. Sandford* (1857), *Plessy v. Ferguson* (1896), *Korematsu v. U.S.* (1944), *Brown v. Board of Education* (1954), and *Heart of Atlanta Motel v. U.S.* (1964).

Just the Facts: U.S. Constitution/Bill of Rights (1999) is a two-part educational video that examines the creation of the Constitution the amendments that became known as the Bill of Rights.

John Adams (2008) is a seven-part HBO series that traces the life of the second president of the United States, and the first 50 years of the new nation. It is based on historian David McCullough's biography of Adams and includes great examples of how John's wife Abigail impacted his life and decision making at the time of the Declaration of Independence and in the years that followed.

2 FEDERALISM: GOVERNMENTAL COMPETITION OR COOPERATION?

Struggling to survive after Hurricane Katrina. Federalism played a role in the inability of local, state, and federal governments to adequately respond to the Katrina disaster. This especially hurt New Orleans' poor and minority population.

The Introduction noted that differences in the American population (i.e., diversity) can have several different applications in U.S. politics and government. One application is in the area of equal rights and justice (including discrimination, equal protection, and due process). In this section, we investigate contemporary examples of how the divided authority of our federated system in the United States has responded to political and legal challenges arising from questions of equal protection, justice, and equal rights.

The important constitutional principle of "dual federalism" divides power and authority between the national government and the states. Many scholars have considered dual federalism to be largely conflict-based because there has been so much disagreement over time about the relative powers and responsibilities of the different levels of government. As related to diversity issues, those disagreements were embodied in the Civil War, public school desegregation, and civil rights legislation.

Beginning in the early twentieth century, selective incorporation of the Bill of Rights "nationalized" a number of provisions in the Constitution's first ten Amendments by applying them to state governments as well as federal government action. The 14th Amendment's equal protection clause also brought state actions under federal review and authority. Throughout the nineteenth and most of the twentieth century, the

27

Commerce Clause of the Constitution was used as the constitutional rationale and vehicle for expanded national government powers over states. In the case of the commerce clause, the federal 1964 Civil Rights Act was upheld by the U.S. Supreme Court (in two 1964 cases: *Heart of Atlanta Motel v. U.S.* and *Katzenbach v. McClung*) because Court Justices unanimously agreed in both cases that prohibiting racial discrimination "in places of public accommodation" was a constitutionally permissible use of Congress' powers *to regulate interstate commerce.* Therefore, in many policy issues, the conflict between the national and state governments often turned on how a problem or issue was defined (and therefore, which government had authority over that area).

Therefore, we can identify some important policy areas where there is a connection between diversity and federalism. In our country's history, different levels of government have taken different approaches to supporting civil rights and equality. It has made a difference whether the federal government or a state government has had authority to deal with a particular issue, such as immigration or welfare policy. There also has been an ongoing set of disputes over the proper division of powers between the federal and state governments. The balance of power has shifted over time, but the disputes continue.

The readings that follow tackle the seemingly disparate issues of immigration law, gay marriage, welfare policy, and the Hurricane Katrina aftermath. However, in each case, the framework of federalism has played a major role in how these policies are made, who makes them, and if and how a problem is solved. Moreover, in examining both Katrina and welfare policy, it has been argued that minority group members have been unfairly affected by the kind and quality of policy or service delivery that emerged from our federalist governmental structure.

The balance and overlap of responsibilities between federal, state, and local government seems to constantly evolve and can varyingly affect governmental action and response to minority group interests. Federalism is one place where the structural design of U.S. democracy directly interacts with the politics of diversity.

*R*ecall the horrifying media images immediately following Hurricane Katrina. We *saw individuals in the United States stranded on the top of highway overpasses and stranded on the top of houses and apartment buildings—for days. Other residents fled to the Superdome where they were greeted by inadequate supplies coupled with inadequate police and support agencies. Businesses were broken into—usually so residents could gain access to much needed water, diapers, and other supplies. Break-ins continued as these basic resources did not make it to New Orleans and the Gulf Coast in a timely fashion. How could this happen? Many people wondered how a major American city could be so crippled and the governmental response so inadequate.*

Enter federalism and the politics of diversity. Though not the only reason for the failed response to Katrina, the interaction of the levels of government operating in a federated system—and the politics of diversity—can be considered a primary reason for such governmental ineffectiveness. Indeed, the connection between federalism and diversity might not be immediately apparent to many observers, but the aftermath of Hurricane Katrina helps make it so. As we saw with Katrina, this nexus can have particular consequences for traditionally aggrieved groups. The Hurricane Katrina disaster revealed major political and administrative deficiencies in the shared-powers nature of the U.S. system. The lack of decision-making and coordinated relief efforts among the federal, state, and local governments contributed to the problems in the Katrina's aftermath. In part, the federal government—in the form of the Federal Emergency Management Agency (FEMA)—waited too long to act (for this, FEMA chief Michael Brown resigned). State and local officials gave little information to citizens—or gave contradictory advice about evacuating the city. The lack of emergency preparedness on the part of local government was evident—for instance, buses and trains that could have been used to evacuate residents sat unused. This was a case where the shared nature of the power in our federal system went wrong, and certainly showed its potential inefficiency and ineffectiveness. While all residents of New Orleans (and the Gulf Coast) were affected by these miscues, our memory of the post-Katrina images reminds us that poor citizens—who are disproportionately African-American—were most affected.

When Government Fails—Katrina's Aftermath

THE ECONOMIST

The pathetic official response to Katrina has shocked the world. How will it change America?

Only those with a special pass, and under armed guard, can now go to the centre of New Orleans. The city, officials will tell you, is far more dangerous than is generally believed. But just a few people, such as scientists needing to retrieve experiments, are being allowed in.

Much of the city is a sea of filthy water. Cars, boats, trees and power-lines float on it in a tangled mass. The water stinks. On higher ground some parts remain oddly untouched, save for massive oaks lying in the road and huge plumes of smoke from various distant fires. But on every side the city is empty. The only sound is of helicopters overhead, dropping water on the fires. The only people are National Guard companies at the intersections, guns at the ready—and, on St Charles Avenue, one lone jogger, running on the streetcar tracks.

Slowly, falteringly and much too late, America began to respond this week to the devastation wrought by Hurricane Katrina. Troops and supplies poured into New Orleans, even as survivors were bused away. The city's Superdome and convention centre, both epicentres of horror in the days after the hurricane, are now empty. The broken levees are being fixed, and water is even being pumped out. By mid-week only 60% of New Orleans, rather than 80%, remained under water. Police were preparing to remove any remaining people by force. The death toll is still unclear, though Ray Nagin, New Orleans's mayor, talks of 10,000 dead.

As relief stumbles along, the political blame-game is in top gear. George Bush and the federal government have come under fierce attack. Though a CNN/USA Today/Gallup poll found that only 13% supposed the president should take most responsibility for the relief effort, or lack of it, both Republicans and Democrats were appalled at Mr. Bush's failure to grasp the scale of the catastrophe; shocked that his senior staff were absent, or on holiday, while thousands of Americans were stranded without food and water; and aghast at the bumbling response of the Federal Emergency Management Agency (FEMA), which is charged with coping when disasters strike. America's enemies, from Cuba to Iran, lined up with unconcealed smirks to offer doctors and aid.

Karl Rove, Mr. Bush's political Svengali, moved into damage-control mode. Top officials, from Donald Rumsfeld to Condoleezza Rice, were packed off to visit the disaster zone. Mr. Bush himself went back again to hug refugees, and said, unpromisingly, that he would launch an investigation. The White House spin-machine whirled into action, trying to shift blame to local and state officials. The federal government, claimed Michael Chertoff, head of the Department of Homeland Security, had only a supporting role to play; it could not, he implied, do much if the locals were incompetent.

Local and state officials jabbed fingers right back. Kathleen Blanco, the Democratic governor of Louisiana, refused to let the federal government take control of the National Guard relief effort in her state, fearing this would allow the Bush team to blame her for any earlier incompetence. Instead, she hired James Lee Witt, the head of FEMA in the Clinton administration, to advise her on disaster relief.

Pundits explained the government's failure in every way they pleased. Anti-war types blamed Iraq, particularly the fact that thousands of National Guard troops had been sent there. Environmental types blamed Mr. Bush's lackadaisical attitude to wetlands. Many Democrats saw it as proof that Mr. Bush and the Republicans cared nothing for America's poor and black. Liberals argued that Katrina showed why, as James Galbraith, a vocal leftist economist at the University of Texas, put it, the "government of the United States must be big, demanding, ambitious and expensive." A Wall Street Journal column, in contrast, argued that the hurricane showed the danger of relying too heavily on inefficient government.

The question of racism bobbed quickly to the surface. Jesse Jackson, a one-time presidential hopeful, set the tone. Inspecting the crowded pavement outside the convention centre in New Orleans, he said: "This looks like the hull of a slave ship."

Absurd though the comparison may be, America's racial rift has been re-opened. Almost all the desperate-looking victims on the television news are black. That partly reflects demography—New Orleans is two-thirds black. It also reflects poverty. Those who failed to leave town typically did so because they had no means of transport. Some 35% of black households lacked a car, compared with 15% of white ones.

Nonetheless, media coverage of Katrina drew furious allegations of subtle bias. Using the term "refugees" for those seeking refuge from the storm was racist, apparently, and Yahoo! News drew flak for picture captions describing a black man as "looting" and whites as "finding" goods. The agencies that supplied the pictures retorted that the captions reflected what their photographers had witnessed.

Many blacks feel that, had it been whites drowning, the federal government would have acted more swiftly to save them. An ABC poll found them 23 percentage points more likely than whites to find fault with Mr. Bush's response. "George Bush doesn't care about black people," suggested Kanye West, a rapper, during a televised appeal to raise money for the victims. His contention is hard to prove. Was the president indifferent, or merely incompetent? Some of Mr. Bush's supporters favour a third explanation: that Mayor Nagin (who is black) proved more adept at berating the federal government on the radio than at implementing the city's pre-prepared emergency plan.

Amid all this name-calling, there were a few odd winners. Wal-Mart, for instance, a company that is often under fire from the left for the way it treats employees, was widely praised for the efficiency and unusual generosity of its response. The firm donated $23 million to the relief effort; promised jobs in other Wal-Marts for all employees dislocated by Katrina; and proved far more adept than the Feds at getting supplies quickly to where they are needed. The state of Florida, too, which is used to these things, immediately launched an impressive pre-planned relief effort that saw more than $40 million in aid, together with teams of doctors and nurses, despatched to neighbouring states.

Around 1 million people have been displaced by Katrina. Texas has been the destination of close to a quarter of them. Many have gone to Houston, already the fourth-biggest city in America, to camp in the Astrodome. Other Texas cities have also pitched in: San Antonio has offered temporary housing for 25,000 (as well as practice fields for New Orleans's displaced football team). In Dallas and Austin, convention centres have become shelters.

Governor Rick Perry has been widely praised for his quick response. He has promised extra teachers for displaced schoolchildren and, with Texas's shelters now crammed, he is coordinating with other states to take survivors. But the real test lies ahead. As time wears on, keeping a few hundred thousand survivors fed and clothed, not to mention pacified, is a huge challenge—especially since nobody knows when, or whether, they will go home. Texas has already had trouble; people have been turned away from the Astrodome with nowhere to go, and those who are there must endure an 11 p.m. curfew.

Race is inevitably a factor. Most of the New Orleanians seeking public shelter are poor and black. Barbara Bush, the president's mother, earned no thanks from him for her remark that because many survivors "were underprivileged anyway," their Astrodome quarters are "working very well for them." Some white Texans (including many in the Republican base) will "feel that we've got enough minorities in Texas already," says Richard Murray, director of the Centre for Public Policy at the

University of Houston. He predicts that the early euphoria associated with aiding survivors will probably fade, and that crime will increase tensions.

Such sentiments are likely to be echoed in other states also accepting refugees. Arkansas, for example, has opened its doors to more than 70,000 of them, turning National Guard armouries into "readiness centers" and mobilising churches to take refugees into their halls. But Arkansas is itself a poor state, with little cash to spare.

States at the other end of the Mississippi river are also preparing for an influx of Katrina victims. Minnesota has agreed to accept between 3,000 and 5,000, and will temporarily house them at a National Guard encampment in the north-west of the state. Officials say they have lined up longer-term housing for 2,000 evacuees. Wisconsin has space for 1,150 Katrina victims, and will put them up at the state fair grounds and in Milwaukee.

Ordinary citizens have also rented buses or driven down in their own cars to pick up Katrina victims. But not many refugees are willing to travel so far north. When one coach was sent down to Houston, most passengers preferred to be dropped off in Dallas. Hundreds of sympathetic families in Wisconsin and Minnesota have offered to take Katrina victims into their homes, but, as yet, few have had their offers accepted.

That may be as well. Both sides are aware of the tensions that might accrue once short-term needs are met. The refugees will overwhelmingly be black, their hosts white; evacuees will come from a place that ranks last in most every measure of civic health and social cohesion, and will end up in states that rank near the top in all of those measures. No wonder the survivors would rather stay closer to home.

Any help offered also has a price. Jim Doyle, Wisconsin's governor, is hoping that Mr. Bush will extend the state of emergency from southern states to northern ones, so that they too can receive federal aid for taking in thousands of people. That may be too much to hope for.

Congress has already agreed to provide $10.5 billion. Since FEMA is currently spending $500 million a day on relief and recovery, that will not last long. The White House has already asked Congress for an additional $52 billion. Together, Florida's four hurricanes in 2004 cost the federal government $14 billion, while insurers paid out much more. This time, the ratio will be reversed.

The insurance industry is in shock. Loss-adjusters still cannot get close enough to assess much of the damage; hundreds of them have fanned out across the region, trying to work their way in from the edge to the centre of the catastrophe. Latest estimates suggest that the damage to homes, businesses and infrastructure is around $100 billion, with private insurance claims as high as $35 billion. Some property owners without flood insurance (which mortgage lenders require of most people living in flood-plains) will get relief from a federal disaster-loan programme. Only about half of property owners in New Orleans hold flood coverage, and even fewer in hard-hit patches of Mississippi and Alabama. Renters and those who own homes outright are most likely to be uncovered.

America's insurers have had some bruises of late: 2004 was the worst year for catastrophes on record, and this year will surpass that. Stricter underwriting means that the industry as a whole is in better shape than it was in 2001, but Katrina will hit profits. Reinsurers, the big firms that provide a safety net in major disasters, will take the brunt of the burden. For now, the majors contend they can handle the fallout from Katrina, but losses—including those for interrupted business—are mounting by the day.

The broader economic fall-out of Katrina remains uncertain. Traditionally, big hurricanes—for all their devastation—have had only a small effect on the macro-economy. Katrina, though, may well be a different case.

Forecasters have cut their expectations for GDP for the rest of the year—the Treasury by half a percentage point, the Congressional Budget Office (CBO) by slightly more. But some have raised them for 2006 as reconstruction efforts boost output. The CBO fears that, from now to the end of the year, 400,000 jobs may be lost, though employment is "likely to rebound" later. The big unknown remains fuel costs and the risk that soaring prices for petrol, let alone physical supply shortages, will hit consumer spending hard.

Financial markets certainly seem gloomier about the country's growth prospects. Before Katrina hit, futures prices suggested the central bank would continue its upward march in interest rates over the next few months. Now, the markets reckon the Federal Reserve will cut this process short. But this week the president of the Chicago Fed sounded a different note, emphasising the risk of higher inflation.

And the fiscal impact could end up being sizeable. Some politicians talked of spending more than $150 billion on recovery and relief. Washington's budget boffins worry that all kinds of other requests will be attached to money for Katrina relief, such as (paradoxically) drought relief for farmers in the mid-west. Moreover, the political aftermath of the hurricane may dampen lawmakers' already tepid enthusiasm for budget-cutting. The 2006 budget—agreed in principle but not in detail—is supposed to include $35 billion in budget cuts over next five years, including in Medicaid, the federal-state health-care programme for the poor. Politicians will be loth [sic] to do any such trimming when America's vulnerabilities, in almost every region of social policy, have been so ruthlessly exposed.

*W*hile it would appear that policy-making authority in the United States is relatively clear, there have been a number of cases where lower levels of government have sought to take action on matters when the federal government has failed to act quickly enough, or when those lower levels of government have disagreed with the positions taken by the federal government.

For example, a number of U.S. cities adopted "nuclear free zone" policies in the 1970s in reaction to the U.S. government's policy of arming warships and fighter planes with nuclear missiles and warheads. While this action might appear to be purely symbolic, for some cities (such as those housing higher education institutions that conducted nuclear-based research), this had a real effect. Similarly, over 250 U.S. city leaders had signed the U.S. Mayor's Climate Agreement document by 2007, pledging to reduce carbon dioxide emissions within a certain time frame. This agree-

ment also reflects sub-national government frustration with the lack of progress by the federal government on climate control.

This selection raises another controversial issue in which some sub-national governments have attempted to take action in lieu of more aggressive federal policy—immigration. The federal government has continued to debate the relative merits of a guest worker program, amnesty for illegal immigrants, and construction of a wall between Mexico and the United States. Without definitive federal action, the city of Hazleton, Pennsylvania adopted a local ordinance seeking to penalize local landlords for renting housing to illegal immigrants or employers who hire them. But this article also notes how federalism has come to affect such local attempts, as a federal judge ruled that local governments do not have proper authority to make such policies; the battle continues, however, because other local governments have continued to pass similar ordinances including Valley Park, Missouri; Riverside, New Jersey; Escondido, California; and Farmers Branch, Texas.

Judge Rejects Hazleton Law on Immigrants; A City Cannot Take Such a National Issue into Its Own Hands, He Says

DAVID G. SAVAGE AND NICOLE GAOUETTE

A federal judge on Thursday struck down a Pennsylvania city's ordinance that sought to punish landlords who rent to illegal immigrants and employers who hire them, ruling that immigration law is the province of the federal government alone.

The measure in Hazleton had become a symbol and an inspiration for a growing movement among state and city officials to enact local laws to combat illegal immigration. Supporters of this effort charge that Washington has failed to control the U.S. borders or deal with the estimated 12 million illegal immigrants who live in the country.

Activists on both sides of the issue said that Thursday's decision—the first after a trial in federal court—dealt a major setback, but not a final defeat, to these local initiatives.

"Immigration is a national issue," U.S. District Judge James M. Munley said in knocking down the ordinance adopted last year in Hazleton, a city of about 30,000 that is 80 miles northwest of Philadelphia.

Led by the city's outspoken mayor, Louis J. Barletta, the City Council voted to fine landlords who rented to illegal immigrants and to revoke business permits of employers who hired them.

But Munley blocked the measures from taking effect and, in Thursday's 206-page decision, concluded that local officials lacked authority to go beyond federal law and impose penalties on businesses for hiring illegal immigrants.

"Allowing states or local governments to legislate with regard to the employment of unauthorized aliens would interfere with congressional objectives" to control immigration policy, Munley said.

The judge also noted that people in the country illegally had the legal right to challenge discriminatory ordinances in court.

"We cannot say clearly enough that persons who enter this country without legal authorization are not stripped immediately of all their rights because of this single illegal act," Munley wrote.

He noted that the Constitution says no person may be deprived of "due process of law." The Supreme Court has said this protection extends to those who have entered the country illegally, he added.

Civil liberties lawyers who sued to void the Hazleton ordinance called the ruling a sweeping victory and said it dealt a "body blow" to other local efforts to regulate illegal immigrants. Hazleton has inspired similar measures nationally.

"Today's decision sends an unmistakable message to local officials across the nation that these types of ordinances are a waste of taxpayers' money, anathema to American values and a violation of the Constitution," said Omar Jadwat of the ACLU Immigrants' Rights Project.

The ruling was also welcomed by the U.S. Chamber of Commerce. "State and local governments have no business setting national immigrant policy," said the agency's National Chamber Litigation Center.

But advocates of stricter measures against illegal immigrants said they were confident the U.S. Supreme Court would uphold a Hazleton-style ordinance.

"What's at stake . . . is the right of local communities to govern how business and commerce are conducted within their jurisdictions," said Dan Stein, president of the Federation for American Immigration Reform. "We are confident when the high court reviews the facts of this case, they will side with the right of local communities to take steps to protect themselves against the destructive impact of mass illegal immigration."

Congress has tried and failed to pass comprehensive immigration legislation for the last two years. States and localities have moved aggressively to fill the vacuum. The Federation for American Immigration Reform estimates that 1,200 local immigration measures are in progress or have passed. The Puerto Rican Legal Defense and Education Fund estimates that more than 100 localities have passed anti-immigration ordinances.

Many of these measures also face legal challenges. Last year, the Escondido, Calif., City Council moved to fine landlords who rented to illegal immigrants but withdrew the ordinance after it was put on hold by a federal judge.

According to the National Conference of State Legislatures, in the first four months of this year, state lawmakers had introduced at least 1,169 bills and resolutions related to immigration—compared with 570 bills introduced last year.

Barletta introduced his proposal in June 2006 after two illegal immigrants from the Dominican Republic were charged with killing a 29-year-old Hazleton man. "Illegal immigrants are destroying the city," Barletta said then. (The homicide charges were dropped three weeks ago because, prosecutors said, key witnesses were unreliable or unavailable. The men were to remain jailed until deportation.)

The former coal town had changed dramatically since Barletta became mayor in 2000, when the city had a population of 23,000, about 5% of whom were Latino. Cheap housing and proximity to farms and factories drew immigrants. By 2006, city officials estimated the town's population at 31,000, with 30% of residents Latino.

During the federal trial in March, lawyers for the American Civil Liberties Union disputed claims that new immigrants were responsible for an increase in crime. They introduced a 2002 study which found that native-born men were five times more likely to be incarcerated than those who were foreign-born.

Marshall Fitz of the American Immigration Lawyers Assn. said the ruling was significant for the same reason Hazleton's ordinance was significant. "It was the first one. If there are enough of these rulings, you are going to see states and localities second-guessing whether they want to go forward with these." Fitz said a ruling by one federal district judge set no precedent but was "an important signal."

Irvine immigration lawyer Angelo Paparelli—president of the Academy of Business Immigration Lawyers, which says it advocates "enlightened business immigration reform"—said the ruling could cool local illegal immigration campaigns.

"I think the cities and states will be given a handy justification for not taking action," he said, "and I hope the pressure will be redirected back at Congress, where it belongs."

In 1996, the federal government passed the Defense of Marriage Act (DOMA), which prevents, among other features, state governments from recognizing gay marriages if approved by another state. This law limits the effects of Article V of the U.S. Constitution, in which the "full faith and credit" clause has been interpreted to mean that laws passed in one state typically are recognized in all other states. Since that time, voters in a number of states have approved amendments to their respective state constitutions banning gay marriages/civil unions.

In this article, Charles Krauthammer from the Washington Post *argues against passing a constitutional amendment banning gay marriage. He is not an advocate of gay marriage—rather, he takes this position in large part because of his view of federalism and federal versus state authority. He believes that states should be allowed to decide within their own political cultures about controversial social policies such as gay marriage or assisted suicide—without the requirement that other states recognize such policies. Moreover, social policies are best decided by voters after much discussion and debate, in Krauthammer's view. He argues that by approving bans on gay marriage that were proposed as amendments to state constitutions, voters have taken the issue out of their own hands and given the ultimate decisions to courts and judicial interpretation. This article summarizes yet another issue of the politics of diversity that turns to a large degree on federalism.*

A Ban We Don't (Yet) Need

CHARLES KRAUTHAMMER

On Wednesday the Senate fell 18 votes short of the two-thirds majority that would have been required to pass a constitutional amendment banning gay marriage. The mainstream media joined Sen. Edward Kennedy in calling the entire debate a distraction from the nation's business and a wedge with which to divide Americans.

Since the main business of Congress is to devise ever more ingenious ways (earmarked and non-earmarked) to waste taxpayers' money, any distraction from the main business is welcome. As for dividing Americans, who came up with the idea of radically altering the most ancient of all social institutions in the first place? Until the past few years, every civilization known to man has defined marriage as between people of opposite sex. To charge with "divisiveness" those who would do nothing more than resist a radical overturning of that norm is a sign of either gross partisanship or serious dimwittedness.

And that partisanship and dimwittedness obscured the rather interesting substance of the recent Senate debate. It revolved around the two possible grounds for the so-called Marriage Protection Amendment: federalism and popular sovereignty.

Federalism. When one state, such as Massachusetts, adopts gay marriage, the full-faith-and-credit clause of the Constitution might reasonably be applied to require other states to recognize such marriages, and thus essentially force it upon the rest of the nation. Federalism, however, is meant to allow states the autonomy of social experimentation (as with Oregon's legalization of assisted suicide) from which other states can learn. It is not intended to force other states to follow.

But it turns out that the Massachusetts experiment has not been forced on other states. No courts have required other states to recognize gay marriages performed in Massachusetts. Gay activists have not pushed it, wisely calculating that it would lead to a huge backlash. Moreover, Congress's Defense of Marriage Act (DOMA) explicitly prevents the state-to-state export of gay marriage.

Should DOMA be overturned, that would justify a constitutional amendment to prevent one state from imposing its will on the other 49. But it has not been overturned. And under the current Supreme Court, it is unlikely to be. The Marriage Protection Amendment is therefore superfluous.

That leaves justification No. 2:

Popular Sovereignty. Gay marriage is a legitimate social issue to be decided democratically. The problem is that imperial judges are legislating their personal preferences, striking down popular will and calling it constitutional law.

Most notoriously, in Massachusetts a total of four judges out of seven decided that the time had come for gay marriage. More recently, in Georgia and Nebraska, judges have overturned (state) constitutional amendments banning gay marriage that had passed with more than 70 percent of the vote.

This is a rerun of the abortion fiasco: judicial fiat that decades later leaves the issue roilingly unsettled and divisive. This is no way to set social policy in a democracy. So why not have a federal constitutional amendment and smite the arrogant solons of Massachusetts, Nebraska and Georgia, and those yet to come, all at once?

Because it is an odd solution for a popular-sovereignty problem to take the gay-marriage issue completely out of the hands of the people. Once the constitutional amendment is passed, should the current ethos about gay marriage change, no people in any state could ever permit gay marriage.

The amendment actually ends up defeating the principle it sets out to uphold. The solution to judicial overreaching is to change the judiciary, not to undo every act of judicial arrogance with a policy-specific constitutional amendment. Where does it end? Yesterday it was school busing and abortion. Today it is flag burning and gay marriage.

It won't end until the Constitution becomes pockmarked with endless policy amendments. The Constitution was never intended to set social policy. Its purpose is to (a) establish the rules of governance and (b) secure for the individual citizen rights against the power of the state. It defaces the Constitution to turn it into a super-leg-islative policy document.

In the short run, judicial arrogance is to be fought democratically with the means still available. Rewording and repassing the constitutional amendment in Georgia, for example. Appealing the Nebraska decision right up to the Supreme Court, which, given its current composition, is extremely likely to terminate with prejudice this outrageous example of judicial interposition.

In the longer run, it means having Supreme Courts that routinely strike down such judicial imperialism. And that means electing presidents who nominate John Roberts and Sam Alito rather than Stephen Breyer and Ruth Bader Ginsburg.

True, this does nothing about today's judicial usurpation in Massachusetts. But that is the problem of its good citizens. If they want to, they have the power to amend their own state constitution. In the meantime, Massachusetts remains quarantined by DOMA.

Therefore, there is no need (yet) to disfigure the U.S. Constitution with a policy amendment.

This next piece examines a policy area that has involved all levels of government—means-tested welfare programs. Historically, there has always been significant localism in administration of welfare benefits but the role of the federal government has fluctuated—especially in terms of oversight and in funding practices. In 1996, under the Clinton administration, the Aid to Families with Dependent Children

(AFDC) program became TANF (Temporary Assistance to Needy Families). With TANF the role of the federal government changed. States were given more authority to administer the program, but without the federal funding that had been attached to the AFDC program. The states had substantial discretion to "get tougher" but could not design programs that they thought served their community by being more generous in particular areas.

Joe Soss and his colleagues take a scholarly view of the effects of state welfare policy-making and the possible racial implications of the policy shifts that allow states more punitive discretion in welfare policy decision-making. This discussion moves the debate away from the legal and constitutional arguments over governmental scope of authority and focuses instead on the results of how policy has been implemented once authority has shifted toward the states. The authors find that the single biggest predictor of whether states chose to be even more restrictive than the new federal guidelines was the racial composition of their welfare clients. States with higher percentages of African-Americans and Hispanics claiming welfare were the ones that, with increased discretion, got tougher on welfare. Compared to whites, individuals of color are more likely to live in states that are tougher on welfare. This article thus highlights places where "local control" can have disparate impact for minorities.

Welfare Policy Choices in the States: Does the Hard Line Follow the Color Line?

JOE SOSS, SANFORD F. SCHRAM, THOMAS P. VARTANIAN, AND ERIN E. O'BRIEN

In the 1990s, federal welfare reform shifted control over many aspects of social provision down to the state level. Some observers predicted the states would act as "laboratories of democracy" seeking out new and better ways to solve problems related to poverty. Others suggested the states would "race to the bottom" in an effort to pare costs and avoid becoming a comparatively generous "magnet" for low-income families. State policy choices, however, are more than just efforts to solve problems, and they can rarely be explained solely by the urge to minimize costs. They are, at root, political decisions, reflecting the wide range of values, beliefs, demands, and constraints that shape governance in a diverse democracy.

Under welfare reform, state lawmakers and their constituents confronted fundamental questions about how and when government should extend aid to the poor. As

Joe Soss, Sanford F. Schram, Thomas P. Vartanian, and Erin O'Brien, "Welfare Policy Choices in the States: Does the Hard Line Follow the Color Line?" *Focus*, newsletter of the Institute for Research on Poverty, vol. 23, no. 1 (Winter 2004), pp. 9–15. © 2004 by the Regents of the University of Wisconsin.

states responded to the new policy prescriptions dictated by the federal welfare law, the political process that sets the terms of relief for poor families was replicated many times, in different places, under different configurations of political forces. In the research summarized here we explore the sources of these decisions, taking advantage of the opportunity to observe how state responses differed within a single time period under a single federal mandate.[1]

Until recently, most quantitative research on the political roots of state welfare policies sought to explain differences in benefit levels and spending patterns.[2] In contrast, we analyze variation in the *institutional form* of welfare provision—the rules and penalties that condition access to resources and structure the treatment citizens receive in government programs. In the 1990s, public officials showed renewed interest in using program rules as tools to modify poor people's behaviors. The 1996 federal law emphasized such aid requirements, and as states responded, their policy changes focused less on the amount of relief offered than on the terms on which aid would be given. Some states adopted a moderate course in this area of reform; others used their enlarged discretion to pursue relatively stringent program rules, with punitive measures for those who did not comply. Here we seek to understand why some states were more likely than others to "use their new authority to limit access to social provision and, most especially, to shift the balance in welfare policy design from rights to obligations." Our findings, as we describe below, suggest that state choices can be traced in significant ways to race-related factors. To a degree that some may find surprising, the "hard line" in welfare reform appears to have followed the color line.

ENDING PERMISSIVENESS, GETTING TOUGH: POLICY CHOICE IN THE STATES

With welfare reform, states gained more authority over eligibility rules and administrative procedures than they had enjoyed since the 1960s. Proponents acclaimed the new, less-regulatory environment, seeing Temporary Assistance for Needy Families (TANF) as a "devolution revolution" that would liberate states from constricting federal rules and allow them to create more effective poverty policies. In a sense, however, the term "revolution" is a bit misleading: states did not gain unprecedented freedom to shape policy. Rather, they recouped many forms of discretion they had lost to the federal government during the welfare rights era of the 1960s. In addition, the federal law imposed new mandates and constraints on the states. For example, it set quotas on the percentage of adult recipients who must participate in "work-related activities," and defined these activities rather narrowly. Likewise, it imposed limits on the length of time states could provide cash assistance to residents.

In principle, states can now make benefits more accessible to poor families and enable clients to pursue new opportunities. Indeed, most states have passed policies that offer clients new services, supply transitional benefits, and allow clients to keep higher amounts of earnings. The political momentum toward welfare reform, however, was fueled largely by the belief that the existing program, Aid to Families with Dependent Children (AFDC), was too permissive. As reform advocate Lawrence Mead puts it, "Today 'welfare reform' largely means that the government seeks to supervise poor citizens"; public officials have embraced the idea that welfare provision is partly about "telling the poor what to do."[4] The federal legislation of 1996 reflected and reinforced this view, with its emphasis on ending welfare dependency and encouraging marriage. In consequence, when it came to program requirements, policy innovation in the states leaned in a restrictive direction. Many states stuck close to the basic federal rules, but the states that deviated from the baseline requirements (for work, time limits, and so on) mostly used their new authority to limit rather than expand access to cash assistance, though some states did increase "work supports" such as child care and transportation assistance.

In selecting policy choices for analysis, we emphasized two goals: covering the major domains of "get-tough" welfare reform (i.e., rules and penalties intended to counter permissiveness) and identifying the policies most salient in public debate and most widely considered by state governments. Surveying scholarly books and articles, policy reports, legislative materials, and mass media, we found a consistent emphasis on four key areas in which federal lawmakers sought to end permissiveness. Each defined a specific policy choice for state governments.

- Imposing obligations in exchange for assistance: states decided whether to demand work from recipients earlier than the federal requirement of 24 months.

- Ending long-term program usage: states decided whether to adopt a lifetime eligibility limit shorter than the federal requirement of 60 months.

- Changing social behavior, especially reproductive choices: states decided whether to impose a family cap denying additional benefits to children conceived by women receiving assistance.

- Imposing meaningful penalties: states decided whether to choose a weak, moderate, or strong sanctions policy for recipients' infractions.

As a group, these program rules define the key terms of participation for citizens seeking aid under TANF; they also capture some of the fundamental goals of 1990s welfare reform. But there are differences among them. Family caps, time limits, and work requirements are widely viewed as complementary tools for combating permissiveness; each is tied to a distinct goal: deterring childbirth among recipients, combating welfare dependency, and demanding work. Sanctions, in contrast, are punitive tools for enforcing a broad range of program rules that may have diverse political constituencies. Because of this greater reach and ambiguity, one might expect sanction choices to be subject to a wider range of political influences.

* * * * *

STATE POLICY CHOICES: TESTING THE HYPOTHESES

. . . [W]e employed a set of 10 independent, state-level variables to structure our analysis: the unmarried birth rate, the caseload-to-population ratio, government ideology, interparty competition, low-income voter turnout, the unemployment rate, change in the incarceration rate, the percentages of Hispanics and blacks, and propensity to welfare innovation.

We began our analysis by assuming that TANF policy choices constituted a single "package" of stringent policies driven by a coherent set of political forces. Our empirical analysis based on a single equation did, indeed, offer some explanatory power. It told a relatively simple story based in race and ideology: states were significantly more likely to make restrictive policy choices if they had conservative governments and if blacks made up a higher percentage of AFDC recipients. No other factors stood out.

. . . [H]owever, the policies we selected express somewhat different political motives and so may actually be influenced by different configurations of political forces. This speculation is strengthened by the fact that states did not in general adopt the entire package of restrictive policies. The median state, indeed, adopted only one, and only five states adopted all four. We thus undertook separate analyses for each of our four policies. . . .

The analyses showed that, in each area, restrictive policy choices were systematically related to the state-level characteristics we identified; 9 of our 10 independent variables were statistically significant in at least one area. For some of the individual hypotheses, the patterns of influence appeared quite strong. To begin with, family caps and strict time limits seemed to arise from virtually identical processes, with each being closely tied to race. All else equal, these policies were significantly more likely in only two kinds of states: those with a higher percentage of blacks and those with a higher percentage of Hispanics in their AFDC caseloads. Our analysis of work requirements also revealed a tight cluster of determining factors—in this case related not to race but to our social control hypotheses. States with larger increases in incarceration from 1990 to 1996 were significantly more likely to adopt strict work requirements, as were states with tighter labor markets.

Sanctions, as we expected, evoked a more complex set of relationships. Race was again prominent: states with larger proportions of blacks in their AFDC caseloads were significantly more likely to adopt strict sanctions. So too were states with conservative governments, less vigorous party competition, higher unmarried birth rates, and smaller AFDC caseloads, and states that were policy innovators. The only characteristic that appeared to have no significant effect on any area of welfare policy was low-income voter turnout—a finding we return to below.

Thus, in three of our four policy domains, the racial composition of welfare recipients turned out to be a significant predictor of state choices, even after the effects of other state differences were taken into account. To gauge the scale of these effects, we made use of an interpretive procedure developed by Gary King and colleagues. First, we created a "hypothetically average" state by setting all our independent variables (except the racial composition of the welfare rolls) at their mean value. We then estimated how the probability of this state making a particular policy choice would change as we shifted the black percentage of its welfare rolls from a low to a high value-assuming that no other state characteristic changed at all. . . . [A]s the percentage of black recipients rises across its full range, so too does the probability that states will adopt strong (full family) sanctions, institute strict time limits, and introduce a family cap policy. The estimated effects of having more Hispanics on the rolls are similarly large. Most dramatically, as the percentage of black recipients rises from moderately low to moderately high, this "average" state's chance of instituting a family cap rises from 9 percent to 75 percent; the same shift for Hispanics produces a parallel change from 19 percent to 63 percent.[12]

This analysis suggests that far from being a pure technocratic search for policy solutions, the construction of public assistance policy in the new era of welfare reform continues to be shaped by forces that are familiar in the history of American welfare politics—particularly race, ideology, and the control of representative institutions. At the same time, it also underscores that important insights may be lost if diverse policy choices are lumped together in a single index and analyzed as an undifferentiated move away from permissive program rules.

THE IMPORTANCE OF RACE

To the question of whether "hard line" policy choices under welfare reform have followed the "color line" in the states, our answer must be a qualified—but unequivocal—yes. In two of our four policy areas, time limits and family caps, we find very strong connections to the black and Hispanic proportion of state welfare rolls, and we find no relationship to any other factor. These results focus attention squarely on race as a central problem for contemporary welfare reform.

In contrast, and despite considerable evidence that welfare politics is bound up with racial stereotypes regarding work effort,[13] our analysis provided no evidence that work mandates have been linked to the racial composition of the rolls. Instead, it pointed to two factors suggested by social control theory: the tightness of state labor markets and the rate of increase in state incarceration rates.

Sanctions policy provided the best example of how racial effects may intersect with other forces to shape state policy choices. Strong sanctions were especially likely in states with large numbers of black welfare recipients. But they were also significantly more likely in states with several other characteristics: conservative governments, less vigorous party competition, higher unmarried birth rates, a history of policy innovation, and smaller AFDC caseloads. We may speculate that the popularity of sanctions is due to their versatility: they raise the stakes for participants who fail to follow any of a variety of new welfare initiatives, and in legislative debates they may not be tied to any specific program goal other than achieving "compliance."

On balance, these results suggest that policy devolution created new openings for racial distortions in U.S. welfare policy. Indeed, because state policy choices have tracked so closely with the racial composition of welfare rolls, black recipients nationwide are now more likely than their white counterparts to be participating under tough welfare policies. For example, a black recipient who conceives a child is now more likely than a white recipient to live in a state that offers no additional aid for the child. Likewise, a black recipient who misses a meeting with a caseworker is now disproportionately likely to live in a state where this single infraction causes family benefits to be terminated. . . . It is hard to know how such different rates of *exposure* to sanction policies actually translate into rates of *being sanctioned*. After all, many intermediary processes are involved within each state. But the numbers do suggest that, if full-family sanctions were applied equally to blacks and whites in each state, national rates of sanctioning would be higher for black recipients than for their white counterparts.

REFLECTIONS AND EXTENSIONS: REVISITING OUR FINDINGS

The research reported in this article was conducted immediately after the passage of welfare reform and has circulated among political scientists for some time now. It is well worth asking how the findings have fared and, as well, whether our findings for race might have represented an evanescent phase—an echo of past policies that disappeared as the system matured. Our central findings regarding the connection between racial composition and hard-line welfare policies proved to be very robust in the face of our own efforts to dislodge them. Statistical tests indicate that they do not, for example, simply reflect the distinctiveness of the American South. Nor do they fade when subjected to additional controls for social behaviors that vary across racial groups.

* * * * *

Beyond the issue of race, it is also worth asking about findings for other political factors reported here—especially our lack of significant results for some variables we expected to play a role. First, our analysis suggested that turnout rates among low-income voters had no discernible influence on TANF policy choices in the states. Yet in a country with very high wage and income inequality, it struck us as unlikely that income and class divisions played no role. Recent evidence suggests we had the right expectations but the wrong measure. Fellowes and Rowe's analysis demonstrates that it is not absolute levels of low-income voting participation, but rather class bias in participation (low-income turnout relative to high-income turnout) that actually matters. And it matters in precisely the direction one would expect: restrictive TANF eligibility and work policies are significantly more likely in states where electoral turnout is more biased toward high-income, as opposed to low-income, residents.

Second, in supplemental analyses reported in our 2001 article, we found that none of our four TANF policies were significantly affected by state resource levels, as measured by per capita income, or by the policies of neighboring states. Although brimming state coffers do not guarantee generous welfare policies, states with more resources may provide higher benefits than less wealthy states.[15] With the shift to block-granted funding, however, many observers became concerned that states could compete to avoid becoming a relatively generous "welfare magnet" (attractive to low-income people from other states), and accordingly would engage in a "race to the bottom." This concern suggested wealthy states might not use their resources to offer greater benefits and would, instead, try to keep pace with the least generous policies of their neighbors. By contrast, our results suggested that neither state resources nor neighboring states' policies exerted a discernible effect on TANF policy choices. Similarly, Fellowes and Rowe find little evidence that state policies responded either to abundant resources in their own state or to the restrictiveness of policies in neighboring states—although their evidence does suggest that states with more slack resources may be more likely to allow clients to continue receiving benefits, even if they are not fully meeting traditional work requirements.

* * * * *

THE FUTURE OF STATE POLICY EXPERIMENTATION

Freedom from the tether of federal regulation hitches welfare policy to the social and political forces that operate in each of the American states. In the first half of the 20th century, such state discretion was used for a variety of social purposes. Welfare policies were used to control women's sexual and parental behaviors (e.g., the "man in the house" rule), and to regulate the labor activities of the poor, absorbing them during slow economic times and impelling work when more hands were needed in the factories or on the farms. Likewise, many states administered benefits in a racially biased manner, withholding aid from people of color and using program rules to punish those who violated race-specific, segregation-enforcing norms of social conduct.

This era largely came to an end with the welfare rights victories of the late 1960s. Today, our post–civil-rights political and legal context makes it unlikely that the TANF system could replicate the worst of earlier practices. Yet TANF policies remain deeply entwined with the politics of gender, class, and race. Recent policies include rules that explicitly target women's sexual and familial behaviors, primarily related to childbearing among unmarried women. Meanwhile, work enforcement remains central. Finally, our central conclusion in this article is that race and ethnicity continue to be major influences on the terms of relief state governments set for poor families. Indeed, as caseloads have become slightly more skewed toward people of color under the TANF program, people of color . . . have become more concentrated in states adopting the stricter policies.

Based on our own study and the research that has followed, we are convinced that the racial composition of the welfare rolls has a significant relationship to state policy choices that "get tough" on TANF recipients. But we also believe this statistical correlation raises more questions than it answers. What does it mean? Do lawmakers operate from different assumptions when they see their policy targets as people of color? Do public preferences change in response to the composition of a state's welfare rolls, and do these constituent views shape policy outcomes? Does the observed relationship between race and TANF policies reflect divergent patterns of political development in states with different levels of racial-ethnic diversity? The search for a compelling causal account continues, What seems more certain, however, is that the "problem of the color line" and troubling questions of racial justice remain very much with us as we move into the second decade of America's new era of welfare provision.

Notes

1. This article summarizes research presented in greater detail in two articles by J. Soss, S. Schram, T. Vartanian, and E. O'Brien, "Setting the Terms of Relief: Explaining State Policy Choices in the Devolution Revolution," *American Journal of Political Science* 45, no. 2 (April 2001): 378–95, and "The Hard Line and the Color Line: Race, Welfare, and the Roots of Get-Tough Reform," Chapter 9 in *Race and the Politics of Welfare Reform*, ed. S. Schram, J. Soss, and R. Fording (Ann Arbor: University of Michigan Press, 2003).

2. See, e.g., C. Howard, "The American Welfare State, or States?" *Political Research Quarterly* 52 (1999): 421–42; R. Plotnick and R. Winters, "A Politico-Economic Theory of

Income Distribution," *American Political Science Review* 79 (1985): 458–73.

4. L. Mead, "Telling the Poor What to Do," Public *Interest* 132 (Summer): 97–112.

12. "Moderately low" to "moderately high" are defined as one standard deviation below the mean and one standard deviation above the mean, respectively. . . .

15. J. Tweedie, "Resources Rather Than Needs: A State-Centered Model of Welfare Policy-Making," *American Journal of Political Science* 38, no. 3 (1994): 651–72.

✖ DISCUSSION QUESTIONS ✖

1. How does U.S. federalism affect the kind of policies that have a diversity focus to them—for example, immigration policy, disaster relief, or welfare policy? Does the kind of governmental system make a difference, or would these issues be resolved in the same way under a different form of government? Which level of government has protected minority rights more? Why?

2. Which system of government (federated, confederated, unitary) do you think can best deal with modern problems? Why did our federated system fail in responding to the Katrina disaster? Some observers have suggested the government's failure to adequately respond to the Katrina aftermath *because* New Orleans had a largely poor and African-American population. Do you agree? Why or why not?

3. Why has it been so unclear as to which level of government has responsibility in a given policy area? Isn't there a distinct separation of powers and authority between the national and state governments? What are the arguments in support of a local government such as Hazleton, Pennsylvania in adopting a local ordinance regarding illegal immigrants? What are the arguments for leaving such policy-making to the national government?

4. Should gay adults have the same rights as heterosexual adults have, including the legal right to marry? Why or why not? There is a federal Defense of Marriage Act—do states need to adopt their own laws (or state constitutional amendments) prohibiting gay marriage too?

5. Based on your reading of the Soss et al. piece on welfare reform, what is your reaction to the changes created by the Personal Responsibility and Work Opportunity Reconciliation Act of 1996? Explain. Are there other social welfare policy areas where federalism and the politics of diversity might be at play?

Additional Resources

http://www.brookings.edu
The Brookings Institution conducts research on a wide variety of issues related to federalism, including those that investigate welfare policy and how the federal government has allocated funding to states and local communities in response to Hurricanes

Katrina, Rita, and Wilma which can be found in the federalism section of its web site (http://www.brookings.edu/topics/federalism.aspx). Brookings also offers a variety of research papers on immigration policy, including "The Impact of Immigration on States and Localities," which looks at the intergovernmental dynamics of current and proposed immigration policy in the United States (http://www.brookings.edu/topics/immigration.aspx).

http://www.heritage.org/
The Heritage Foundation conducts research on a variety of public policy issues, including several that relate to gay marriage and federal/state/local policy. Among the papers written on the subject include "Federalism—Marriage Amendment Protects Federalism" (http://www.heritage.org/Research/Family/wm531.cfm) and "A Defining Moment: Marriage, the Court, and the Constitution," a "backgrounder" paper (http://www.heritage.org/Research/LegalIssues/bg1759.cfm).

http://www.cato.org/
The Cato Institute promotes "limited representative government" through its wide-ranging research efforts. Areas of interest include "Government and Politics" (with a focus on federalism, elections, and campaign finance), as well as "Law and Civil Liberties," "Immigration and Labor Markets," and "Health, Welfare, and Entitlements" (http://www.cato.org/researchareas.php). Publications include "The Federal Marriage Amendment: Unnecessary, Anti-Federalist, and Anti-Democratic" (http://www.cato.org/pub_display.php?pub_id=6379).

http://www.fed-soc.org/
The Federalist Society for Law and Public Policy Studies is a self-proclaimed "group of conservatives and libertarians" advocating strict constructionist interpretation of the Constitution. Among its committees and subcommittees includes a group focused on federalism and the role of state courts in the federal system.

http://www.landmarkcases.org/
This site provides a forum to discuss and analyze various landmark U.S. Supreme Court cases. Among the cases discussed include those involving interpretations of the Commerce Clause and civil rights (*Heart of Atlanta Motel v. U.S.*, 1964) and whether the federal government had the authority to enact the 1964 Civil Rights Act. Other relevant cases discussed include *U.S. v. Lopez* (1995).

The Last Abortion Clinic (2005) is a PBS *Frontline* video that traces the pro-life and pro-choice movements at each level of government and how U.S. Supreme Court decisions have raised issues of federalism with regard to abortion policy.

Immigration on Main Street (2007) is a PBS *NOW* program that traces how the mayors of two New Jersey communities have responded in different ways to federal policy and enforcement on illegal immigration.

3

AMERICAN POLITICAL CULTURE:
NOTIONS AND BOUNDARIES

American Dream ideology . . . all spelled out by *The Office*'s character "Dwight". American Dream ideology is one of the most pervasive aspects of American political culture, but, as Dwight's firm belief suggests, there is considerable debate as to whether the dream is myth or reality.

There are at least two major tensions in American political culture that bear directly upon demography and diversity. The first tension involves the degree to which a single American political culture actually exists. Just how shared is political culture in the United States? Is there a core set of values, beliefs, or political norms that most people in the United States agree upon? Or, alternatively, is American political culture inherently contested? Are one's political values and beliefs so determined by one's social position that there is relatively little that Americans can agree define our political culture? These questions reflect the debate between the viewpoints that U.S. political culture is either based on "shared values or is demographically contested." The "*shared values versus demographically contested*" debate has major ramifications for the polity and the ability of government to function effectively. If, for instance, one agrees that there is a commonly shared set of values that define our politics, then it is not hard to image a polity where political outcomes—even those one does not favor— are viewed as legitimate. If, however, one sees American political culture as inherently contested, then a more critical stance toward governmental actors and the legitimacy of their decisions is natural.

The second major tension involving political culture and diversity shifts debate from "who believes what" to "is what 'we' believe accurate?" This "*myth versus reality*" debate considers potential tensions between what many Americans say defines our political culture (equality, individualism, popular sovereignty) against the hard-nosed realities of day-to-day American life. For the politics of diversity and equality, these comparisons can suggest that some of America's most highly esteemed political values do not always correspond with the lived experiences of many Americans. Those who experience these gaps are more likely to be female, of color, and less affluent. Potential responses to this state of affairs depend on where one thinks the United States is headed. If, for instance, one sees equality as an eventual reality (perhaps citing legal changes over the past 50 years), then divergence between American political promise and current reality is perhaps not a cause for alarm. We will get there. If, however, one sees equality as stalled and increasingly embedded in social and economic practices, then the gap between myth and reality for particular groups is likely cause for alarm.

Taken together, the articles that follow tug on these two tensions in American political culture and highlight the ways in which debates surrounding American political culture are inextricably linked to diversity. The tension of "*shared versus demographically contested political culture(s)*" calls for us to examine potential group-based differences in what it means to be an American and what living in America is like. It begs the questions of what, if anything, must Americans share when it comes to political values in order for a government to function and be viewed as legitimate. The "*myth versus reality*" tension shines light on differences between the views individual Americans regularly endorse and the multiple realities of American life. The articles all suggest the American Dream is potent—but take differential stances on (1) whether it really is just a dream; and, (2) for whom the Dream serves.

*T*his first selection comes from Jennifer Hochschild's book Facing Up to the American Dream. *In it, Hochschild focuses on an aspect of political culture that those living in the United States almost universally endorse: the American Dream. Hochschild identifies four main aspects of the Dream: (1) everyone can pursue it regardless of demographic characteristics; (2) one may reasonably anticipate success in America; (3) success is pursued and rewarded via individual effort; and, (4) success is associated with virtue. That Americans believe this is not contested—Hochschild shows how belief in the American Dream is a shared aspect of U.S. political culture.*

In turning to differences between what we believe and whether it is descriptively accurate (i.e., "myth versus reality"), however, Hochschild's analysis identifies flaws in the Dream. There are places where it is simply not descriptively accurate and her analysis indicates that this gap has particular ramifications for individuals of color, those of lower economic status, and women. In an ironic twist, formulating a political community adept at addressing these gaps is encumbered by often steadfast belief in the American Dream.

What Is the American Dream?

JENNIFER HOCHSCHILD

"In the beginning," wrote John Locke, "all the world was *America*."[1] Locke was referring specifically to the absence of a cash nexus in primitive society. But the sentence evokes the unsullied newness, infinite possibility, limitless resources that are commonly understood to be the essence of the "American dream." The idea of the American dream has been attached to everything from religious freedom to a home in the suburbs, and it has inspired emotions ranging from deep satisfaction to disillusioned fury. Nevertheless, the phrase elicits for most Americans some variant of Locke's fantasy—a new world where anything can happen and good things might.

. . . But one cannot address that subject, not eventually move beyond it to evaluate the future of the American dream and its society, without knowing what the dream is and how it operates. That knowledge is the goal of this chapter.

THE MEANING OF SUCCESS

The American dream consists of tenets about achieving success. Let us first explore the meaning of "success" and then consider the rules for achieving it.

* * * * *

. . . Success can be measured in at least three ways, with important normative and behavioral consequences. First, it can be *absolute*. In this case, achieving the American dream implies reaching some threshold of well-being, higher than where one began but not necessarily dazzling. As Bruce Springsteen puts it, "I don't think the American dream was that everybody was going to make . . . a billion dollars, but it was that everybody was going to have an opportunity and the chance to live a life with some decency and some dignity and a chance for some self-respect."[6]

Second, success can be *relative*. Here achieving the American dream consists in becoming better off than some comparison point, whether one's childhood, people in the old country, one's neighbors, a character from a book, another race or gender—anything or anyone that one measures oneself against. Relative success implies no threshold of well-being, and it may or may not entail continually changing the comparison group as one achieves a given level of accomplishment. A benign version of relative success is captured by James Comer's "kind of competition . . . we had . . . going on" with "the closest friends that we had":

> When we first met them, we had a dining room and they didn't. They went back and they turned one of their bedrooms into a dining room. . . . After that we bought this big Buick car. And we came to their house and they had bought another car. She bought a fur coat one year and your dad bought me one the

next. But it was a friendly thing, the way we raced. It gave you something to work for, to look forward to. Every year we tried to have something different to show them what we had done, and they would have something to show us.

William Byrd II articulated a more malign version in 1736: slaves "blow up the pride, and ruin the industry of our white people, who seeing a rank of poor creatures below them, detest work for fear it should make them look like slaves."[7]

Success can, alternatively, be *competitive*—achieving victory over someone else. My success implies your failure. Competitors are usually people, whether known and concrete (opponents in a tennis match) or unknown and abstract (all other applicants for a job) . . .

TENETS OF SUCCESS

The American dream that we were all raised on is a simple but powerful one—if you work hard and play by the rules you should be given a chance to go as far as your God-given ability will take you.
—President Bill Clinton, speech to Democratic Leadership Council, 1993

In one sentence, President Clinton has captured the bundle of shared, even unconsciously presumed, tenets about achieving success that make up the ideology of the American dream. Those tenets answer the questions: Who may pursue the American dream? In what does the pursuit consist? How does one successfully pursue the dream? Why is the pursuit worthy of our deepest commitment?

The answer to "who" in the standard ideology is "everyone, regardless of ascriptive traits, family background, or personal history." The answer to "what" is "the reasonable anticipation, though not the promise, of success, however it is defined." The answer to "how" is "through actions and traits under one's own control." The answer to "why" is "true success is associated with virtue." Let us consider each rule in turn.

WHO MAY PURSUE SUCCESS?

The first tenet, that everyone may always pursue their dream, is the most direct connotation of Locke's "in the beginning . . . "

[F]ewer than one-fifth [of Americans] see race, gender, religion, or class as very important for "getting ahead in life." Even two-thirds of the poor are certain that Americans like themselves "have a good chance of improving our standard of living," and up to three times as many Americans as Europeans make that claim.[10] In effect, Americans believe that they can create a personal mini-state of nature that will allow them to slough off the past and invent a better future.

WHAT DOES ONE PURSUE?

The second tenet, that one may reasonably anticipate success, is less straightforward. "Reasonable anticipation" is far from a guarantee, as all children on the morning of their birthday know. But "reasonable anticipation" is also much more than simply longing; most children are fairly sure of getting at least some of what they wish for on their birthday. On a larger scale, from its inception America has been seen by many as an extravagant birthday party:

Seagull: A whole countrie of English is there, man, . . . and . . . the Indians are so in love with 'hem that all the treasure they have they lay at their feete . . . Golde is more plentiful there than copper is with us. . . . Why, man, all their dripping pans and their chamberpots are pure golde; and all the chaines with which they channe up their streets are massie golde; all the prisoners they take are fettered in golde; and for rubies and diamonds they goe forthe on holy dayes and gather 'hem by the sea shore to hang on their childrens coats.[11]

Presumably few Britons even in 1605 took this message literally, but the hope of abundant riches—whether material, spiritual, or otherwise—persists.

Thus Americans are exhorted to "go for it" in their advertisements as well as their commencement addresses. And they do; three-quarters of Americans, compared with only one-third of Britons, West Germans, and Hungarians (and fewer Dutch), agree that they have a good chance of improving their standard of living. Twice as many Americans as Canadians or Japanese think future generations of their nationality will live better than the present generation.[12]

HOW DOES ONE PURSUE SUCCESS?

The third premise, for those who do not take Seagull literally, explains how one is to achieve the success that one anticipates. Ralph Waldo Emerson is uncharacteristically succinct on the point: "There is always a reason, in the man, for his good or bad fortune, and so in making money."[13]

* * * * *

[S]urveys unanimously show Americans' strong support for rewarding people in the marketplace according to their talents and accomplishments rather than their needs, efforts, or simple existence.[15] And Americans mostly believe that people are in fact rewarded for their acts. In 1952, fully 88 percent of Americans agreed that "there is plenty of opportunity and anyone who works hard can go as far as he wants"; in 1980, 70 percent concurred.[16]

Comparisons across space yield the same results as comparisons across time. In a 1973 survey of youth in ten nations, only Swedes and British disagreed more than did Americans that a man's [sic] future is "virtually determined" by his family background. A decade later only 31 percent of Americans agreed that in their nation "what you achieve in life depends largely on your family background," compared with over 50 percent of Austrians and Britons, and over 60 percent of Italians.[17] Most pointedly, half of American adolescents compared with one-fourth of British adolescents agreed in 1972 that "people get to be poor . . . [because] they don't work hard enough."[18]

Americans also believe more than do Europeans that people ought not to be buffered from the consequences of their actions, so long as they have a fair start in life. Thus up to four times as many more Americans think college opportunities should be increased, but roughly half as many think the government should reduce the income disparity between high- and low-income citizens, or provide jobs or income support for the poor.[19]

WHY IS SUCCESS WORTH PURSUING?

Implicit in the flows of oratory and survey responses is the fourth tenet of the American dream, that the pursuit of success warrants so much fervor because it is associated with virtue. "Associated with" means at least four things: virtue leads to success, success makes a person virtuous, success indicates virtue, or apparent success is not real success unless one is also virtuous.

* * * * *

[Americans] distinguish between the worthy and unworthy rich, as well as the deserving and undeserving poor. For example, most Americans characterize "yuppies" as people who "play fashionable games" and "eat in trendy restaurants," and on the whole they enjoy watching such forms of conspicuous consumption. But they also characterize yuppies as selfish, greedy, inclined to flaunt their wealth, and imbued with a false sense of superiority. These traits they mostly find unacceptable. Overall, Americans overwhelmingly deplore the 1980s sentiment of "making it fast while you can regardless of what happened to others."[21] This is not simply a reaction against the Reagan years. In surveys throughout the 1970s, four in ten Americans deemed honesty to be the most important quality for a child to learn, compared with 2 percent proclaiming that a child should try hard to succeed. Virtually all Americans require that their friends be "honest" and "responsible"—core components of the third and fourth tenets.[22]

Americans also focus more on virtue than do citizens of other nations, at least in their self-descriptions. A survey of youth in ten nations found that more Americans than people in any other country described their chief goal in life as "sincerity and love between myself and others," and in only one other nation (the Philippines) did more youth seek "salvation through faith." Conversely, only in Sweden did fewer youths seek "money and position," and only in three other countries did fewer seek "freedom from restrictions." More Americans than Europeans gain strength from religion, report prayer to be an important part of their daily life, and agree that there are universally applicable "clear guidelines about what is good or evil."[23] In short, "this country succeeds in living a very sinful life without being deeply cynical. That is the difference between Europe and America, and it signifies that ethics *means* something here."[24]

* * * * *

VIRTUES OF THE AMERICAN DREAM

. . . If one measures success absolutely and accepts a wide array of indicators of success, the ideology portrays America as a land of plenty, and Americans as "people of plenty."[25]

* * * * *

If success is measured competitively and defined narrowly, however, the ideology portrays a different America. Hard work and virtue combined with scarce resources produce a few spectacular winners and many dismissible losers. . . .

. . . Americans prefer the self-image of universal achievement to that of a few stalwarts triumphing over weaker contenders.[28] What matters most, however, is not any single image but rather the elasticity and range of the ideology of the American dream. People can encourage themselves with soft versions, congratulate themselves with harder ones, and exult with the hardest, as their circumstances and characters warrant.

Thus the American dream is an impressive ideology. It has for centuries lured people to America and moved them around within it, and it has kept them striving in horrible conditions against impossible odds. Most Americans celebrate it unthinkingly, along with apple pie and motherhood; criticism typically is limited to imperfections in its application. But like apple pie and motherhood, the American dream turns out upon closer examination to be less than perfect. Let us look, then, at flaws intrinsic to the dream.

FLAWS IN THE TENETS OF THE AMERICAN DREAM

The First Tenet

The first tenet, that everyone can participate equally and can always start over, is troubling to the degree that it is not true. It is, of course, never true in the strongest sense; people cannot shed their existing selves as snakes do their skin. So the myth of the individual mini-state of nature is just that-a fantasy to be sought but never achieved.

Fantasies are fine so long as people understand that that is what they are. For that reason, a weaker formulation of the first tenet—people start the pursuit of success with varying advantages, but no one is barred from the pursuit—is more troubling because the gap between ideological claim and actual fact is harder to recognize. As a factual claim, the first tenet is largely false; for most of American history, women of any race and men who were Native American, Asian, black, or poor were barred from all but a narrow range of "electable futures." [29] Ascriptive constraints have arguably been weakened over time,[30] but until recently no more than about a third of the population was able to take seriously the first premise of the American dream.

This flaw has implications beyond the evident ones of racism and sexism. The emotional potency of the American dream has made people who *were* able to identify with it the norm for everyone else. White men, especially European immigrants able to ride the wave of the Industrial Revolution (and to benefit from the absence of competition from the rest of the population) to comfort or even prosperity, are the epitomizing demonstration of America as the bountiful state of nature. Those who do not fit the model disappear from the collective self-portrait. Thus the irony is doubled: not only has the ideal of universal participation been denied to most Americans, but also the very fact of its denial has itself been denied in our national self-image

* * * * *

The Second Tenet

The flaws of the second tenet of the American dream, the reasonable anticipation of success, stem from the close link between anticipation and expectation. That link presents little problem so long as there are enough resources and opportunities that everyone has a reasonable chance of having some expectations met. . . .

. . . But if they do not, worse yet, if they used to but do no longer—then the dream rapidly loses its appeal. . . .

[T]he right to aspire to success works as an ideological substitute for a guarantee of success only if it begins to approach it. When people recognize that chances for success are slim or getting slimmer, the whole tenor of the American dream changes dramatically for the worse.

* * * * *

This logic suggests a dynamic: as resources become tighter or success is more narrowly defined, Americans are likely to shift their understanding of success from absolute to relative to competitive. Before the 1980s, claims one journalist, "there was always enough to go around, plenty of places in the sun. It didn't even matter much about the rich so long as everyone was living better, it seemed the rich couldn't be denied their chance to get richer." But "today [in 1988] that wave [of prosperity] has crested. . . . Now when the rich get richer, the middle class stagnates—and the poor get decidedly poorer. If left unchecked, a polarization of income . . . is likely to provoke consequences that will affect America's politics and power, to say nothing of its psyche."[35]

The risks of anticipating success do not stop with anticipation. Attaining one's dreams can be surprisingly problematic. From William Shakespeare to William Faulkner, writers have limned the loneliness of being at the top, the spiritual costs of cutthroat competition, the shallowness of a society that rewards achievement above all else.

* * * * *

The problems of success, however, pale beside the problems of failure. Because success is so central to Americans' self-image, and because they expect as well as hope to achieve, Americans are not gracious about failure. Others' failure reminds them that the dream may be just that—a dream, to be distinguished from waking reality. Their own failure confirms that fear. As Zora Neale Hurston puts it, "there is something about poverty that smells like death."[40]

Furthermore, the better the dream works for other people, the more devastating is failure for the smaller and smaller proportion of people left behind. In World War II, members of military units with a high probability of promotion were less satisfied with advancement opportunities than members of units with a much lower probability of promotion, because failure to be promoted in the former case was both more salient and more demonstrably a personal rather than a systemic flaw. The "tunnel effect" is a more nuanced depiction of this phenomenon of relative deprivation. The first stage is one of relative gratification, in which others' success enhances one's own well-being. After all, drivers in a traffic jam in a tunnel are initially pleased when cars in the adjacent lane begin to move "because advances of others supply information about a more benign external environment; receipt of this information produces gratification; and this gratification overcomes, or at least suspends, *envy*." At some point, however, those left behind come to believe that their heightened expectations will not be met; not only are their hopes now dashed, but they are also worse off than when the upward mobility began. "Nonrealization of the expectation ["that my turn to move will soon come"] will at some point result in my 'becoming furious.'"[41] And one is still stuck in the tunnel. In short, the ideology of the American dream includes no provision for failure; a failed dream denies the loser not only success but even a safe harbor within which to hide the loss.

The Third Tenet

Failure is made more harsh by the third premise of the American dream—the belief that success results from actions and traits under one's own control. Logically, it does not follow that if success results from individual volition, then failure results from lack of volition. All one needs in order to see the logical flaw here is the distinction between necessary and sufficient. But that distinction is not obvious or intuitive, and in any case the psychologic of the American dream differs from strict logic. In the psychologic, if one may claim responsibility for success, one must accept responsibility for failure.

Americans who do everything they can and still fail may come to understand that effort and talent alone do not guarantee success. But they have a hard time persuading others. After all, they are losers—why listen to them? Will we not benefit more by listening to winners (who seldom challenge the premise that effort and talent breed success)?

The Fourth Tenet

Failure, then, is unseemly for two reasons: it challenges the blurring between anticipation and promise that is the emotional heart of the American dream, and people who fail are presumed to lack talent or will. The coup de grace comes from the fourth tenet of the dream, the association of success with virtue. By the psychologic just described, if success implies virtue, failure implies sin.

*****

Small wonder that in the late twentieth century even the poor blame the poor for their condition. Despite her vivid awareness of exploitation by the rich, an aging cleaning woman insists that many people are poor because they "make the money and drink it all up. They don't care about the kids or the clothes. Just have a bottle on that table all the time." Losers even blame themselves: an unemployed factory worker, handicapped by a childhood accident, "wish[es] to hell I could do it [save money for his children]. I always said for years, 'I wanna get rich, I wanna get rich.' But then, phew! My mind doesn't have the strong will. I say, 'Well, I'm *gonna* do it.' Only the next day's different." These people are typical . . .

The equation of failure with evil and success with virtue cannot be attributed to poor education or low status. College students "who learned that a fellow student had been awarded a cash prize as a result of a random drawing were likely to conclude that he had in fact worked especially hard." In another experiment, subjects rated a presumed victim of electric shocks who was randomly selected to receive compensation for her pain more favorably than a victim who would not be compensated. "The sight of an innocent person suffering without possibility of reward or compensation motivated people to devalue the attractiveness of the victim in order to bring about a more appropriate fit between her fate and her character."[45] Devaluing losers allows people to maintain their belief that the world is fundamentally just, even when it patently is not.

Losers are obviously harmed by the association of success with virtue. But the association creates equally important, if less obvious, problems for winners. . . . If I continue to win, all is well; if I falter, I lose my *amour propre* as well as my wealth or power. Alternatively, if I recognize that I partly owe my success to lying to a few clients, evading a few taxes, cheating a few employees, then I am likely to feel considerable guilt. This guilt might induce reform and recompense, but it may instead induce drinking to assuage the unease, persecuting other nonvirtuous winners, striving to show that losers are even more sinful, or simple hypocrisy.[47]

These problems intensify when patterns of group success rather than the idiosyncrasies of individual success are at issue. When members of one group seem disproportionately successful, that group acquires a halo of ascribed virtue. Consider a 1907 article by Burton J. Hendrick on "The Great Jewish Invasion" in *McClure's Magazine*. The author's name, the publication, the date, and the title all lead one to expect an (at best, thinly veiled) anti-Semitic diatribe. The first few pages seem to confirm that expectation, with their claims that "the real modern Zion, greater in numbers and wealth and power than the old, steadily gathers on Manhattan Island," and that "the Jews are active, and invariably with success, in practically every business, professional, and intellectual field. The New Yorker constantly rubs shoulders with Israel." These feats are all the more "remarkable" because "the great mass of its [New York's] Jews are not what are commonly regarded as the most enlightened of their race" since they come from eastern Europe. After all, "no people have had a more inadequate preparation, educational and economic, for American citizenship."[48]

Yet the article goes on to describe in careful and admiring detail how these dirt-poor, ignorant, orthodoxly non-Christian immigrants work, save, cooperate, sacrifice for their children—and end up wealthy beyond anyone's wildest imaginings. Nor are they merely money-grubbers; Russian Jews are "individualist[s]," the "city's largest productive force and the greatest contributor to its manufacturing wealth," demonstrating "intense ambition," abstinence, and foresight. In his highest accolade, Mr. Hendrick even insists that the Russian Jew's

> enthusiasm for America knows no bounds. He eagerly looks forward to the time when he can be naturalized. . . . The rapidity with which the New York Jew adopts the manners and trappings of Americans almost disproves his ancient heritage as a peculiar people. . . . Better than any other element, even the native stock, do they meet the two supreme tests of citizenship: they actually go to the polls, and when once there, vote independently.[49]

In short, in one generation the east European Jewish immigrant has gone from an unassimilable, bovine drag on the American spirit to the epitome of all the American virtues. Nothing succeeds like success.

The contemporary equivalent of Mr. Hendrick's amazing Jews are Southeast Asians. A century ago, Chinese and Japanese immigrants could hardly be derogated enough . . . Now newspapers have a seemingly endless supply of rags-to-riches stories about destitute boat people whose daughter became the high school valedictorian a scant five years later and is now a pre-med student at Stanford. Such success is inevitably attributed to hard work, self-discipline, family support, and refusal to follow the bad example set by American-born peers.[51] This portrayal is so ubiquitous that spokespeople for Asian immigrants feel impelled to insist publicly that not all Asians escape poverty, crime, and discrimination, and that even the successful pay a heavy emotional cost.[52]

It would be churlish to argue that excessive praise is as bad as racism or ethnic slurs. But newly anointed groups are too often used to cast aspersions on some despised group that has not managed to fulfill the American dream. In Burton Hendrick's case, the main negative reference group is the Irish, who drink and gamble, yield their productive jobs to Jews, and—worst of all—band together in labor unions, in the "Irish vote," and in political party machines. In the case of immigrant Asians, the usual (if slightly more subtle) message is "Why can't African Americans do the same thing? At least they speak English when they start school." This dynamic adds yet another component to the nightmare of a failed American dream. Members of a denigrated group are disproportionately likely to fail to achieve their goals; they are blamed as individuals (and perhaps blame themselves) for their failure; and they carry a further stigma as members of a nonvirtuous (thus appropriately denigrated) group.

This effect of the fourth tenet can be taken a further, and most dangerous, step. For some Americans always, and for many Americans in some periods of our history, virtuous success has been defined as the dominance of some groups over others. This phenomenon extends the idea of competitive success from individual victories to collective hierarchies. If women are weak and emotional, it is *right* for men to control their bodies and wealth; if blacks are childlike pagans, it is *right* for whites to ensure their physical and spiritual survival through enslavement and conversion; if citizens of other nations refuse to recognize the value of capitalism and free elections, it is *right* for Americans to install a more enlightened government in their capitol. I find it hard to present these sentiments with a straight face, but they have arguably done almost as much as the American dream to shape Americans' beliefs, practices, and institutions.[53]

FLAWS IN THE AMERICAN DREAM TAKEN AS A WHOLE

Atomistic Individualism

Not only each tenet, but also the ideology of the American dream as a whole, is flawed. One problem stems from the radical individualism often associated with the dream (although the ideology entails nothing that prohibits groups from pursuing collective success). Achievers mark their success by moving away from the tenement, ghetto, or holler of their impoverished and impotent youth, thus speeding the breakup of their ethnic community. This is a bittersweet phenomenon. The freedom to move up and out is desirable, or at least desired. But certainly those left behind, probably those who leave, and arguably the nation as a whole lose when groups of people with close cultural and personal ties break those ties in pursuit of or after attaining "the bitch-goddess, success."[54] The line between autonomy and atomism is hard to draw.

American culture is full of stories about the mixed effects of success on communities and their residents. A Polish-American folk song tells of a man who emigrated to America, worked for three years in a foundry, returned home with "gold and silver," but found that "my children did not know me, for they fled from me, a stranger."

Only irresponsible romanticism permits the wish that peasants and villagers would opt for tradition rather than opportunity. It is surely significant that across the world and throughout centuries, they almost never do.[56] But one can still regret what is lost. And Thomas Hooker's warning cannot be shrugged off. "For if each man may do what is good in his owne eyes, proceed according to his own pleasure, so that none may crosse him or control him by any power, there must of necessity follow the distraction and desolation of the whole."[57]

* * * * *

THE DREAM AS A FRAMEWORK FOR SUCCESS

Tocqueville assured his readers that "up to now the Americans have happily avoided all the reefs I have just charted."[65] Some Americans continue, 150 years later, to sail free, and perhaps they always will. But some have wrecked, and some have never gotten anywhere near the boat. For those afloat, the ideology of the American dream is a vindication, a goad to further efforts, a cause for celebration—and also grounds for anxiety, guilt, and disillusionment. For the shipwrecked and drifters, the dream is a taunt, a condemnation, an object of fury—and also grounds for hope, renewed striving, and dreams for one's children . . .

Notes

---

1. Locke (1980: sec. 49, p. 29).

6. Marsh (1987: 264).

7. Comer (1988: 83–85); Letter to Lord Egmont, July 12, 1736, quoted in Greenberg (1977: 454).

10. Ladd (1993: 21; 1994: 67, 76; see also 53–56, 66).

11. Ben Jonson, George Chapman, and John Marston, *Eastward Ho!* (1605), quoted in Beeman (1971: 618–19).

12. Tom Smith (1988: 14); "Public Opinion and Demographic Report" (1993b: 89); see also "Public Opinion and Demographic Report" (1993a: 85, 87).

13. Emerson (1863: 86).

15. Miller (1992: 564–70); Ladd (1994: 55–58)

16. Kluegel and Smith (1986: 44). See also Lynd and Lynd (1930: 65); Huber and Form (1973); Caplow and Bahr (1979: table 1); Ladd (1994: 53–56, 68–69). In 1993 fully 94% of Americans agreed that hard work was crucial to success; the next most popular choice was God's will, with 53% agreement (Marsden and Swingle 1994: 277).

17. *Gallup Opinion Index* (1973: 28); Tom Smith (1987a: 411). See also Tom Smith (1987b); Miller (1992: 586–88); Ladd (1994: 79). Working-class respondents in all Western countries are slightly less committed to the third tenet than are members of the middle class. But the most striking feature of comparisons by class is the degree to which the poor, especially in the United States, support norms that benefit the rich more than themselves (Miller 1992: 582–86; see also Ladd 1994: 80; Hochschild 1981).

18. Stern and Searing (1976: 198). Perhaps the equation of poverty with laziness makes fewer American youths than youths of ten other countries (except for India) agree that "it is important . . . to take it easy and not to work too hard" (*Gallup Opinion Index* 1973: 36).

19. Ladd (1994: 75, 79, 80).

21. Louis Harris (1986; 1990: 2).

22. Davis and Smith (1982: vars. 127–129); Marsden and Swingle (1994: 279). Other desirable features of friends, such as being fun-loving or intelligent, received considerably less than unanimous support.

23. *Gallup Opinion Index* (1973: 34); Ladd (1994: 72–73).

24. Gunnar Myrdal, in Baldwin et al. (1964: 33). Lamont (1992; forthcoming) analyzes the greater weight placed by Americans than by the French on including morality in their definition of success. Nackenoff (1993) shows the interactions of virtue and material success in modern American history.

25. Potter (1954).

28. My thanks to Walter Lippincott and Hugh Van Dusen for providing me with these figures.

29. The phrase is from Rae (1988).

30. Although not without backsliding, as a survivor of Japanese internment camps points out: "The American Dream? I think: for whites only. I didn't feel that way before World War Two" (Terkel 1980: 161–171; more generally, see Rogers Smith 1993).

35. Goldstein (1988: 77).

40. Hurston (1942: 116).

41. Stouffer et al. (1949: 250–57); Hirschman (1981: 41, 47). In the Latin American context that he was studying, Hirschman equated "becoming furious" with "turning into an enemy of the established order." That sometimes happens in the United States, as will be seen in succeeding chapters. But "becoming furious" may also result in spouse-battering, a lawsuit, or "the embrace of victimhood" (Sykes 1992; John Taylor 1991; Hughes 1992).

45. Rubin and Peplau (1975: 67, 68); Lerner (1980); see also Rubin and Peplau (1973); Lerner and Lerner (1981).

47. Huntington (1981: 30–41, 61–70), Shklar (1984: 67–78), and McWilliams (1990: 177) examine hypocrisy in American liberal democracy. Mark Twain remains, however, its best analyst.

48. Some earlier Jewish immigrants concurred:

> They are a bane to the country and a curse to the Jews. The Jews have earned an enviable reputation in the United States, but this has been undermined by the influx of thousands who are not ripe for the enjoyment of liberty and equal rights, and all who mean well for the Jewish name should prevent them as much as possible from coming there. The experience of the charity teaches that organized immigration from Russia, Roumania, and other semi-barbarous countries is a mistake and has proved a failure. It is no relief to the Jews of Russia, Poland, etc., and it jeopardizes the well-being of the American Jews.

Document of the United Jewish Charities of Rochester, New York, 1893, quoted in Szajowski (1951: 232).

49. Hendrick (1907).

51. An article headlined "Honor, Family, Work: Success" (Dillon 1988) says it all. A high-quality example of the genre is Butterfield (1986).

52. Ueda (1989); Hurh and Kim (1989); Kim (1993).

53. Rogers Smith (1993).

54. James (1920: 260). Here, as elsewhere, success is highly gendered. In this case, perhaps because James is challenging its desirability, it is cast as a woman; more often, perhaps because those discussing it want to achieve "mastery" or to encourage others to seek it, success is cast as a male or men are used as exemplars (and women as exemplars of failure). One could do a fascinating analysis of the gendered nature not only of who succeeds in America but also of the very terms of the ideology.

56. Stack and Cromartie (n.d., c. 1990) and Cromartie and Stack (1989) describe the rarity of return migration.

57. "A True Sight of Sin," in Miller and Johnson (1963: 295).

65. de Tocqueville (1969: 541).

References

Baldwin, James, et al. (1964) "Liberalism and the Negro: A Round-Table Discussion," *Commentary* 37, 3: 25–42.

Beeman 1971.

Butterfield, Fox (1986) "Why Asians Are Going to the Head of the Class," *NYT*, Aug. 3: sec. 12 ("Education Life"): 18–23.

Caplow, Theodore, and Howard Bahr (1979) "Half a Century of Change in Adolescent Attitudes: Replications of a Middletown Survey by the Lynds," *Public Opinion Q.* 43, 1: 1–17.

Comer, James (1988) *Maggie's American Dream* (New Am. Library).

Cromartie, John, and Carol Stack (1989) "Reinterpretation of Black Return and Nonreturn Migration to the South, 1975–1990," *Geographic Perspectives* 79, 3: 297–310.

Davis, James, and Tom Smith (1982) *General Social Surveys, 1972–1982: Cumulative Codebook* (U. of Chicago, National Opinion Research Center).

de Tocqueville, Alexis (1969 [1848]) *Democracy in America*, trans. George Lawrence, ed. J. P. Mayer (Doubleday).

Dillon, Pat (1988) "Honor, Family, Work: Success," *San Jose Mercury News*, Mar. 29: B1.

Emerson, Ralph Waldo (1863) "Wealth," in *The Conduct of Life* (Ticknor and Fields), 71–110.

Gallup Opinion Index (1973) Report no. 100, Oct.

Goldstein, Mark (1988) "The End of the American Dream?" *Industry Week*, April 4: 77–80.

Harris, Louis (1986) "Yuppie Lifestyle Felt To Be Unattractive to Americans" (N. Y. Harris Survey), Feb. 3.

Hendrick, Burton (1907) "The Great Jewish Invasion," *McClure's Magazine* 28, 3: 307–21.

Hirschman, Albert (1981) *Essays in Trespassing* (Cambridge U. Press).

Hochschild, Jennifer (1981) *What's Fair? American Beliefs about Distributive Justice* (Harvard U. Press).

Huber, Joan, and William Form (1973) *Income and Ideology* (Free Press).

Hughes, Robert (1992) *The Culture of Complaint* (Oxford U. Press).

Huntington, Samuel (1981) *American Politics: The Promise of Disharmony* (Harvard U. Press).

Hurh, Won Moo, and Kwang Chung Kim (1989) "The 'Success' Image of Asian Americans," *Ethnic and Racial Studies* 12, 4: 512–38.

Hurston, Zora Neale (1942) *Dust Tracks on a Road*, 2d. ed. (U. of Illinois Press).

James, William (1920) Letter to H. G. Wells, in *The Letters of William James*, ed. Henry James (Atlantic Monthly Press), 2: 260.

Kim, Claire (1993) "A Model Minority Compared to Whom? Myths, Hierarchy, and the New Convergence on Race" (Yale U., Dept. of Political Science).

Kluegel, James, and Eliot Smith (1986) *Beliefs about Inequality* (Aldine de Gruyter).

Ladd, Everett (1993) "Thinking About America," *Public Perspective* 4, 5: 19–34.

Ladd, Everett (1994) *The American Ideology* (Storrs, CT: Roper Center for Public Opinion Research).

Lamont, Michéle (1992) *Money, Morals, and Manners* (U. of Chicago Press).

Lamont, Michéle (forthcoming) "National Identity and National Boundary Patterns in France and the United States" *French Historical Studies*, fall.

Lerner, Melvin (1980) *Belief in a Just World* (Plenum Press).

Lerner, Melvin, and Sally Lerner, eds. (1981) *The Justice Motive in Social Behavior* (Plenum Press).

Locke, John (1980 [1690]) *Second Treatise of Government*, ed. C. B. MacPherson (Hackett).

Lynd, Robert, and Helen Lynd (1930) *Middletown* (Harcourt, Brace, and Co.).

Marsden, Peter, and Joseph Swingle (1994) "Conceptualizing and Measuring Culture in Surveys," *Poetics* 22: 269–89.

Marsh, Dave (1987) *Glory Days: Bruce Springsteen in the 1980s* (Pantheon).

McWilliams, Wilson Carey (1990) "*Pudd'nhead Wilson* on Democratic Governance," in Susan Gillman and Forrest Robinson, eds., *Mark Twain's Pudd'nhead Wilson* (Duke U. Press), 177–89.

Miller, David (1992) "Distributive Justice: What the People Think," *Ethics* 102, 3: 555–93.

Miller, Perry, and Thomas Johnson, eds. (1963) *The Puritans*, vol. 1 (Harper Torchbooks).

Nackenoff, Carol (1994) *The Fictional Republic: Horatio Alger and American Political Discourse* (Oxford U. Press).

"Public Opinion and Demographic Report," *Public Perspective*: (1993a) 4, 4: 82–104

"Public Opinion and Demographic Report," *Public Perspective*: (1993b) 4, 5: 82–104

Rae, Douglas (1988) "Knowing Power," in Ian Shapiro and Grant Reeher, eds., *Power, Inequality, and Democratic Politics* (Westview Press), 17–49.

Rubin, Zick, and Letitia Peplau (1973) "Belief in a Just World and Reactions to Another's Lot," *J. of Social Issues* 29, 4: 73–93.

Rubin, Zick, and Letitia Peplau (1975) "Who Believes in a Just World?" *J. of Social Issues*, 31, 3: 65–89.

Shklar, Judith (1984) *Ordinary Vices* (Harvard U. Press).

Smith, Rogers (1993) "Beyond Tocqueville, Myrdal, and Hartz," *APSR* 87, 3: 549–66.

Smith, Tom (1987a) "The Welfare State in Cross-national Perspective," *Public Opinion Q.* 51, 3: 404–21.

Smith, Tom (1987b) "Public Opinion and the Welfare State: A Crossnational Perspective," paper at the annual meeting of the ASA, Chicago.

Smith, Tom (1988) "Social Inequality in Cross-National Perspective" (U. of Chicago, National Opinion Research Center).

Stack, Carol, and John Cromartie (c. 1990) "The Journeys of Black Children" (U. of California, Berkeley, School of Education).

Stern, Alan, and Donald Searing (1976) "The Stratification Beliefs of English and American Adolescents," *British J. of Political Science* 6, part 2: 177–201.

Stouffer, Samuel, et al. (1949) *The American Soldier: Adjustment during Army Life* (Princeton U. Press).

Sykes, Charles (1992) *A Nation of Victims: The Decay of the American Character* (St. Martin's Press).

Szajowski, Zosa (1951) "The Attitude of American Jews to East European Jewish Immigration (1881–1893)," *Publications of the Am. Jewish Historical Society*, 40, part 3: 221–80.

Taylor, John (1991) "Don't Blame Me!: The New Culture of Victimization," *New York*, June 3: 26–34

Terkel, Studs (1980) *American Dreams, Lost and Found* (Pantheon).

Ueda, Reed (1989) "False Modesty," *New Republic*, July 3: 16–17.

*T*he following article, originally entitled "Many Find Themselves Crossing the Poverty Line," also taps the "myth versus reality" tension in American political culture. On the one hand, shows like MTV's Cribs and My Super Sweet 16 or any of VH1's features on how celebrities live can paint the picture that material abundance is the norm (or goal) in the United States. Hopfensperger's piece, however, reports on a study that found 42 percent of Americans will live in poverty for at least one year by the time they reach age 50, and 60 percent of those who reach age 75 will do so. Near majorities of Americans thus experience poverty in their lifetime. As students of politics, we know that income and wealth enlarge political voice. This article therefore challenges us to at least consider how our political culture is defined by having near majorities of Americans denied that microphone for at least some period of their life and what this then means for success and opportunity in America.

Poverty Weaves Through the Lives of Many Americans

JEAN HOPFENSPERGER

+ About 40 years ago, University of Minnesota President Robert Bruininks was a poor teenager working alongside migrant workers in the fields.

+ Thirty years ago, state Sen. Linda Berglin was a newly divorced graphic artist surviving on eggs and bread.

Jean Hopfensperger, "Many Find Themselves Crossing the Poverty Line; Two Out of Five Americans Fall Into Poverty at Some Point," *Star Tribune*, October 18, 2003. Copyright © 2003 Star Tribune. Reprinted by permission of the Star Tribune, Minneapolis, MN.

✦ Twenty years ago, Franklin Bank CEO Dorothy Bridges was a poor single mother trying to finish college.

Their bouts with poverty reflect findings from a surprising study, which found that about 42 percent of Americans will have fallen into poverty for at least one year by the time they reach age 50. Sixty percent will have by the time they reach 75. The study was based on data from nearly 8,000 families that have been tracked for three decades. It complements recent poverty numbers from the U.S. Census Bureau, which showed 12 percent of Americans living in poverty in 2002.

"For most people, the words poverty and welfare conjure up images of people on the fringes of society," said Prof. Mark Rank of Washington University in St. Louis, whose findings recently appeared in a publication of the American Sociological Association. "But most of us will experience poverty in our lifetimes," he said. "Losing a job, a family splitting up, health problems . . . are big reasons people fall into poverty during the working years."

Rank's findings are drawn from data running from 1968 to 1992, but the conclusions hold true today, he said. For one thing, national poverty rates were the same during that period as in the past decade. Plus the results are consistent with newer government studies, he said. For example, a federal study found that about 25 percent of Americans, including 34 percent of children, had experienced poverty from 1987 to 1996.

The results don't surprise Sen. Berglin, DFL–Minneapolis, who grew up in a house without plumbing. She was a self-employed graphic designer with not much work when she was divorced in the early 1970s. She drove a junker car, used free health clinics and didn't go grocery shopping very often. Berglin likens the study's findings to her observations about the lower-income neighborhood she represents. Many people move in, often during hard times, then move out with little fanfare as they're able to afford it, she said. "I'm always running into people who tell me, 'I lived in your district once,'" Berglin said. "I like to say everyone has, or will, live here," she joked. "I guess that correlates with the study."

DRIVING FORCES

The two biggest reasons people fall into poverty are loss of earnings (43 percent) and change in family structure (40 percent), said Rebecca Blank, a University of Michigan public policy professor who studies poverty trends. Such events as a divorce, death of a spouse or birth of a child frequently upset financial stability, she said. "You never think it's going to happen to you, or someone that you know," said former Minnesota Secretary of State Joan Growe, who fell into poverty after a divorce years back. "But it can."

* * * * *

BOUNCING BACK

When Franklin Bank CEO Bridges moved to Montana in the late 1970s to attend college, she was a single parent with a young child. She was lucky, she says, because she was able to get child care and housing subsidies, as well as welfare, while she attended classes. "We lived in subsidized housing when I was growing up," said Bridges, who grew up poor in Louisiana. "But I viewed poverty as a condition you can overcome. I saw this [help in Montana] as tools to assist you at a point in life."

While rising from poverty to become a bank executive may be rare, many poor people do land on their feet. Mickey Mikeworth, for example, was on welfare until several years ago. When she landed a part-time job at a financial planning office, she realized, "I can do that." Mikeworth, 37, now has a financial planning business in Edina. She also works with nonprofit groups, helping low-income parents learn to manage budgets and increase their savings. Getting out of poverty is one thing, she said. Climbing into the middle class is another. "The most difficult part is the emotional baggage, the shame and blame," said Mikeworth of Minneapolis. "Transitioning out of a survival mentality into a growth mentality is difficult. There wasn't any money six months from now, so people didn't plan out that far."

Rank says his research underscores that poverty is not a perpetual state for most Americans. Of those who had fallen into poverty by the time they reached age 50, 42 percent were poor for one to two years and 31 percent for two to three years. Sixteen percent were poor for five years or more. Similarly, the Census Bureau looked at poverty from 1996 to 1999, and found that about half of the people who were poor in 1996 no longer were in 1999. . . . "This is a different way of thinking about the risk of poverty," Rank said. "It looks at poverty across adulthood. And it fills out the story behind the census numbers" recently released.

POVERTY'S REACH

Here's a look, by age, at the percentages of adult Americans who have experienced poverty at some point in their lives. . . .

Table 3.1: Percentage Who Have Lived Below the Poverty Line

Age	Percentage
20	10.6%
25	21.6%
30	27.1%
35	31.4%
40	35.6%
45	38.8%
50	41.8%
55	45%
60	48.2%
65	51.4%
70	55%
75	58.5%

Source: Mark Rank, Washington University, St. Louis, analysis of data from Panel Study of Income Dynamics, based at the University of Michigan.

Table 3.2: Federal Poverty Level, 2003

Household Size	Income
One	$8,980
Two	$12,120
Three	$15,260
Four	$18,400

*I*n this selection, David Wessel describes a series of experiments. One of these involved young men posing as job applicants in low-wage service jobs. The men were matched for similarity in all categories except race and criminal history. White applicants told potential employers they had served 18 months in prison for possession of cocaine with intent to sell and the black applicants did not have criminal records. The white applicants were nonetheless called back slightly more often.

Findings like these help explain why whites and blacks diverge on the issue of whether or not racial minorities have the same opportunities as whites—hence, raising the issue of "universally shared versus demographically contested political culture(s)." One's race is the single best predictor of one's views on the prevalence of discrimination in America. The findings Wessel reports on also identify places where the discrimination that African-Americans face in the job market buttresses against the general belief that opportunity for advancement is abundant in the U.S. The "myth v. reality" tension in American political culture again appears.

Racial Discrimination Still at Work

DAVID WESSEL

Two young high-school graduates with similar job histories and demeanors apply in person for jobs as waiters, warehousemen or other low-skilled positions advertised in a Milwaukee newspaper. One man is white and admits to having served 18 months in prison for possession of cocaine with intent to sell. The other is black and hasn't any criminal record.

David Wessel, "Racial Discrimination Is Still at Work," *Wall Street Journal*, September 4, 2003, p. A2. Copyright 2003 by Dow Jones & Company, Inc. Reproduced with permission of Dow Jones & Company, Inc. in the format Textbook via Copyright Clearance Center.

Which man is more likely to get called back?

It is surprisingly close. In a carefully crafted experiment in which college students posing as job applicants visited 350 employers, the white ex-con was called back 17% of the time and the crime-free black applicant 14%. The disadvantage carried by a young black man applying for a job as a dishwasher or a driver is equivalent to forcing a white man to carry an 18-month prison record on his back.

Many white Americans think racial discrimination is no longer much of a problem. Many blacks think otherwise. In offices populated with college graduates, white men quietly confide to other white men that affirmative action makes it tough for a white guy to get ahead these days. (If that's so, a black colleague once asked me, how come there aren't more blacks in the corporate hierarchy?)

A recent Gallup poll asked: "Do you feel that racial minorities in this country have equal job opportunities as whites, or not?" Among whites, the answer was 55% yes and 43% no; the rest were undecided. Among blacks, the answer was 17% yes and 81 % no.

The Milwaukee and other experiments, though plagued by the shortcomings of research that relies on pretense to explain how people behave, offer evidence that discrimination remains a potent factor in the economic lives of black Americans. "In these low-wage, entry-level markets, race remains a huge barrier. Affirmative-action pressures aren't operating here," says Devah Pager, the sociologist at Northwestern University in Evanston, Ill., who conducted the Milwaukee experiment and recently won the American Sociological Association's prize for the year's best doctoral dissertation. "Employers don't spend a lot of time screening applicants. They want a quick signal whether the applicant seems suitable. Stereotypes among young black men remain so prevalent and so strong that race continues to serve as a major signal of characteristics of which employers are wary."

In a similar experiment that got some attention last year, economists Marianne Bertrand of the University of Chicago and Sendhil Mullainathan of the Massachusetts Institute of Technology responded in writing to help wanted ads in Chicago and Boston, using names likely to be identified by employers as white or African-American. Applicants named Greg Kelly or Emily Walsh were 50% more likely to get called for interviews than those named Jamal Jackson or Lakishe Washington, names far more common among African-Americans. Putting a white-sounding name on an application, they found, is worth as much as an extra eight years of work experience.

These academic experiments gauge the degree of discrimination, not just its existence. Both suggest that a blemish on a black person's resume does far more harm than it does to a white job seeker and that an embellishment does far less good.

In the Milwaukee experiment, Ms. Pager dispatched white and black men with and without prison records to job interviews. Whites without drug busts on their applications did best; blacks with drug busts did worst. No surprise there. But this was a surprise: Acknowledging a prison record cut a white man's chances of getting called back by half, while cutting a black man's already-slimmer chances by a much larger two-thirds.

"Employers, already reluctant to hire blacks, are even more wary of blacks with proven criminal involvement," Ms. Pager says. "These testers were bright, articulate college students with effective styles of self-presentation. The cursory review of entry-level applicants, however, leaves little room for these qualities to be noticed." This is a big deal given that nearly 17% of all black American men have served some time, and the government's Bureau of Justice Statistics projects that, at current rates, 30% of black boys who turn 12 this year will spend time in jail in their lifetimes.

In the Boston and Chicago experiment, researchers tweaked some resumes to make them more appealing to employers. They added a year of work experience, some military experience, fewer periods for which no job was listed, computer skills and the like. This paid off for whites: Those with better resumes were called back for interviews 30% more than other whites. It didn't pay off for blacks: Precisely the same changes yielded only a 9% increase in callbacks.

Someday Americans will be able to speak of racial discrimination in hiring in the past tense. Not yet.

*L*awrence E. Harrison's "The End of Multiculturalism" completes our treatment of diversity and political culture. In it, he weighs in on the argument about universally shared versus demographically contested political culture(s). Harrison's thesis is that the cultures that dominate in some countries are better for fostering "democratic continuity, social justice, and prosperity." He argues that this view has not dominated George W. Bush's policies in Iraq and on immigration from Latin America. Instead, he contends Bush's policies in these areas are rooted in a "cultural relativism" whereby all cultures are recognized as equal, with no culture being better than another. Harrison suggests this belief has had perilous consequences. In Iraq, it has meant a war waged without truly recognizing the difficulties in promoting a sustainable democracy in a country where trust and other bedrocks of democracy are so low. In immigration policy, the influence of cultural relativism has translated into policies that make it easier for immigrants from Latin America not to assimilate—indeed to maintain cultural norms from their countries of origin despite the fact some of these norms contradict the "Anglo-Protestant cultural tradition." Harrison believes that many immigrants from Latin America reject the "universally shared" American political culture, current policy makes it easier for them to do so, and all this threatens the health of U.S. democracy and civil society.

The End of Multiculturalism

LAWRENCE E. HARRISON *

Future generations may look back on Iraq and immigration as the two great disasters of the Bush presidency. Ironically, for a conservative administration, both of these policy initiatives were rooted in a multicultural view of the world.

Since the 1960s, multiculturalism has become a dominant feature of the political and intellectual landscape of the West. But multiculturalism rests on a frail foundation: cultural relativism, the notion that no culture is better or worse than any other—it is merely different.

When it comes to democratic continuity, social justice, and prosperity, some cultures do far better than others. Research at Tufts University's Fletcher School of Law and Diplomacy, summarized in my recent book, "The Central Liberal Truth: How Politics Can Change a Culture and Save It from Itself," makes this clear.

Extensive data suggest that the champions of progress are the Nordic countries—Denmark, Finland, Iceland, Norway, and Sweden—where, for example, universal literacy was a substantial reality in the 19th century. By contrast, no Arab country today is democratic, and female illiteracy in some Arab countries exceeds 50 percent.

Culture isn't about genes or race; it's about values, beliefs, and attitudes. Culture matters because it influences a society's receptivity to democracy, justice, entrepreneurship, and free-market institutions.

What, then, are the implications for a foreign policy based on the doctrine that "These values of freedom are right and true for every person, in every society"? The Bush administration has staked huge human, financial, diplomatic, and prestige resources on this doctrine's applicability in Iraq. It is now apparent that the doctrine is fallacious.

A key component of a successful democratic transition is trust, a particularly important cultural factor for social justice and prosperity. Trust in others reduces the cost of economic transactions, and democratic stability depends on it.

Trust is periodically measured in 80-odd countries by the World Values Survey. The Nordic countries enjoy very high levels of trust: 58 to 67 percent of respondents in four of these countries believe that most people can be trusted, compared with 11 percent of Algerians and 3 percent of Brazilians.

The high levels of identification and trust in Nordic societies reflect their homogeneity; common Lutheran antecedents, including a rigorous ethical code and heavy

Lawrence E. Harrison, "The End of Multiculturalism," *Christian Science Monitor*, February 26, 2008. Reprinted by permission of the author. © 2008 by Lawrence E. Harrison.

* Lawrence E. Harrison directs the Cultural Change Institute at the Fletcher School at Tufts University, where he also teaches. This article is adapted from a longer essay in the January–February 2008 issue of *The National Interest*.

emphasis on education; and a consequent sense of the nation as one big family imbued with the golden rule.

Again, culture matters—race doesn't. The ethnic roots of both Haiti and Barbados lie in the Dahomey region of West Africa. The history of Haiti, independent in 1804 in the wake of a slave uprising against the French colonists, is one of corrupt, incompetent leadership; illiteracy; and poverty. Barbados, which gained its independence from the British in 1966, is today a prosperous democracy of "Afro-Saxons."

IMMIGRATION

Hispanics now form the largest U.S. minority, approaching 15 percent—about 45 million—of a total population of about 300 million. They're projected by the Pew Research Center to swell to 127 million in 2050—29 percent of a total population of 438 million. Their experience in the United States recapitulates Latin America's culturally shaped underdevelopment. For example, the Hispanic high school dropout rate in the U.S. is alarmingly high and persistent—about 20 percent in second and subsequent generations. It's vastly higher in Latin America.

Samuel Huntington was on the mark when he wrote in his latest book "Who Are We? The Challenges to America's National Identity": "Would America be the America it is today if it had been settled not by British Protestants but by French, Spanish, or Portuguese Catholics? The answer is no. It would not be America; it would be Quebec, Mexico, or Brazil."

In "The Americano Dream," Mexican-American Lionel Sosa argues that the value system that has retarded progress in Latin America is an impediment to upward mobility of Latino immigrants. So does former U.S. Rep. Herman Badillo, a Puerto Rican whose book, "One Nation, One Standard," indicts Latino undervaluing of education and calls for cultural change.

The progress of Hispanic immigrants, not to mention harmony in the broader society, depends on their acculturation to mainstream U.S. values. Efforts—for example, long-term bilingual education—to perpetuate "old country" values in a multicultural salad bowl undermine acculturation to the mainstream and are likely to result in continuing underachievement, poverty, resentment, and divisiveness. So, too, does the willy-nilly emergence of bilingualism in the U.S. No language in American history has ever before competed with English to the point where one daily hears, on the telephone, "If you want to speak English, press one; Si quiere hablar en espanol, oprima el boton numero dos."

Although border security and environmental concerns are also in play, the immigration debate has been framed largely in economic terms, producing some odd pro-immigration bedfellows, for example the editorial pages of *The New York Times* and *The Wall Street Journal*. Among the issues: whether the U.S. economy needs more unskilled immigrants; whether immigrants take jobs away from U.S. citizens; to what extent illegal immigrants drain resources away from education, healthcare, and welfare; and whether population growth, largely driven by immigration, is necessary for a healthy economy.

But immigration looks very different when viewed in cultural terms, particularly with respect to the vast legal and illegal Latino immigration, a million or more people a year, most of them with few skills and little education. To be sure, the U.S. has absorbed large numbers of unskilled and uneducated immigrants in the past, and today the large majority of their descendants are in the cultural mainstream. But the numbers of Latino immigrants and their geographic concentration today leave real doubts about the prospects for acculturation: 70 percent of children in the Los Angeles public schools and 60 percent in the Denver schools are Latino.

In a letter to me in 1991, the late Mexican-American columnist Richard Estrada captured the essence of the problem:

"The problem in which the current immigration is suffused is, at heart, one of numbers; for when the numbers begin to favor not only the maintenance and replenishment of the immigrants' source culture, but also its overall growth, and in particular growth so large that the numbers not only impede assimilation but go beyond to pose a challenge to the traditional culture of the American nation, then there is a great deal about which to be concerned."

SOME RECOMMENDATIONS

If multiculturalism is a myth, how do we avoid the woes that inevitably attend the creation of an enduring and vast underclass alienated from the upwardly mobile cultural mainstream? Some policy implications, one for Latin America, the others for the U.S. and Canada, are apparent.

We must calibrate the flow of immigrants into the U.S. to the needs of the economy, mindful that immigration has adversely affected low-income American citizens, disproportionately African-American and Hispanic, as Barbara Jordan stressed as chair of the 1990s immigration Reform Commission. But the flow must also be calibrated to the country's capacity to assure acculturation of the immigrants.

We must be a melting pot, not a salad bowl. The melting pot, the essence of which is the Anglo-Protestant cultural tradition, is our way of creating the homogeneity that has contributed so much to the trust and mutual identification—and progress—of the Nordic societies.

As with immigration flows of the late 19th and early 20th centuries, an extensive program of activities designed to facilitate acculturation, including mastery of English, should be mounted. A law declaring English to be the national language would be helpful.

The costs of multiculturalism—in terms of disunity, the clash of classes, and declining trust—are likely to be huge in the long run. All cultures are not equal when it comes to promoting progress, and very few can match Anglo-Protestantism in this respect. We should be promoting acculturation to the national mainstream, not a mythical, utopian multiculturalism. And we should take care that the Anglo-Protestant virtues that have brought us so far do not fall into disrepair, let alone disrepute.

1. What are the attributes, values, and norms commonly shared in America? How might an individual or members of a particular demographic or social group disagree with you? Does this disagreement matter for American government, civil society, and/or politics? Why or why not? Is a shared political culture necessary for the polity to function effectively?

2. What would happen if majorities of Americans no longer believed in the American Dream? What if those in particular groups (potential examples: whites, poor, Latina, men, gay/lesbian/transgender, etc.) stopped believing in the Dream while others remained steadfast in their belief? What, if anything, would this mean for American governance?

3. Hopfensperger and Wallace both detail places where life experiences in the United States fall short of values such as equality and opportunity. How is it that so many believe these values define America despite their own experiences to the contrary? What does this mean for politics?

4. At the end of his article Harrison offers several recommendations related to Latino immigration. These include passing an "English-only" law, limiting immigration from Latin America, and aggressively promoting acculturation of Latino immigrants to Anglo-Protestant virtues. Harrison argues these recommendations will benefit Latinos and others in the United States by preserving American values and civil society. Is he right? Would his recommendations be beneficial or detrimental? Why?

5. What if we turn Harrison's argument "upside down"? Is it that today's Hispanic immigrants do not want to assimilate or face unique challenges in being accepted? How, if at all, does posing the question this way inform understandings of American political culture?

Additional Resources

Roger and Me (1989) is a film that follows the cultural responses to General Motors' decision to close several of their plants in Flint, Michigan. Depicted are social class differences, responses to globalization, and the unique relationship between businesses and local communities in the United States.

http://www.theasa.net
The American Studies Association is the professional organization representing scholars "devoted to the interdisciplinary study of American culture and history."

http://www.loc.gov
Included as part of the Library of Congress' web site is their American Memory Project. (http://lcweb2.loc.gov/ammem/index.html). This web site allows access to the archived materials documenting American political culture housed by the Library of Congress. Materials vary widely and include Sunday school books, sheet music, original papers, first-person narratives, and other source documenting American political experiences.

http://www.sentencingproject.org
The Sentencing Project is a Washington, D.C.–based nonprofit organization. It documents the sheer number of individuals involved in the American criminal justice system, the racial, ethnic, and social class biases in these numbers, and researches the corresponding policy issues that arise.

http://www.politicalcompass.org
This web site provides a test that locates one's political views on a more complete two-dimensional matrix of "right–left" and "authoritarian–libertarian."

http://csrpc.uchicago.edu
This center is housed at the University of Chicago and takes an explicitly intersectional approach to the politics of race, ethnicity, and political culture.

http://www.heritage.org
The Heritage Foundation is a Washington, D.C.–based think tank that conducts research on both domestic and foreign policy issues. An entire section of its web site is devoted to issues relating to poverty and/or inequality (http://www.heritage.org/Research/welfare/povertyinequality.cfm).

http://www.aei.org
The American Enterprise Institute (AEI) is a Washington, D.C.–based "private, non-partisan, not-for-profit institution dedicated to research and education on issues of government, politics, economics, and social welfare." Scholars there do research and hold events related to a wide variety of issues. A recent event highlighted the issue of illegal immigration and the economic and social factors that influence the flow of illegal migrants from Mexico. Video of the conference can be found at http://www.aei.org/events/filter.social,eventID.1440/event_detail.asp.

PUBLIC OPINION: MANY VOICES?

Gay marriage in the United States is hotly contested. These protesters firmly believe in the right of same-sex couples to wed, while others strongly disagree. This is just one of the many policy issues where public opinion and diversity interact to produce deeply felt political debate.

Men Are from Mars, Women Are from Venus. So goes the title of a bestselling book so popular that none other than Oprah featured its author on her talk show. The gender differences described in that book not only interest daytime television viewers, they echo differences between genders in the political realm. For example, we know that men and women tend to differ on political party affiliation, their views on a variety of public policy issues, and in support for particular political candidates (see Sections 5 and 6, for examples). Political scientists have called these differences the *gender gap*.

The influence of diversity on public opinion extends beyond just gender. Research on public opinion suggests that the development of an individual's opinions is often influenced by their social group memberships (e.g., race, ethnicity, religion, gender, and income level) in addition to one's socialization experiences (influence of parents, peers, schools, and the media). This helps us better predict public opinion. For example, if you are asked to guess how a stranger feels about social welfare spending, George W. Bush, or gay marriage, your guess is more likely to be more accurate if you know their gender, race, ethnicity, social class, and religious views.

When public opinion pollsters conduct nationwide polls they recognize these trends and regularly identify important subgroups of the population based on key demographic characteristics. All four of the readings in this section make this clear. In the first reading, Roberta Sigel identifies a gender gap in how men and women view gender equity. The other readings in this section respectively examine differences in public opinion among the following demographic groups: blacks, whites, and Latinos; those with particular (and no) religious affiliation; and, parents and nonparents. In short, there is substantial evidence that demographic groups interpret policy issues, political institutions, and candidates differently. The reality of these differences is given voice in the selections that follow.

Research on public opinion also suggests its complexity within this truism. Popular culture or the mass media can sometimes oversimplify these complexities and thereby mask the considerable nuances that characterize American public opinion. The readings in this section illuminate these nuances as well. For instance, group labels such as "men" and "women" are not necessarily straightforward. Put all the men on one side of your classroom and you will likely see that these men differ in terms of age, race, religion, and ethnicity. If you made each man show the contents of his wallet, you would likely also see that not every man in your class has the same access to money. With more questioning, you would likely also find out that some of the men are Republican and others Democrats. Some are straight, some gay, some bisexual, and some may be transgender. This simultaneous recognition of the various groups one can belong to is called as *intersectionality*. The reality of intersectionality, and its impact for public opinion, is sometimes masked by the reporting of public opinion using singular categories like "men." The findings in the readings that follow caution against this. For example, Roberta Sigel demonstrates how both gender and income influence one's opinion on matters of gender equity. The second reading by Brook and Jeon-Slaughter similarly points to how an intersectional perspective brings nuance in understanding public opinion on the courts among Latinos, African-Americans, and whites of various income levels. Terry Moe continues this trend in the last selection in his examination of public opinion on school vouchers. In this regard, understanding intersectionality and the role of multiple influences increases our ability to understand the complexities of public opinion in the United States.

The notion of multiple and competing influences suggests another, often overlooked nuance about public opinion and diversity: There is considerable overlap among groups. Saying that women are more likely to vote for Democrats, for example, is true but does not negate the fact that considerable numbers of men and women vote for the same party. Differences may be very real but they are usually at the margins. Public opinion is influenced by demographic group membership, but this does not mean demographic groups are always diametrically opposed on matters of politics and public policy. We see this pattern for a variety of demographic cleavages throughout the readings in this section.

The final nuance regarding public opinion and diversity reflected in the readings is that of shifting public opinion. One might assume that public opinion does not change once it is formed. Each reading in this section calls this assumption into question.

Terry Moe does so most overtly, demonstrating how views on school vouchers shift as Americans learn more about the issue.

The selections in this section reflect a political truism: Demography matters when it comes to public opinion, but simplistic demographic breakdowns mask considerable nuance. Intersectional analysis shows there is usually considerable overlap among demographic difference in opinion, public opinion remains malleable, and groups do not always act "as expected" when it comes to public opinion. The notion that "men are from Mars, women are from Venus" is a starting point for our discussion of demographic influences on public opinion, not a conclusion.

*I*n this selection, Roberta Sigel investigates how men and women view gender politics. Her analysis demonstrates that it is not that men and women view gender equality, the division of labor within the home, and gender discrimination in completely opposite ways. Rather, there are both differences and areas where the views of the genders overlap. Men agree with women that gender inequity still exists and poses a barrier in women's lives. Men are simply less apt to make these issues major political priorities and do not prioritize issues surrounding gender inequity the same way that women do. This suggests that men and women have grown toward one another when it comes to views on gender equity, but differences still exist in terms of how pervasive men and women view gender inequity.

Sigel's work also highlights the importance of an intersectional analysis of public opinion, as lower-income men and more affluent men register different opinions from one another on issues of gender equity. Public opinion is malleable over time on these issues and influenced by a variety of demographic group cleavages.

The Male Perspective

ROBERTA SIGEL

. . . How similar or dissimilar are men's and women's perceptions [on gender relations] and what is the impact of these dis/similarities on the character of gender relations? . . .

* * * * *

. . . Put in a nutshell, men's views of today's gender relationships reflect a good deal of ambivalence as well as occasional insensitivity. On the one hand, they are fully cognizant that women's traditional sex roles are in a state of flux. Moreover, most men—some more than others—are sympathetic to women's desire for equality with men. At the same time, many are uncomfortable and a bit alarmed over the changes they see taking place. They worry what the recent developments might mean for their own lives—their family lives, their work lives, and their social relations. A certain sense of regret permeates their recognition that the "good old days" of male dominance might be coming to an end (when in the words of one focus group member, "a man's word was law"), but they also believe that the change "is only fair" (to cite another) and, besides, there is nothing they can do about it; the clock cannot be turned back. So they are learning to adjust to the inevitable.[4] But whereas gender inequality is a matter of central concern for the New Jersey women, it is not for the men. Not that they are ignorant of women's distress. Quite the contrary; . . . they understand that distress, but . . . they consider it a fact of life which does not engage their interest, let alone their commitment.

*****

DISCRIMINATION AWARENESS

Not only is the proportion of men who saw discrimination considerably smaller than the proportion of women who perceived it, but even in their recognition of discrimination, men's assessment of its nature was less emphatic than was the women's. Thus, they believed that it occurs less frequently, or if it does occur, is less severe [see Table 4.1]. That men believed that discrimination is less pronounced became particularly noticeable when respondents were asked to decide how strongly they agree or disagree with a given discrimination-related statement. In most of those instances, men perceived discrimination but tended to consider it to be negligible or moderate; women, on the other hand, were inclined to choose the more emphatic option (such as seeing a great deal of it). For example, majorities of males and females (57 and 70 percent, respectively) saw evidence of much discrimination in today's society; among the remaining men, 40 percent recognized the persistence of discrimination but believed it to be of minor proportion, and 4 percent denied its existence. . . . Men are simply less likely than females to note discrimination in all of its pervasiveness and severity.

*****

Table 4.1: Discrimination Awareness by Gender

Percentage Agreeing That*	Men	Women
Men are treated better in society	48	69
There is much sex discrimination in U.S. society	57	70
It is still a man's world	34	50
Women are often treated as second-class citizens	23	50
A woman has to be better than a man to get ahead	43	64
Even if accomplished, women get less recognition	35	45
Women's opinions get less reaction than men's	44	59

*Only those respondents who agree "a lot."

The male/female awareness-gulf narrowed substantially with respect to some largely economic practices (see Table 4.2). In fact, in a few of them the two genders find themselves in almost complete agreement. . . .

Table 4.2: Discrimination Awareness in Specific Economic Areas

Percentage Agreeing That	Men	Women
Men are treated better in mortgage applications	56*	67
Men get better jobs in business management	65	72
Men are treated better with respect to pay	81	80
Men are more likely to get top government jobs	77	83

*All correlations significant at the .01 level.

That similarity in perspective when dealing with concrete, so-called bread-and-butter issues stands in sharp contrast to reactions to more ephemeral, hard to document signs of bias, such as the lack of respect accorded women's opinions or society's inadequate recognition of their achievements. There men showed themselves to be less sensitive . . .

The Discrimination Awareness index gives further evidence that men are less aware than women of the prevalence of gendered inequality . . . As might have been predicted, fewer men than women scored high on that index . . .

One important difference—as stated before—is that women see discrimination pervading almost all social interactions and spheres of life, whereas men notice it in a narrower range of life experiences, and even there they consider it to be less frequent and less severe than do women. It would be wrong, however, to declare that most men are either oblivious of or choose to ignore subtle and not-so-subtle manifestations of gender-based inequality. But it is correct to assert that considerably fewer among them are aware of it, and where they are aware, they see it as a less serious issue than do women. To quote an old see-saw, it is as though both genders agree the glass of equality is not completely full, but men judge it to be half full and women to be half empty.

* * * * *

THE PRINCIPLE OF GENDER EQUALITY

Perhaps even more revealing than their recognition of the persistence of inequalities is the way in which men deal with that recognition. . . . [W]hen the discussion turned to women in the workforce, males had no trouble agreeing that women are entitled to equal opportunity and treatment, including equal pay for equal work. But some men also had no trouble finding reasons why in their own work situation women ought to be treated differently from men. Either women's work was seen as less difficult, or as performed in more pleasant surroundings, or performance standards expected of women were lower, or a host of other reasons why the women they encountered at the workplace really did not "deserve" equal status or equal pay. In this way, the men could then avoid having to deal forthrightly with the issue of equal pay and equal opportunity. Their redefinition of the situation permitted them to minimize the issue of pay discrimination without appearing to be unfair or biased against women. . . . [A] young man, performing heavy physical labor, believed that physical strength and agility deserve more recognition and pay than "mere" clerical skills and asserted that it "is not fair" for secretaries or other "girls" performing physically nondemanding tasks to demand pay equivalent to his own. "So, I'm for a woman coming out and being a mechanic or climbing a pole and finding out, this is what you have to do to make this salary. If you don't want to do it, then fine. Go back into the office and make less money." He concluded his case for rewarding physical skill more than clerical skill with the comment: "What's happening now is that these ERAs pushing for this equal pay for equal job, I'm really against that."

* * * * *

Nevertheless, it would be unfair to characterize any of these men as hostile to women's progress. They are apprehensive, yes, and at times resentful, but they are rarely, if ever; hostile. Instead, I am inclined to characterize their reaction as primarily one of ambivalence. In principle, they believe in equality, at least equality of opportunity, but they are uncertain what this might mean in practice for them . . .

How do men cope with the tension between their principled beliefs (such as the belief in gender equality) and the natural tendency to hold on to accustomed privileges as they go about their everyday activities? For answers to that question, the next section will examine male attitudes and behaviors in three related realms: employment, family life (especially the impact of wives entering the work or reactions to the recent changes in women's positions [and division of labor] . . .

EMPLOYMENT

The conflict between principled beliefs and long-ingrained behavior patterns becomes particularly acute in the case of working-class males. That working-class males should be especially conflicted is not surprising since this is the group most vulnerable to or threatened by current changes. These men see themselves being made obsolete by technological advances, by demands for new skills for which they have not been trained, and by the ever-present threat of losing their jobs. To these technological predicaments is now added the possibility of having to work alongside women in formerly all-male jobs and possibly even be "displaced by women," as one man phrased it. Women's massive entrance into the workforce touches their lives very directly and, judging from their conversations, causes them a good deal of anxiety. It has forced many to cope with novel situations with which they have not yet come to terms.[10]

The situation confronts them on two separate, yet related fronts: at home as their wives take on paid employment and in their own workplace as they have to work side-by-side and perhaps even compete with women on jobs previously characterized as "a man's job"; a designation meant to imply women would be unable to discharge satisfactorily the duties of the job . . .

Their anxieties about the impending changes are expressed in a variety of ways. Some, as mentioned before, denigrated their female co-workers' suitability for the job by attributing their employment to affirmative action mandates ("quotas" as they preferred to call it). Others attributed female success to male coworkers' help with the assigned tasks.[11] "Technically, you're a male. But they are women, right? They have to do men's work. And if they can't handle the job, you've got men that will help them do their job. Which I don't think is right," said Luigi, a skilled maintenance worker in an industrial plant. Not that Luigi himself is inclined to help them! In fact, he refused to do so. He almost looks upon such help as a kind of sabotage of the male prerogative to perform certain types of labor. Another technique, also observed by Crosby, is "to see each competent woman as an exception while maintaining that any mistake made by a female was proof of the inferiority of the entire female gender [in the workforce]. Through the use of these and a number of other devices, the men managed to be, simultaneously, supportive and resistant" (1991: 188). . . .

* * * * *

In the middle-class male group, the topic of women in the workforce did not arouse the same controversy, let alone anxiety—at least not overtly. The middle-class men gave the impression that the whole issue has no immediate relevance for them . . . Their concerns however, were more likely expressed in terms of reservations about the general principle of affirmative action or other abstract issues. So long as the discussion turned around the abstract topic of equal opportunity, the men were generally approving, but when they recalled personal encounters in their own work situation, they too hedged their seemingly strong approval with a host of qualifying statements. They told one another that women are sometimes hard to work with because they are apt to equate a compliment or a friendly gesture with sexual harassment. They voiced the opinion that when women rise in the hierarchy, they become picky, "very, very over conscientious" or bossy, aggressive, and in the voice of Robert, a middle-level corporate manager, "overly assertive because they are so anxious to do a good job, and it makes it very difficult for a male to come in and to try and contend with that because you're always being put on your mettle to prove, and they're trying to prove that they're right. . . ." Should we not, therefore, infer that these men too may be ambivalent about women's ambitions? They may well be sincere in their support of women's desire to enter the workforce on an equal footing with men, but they can muster a host of reasons why in their particular case the female colleague is perhaps not quite equal and, therefore, not quite as deserving as they are. . . .

* * * * *

FAMILY

The recent changes in women's lives have a direct impact on family life, but again the impact varies by social class. Nowhere does the men's ambivalence and the sense of loss become more apparent than when middle-aged and older blue-collar males discussed their wives' employment history. The need to depend in part on income from the wife's employment diminishes their traditional roles as providers and, indirectly, their exclusive authority over the family. Here their anxieties about status and economic security become clearly visible.[15] The focus groups reveal most poignantly what a strong hold traditional definitions of gender relations still have on these men (Crosby 1987; Hertz 1986; Weiss 1987), although many would probably reject the idea that their outlook is traditional. . . . Tony is an electrical worker in his mid-forties whose wife, much to his chagrin, now holds a full-time clerical position. "I wouldn't let my wife work. I told her; I said 'Look, you got the kids, you stay home. When the kids go to school all day, then you work.' That's fine, up to a point, I tried to do it on my own. Working 20 hours a day to make everything go. She said 'hey look I gotta go to work.' Well, I was against it, but it had to be done. As far as I was brought up, Pop did the work; Mom stayed home with the kids. Alright? I was raised that way, and that's the way I saw it." That is also pretty much the way the other middle-aged and older blue-collar men saw the situation. The husband as the breadwinner and the wife as the homemaker describes their image of the normal and good life. . . . And so they "permit" their wives to work.[16] I was struck by how often the term "permit" is used, and how often they asserted that initially they "had not allowed" their wives to work. Comments such as these suggest two things. First, by permitting or forbidding, the role of the man as authority figure is maintained, his personal power over the family is not diminished. Second, only economic necessity justifies deviating from the traditional family structure in which the wife's role is exclusively defined as that of homemaker. The wife's employment thus is seen as a means to an end, the end being the family . . . The employed wife is the helper; her employment serves family, not personal, needs; it serves essentially the same needs as do the domestic activities, namely, the maintenance of the family . . .

* * * * *

While most blue-collar men referred to their wives' employment strictly in terms of family needs, middle-class men were more apt to refer to the fulfillment their partners derived from their work and/or the opportunity to utilize their training . . .

* * * * *

It is best, however, not to exaggerate just how "liberated" middle-class men are. They may not be as outspoken as working-class men in their preferences, but essentially they too opted for a fairly traditional family pattern. Although not voicing opposition in principle to their wives seeking employment, they voiced plenty of reservations. The presence of children in the family gave rise to a number of them, and the "latch-key" child became a reason for resisting a wife's entrance in the labor force . . .

* * * * *

DIVISION OF LABOR

The inequitable division of labor in the household was one of the major sources for women's complaints . . . [M]en simply ignored the subject, as though it were quite natural to expect women to work two shifts. . . . Asked how labor should be divided in the household when both partners are employed, over two-thirds believed it should be divided evenly (an opinion held by 90 percent of the women), and virtually no man believed that men should be exempt from domestic responsibilities. F. J. Crosby (1991: 148) cites a national survey conducted in 1978 in which 67 percent of the men expressed the same sentiments. Apparently not much has changed since; good intentions there were aplenty then and still are. However, only a small segment of the males in our study (14 percent) believed that equal sharing actually takes place.

* * * * *

Where men and women really part company is in their emotional reactions to observed discrimination. Males did not give the impression that the persistence of discrimination causes them pain, rather they see it as a fact of life—perhaps not a desirable one, but a fact of life nonetheless. . . . The women expressed much anger over discrimination; men expressed none. . . . For example, even though most men (70 percent) believed that society treats men better than women and thought that this is unfair, they were not greatly upset by it. Almost two-thirds (62 percent) accepted it as a fact of life, and only 30 percent (compared with 44 percent for women) told the interviewer that it bothers them. Even so, each man thought that he is more bothered by this injustice than are his fellow men. Where 20 percent declared themselves to be bothered "a lot" by societal discrimination, they granted similar concerns to only 6 percent of the rest of the male population. Women share men's assessment of the male population, but think that other women are greatly disturbed by discrimination.

* * * * *

CONCLUSION

. . . The conclusion has to be that the men who participated in our study are quite aware of the "subtle revolution" and are aware that many or most women no longer are willing to accept the subordinate status their mothers took for granted. The men not only understand that desire but support it and support it in a way that I believe to be genuine. However, they support the ideal in an abstract sense, as a principle. The problem for them becomes acute when they reflect on its ramifications and on what gender equality would mean for their own lives. It is then that their ambivalence comes to the fore. . . .

Notes

---

4. As one focus group participant, whose wife's employment has become crucial for the family's financial well-being, put it when reflecting on the altered power balance in his home, "I roll with the punches. Nothing fazes me any more."

10. The anxieties expressed by these men don't seem to be atypical. Judging from the many media reports which appeared soon after the 1994 November election, fear and anxiety over becoming displaced by women, minorities, or machines fueled the resentment of many white males. Much in this vein, Secretary of Labor Reich referred to the election results as "the revolt of the anxious."

11. That such help seems to be the exception rather than the rule can be seen from the anecdotal evidence cited. While some women, as we have seen, are of the firm conviction that men actually work at making women fail, I found no evidence of that in the focus group. But I also found little evidence that men went out of their way to help women learn the trade as they might do for new male co-workers. Kessler-Harris's (1982) pioneering study of working women documents that in some trade unions men actually were fined by their unions if they helped women.

15. A great number of studies exist to the effect that men's sense of well-being and even their self-esteem is closely connected to their sense of power and authority over their families, including their wives (Bernard 1972 and 1981; Gilbert 1985; Guttenberg and Secord 1983; Kahn 1984; Pleck 1983 and 1985).

16. Arlene Hochschild (1989: 60) made a similar observation when she wrote that working-class men spoke of "letting my wife work."

References

Bernard, J. 1981. *The Female World*. Glencoe, IL: Free Press.

_____. 1972. *The Future of Marriage*. New York: World.

Crosby, F. J. 1991. *Juggling: The Unexpected Advantages of Balancing Career and Home for Women and Their Families*. New York: The Free Press.

_____, ed. 1987. Spouse, Parent, Worker: On Gender and Multiple Roles. New Haven, CT: Yale University Press.

Gilbert, L. A. 1985. Men *in Dual-Career Families: Current Realities and Future Prospects*. Hillsdale, NJ: Lawrence Erlbaum Associations.

Guttentag, M., and P. F. Secord. 1983. *Too Many Women? The Sex-ratio Question*. Beverly Hills, CA: Sage Publishers.

Hertz, Rosanna. 1986. *More Equal Than Others: Women and Men in Dual-Career Marriages*. Berkeley: University of California Press.

Hochschild, Arlene R. 1989. *Second Shift: Working Parents and the Revolution at Home*. New York: Viking Press.

Kahn, A. 1984. "The Power War: Male Responses to Power Loss Under Equality." *Psychology of Women Quarterly* 8: 234–47.

Pleck, J. H. 1985. *Working Wives, Working Husbands*. Newbury Park, CA: Sage Publications.

_____. 1983. "Husband's Paid Work and Family Roles: Current Research Issues." In *Research in the Interweave of Social Roles: Families and Jobs*, vol. 3, edited by H. Lopata and J. H. Pleck, pp. 251–333. Greenwich, CT: JAI Press.

Weiss, Robert S. 1987. "Men and Their Wives' Work." In *Spouse, Parent, Worker: On Gender and Multiple Roles*, edited by F. J. Crosby, pp. 109–38. New Haven: Yale University Press.

*R*ichard R. W. Brooks and Haekyung Jeon-Slaughter's analysis should make readers wary of overestimating the influence of an individual's demographic characteristics on their opinion. As many expect, the authors do find that African-Americans have less confidence in the U.S. courts compared to whites and Latinos. African-Americans are less apt to agree that they are treated equally in the various layers of the court system. That said, middle-class African-Americans are more satisfied than low-income African-Americans, suggesting again the importance of intersectionality. Confidence in the courts by middle-class African-Americans stands in contrast to larger trends where poor and working-class African-Americans are more satisfied than middle-class African-Americans when it comes to other political institutions and in endorsing American Dream ideology. In this manner, we see that race does not *determine views on the courts. Rather, more nuanced relationships are the norm and not always the patterns we might expect.*

Race, Income, and Perceptions of the U.S. Court System

RICHARD R. W. BROOKS AND HAEKYUNG JEON-SLAUGHTER

INTRODUCTION

This article reports on the effect of income within race on citizen perception of the courts. Specifically, we identify and discuss a pattern of skepticism and distrust concerning the court system by higher-income African Americans.

* * * * *

Our findings are somewhat consistent with the previous research on black middle-class dissatisfaction. That is, unlike whites and Latinos in our study, we find that higher-income African Americans are more skeptical of the notion that blacks receive equal treatment in the courts. This same group also reported less confidence in the court's handling of specific types of case (e.g., civil, criminal, and juvenile delinquency cases). However, better-off blacks were more likely to have confidence in the U.S. Supreme Court and community courts. This finding is likely rooted in continued diffused support for the U.S. Supreme Court and the court system generally among "rights conscious" blacks. It appears that better-off blacks are dissatisfied with the courts' effectiveness when it comes to specific issues, such as African American defendants and the handling of criminal cases. However, as a general matter, this group remains more confident in the courts than do poor blacks. Thus, the general wave of black middle-class dissatisfaction with American political and economic institutions may not have yet reached the shores of the judiciary.

RESEARCH ON PERCEPTIONS OF THE AMERICAN LEGAL SYSTEM

Public opinion and attitudes concerning the legal system and criminal law enforcement have been extensively studied. . . . Few studies, however, have considered the effect of income within race on citizen perception of the courts . . .

* * * * *

. . . (see Table 4.3). Almost 64% of African Americans feel that the courts treat them worse than others, while 22% feel that they are treated equally in the courts. African Americans' perceptions of fairness in the American court system are more

Richard R. W. Brooks and Haekyung Jeon-Slaughter, "Race, Income, and Perceptions in the U.S. Court System," *Behavioral Sciences and the Law,* vol. 19, no. 2 (May 2001), pp. 249–264. Copyright © 2001 John Wiley & Sons Limited. Reproduced by permission of John Wiley & Sons Limited.

likely to be negative compared with other racial groups according to findings from this sample. Perhaps surprisingly, however, this study found that more than 60% of African Americans have "some" or "a great deal" of confidence in the U.S. Supreme Court and community courts, while only 13 to 17% of African Americans believe that the courts handle civil and small claims cases poorly, and around 30% believe that the courts handle criminal and juvenile delinquency cases poorly. Since these findings contradict each other somewhat, we . . . will explore the relationship between confidence of African Americans in the U.S. court system and their income status . . .

Table 4.3. Summary Statistics for . . . African American Sub-Sample

Q1: What kind of treatment do blacks receive in courts?

Far better	6	(1.4)[a]
Somewhat better	28	(6.5)
Same treatment	93	(21.7)
Somewhat worse	150	(35.0)
Far worse	124	(28.9)
Don't know	26	(6.1)
No answer	2	(0.5)

[a] Numbers in parentheses are the percentages.

Q2 & Q3: What is your level of confidence in the	*Supreme Court?*	*Community courts?*
A great deal	67 (15.6)	55 (12.8)
Some	205 (47.8)	208 (48.5)
Only a little	92 (21.5)	87 (20.3)
No confidence	44 (10.3)	64 (14.9)
Don't know	21 (4.9)	15 (3.5)
No answer	0 (0.0)	0 (0.0)

Q4–Q7: In what manner do the courts handle	*Civil cases?*	*Criminal cases?*	*Small claims?*	*Juvenile delinquency?*
Excellent	22 (5.1)	32 (7.5)	19 (4.4)	27 (6.3)
Good	107 (24.9)	93 (21.7)	99 (23.1)	73 (17.0)
Fair	195 (45.5)	146 (34.0)	159 (37.1)	134 (31.2)
Poor	57 (13.3)	127 (29.6)	73 (17.0)	141 (32.9)
Don't know	46 (10.7)	27 (6.3)	75 (17.5)	51 (32.9)
No answer	2 (0.5)	4 (1.0)	4 (1.0)	3 (1.0)

* * * * *

RESULTS

. . . By and large, we found income and gender have more significant effects on confidence or trust of African Americans in the U.S. court system than other demographic variables: better-off African Americans and African American women have lower confidence in the courts than the poor and men, respectively.[23] In the question about how the courts treat African Americans, we found the likelihood of responding somewhat worse treatment relative to equal treatment is greater for better-off African Americans than for lower-income African Americans. As income level increases further, respondents' confidence in the court treatment of African Americans begins to increase slightly. By contrast, confidence in the U.S. Supreme Court and community courts is higher for better-off African Americans than for poorer African Americans.

Perceptions of courts' handling of civil, criminal, and juvenile delinquency cases follow a similar pattern to that observed in the question regarding court treatment of African Americans. That is, the likelihood of answering *poor* relative to *excellent* is greater for middle-income African Americans than those with lower income. Confidence levels increased slightly for the wealthiest respondents in the sample. Perceptions of courts' handling of small-claims cases, however, follow the opposite pattern. Again, African American females show less confidence than African American males in courts' handling civil cases and the U.S. Supreme Court. Education was significantly correlated with lack of confidence in the courts handling of criminal cases. This result was also found among better educated Latinos in the sample, but not among whites.

DISCUSSION

The results in the previous section are somewhat consistent with the research on black middle-class discontent. Higher-income African Americans express more skepticism about the chances of blacks to receive equal treatment in the courts. Additionally, better-off African Americans have less confidence in the court's handling of specific types of case (e.g., civil, criminal, and juvenile delinquency cases[24]). In contrast with the trend identified in the recent research literature however, our analysis found that better-off blacks were more likely to have confidence in the U.S. Supreme Court and community courts. This finding is consistent with the notion of diffused support for the courts among blacks, particularly those concerned with civil rights. For instance, Gibson and Caldeira (1992) found, on the one hand, that blacks were more critical of specific court outputs and policies; and on the other hand, that blacks reported general or diffuse support for the institution of the Court. They explained this diffuse support as good will generated by the role that the Court played in assuring the rights of African Americans: "[from] the early days of the Warren Court onward through the beginning of the 1960s, the Court stood as a beacon of hope and light for black Americans amidst an otherwise hostile political system . . . [B]lack Americans had good reason to hold the Supreme Court in high esteem" (p. 1123).[25] Thus the general pattern of black middle-class dissatisfaction with American political, economic and legal institutions may stop short of the judiciary. Still, the fact that higher-income blacks are more inclined to express lack of confidence on specific issues, such as the courts' treatment of blacks and criminal cases, suggests that their general support for the courts may erode unless steps are taken to counter such a trend.[26]

* * * * *

Notes

23. Analysis of the survey did not reveal a similarly significant income effect for whites. There was some indication that higher-income Latinos had more confidence in the courts than do poor Latinos. However, this pattern is neither as consistent nor as pervasive as the alternate pattern of distrust among higher income African Americans . . .

24. As mentioned in the results section, with respect to the handling of small-claims cases the pattern appears reversed. However, compared to the results concerning the handling of civil, criminal, and juvenile delinquency cases (which were significant at the 5% level), the result regarding small-claims cases was significant at only the 10% level.

25. Gibson and Caldeira find support for this hypothesis by dividing their sample into three cohorts, and observe that those blacks who came of age during the Warren Court were most supportive of the Court. We used the same cohort categories as Gibson and Caldeira in our analysis, but found no consistent results with regard to confidence in community courts and the Supreme Court.

26. Political scientists, such as David Easton (1965), have long predicted that diffused support for institutions will subside as specific support falls off over time.

References

Easton, David. 1965. *A Framework for Political Analysis*. Englewood Cliffs, NJ: Prentice-Hall.

Gibson JL, Caldeira GA. 1992. "Blacks and the United States Supreme Court: Models of Diffuse Support." *Journal of Politics 54*: 1120–1145.

*T*his article comes from the journal Social Science Quarterly. *In it, Laura Olson, Wendy Cadge, and James Harrison examine the effects of religious affiliation and religiosity on views about gay marriage, civil unions, and a constitutional amendment to ban gay marriage. The effect of religious affiliation is felt most deeply for gay marriage with non-Protestants being less opposed to gay marriage. But, here again, these differences are both very real but not at the expense of any overlap between various religious groups. Visualize each ring in the famous five-circle Olympic symbol as religious affiliations. Now condense the rings more than they are typically depicted in the Olympic symbol. The places of overlap among circles are where many among the religious traditions agree on gay marriage. The places where overlap does not occur represents the manner in which particular religious traditions tend to have different opinions regarding gay marriage.*

This reading thus presents the reality of demographic influence on public opinion—in this case, religion—as well as the fact that public opinion regularly overlaps across various demographic demarcations.

Religion and Public Opinion about Same-Sex Marriage

LAURA R. OLSON, WENDY CADGE, AND JAMES T. HARRISON

Exit polls conducted on Election Day 2004 (and much debated since then) show that 22 percent of the American electorate claimed to be motivated by moral values when they turned out to vote in the presidential election between George W. Bush and John Kerry (Edison Media Research and Mitofsky International, 2004). Gay marriage was one of the most significant moral issues lurking below these exit poll results. Recent analyses show that the issue had a significant influence on individual voters and state vote totals in several regions of the United States (Lewis, 2005).

Public debates and related court battles about gay marriage began in the United States more than 10 years before the 2004 presidential election (Andersen, 2005; D'Emilio and Freedman, 1988; Mello, 2004; Strasser, 1999). The issue took on renewed national visibility recently in response to *Goodridge v. Department of Public Health* (2003), which legalized same-sex marriage in Massachusetts. People of faith, especially evangelical Protestants (who have long been a prominent force in anti-gay rights efforts in the United States), mobilized in response to the *Goodridge* decision, successfully leading efforts to amend numerous state constitutions to prohibit same-sex marriage (Green, 2000; Herman, 2000; Soule, 2004). Led largely by religious conservatives, voters in 11 states (Arkansas, Georgia, Kentucky, Michigan, Mississippi, Montana, North Dakota, Ohio, Oklahoma, Oregon, and Utah) approved related amendments in the November 2004 elections, and legislation and litigation in several other states is pending (see, e.g., Damore, Jelen, and Bowers, forthcoming). At the federal level, resolutions were introduced in Congress following the *Goodridge* decision to amend the U.S. Constitution to restrict marriage to heterosexual couples. The U.S. Senate rejected the Federal Marriage Amendment in July 2004, though some activists continued to push for such an amendment in 2005 (Easton, 2005; Liu and Macedo, 2005).

. . . [We] examine how religion (as measured by both religious affiliation and religiosity) influences attitudes about gay marriage, as well as attitudes about civil unions and a Federal Marriage Amendment that would restrict marriage to heterosexual couples . . .

BACKGROUND

* * * * *

Recent polls indicate that demographic factors such as education, gender, and age have significant influences on public opinion about homosexuality, as does the degree of personal contact individuals have with gay men and lesbians, and attitudes toward

---

Laura R. Olson, Wendy Cadge, and James T. Harrison, "Religion and Public Opinion about Same-Sex Marriage," *Social Science Quarterly*, vol. 87, no. 2 (June 2006), pp. 340–360. © 2006 by the Southwestern Social Science Association. Reprinted by permission of Blackwell Publishing.

traditional morality (Brewer, 2003; Davis, 1992; Ellison and Musick, 1993; Finlay and Walther, 2003; Gibson and Tedin, 1988; Glenn and Weaver, 1979; Herek, 2002; Herek and Capitanio, 1996; Herek and Glunt, 1993; Kerns and Fine, 1994; Kite and Whitley, 1996; Loftus, 2001). Religion, as measured by individuals' religious affiliations, behaviors, and beliefs, also has a clear and consistent influence on their opinions about homosexuality. Religious affiliation has an especially strong impact: Jews, liberal Protestants, and people who are religiously unaffiliated have the most liberal attitudes, in part because many of their religious traditions have not systematically condemned homosexual behaviors in recent years. Catholics and moderate Protestants tend to espouse moderate but generally tolerant attitudes. Evangelical Protestants have the most conservative attitudes, reflecting their theological beliefs and official denominational and congregational positions on homosexuality (Cochran and Beeghley, 1991; Cotten-Huston and Waite, 2000; Finlay and Walther, 2003; Fisher et al., 1994; Glenn and Weaver, 1979; Herek and Glunt, 1993; Irwin and Thompson, 1977; Kirkpatrick, 1993; Roof and McKinney, 1987). Religiosity, as measured by frequency of attendance at religious services, is also a significant predictor of individuals' opinions about homosexuality. People who attend services frequently have more conservative attitudes, at least in part because many of them are evangelical Protestants (Beatty and Walter, 1984; Cochran and Beeghley, 1991; Fisher et al., 1994; Herek, 1984; Herek and Glunt, 1993). . . . People whose social networks are deeply tied to a religious congregation tend to be less accepting of homosexuality . . . (Petersen and Donnenwerth, 1998).

* * * * *

DATA

To examine the relationship between religion and attitudes toward same-sex marriage, we examine data collected in a telephone survey designed and administered by Greenberg Quinlan Rosner Research, Inc. The survey . . . was conducted . . . about one month after media attention focused on same-sex marriages being performed in the City of San Francisco . . .

* * * * *

The . . . survey asked respondents to indicate their attitudes about three distinct aspects of the same-sex marriage debate. First, respondents were asked: "Do you strongly favor, favor, oppose, or strongly oppose allowing gays and lesbians to marry legally?" Second, they were asked: "Would you strongly favor, favor, oppose, or strongly oppose a law that would allow homosexual couples to legally form civil unions, giving them some of the rights of married couples?" Third, only those respondents who stated that they opposed or strongly opposed gay marriage were asked: "Should the U.S. Constitution be amended to ban gay marriage, or is it enough to prohibit gay marriage by law without changing the Constitution?" . . . 60.9 percent of the sample said they either oppose or strongly oppose gay marriage; an even larger proportion oppose or strongly oppose civil unions (72.6 percent). These opponents of same-sex unions are split on the question of how to prohibit gay marriage under law, however; only two in five favor a Federal Marriage Amendment as opposed to statutory prohibitions against gay marriage.

* * * * *

Because we are investigating the extent to which religion shapes public opinion on gay marriage, our principal independent variables tap two dimensions of religious life: religious affiliation and religiosity . . . [W]e operationalize religious affiliation using . . . : African-American Protestant, evangelical Protestant, mainline Protestant, Roman Catholic, Jewish, other religion, and unaffiliated.[1] We expect to find evangelical Protestants and African-American Protestants to be especially opposed to same-sex unions because their religious traditions consistently teach that the practice of homosexuality is sinful . . .

The political relevance of religion cannot be measured by religious tradition alone, however, so we also include measures of religiosity in our analyses . . . The key measure of religiosity is frequency of attendance at worship services, and we include this . . . along with other measures of religious activity in a "religious activity" index (see Guth et al., 1997). . . . We expect to show that involvement in religious activity increases opposition to same-sex unions because voices of organized religion do not frequently speak out in support of gay couples (but see Cadge, 2002). The more involved one is in organized religion, the more likely he or she might be to hear messages denouncing same-sex unions from the pulpit, in congregational forums and adult education classes, and in the course of informal discussion.

* * * * *

Table 4.4: Descriptive Statistics

Attitude Toward Gay Marriage

Strongly favor	185 (12.8%)
Favor	380 (26.3%)
Oppose	294 (20.3%)
Strongly oppose	588 (40.6%)

Attitude Toward Civil Unions

Strongly favor	150 (10.5%)
Favor	242 (16.9%)
Oppose	286 (20.0%)
Strongly oppose	752 (52.6%)

Attitude Toward Const. Amendment

Amend the Constitution	385 (40.1%)
It is enough to prohibit by law	575 (59.9%)

Religious Tradition

African-American Protestant	136 (8.7%)
White Evangelical Protestant	561 (35.7%)
Mainline Protestant	172 (11.0%)
Roman Catholic	313 (19.9%)

Table 4.4: Descriptive Statistics (continued)

Attitude Toward Gay Marriage

Jewish	16 (1.0%)
Other religion	170 (10.8%)
Unaffiliated	162 (10.3%)
Friends in Congregation	
All	93 (6.0%)
Most	255 (16.4%)
About half	268 (17.3%)
Some	504 (32.5%)
None/not applicable	432 (27.8%)
Worried Society Becoming Too Secular	
Very worried	457 (31.5%)
Somewhat worried	510 (35.2%)
Not too worried	268 (18.5%)
Not worried at all	214 (14.8%)
Ideology	
Conservative	655 (44.8%)
Moderate	541 (37.0%)
Liberal	267 (18.2%)
Gender	
Female	817 (52.0%)
Male	753 (48.0%)
Education	
1st–11th grade	143 (9.2%)
High school graduate	426 (27.4%)
Noncollege course(s) after high school	34 (2.2%)
Some college	382 (24.6%)
College graduate	410 (26.4%)
Postgraduate school	158 (10.2%)
Marital Status	
Married	859 (55.4%)
Single	389 (25.1%)
Separated/divorced	178 (11.5%)
Widowed	124 (8.0%)

Total N = 1,610.

Source: Greenberg Quinlan Rosner poll for *Religion & Ethics Newsweekly* (2004).

FINDINGS AND DISCUSSION

* * * * *

The results . . . lead us to two conclusions. First, religion (especially as measured by religious affiliation and attitudes about morality and secularism) has a powerful effect on attitudes toward same-sex unions. Being a member of a non-Protestant religious tradition appears to lead individuals away from opposition to both gay marriage and civil unions, whereas espousing traditional attitudes on morality and secularism makes individuals more likely to oppose same-sex unions. Second, our strong findings regarding the impact of prioritizing moral values on attitudes toward gay marriage and civil unions remind us of the much-discussed exit poll result from November 2004 (Edison Media Research and Mitofsky International, 2004). Prioritization of moral values above other issues is clearly a significant predictor of opposition to gay marriage. Thus it may well be correct to assume that opposing gay rights is a key component of the rhetorically nebulous notion of "morality" as a political issue.

Our final question is whether opponents of gay marriage also support a federal constitutional amendment that would define marriage as the union between one man and one woman. Theoretically, we could find the strongest relationship between religion and a Federal Marriage Amendment because such an amendment could be seen as the strongest way to prohibit same-sex marriage nationally. However, some conservatives might not support amending the Constitution under any circumstances (see Reeves and Stewart, 2002), so it is somewhat more difficult to generate hypotheses about the factors that should be expected to structure attitudes about a Federal Marriage Amendment.

Recall that the question about amending the Constitution was asked only of respondents who expressed some level of opposition to gay marriage. The item asked whether "it is enough to prohibit gay marriage by law" or if it would be better to "amend the Constitution." Thus our analysis attempts to identify the factors that drive people to the strongest possible level of opposition to gay marriage.

Here, we see that religious affiliation on its own cannot explain all the nuances of opinion about gay marriage. . . . None of the religious tradition . . . variables are statistically significant. . . . The only significant finding regarding any religion variable is that high levels of religious activity contribute to support for a constitutional amendment, although the substantive significance . . . is again rather small. Among the statistically significant predictors in the model, political conservatism is by far the strongest predictor of support for a Federal Marriage Amendment. As such, we conclude that while religion plays strong roles in structuring attitudes toward gay marriage and civil unions, it does not help us differentiate between those who wish to amend the Constitution to prevent same-sex unions and those who prefer statutory prohibitions. Being highly involved in religious life thus promotes opposition to same-sex unions, but it does not go particularly far in helping us understand people's attitudes about how government should prohibit such unions . . .

CONCLUSION

Religion, as measured both by religious affiliation and religiosity, has a powerful effect on public opinion about same-sex marriage and related issues in the United

States. In particular, non-Protestants are much more likely to support same-sex unions, and individuals with conservative attitudes on morality and secularism and (to a lesser extent) those who participate actively in religious life are more likely to oppose such unions. The fact that our religion variables perform better than demographic measures in our models clearly shows how important religion is in the shaping of attitudes about same-sex unions.

. . . [O]ur findings about religiosity . . . point to the ways informal friendship networks in religious contexts might enhance opposition to gay rights. People with many close friends in their religious congregation are most enmeshed in their congregation. The more friends a person has in his or her congregation, the more he or she will be invested in the congregation's future, and the more his or her sociopolitical viewpoints will be structured by the consensus of the congregation, or at least the consensus of the friendship network within the congregation. Congregations, regardless of their specific religious affiliation, can be highly cohesive political communities in which opinion tends to converge on certain issues, particularly those that are morally charged (Gilbert, 1993; Wald, Owen, and Hill, 1988, 1990) . . .

Our results also offer a suggestion that Americans who profess concern about moral values (as did 22 percent of the American electorate on Election Day [Edison Media Research and Mitofsky International, 2004]) are motivated to do so at least in part by their opposition to gay rights. Our analyses show that identifying moral values among one's top two issue concerns is a strong and significant predictor of opposition to both gay marriage and civil unions. Moreover, the Republican mobilization effort directed toward evangelicals and traditional Catholics emphasized gay marriage as an issue of crucial importance (Green et al., 2004; IVoteValues.com, 2004)— and attracted many of the faithful across religious traditions to vote for President Bush (Green et al., 2004; Pew Forum on Religion and Public Life, 2004a; Pew Research Center for the People and the Press, 2004).

More broadly, our results suggest that without a change in opinion among religious individuals and organizations in the United States, the tide is not likely to turn in favor of same-sex marriages or civil unions without some reframing of the issue. Battles about homosexuality are being waged in religious organizations across the country, although this has been the case to a greater extent in mainline Protestant and Jewish circles than in other religious traditions, most notably evangelicals (Cadge, 2002; Zuckerman, 1999). It is useful to remember that American religion is not uniformly opposed to same-sex unions (Cadge, 2002), but opponents do vastly outnumber supporters. Congregations are important crucibles of public opinion, particularly on charged moral issues. It is clear from our analysis that religious context has a powerful effect on citizen opinion about same-sex unions.

Note

1. *Editors' Note*: This procedure was developed by Brian Steensland and colleagues (2000) and was noted as such by original authors.

References

Andersen, Ellen. 2005. *Out of the Closets and into the Courts: Legal Opportunity Structure and Gay Rights Litigation*. University of Michigan Press.

Beatty, Kathleen M., and Oliver Walter. 1984. "Religious Preference and Practice: Reevaluating Their Impact on Political Tolerance." *Public Opinion Quarterly* 48:318–29.

Brewer, Paul. 2003. "The Shifting Foundations of Public Opinion about Gay Rights." *Journal of Politics* 65:1208–20.

Cadge, Wendy. 2002. "Vital Conflicts: The Mainline Protestant Denominations Debate Homosexuality." In Robert Wuthnow and John H. Evans, eds., *The Quiet Hand of God: Faith Based Activism and the Public Role of Mainline Protestantism*. University of California Press.

Cochran, John K., and Leonard Beeghley. 1991. "The Influence of Religion on Attitudes Toward Nonmarital Sexuality: A Preliminary Assessment of Reference Group Therapy." *Journal for the Scientific Study of Religion* 30:45–62.

Cotten-Huston, Annie, and Bradley M. Waite. 2000. "Anti-Homosexual Attitudes in College Students: Predictors and Classroom Interventions." *Journal of Homosexuality* 38:117–33.

Davis, James A. 1992. "Changeable Weather in a Cooling Climate Atop the Liberal Plateau: Conversion and Replacement in Forty-Two General Social Survey Items, 1972–1989." *Public Opinion Quarterly* 56:261–306.

D'Emilio, John, and Estelle Freedman. 1988. *Intimate Matters: A History of Sexuality in America*. Chicago: University of Chicago Press.

Easton, Nina J. 2005. "Mood Dampened for Conservatives: Bush Won't Press Gay Marriage Issue." *Boston Globe* January 20.

Edison Media Research and Mitofsky International. 2004. *Election 2004 Exit Polls*. Available at www.exit-poll.net.

Ellison, Christopher G., and Marc A. Musick. 1993. "Southern Intolerance: A Fundamentalist Effect?" *Social Forces* 72:379–98.

Finlay, Barbara, and Carol S. Walther. 2003. "The Relation of Religious Affiliation, Service Attendance, and Other Factors to Homophobic Attitudes Among University Students." *Review of Religious Research* 44:370–93.

Fisher, Randy D., Donna Derison, Chester F. I. Polley, Jennifer Cadman, and Dana Johnston. 1994. "Religiousness, Religious Orientation, and Attitudes Towards Gays and Lesbians." *Journal of Applied Social Psychology* 24:614–30.

Gibson, James L., and Kent L. Tedin. 1988. "The Etiology of Intolerance of Homosexual Politics." *Social Science Quarterly* 69:587–604.

Glenn, Norval D., and Charles N. Weaver. 1979. "Attitudes Toward Premarital, Extramarital, and Homosexual Relations in the U.S. in the 1970s." *Journal of Sex Research* 15:108–18.

Green, John C. 2000. "Antigay: Varieties of Opposition to Gay Rights." In Craig A. Rimmerman, Kenneth D. Wald, and Clyde Wilcox, eds., *The Politics of Gay Rights*. University of Chicago Press.

Green, John C. 2004. *The American Religious Landscape and Political Attitudes: A Baseline for 2004*. Available at www.uakron.edu/bliss/research.php.

Green, John C., Corwin E. Smidt, James L. Guth, and Lyman A. Kellstedt. 2004. *The American Religious Landscape and the 2004 Presidential Vote*. Available at www.uakron.edu/bliss/research.php.

Guth, James L., John C. Green, Corwin E. Smidt, Lyman A. Kellstedt, and Margaret M. Poloma. 1997. *The Bully Pulpit: The Politics of Protestant Clergy.* University Press of Kansas.

Herek, Gregory M. 1984. "Beyond 'Homophobia': A Social Psychological Perspective on Attitudes Toward Lesbians and Gay Men." *Journal of Homosexuality* 10:1–21.

Herek, Gregory M. 2002. "Gender Gaps in Public Opinion about Lesbians and Gay Men." *Public Opinion Quarterly* 66:40–66.

Herek, Gregory M., and Capitanio, John P. 1996. "'Some of My Best Friends': Intergroup Contact, Concealable Stigma, and Heterosexuals' Attitudes Toward Gay Men and Lesbians." *Personality and Social Psychology Bulletin* 22:412–24.

Herek, Gregory M., and Eric K. Glunt. 1993. "Interpersonal Contact and Heterosexuals' Attitudes Toward Gay Men: Results from a National Survey." *Journal of Sex Research* 30:239–44.

Herman, Didi. 2000. "The Gay Agenda Is the Devil's Agenda: The Christian Right's Vision and the Role of the State." In Craig A. Rimmerman, Kenneth D. Wald, and Clyde Wilcox, eds., *The Politics of Gay Rights.* University of Chicago Press.

Irwin, Patrick, and Norman L. Thompson. 1977. "Acceptance of the Rights of Homosexuals: A Social Profile." *Journal of Homosexuality* 3:107–21.

IVoteValues.com. 2004. Website at www.ivotevalues.com.

Kerns, John G., and Mark A. Fine. 1994. "The Relation Between Gender and Negative Attitudes Toward Gay Men and Lesbians: Do Gender Role Attitudes Mediate This Relation?" *Sex Roles* 31:297–307.

Kirkpatrick, Lee. 1993. "Fundamentalism, Christian Orthodoxy, and Intrinsic Religious Orientation as Predictors of Discriminatory Attitudes." *Journal for the Scientific Study of Religion* 32:256–68.

Kite, Mary E., and Bernard E. Whitley, Jr. 1996. "Sex Differences in Attitudes Toward Homosexual Persons, Behaviors, and Civil Rights: A Meta-Analysis." *Personality and Social Psychology Bulletin* 22:336–53.

Lewis, Gregory B. 2005. "Same-Sex Marriage and the 2004 Presidential Election." *PS: Political Science & Politics* 38:195–99.

Liu, Frederick, and Stephen Macedo. 2005. "The Federal Marriage Amendment and the Strange Evolution of the Conservative Case Against Gay Marriage." *PS: Political Science & Politics* 38:211–15.

Loftus, Jeni. 2001. "America's Liberalization in Attitudes Toward Homosexuality, 1973 to 1998." *American Sociological Review* 66:762–82.

Mello, Michael. 2004. *Legalizing Gay Marriage.* Temple University Press.

Petersen, Larry R., and Gregory V. Donnenwerth. 1998. "Religion and Declining Support for Traditional Beliefs about Gender Roles and Homosexual Rights." *Sociology of Religion* 59:353–71.

Pew Forum on Religion and Public Life. 2004a. *How the Faithful Voted.* Available at pewforum.org/events/index.php?EventID=64.

Pew Forum on Religion and Public Life. 2004b. *Religious Beliefs Underpin Opposition to Homosexuality.* Available at pewforum.org/docs/index.php?DocID=37.

Pew Research Center for the People and the Press. 2004. *Religion and the Presidential Vote: Bush's Gains Broad Based.* Available at people-press.org/commentary/display.php3?AnalysisID=103.

Reeves, Andree, and Joseph Stewart, Jr. 2002. "Old Times in the New South? The Alabama Antimiscegenation Repeal Vote, 2000." Paper presented at the Annual Meeting of the Southern Political Science Association. Savannah, GA.

Roof, Wade Clark, and William McKinney. 1987. *Mainline American Religion: Its Changing Shape and Future*. Rutgers University Press.

Soule, Sarah. 2004. "Going to the Chapel? Same-Sex Marriage Bans in the United States, 1973–2000." *Social Problems* 51:453–77.

Strasser, Mark. 1999. *The Challenge of Same-Sex Marriage: Federalist Principles and Constitutional Protections*. Praeger.

Zuckerman, Phil. 1999. *Strife in the Sanctuary: Religious Schism in a Jewish Community*. Alta Mira.

*I*n the final piece in this section, political scientist Terry Moe uses nationally representative survey data in order to obtain a fuller understanding of public support and opposition for school vouchers. Moe recognizes that Americans are busy, have a wide variety of information being thrown their way, and he is cognizant of the fact that most Americans cannot become fully informed on every issue—nor do they want to. In light of this, he garners baseline or "top of the head" support measures for school vouchers and finds roughly 60 percent support vouchers (however this varies across race, income, and other demographic categories), 32 percent do not, and 7 percent are undecided. He then administered a series of follow-up questions that inform respondents about school vouchers and asks more specific questions about various aspects of the issue. Views often, though not always, changed. This demonstrates how Americans are able to form consistent views but these views can change with new/more information, question wording, and purposeful framing. As students of diversity and public opinion, we are reminded that opinions on the most contested issues of the day are far from intractable. Views can and do change.

Moe's analysis also reveals that the issue of school vouchers is far from simply one of being a Democrat or a Republican. Rather, public opinion is predicted by how a host of factors fit together including: whether or not one is a parent, one's socioeconomic status, and one's religion. How these memberships fit together best predict voucher opinion and make for some seemingly unlikely allies: minority parents, individuals in lower income brackets, Republicans, Catholics, and born-again Christians. All things being equal, these groups are all more likely than their counterparts to support school vouchers.

Support for Vouchers

TERRY MOE

. . . To what extent do Americans support vouchers?

This is the question elites on both sides of the issue care about most. They all recognize that, in a democracy, the polling numbers matter—for the numbers tell elected officials what decisions are likely to meet with public approval, and thus what positions they can take to enhance their own popularity and reelection prospects. The more Americans support vouchers, the more inclined policymakers will be to move in that direction.

But what exactly *are* the numbers? On this there is disagreement. Advocates want to argue that most Americans support vouchers. Critics want to argue the opposite. And both point to scientifically designed polls, carried out by reputable organizations, that seem to bolster their positions.

To some extent, this conflict over the facts is a natural outgrowth of politics. On virtually any policy issue, partisans can be expected to take a selective approach to the evidence and to use it strategically in trying to win over the uncommitted. In politics, evidence often has little to do with the search for truth. It is just another weapon in the struggle for victory.

With the voucher issue, however, and with many other policy issues as well, there is another reason why the truth is so elusive and competing claims so prevalent. The reason is that there *isn't* a simple truth to be discovered. This may sound a bit melodramatic, but the problem is unavoidable. For if most Americans have never heard of the concept, much less thought about it in any depth, they cannot have well-developed opinions. Indeed, it is not even clear that they can have opinions at all. And once we question the meaning and validity of their opinions and recognize how easily their views can change, the notion that there is a true level of public support—a true level that surveys are supposedly measuring—becomes untenable.

To understand support for vouchers, then, we cannot take public opinion at face value. . . . The challenge is to determine whether, in a population of people who are largely uninformed about vouchers, public opinion tells us much of anything about what Americans really want for themselves, their communities, and their country.

This chapter will try to provide some answers. It is an effort to direct attention away from simple questions of support and opposition—the questions that have so monopolized attention in politics and the media—and to construe the subject in a way that helps us understand what is actually going on.

WHAT IS PUBLIC OPINION?

Political scientists began to study public opinion and voting behavior in the 1940s. . . . The typical American, they found, is poorly informed about government and public policy and lacking in coherent, stable attitudes about important public issues.

*****

More recent work has painted a more charitable picture, but not by a lot. . . .

Today, probably the most influential framework for thinking about attitudes and public opinion comes from John Zaller.[6] Zaller agrees that ordinary people are poorly informed about public policy issues, largely incapable of thinking in a consistent, coherent way about them, and when answering questions on a survey, are essentially just making up their opinions as they go along. . . . Yet . . . he does not claim that nothing is going on inside the respondent's mind. Quite the contrary: a great deal is going on, and it is quite meaningful.

In Zaller's view, people may see all sorts of interests, values, and beliefs as relevant to a given policy issue, and their response to a survey item depends on which "considerations" come to mind during the interview process. Among people who are politically knowledgeable, many considerations often come to mind and these considerations are integrated to produce attitudes that are meaningful, consistent, and relatively stable over time. For the great majority, however, things are not so neat. Many considerations may be relevant, but they exist as separate concerns that are never fully reconciled with one another, and only a few of them (if that) actually come to the "top of the head" during the interview. Those that do, moreover, will often emerge not because of the substance of the issue being raised (for people who are too poorly informed to make the connection), but because of specific cues contained within the survey itself—due especially to the wording of questions. In effect, most people use the survey and its cues to figure out what considerations are relevant, and then to figure out what their position on issues ought to be.[7]

Zaller argues that, beneath the surface, people tend to be ambivalent. On a given policy issue, they could come down positively or negatively. It all depends on what considerations happen to be evoked by the survey, and on the cues embedded in the survey itself. From one survey to the next, then, individuals might well express very different positions on the same issue. And even within a single survey, individuals may give inconsistent responses as they react to newly emerging considerations and cues during the course of the interview. Nonetheless, the opinions they express are not random . . . and not simple attempts to please the interviewer or avoid appearing ignorant. Opinions arise from considerations that matter, and they tell us something about people's interests, values, and beliefs.

*****

. . . Zaller's theory . . . may be compatible with some degree of "real thinking" on the part of ordinary people . . . [O]ur analysis will give us a basis for judging whether Americans are engaging in "real thinking" about the voucher issue.

*****

THE APPROACH OF THIS STUDY

. . . The purpose here . . . is to understand what matters to people as they think about the [school voucher] issue, and whether they seem to be engaging in "real thinking."

The survey helps us do this. . . . [T]he first part of the survey is about . . . educational issues and does not mention vouchers. Midway through . . . the concept is first introduced. . . . With the subject of vouchers thus raised, respondents are then presented with an initial support question. . . . [which] asks them how they would feel about such a reform. . . .

The survey . . . [then] follow[s] up the initial support item with a large number of additional questions about vouchers . . . addressing the full range of issues in the national debate, from competition to race to religion to social class.

Once respondents have had a chance to reflect more fully on the issues, they are presented with the same support question they were asked at the beginning. . . . The initial question on support for vouchers [thus] serves as a baseline. . . . representing their first attempt—usually based on very little knowledge or sense of the issue—to take a stand. . . .

. . . [A]fter the initial support question is asked the survey provides respondents with much more to work with: a whole range of new considerations that are related (they now know) to vouchers.

. . . [B]ecause respondents are re-asked the same support question at the end of the interview, we are able to gain new insights into their thinking on the [voucher] issue.

*****

INITIAL SUPPORT FOR VOUCHERS

Now let's turn to the evidence, beginning with the first question on support for vouchers. Again, this item provides an important baseline, because it measures support for vouchers before people have had much opportunity to think much about the issue, which is the way it is typically measured on other surveys.

SIMPLE AGGREGATE RESULTS

The aggregate results are set out in Table 4.5. They show that 60 percent of the general public express support for the idea of vouchers, with 32 percent opposed and 7 percent undecided. We have to be careful not to view these results as measuring the "true" level of popular support for vouchers. They would have been different had the question been worded differently or even asked on a different survey. . . .

It seems fair to say that Americans are open to the general concept of vouchers, at least when they first think about it, and when it is defined as a means of expanding choice for all parents. . . .

Table 4.5: Who Supports Vouchers? Initial Responses

Percent, unless otherwise indicated[a]

Position on vouchers	Total population	Non-parents	Public school parents	Private school parents	Inner-city parents
Oppose	32	36	26	13	14
Support	60	57	66	81	77
Don't know	7	7	8	6	9
N[b]	(4,700)	(1,617)	(2,553)	(530)	(539)

a. Percentages are based on weighted data. They may not sum to 100 due to rounding.

b. N is the unweighted number of respondents.

We should be less interested in the level of support per se, though, than in how support *varies* across groups, and in what this can tell us about why people see the issue as they do. Existing surveys provide almost no analysis along these lines, but they do offer a glimpse of what is going on beneath the surface. They reveal patterns that are much the same for all surveys, whether or not the questions are well worded and regardless of how high or low the level of support seems to be. What they show, notably, is that parents are more supportive of vouchers than nonparents, that private parents are more supportive than public parents, and that blacks and Hispanics are more supportive than whites. This begins to suggest that people with the strongest *incentives* are the ones who are the most sympathetic, and that there is an underlying *structure* to the issue that makes sense. Our job is to pursue this in greater depth.

For starters, our own survey shows that public parents are more supportive of vouchers than nonparents are, by 66 percent to 57 percent. . . .

This difference between parents and nonparents is a mixed blessing for the voucher movement. On the one hand, parents have a greater stake in vouchers, and their support is crucial if policymakers are to go along. On the other hand, nonparents make up some two-thirds of the electorate, and their more negative inclinations—especially if played upon by critics during political campaigns—may threaten the movement's success.

Another basic finding from Table 4.5 is that private parents are enthusiastic about vouchers, with 81 percent of them expressing support . . .

Table 4.5 also shows that low-income public parents from the inner city are much more sympathetic toward vouchers than public parents are in general. Seventy-seven percent of them express support, with just 14 percent opposed . . . Inner-city parents face the most troubled educational contexts, and we know [from an earlier chapter, "The Attraction of Private Schools"] . . . that they are eager to gain access to the private sector. Vouchers allow them to do that, and these parents are highly supportive of a policy that would put vouchers in their hands. It is reasonable to presume, moreover, that these results for the inner city are just the tip of the iceberg, and that vouchers are attractive to disadvantaged populations generally.

Table 4.6 bears this out. Among public parents, vouchers are supported by 73 percent of those with family incomes below $20,000 per year, compared to 57 percent of those with incomes above $60,000. For education, the story is much the same: voucher support is 70 percent among parents with less than a high school education, but 49 percent among those with postgraduate educations. Minority parents also tend to be more supportive: 75 percent of black parents and 71 percent of Hispanic parents express sympathy for vouchers, compared to 63 percent of white parents. And we find the same asymmetry across school districts: 72 percent of parents in the bottom tier of districts favor vouchers, while 59 percent of those in the top tier do.

Table 4.6: Background, Context and Initial Support for Vouchers

Percent, unless otherwise indicated[a]

Background variable		Public school parents' position on vouchers				Nonparents' position on vouchers			
		Support	Oppose	Don't know	N[b]	Support	Oppose	Don't know	N[b]
Annual Income ($)									
Less than 20,000		73	19	8	(458)	53	38	9	(276)
21,000–30,000		70	21	9	(488)	60	32	8	(267)
31,000–40,000		67	28	5	(401)	57	40	3	(261)
41,000–60,000		61	32	6	(534)	62	33	5	(305)
More than 60,000		57	36	8	(336)	57	38	5	(237)
Education									
Less than high school		70	18	11	(254)	59	34	7	(157)
High school		70	23	7	(925)	56	36	7	(489)
Some college		64	27	8	(656)	59	33	8	(406)
College graduate		58	35	7	(501)	55	40	5	(383)
Postgraduate		49	47	4	(196)	50	45	6	(172)
Ethnic background									
White		63	30	7	(1,616)	55	39	7	(1,312)
Black		75	16	9	(529)	64	27	9	(146)
Hispanic		71	17	12	(286)	70	22	8	(79)
[School] District context									
Disadvantaged	1	72	19	9	(720)	50	41	10	(229)
	2	72	22	7	(526)	60	33	7	(406)
	3	62	29	9	(545)	60	34	5	(389)
Advantaged	4	59	33	8	(583)	54	39	7	(401)

Table 4.6: Background, Context and Initial Support for Vouchers (continued)

Percent, unless otherwise indicated[a]

Background variable	Public school parents' position on vouchers				Nonparents' position on vouchers			
	Support	Oppose	Don't know	N[b]	Support	Oppose	Don't know	N[b]
Party identification								
Democrat	66	27	7	(1,150)	55	38	7	(614)
Independent	69	24	7	(674)	55	38	7	(401)
Republican	67	26	7	(595)	61	34	4	(510)
Religion								
Catholic	72	20	8	(637)	59	33	7	(427)
Protestant	62	32	6	(731)	55	39	6	(536)
Born-again	67	26	7	(187)	70	24	6	(114)
Public school performance								
Low-performing 1	75	18	6	(535)	61	33	6	(458)
2	71	22	8	(589)	64	30	6	(400)
3	65	26	9	(634)	55	37		(392)
High-performing 4	57	33	10	(795)	46	47	8	(367)
Desire to go private								
Yes	78	15	7	(1,380)				
No	53	38	9	(1,041)				

a. Percentages are based on weighted data. They may not sum to 100 due to rounding.
b. N is the unweighted number of respondents

Race aside, these relationships don't obtain for nonparents. But nonparents have less stake in the issue. . . . Somehow, even though most parents (particularly those who are less advantaged) are uninformed about the issue, they seem to be connecting their own concerns and interests to their positions on vouchers [documented in an earlier chapter].

What about the traditional wing of the voucher movement [which includes Republicans, Catholics, and born-again Christians—as discussed earlier in the book]? In the aggregate, at least, there is little evidence that political party matters much. Republicans are slightly more supportive of vouchers than Democrats, but the differences are small: a 6 percent margin among nonparents and a 1 percent margin among public parents . . .

Religion seems to be more influential. Among public parents, 72 percent of Catholics and 67 percent of born-again Christians express initial support for vouchers, compared to 62 percent of the baseline group of Protestants. Among nonparents, it is born-again Christians who are most supportive, at 70 percent, followed by Catholics at 59 percent and Protestants at 55 percent. These effects hardly testify to a religious fervor for vouchers at the grass roots. . . . Still, it is clearly relevant to many people and, even in the absence of much initial information about vouchers, it influences their stand on the issue.

A broad-brush look at the data, [the modern wing consists of poor and minority constituencies—as discussed earlier in the book] then, suggests that both the traditional and modern wings of the voucher movement are mirrored in the way Americans think about the issue. But what brings the two wings together, in the eyes of voucher leaders, is a shared concern about the performance of the public schools and a shared belief in the greater benefits of going private. These are the fundamental grounds on which the movement has always depended for attracting constituents to the political cause.

* * * * *

It appears, then, that many people are able to make a connection between [school] performance and their stand on public policy.

* * * * *

STABILITY AND CHANGE

To this point . . . people were asked an initial question about support for vouchers, with no prior discussion of the issue, and they gave responses. What we've found is that those responses are surprisingly meaningful, connected to people's values, beliefs, and interests in ways that make sense. . . .

Our survey, however, does not abandon the voucher issue once its out-of-the-blue question is asked. It goes on to explore the topic in some depth, often by raising issues salient in the national debate—and then asks respondents again . . . whether they support vouchers as public policy. . . .

What happens to support for vouchers the second time around? Do many people change their mind? . . . [W]hy? Is it essentially a random process with little rhyme or reason . . . ? Is it a quasi-rational response to new considerations arising during the survey, as Zaller would argue?

. . . [P]eople became more favorable toward vouchers during the course of the survey. . . . [S]upport increased from 60 percent to 68 percent. . . .

[Analysis shows that] the roles of social class, the various attitudes, [school] performance, and parental interest in going private are all much the same as before. Peeking through all the similarities, however, are some important differences that suggest that people *have* been doing some new thinking, and have arrived at a more coherent view of how vouchers connect to the things that matter to them.

[T]he most compelling evidence . . . is contained in the findings on attitudes . . . among uninformed nonparents—the group most open to new information and change [because they have no direct stake in the issue]—attitudes are now a much more potent force in determining where they stand on vouchers. . . . The impact of racial diversity—indicating that those who *support* diversity are the ones who support vouchers—jumps from .11 on the first item to .24 on the second. And the impact of inequity—indicating that those who perceive the public system as inequitable are inclined to support vouchers—jumps from .14 on the first item to .38 on the second. These are huge increases, and strongly suggest that uninformed nonparents have emerged from the survey with a different view of what vouchers are about. . . . [T]hey are thinking less like traditionalists and more like modernists. And there is simply more substance to their positions.

Uninformed parents are better grounded [because they do have a direct stake in the issue] and less subject to shifting than uninformed nonparents are, so we should expect . . . less dramatic effects. Which is indeed the case. But, still, the basic pattern is similar: the uninformed parents make a stronger connection between attitudes and voucher support the second time around . . . and they put much more emphasis on the liberal social values of diversity and equity.

[The analysis as a whole—which includes additional evidence on the impacts of religion, party, and school performance—shows that] respondents' thinking seems to have evolved in a meaningful, systematic way during the survey. Having had a chance to mull things over and process new information, they seem to have arrived at a more coherent sense of the voucher issue. . . . Connections have been strengthened. New values have come to the fore. There seems to be some "real thinking" going on here.

CONCLUSION

Virtually all surveys on the voucher issue rivet attention on just one number: the percentage of Americans who express support for vouchers. In an intensely democratic society, this number is freighted with profound significance. If most Americans support vouchers, there are normative grounds for arguing that government ought to follow through, and there are practical grounds for arguing that policymakers who value their jobs would be wise to respond. Little wonder, then, that voucher advocates want the magic polling numbers to be high and often latch onto the biggest numbers available. And little wonder that critics want the magic numbers to be low, and often tout the smallest figures they can find.

These numbers don't mean very much. . . . Many could find themselves on either side of the issue, depending on which considerations are evoked.

Our own survey shows that 60 percent of Americans initially express support for vouchers, and that 68 percent do so the second time through, after they have had a chance to think about things. . . .

. . . Our challenge has been to determine how people connect the voucher issue to their own values, beliefs, and interests, and whether their expressions of support and opposition are thus meaningful reflections of what they care about.

. . . Although most people are unfamiliar with the voucher issue, they do a much better job of formulating their opinions than skeptics would lead us to expect. . . .

Which brings us to the substance of the issue. When Americans take positions on the voucher issue, what *does* matter to them? The evidence points to several basic conclusions:

(1) For parents, an interest in going private is by far the most important determinant of their support for vouchers.

(2) Support for vouchers is especially strong among parents who are low in social class, minority, and from low-performing school districts: the same types of parents who are especially interested in going private. . . . It is clear that vouchers have a constituency among the less advantaged, and that the modern movement is cultivating a clientele that is very receptive indeed.

(3) The traditional wing of the movement also finds its reflection in public opinion. This is particularly true for religion, with both Catholics and born-again Christians especially supportive of vouchers. For party, however, the traditional connection—with Republicans more supportive than Democrats—only shows up among the informed, whose views are framed by the political battle lines of the national debate. Among the uninformed, party has no relevance to the voucher issue initially, but it becomes relevant during the course of the survey-and it is the Democrats among them who come to express greater sympathy for vouchers. This is a shift with substantive meaning, for the modern movement has special appeal to the disadvantaged and to people who put special weight on diversity and equity, and these are constituencies and values associated with the Democratic party. Without the traditional framing, to which the uninformed are oblivious, vouchers look very much like a Democratic issue.

(4) Support for vouchers is influenced by a whole range of attitudes, reflecting the specific concerns Americans have about their public schools. People tend to support vouchers when they think the public school system is inequitable and when they think diversity is an important social goal. They also tend to support vouchers when they believe in school prayer, when they want more influence for parents, when they prefer smaller schools to larger ones, and when they think competition and market-based incentives are conducive to school performance. They are less likely to support vouchers, on the other hand, when they believe in the public school system and are normatively committed to it.

* * * * *

In most respects, the findings of this chapter bode well for the voucher movement and its political prospects. Vouchers appeal to broad constituencies: the American public is open to the idea, with no evidence of widespread resistance; public parents are attracted to private schools, and have a self-interested stake in vouchers; and the kinds of arguments that voucher advocates make on issues ranging from equity to markets to school size find a receptive audience. At the same time, vouchers also appeal to the more targeted constituencies that have propelled the movement's politics: they are popular among the less advantaged and among people who are concerned about diversity and social equity; they are also popular among Catholics, born-again Christians, and (informed) Republicans.

These combinations . . . are potentially very powerful. They give the movement a lot to work with in mobilizing public support and in fashioning the kind of heterogeneous coalition necessary for real political progress.

Unavoidably, its efforts will be fraught with uncertainty. Most Americans do not have well-developed opinions, and, as the political battle generates new information, the contours of public opinion could change, possibly in ways adverse to the voucher movement. There are no guarantees. But even so, our analysis suggests that Americans are not mere ciphers whose views are totally up for grabs. There is a structure to their thinking about vouchers, a consistency to the way they connect their values, beliefs, and interests to the issue—and these elements should provide a fairly stable core to public opinion and lend a certain form and predictability to the larger political struggle.

Notes

6. John Zaller, *The Nature and Origins of Mass Opinion* (Cambridge University Press, 1992); and John Zaller and Stanley Feldman, "A Simple Theory of the Survey Response: Answering Questions versus Revealing Preferences," *American Journal of Political Science*, vol. 36 (August 1992), pp. 579–616.

7. It is well known that survey responses are sensitive to the way questions are worded and the ordering in which they appear. See, for example, Howard Schuman and Stanley Presser, Questions and Answers in Attitude Surveys: Experiments on Question Form, Wording, and Context (Academic Press, 1981); and Seymour Sudman and Norman M. Bradburn, Asking Questions (Jossey-Bass, 1982).

◈ DISCUSSION QUESTIONS ◈

1. Suppose all news agencies and journalists began to take an intersectional approach to reporting public opinion on the major issues of the day. How, if at all, would the average American's views on how splintered or divided we are as a country likely change? Why?

2. When it comes to gender and racial equity, are we "getting better" or are we "getting worse"? Roberta Sigel points to places where men and women have considerable overlap when it comes to takes on gender equity, family norms, and related issues. Brooks and Jeon-Slaughter find that African-Americans are more apt to lack confidence that civil, criminal, and juvenile delinquency courts will treat blacks fairly but that this does not extend to the Supreme Court. Do these patterns suggest progress or that progress is far from linear or inevitable?

3. Public opinion is malleable. It changes over time and by question wording or even because of the order in which the questions are asked. What does this mean for emotionally charged topics such as welfare, affirmative action, or terrorism? Can or should public opinion be used to craft public policies in these (and other) areas if it is so subject to change?

4. Religious affiliation and religiosity clearly influence opinion on gay marriage. Where else do you think these factors matter for political opinions? Is religion the next major topic for students of diversity and public opinion?

5. Describe yourself using characteristics that are important to you. How many of these characteristics are important in contemporary U.S. politics? Which aren't

and why? How might some combination of these characteristics change or influence your opinion about a public policy matter such as gay marriage or affirmative action?

Additional Resources

Farmingville (2004) is a film that examines the responses of those living in the suburban town of Farmingville, New York following an influx of Hispanic immigrations to the area and the murder of two Mexican immigrants seeking employment.

Merchants of Cool (2001) is a PBS *Frontline* special that examines teen culture and the marketing practices purposefully aimed at influencing teens' wants, desires, and overall notions of what is "cool."

http://www.worldpublicopinion.org
This organization was created by the University of Maryland's Program on International Policy Attitudes. Their web site includes various reports that document the views of Americans on other countries/groups as well as other countries/groups views on the United States and U.S. policy actions.

http://www.pewresearch.org
The Pew Charitable Trusts conducts and sponsors research on a variety of political and public policy issues in American politics. One recent study, "Muslim Americans: Middle Class and Mostly Mainstream," is the "first-ever, nationwide, random sample survey of Muslim Americans," and can be found at http://www.pewresearch.org/assets/pdf/muslim-americans.pdf.

5 | POLITICAL PARTICIPATION: DEFINITIONS, PATTERNS, AND CONSEQUENCES

One person, one vote . . . but who usually has to wait in line longer? Voting in America is a deeply revered form of political participation, but many indicate that it is often harder for poor and minority citizens to cast their ballot.

Picture it: presidential Election Day. You are on a busy subway or in one of your town's most populated shopping areas. Look around. How many people do you see with one of those "I voted today" stickers? Probably a fair number. Political scientists spend a fair amount of time trying to systematically predict who is most likely to be sporting one of those stickers, as well as who is most apt to participate in ways beyond the ballot. If you open a typical American politics textbook, you would likely read about the importance of factors such as socialization, socioeconomic status, eligibility rules, time, interest in politics, and perceptions of political efficacy in predicting whether or not one participates. The readings in this section consider patterns of participation and nonparticipation—as well as our common explanations for these patterns—from a diversity perspective. Three themes organize the section.

The first theme defines political participation and considers which groups are more or less "political." After all, in deciding what activities count as political, we are inevitably making decisions that determine who will be conceptualized as political. The American Political Science Association (APSA) report that follows, for instance, defines participation to include things such as voting, contacting a public official, and donating to political campaigns. On all these indicators, individuals of low-income participate much less frequently than those with higher incomes. The selection by Erin E. O'Brien, however, focuses exclusively on women's social movement organizing and its long-term effects for women of color and low-income women.

The second theme in this section offers reasons *why* particular individuals and groups are more or less likely to participate. The APSA report noted above explains the economic bias in participation (and corresponding racial, ethnic, and gender biases) by looking to advantages in time, civic skills, social networks, and efficacy/motivation that the affluent are more likely to acquire through advanced education as well as public policies the more and less affluent typically interact with. In "Mass Imprisonment and Disappearing Voters," Marc Mauer turns our attention to structural reasons for why particular groups are more or less likely to participate. Michael Powell and Peter Slevin follow suit in their *Washington Post* article "Several Factors Contributed to 'Lost' Voters in Ohio."

The final theme in this section involves the consequences of the participatory patterns uncovered. The APSA report makes clear that while there have been real improvements in legal access to participation for women and racial minorities, the voices elected officials hear from are systematically skewed toward the affluent. The Mauer piece, as well as Powell and Slevin's, each call into question the legitimacy of some electoral outcomes. Seemingly group-blind policies such as felony disenfranchisement or certain electoral practices disproportionately impact individuals of color, women, and the less affluent; groups who are more likely to vote for Democrats. These articles at least suggest then that the rules and practices surrounding voting eligibility and day-of voting practices impact election outcomes in ways that sometimes skew the voice of Americans.

The selections that follow speak to key considerations in American political participation—access, voice, legitimacy, and representative democracy. In placing the diversity lens on these issues, we witness places of improvement and enduring challenges.

*T*his selection comes from a task force organized by the American Political Science Association (APSA). In it, the leading scholars on political participation evaluate the status of political participation in America from the perspective demography and equality. Looking at activities such as voting, making financial contributions, working on a campaign, contacting a public official, joining a political organization, and demonstrating the report concludes that America has become both more and less egalitarian on these participatory indicators.

Many legal barriers to participation by women and individuals of color have been removed in recent decades. However, massive and increasing wealth and income inequality has also defined this time period. Ramifications for participation are striking: every type of political participation the report looks at skews dramatically in favor of more affluent Americans. The voice government hears from is markedly upper class. This "increases the probability of policies that tilt toward maintaining the *status quo and continue to reward the organized and already well off." Given the ways that race and ethnicity correlate with social class, the income skew in participation also means that individuals of color are less likely to be heard from by government. The report concludes that these patterns pose a fundamental threat to the most basic of American participatory principles: representative democracy.*

American Democracy in an Age of Rising Inequality

AMERICAN POLITICAL SCIENCE ASSOCIATION TASK FORCE ON INEQUALITY AND AMERICAN DEMOCRACY

Equal political voice and democratically responsive government are cherished American ideals. Indeed, the United States is vigorously promoting democracy abroad. Yet, what is happening to democracy at home? Our country's ideals of equal citizenship and responsive government may be under growing threat in an era of persistent and rising inequalities. Disparities of income, wealth, and access to opportunity are growing more sharply in the United States than in many other nations, and gaps between races and ethnic groups persist. Progress toward realizing American ideals of democracy may have stalled, and in some arenas reversed.

We have reached this conclusion as members of the Task Force on Inequality and American Democracy formed under the auspices of the 14,000-member American Political Science Association (APSA). . . .

Generations of Americans have worked to equalize citizen voice across lines of income, race, and gender. Today, however, the voices of American citizens are raised and heard unequally. The privileged participate more than others and are increasingly well organized to press their demands on government. Public officials, in turn, are much more responsive to the privileged than to average citizens and the least affluent. Citizens with low or moderate incomes speak with a whisper that is lost on the ears of inattentive government, while the advantaged roar with a clarity and consistency that policy makers readily heed. The scourge of overt discrimination against African Americans and women has been replaced by a more subtle but still potent threat—the growing concentration of the country's wealth and income.

EQUAL RIGHTS, RISING ECONOMIC INEQUALITY, AND AMERICAN DEMOCRACY

American society has become both more and less egalitarian in recent decades. Following the civil rights revolution of the 1950s and 1960s, racial segregation and

---

American Political Science Association Task Force on Inequality and American Democracy, "American Democracy in an Age of Rising Inequality," *Perspectives on Politics*, vol. 2, no. 4 (December 2004), pp. 651–666. © 2004 by the American Political Science Association. Reprinted with the permission of Cambridge University Press. The full report is available at www.apsanet.org/imgtest/taskforcereport.pdf.

exclusion were no longer legally or socially acceptable. Whites and African Americans began to participate together in schools and colleges, the job market, and political and civic organizations. Gender barriers have also been breached since the 1960s, with women now able to pursue most of the same economic and political opportunities as men. Many other previously marginalized groups have also gained rights to full participation in American institutions and have begun to demand—and to varying degrees enjoy—the dignity of equal citizenship.[2]

But as U.S. society has become more integrated across barriers of race, ethnicity, gender, and other longstanding forms of social exclusion, it has simultaneously suffered growing gaps of income and wealth. Gaps have grown not just between the poor and the rest of society, but also between privileged professionals, managers, and business owners on the one hand, and the middle strata of regular white- and blue-collar employees on the other hand. Many middle-class families are just barely staying afloat with two parents working.[3] And many African Americans, Latinos, and women who head families find themselves losing ground. There are signs of increased segregation by, for example, income and race in public schools.[4] Meanwhile, the rich and the super-rich have become much more so—especially since the mid-1970s. Indeed, the richest 1 percent of Americans has pulled away from not only the poor but also the middle class.

. . . In 2001 the most affluent fifth received 47.7 percent of family income; the middle class (the third and fourth fifths) earned 15.5 percent and 22.9 percent, respectively while the bottom two quintiles each received less than 10 percent. (Twenty-one percent of family income went to the top 5 percent.) Put simply, the richest 20 percent obtained nearly half of the country's income.

* * * * *

Even as the distribution of income has moved rapidly to the top, the most affluent have attained a larger slice of the country's wealth (as defined by stock holdings, mutual funds, retirement savings, ownership of property, and other assets). . . . The top 1 percent of households drew 16.6 percent of all income but commanded more than double this proportion of the country's wealth (38.1 percent). By contrast, the supermajority of the country—the bottom 90 percent of households—earned the majority of household income (58.8 percent) but controlled only 29 percent of the country's wealth.[7]

* * * * *

. . . The absolute economic circumstances of minorities have improved. The civil rights movement and the challenges to overt discrimination made important contributions to these improvements. Nonetheless, gaps remain. The median white household earned 62 percent more income and possessed twelve times more wealth than the median black household; nearly two-thirds of black households (61 percent) and half of Hispanic households have no net worth, while only a quarter of white Americans are in this predicament. . . .

* * * * *

How concerned should we be about persistent and rising socioeconomic inequalities?

* * * * *

We find disturbing inequalities in the political voice expressed through elections and other avenues of participation. We find that our governing institutions are much more responsive to the privileged than to other Americans. And we find that the policies fashioned by our government today may be doing less than celebrated programs of the past to promote equal opportunity and security, and to enhance citizen dignity and participation. . . . Such a negative spiral can, in turn, prompt Americans to become increasingly discouraged about the effectiveness of democratic governance, spreading cynicism and withdrawal from elections and other arenas of public life.

UNEQUAL VOICES

* * * * *

Our review of research on inequality and political participation as well as other components of American political life demonstrates an extraordinary association between economic and political inequality. . . .

THE HALF OF AMERICANS WHO VOTE

Voting is the most obvious means for Americans to exercise their rights of citizenship, yet only a third of eligible voters participate in midterm congressional elections and only about half turn out for today's presidential elections. Even voters in presidential elections tend to be from the ranks of the most advantaged Americans. . . . Nearly 9 out of 10 individuals in families with incomes over $75,000 reported voting in presidential elections while only half of those in families with incomes under $15,000 reported voting.

* * * * *

Although electoral participation ticks up somewhat when contests are closely fought and parties make extra efforts to mobilize voters, a number of ongoing trends discourage voting and reinforce inequalities in voter turnout. Rising economic inequality may discourage less privileged voters.[16] And part of the decline in voting since the early 1970s results from laws in many states that forbid former (as well as current) prisoners from voting, sometimes for their entire lives. Millions of Americans, especially minority men, have been excluded from basic participation in our democracy by such laws.[17] The selective outreach of the Democratic and Republican parties contributes to the stratification of voting, as we discuss below.

In sum, less advantaged Americans vote less because they lack the skills, motivation, and networks that the better-advantaged acquire through formal education and occupational advancement.

BEYOND VOTING

Low and unequal voting is sobering in part because casting a ballot is America's most widespread form of political participation. Many fewer than half of the Americans who vote in presidential elections take part in more time-consuming and costly political activities, such as making financial contributions to candidates, working in electoral campaigns, contacting public officials, getting involved in organizations that take political stands, and demonstrating for or against political causes.

Campaign contributors are the least representative group of citizens. Only 12 percent of American households had incomes over $100,000 in 2000, but a whopping 95 percent of the donors who made substantial contributions were in these most affluent households. . . . [18] Contributing money to politicians is a form of citizen activity that is, in practical terms, reserved for a select group of Americans. As wealth and income have become more concentrated and the flow of money into elections has grown, campaign contributions give the affluent a means to express their choices that is unavailable to most citizens, thus further aggravating inequalities of political voice.

. . . These disparities in resources and skills are evident in a host of political activities. . . .

- ✦ Nearly three-quarters of the well-off are affiliated with an organization that takes political stands (like the AARP or advocacy groups) as compared with only 29 percent of the least affluent.

- ✦ Half of the affluent contact public officials, as compared with only 25 percent of those with low incomes.

- ✦ Thirty-eight percent of the well-off participate in informal efforts to solve community problems, compared with only 13 percent of those in the lowest income groups.

- ✦ Even protesting, which might appear to demand little in the way of skills or money and is often thought of as "the weapon of the weak," is more prevalent among the affluent.

- ✦ Seven percent of the better-off protest to promote such causes as abortion rights or environmentalism, compared with 3 percent among the poor.

* * * * *

INTEREST GROUPS FOR THE WELL-OFF DOMINATE WASHINGTON

Citizens express preferences not just by individual acts, but also through the organized groups they support. . . . But even as the number of organizations speaking for underrepresented interests and preferences has grown, corporate managers and professionals have also increased their sway for a number of reasons.

* * * * *

In short, the number of interest groups has grown, and they have become more diverse; many formerly marginalized Americans have gained some voice in public debates. Yet the dominance of the advantaged has solidified, and their capacities to speak loudly and clearly to government officials have been enhanced.

CONTEMPORARY POLITICAL PARTIES EXACERBATE INEQUALITIES

Most interest groups are the instrument of the few who want to press for particular benefits. Political parties, on the other hand, are the vehicle for reaching and mobilizing the broad public. . . . The problem today is that this mechanism for a broad and inclusive democracy caters to some of the same narrow segments of American society that also disproportionately deploy interest groups on their behalf. Advantage begets additional advantage.

Both of the major political parties intensify the skewed participation in U.S. politics by targeting many of their resources on recruiting those who are already the most privileged and involved.[26] Democrats and Republicans alike have become highly dependent on campaign contributors and activists and have become accustomed to competing for just over half of a shrinking universe of voters. What is more, political parties ignore parts of the electorate that have not turned out at high rates in past elections; the major parties have both become less likely to personally contact large numbers of less privileged and less active citizens—even though research tells us that personal contact is important in encouraging citizens to vote. . . . [27]

THE UNEVEN PLAYING FIELD

Disparities in participation mean that the concerns of lower- or moderate-income Americans, racial and ethnic minorities, and legal immigrants are systematically less likely to be heard by government officials. In contrast, the interests and preferences of the better-off are conveyed with clarity, consistency, and forcefulness.

* * * * *

Unequal political voice matters because the advantaged convey very different messages to government officials than do the rest of the citizenry. . . . Those Americans who would be most likely to raise issues about basic opportunities and needs—from escaping poverty to securing jobs, education, health care, and housing—tend to be the least likely to participate in politics. . . . Political voice is also unequal because Americans who are very active in politics often have more intense or extreme views than average citizens. They tend, for instance, to identify themselves as far more conservative or liberal. . . . The intense and unrelenting expressions of "extremists" . . . make it harder for government to work out compromises or to respond to average citizens, who may have more middle-of-the-road opinions about a range of important matters, from abortion to tax cuts.[29]

HOW GOVERNMENT RESPONDS

Generations of reformers have understood a simple truth: What government officials hear influences what they do. . . . Because government officials today hear more clearly and more often from privileged and highly active citizens, policy makers are less likely to respond readily to the concerns of the majority. The skew in political participation toward the advantaged increases the probability of policies that tilt toward maintaining the status quo and continue to reward the organized and already well-off.

MONEY BUYS ATTENTION

Today politicians are *not* usually directly bribed by political contributors or moneyed interests. . . . What wealthy citizens and moneyed interests do gain from their big contributions is influence over who runs for office and a *hearing* from politicians and government officials.

Money is the oxygen of today's elections, given the reliance of candidates on high-priced consultants and expensive media advertisements.[31] Big contributors have the power to discourage or perhaps suffocate unfriendly candidates by denying them early or consistent funding. After the election, moreover, government officials need information to do their jobs, and research shows that big contributors earn the privilege of meeting regularly with policy makers in their offices. Money buys the opportunity to present self-serving information or raise some problems for attention rather than others.

* * * * *

CONGRESS FAVORS THE ORGANIZED

Recent changes in how Congress designs legislation reinforce and expand the advantages of the organized. Government money to fund projects—from building highways and waterways to constructing buildings—has long been allocated to well-organized and vocal groups with connections inside Washington.

* * * * *

WHO GETS THE POLICIES THEY WANT?

Skewed participation among citizens and the targeting of government resources to partisans and the well-organized ensure that government officials disproportionately respond to business, the wealthy, and the organized when they design America's domestic and foreign policies.[34]

Recent research strikingly documents that the votes of U.S. senators are far more influenced by the policy preferences of each senator's rich constituents than by the preferences of the senator's less-privileged constituents.[35] In particular, income-weighted preferences were much more influential than simple averages of state opinion, especially for Republican senators. Constituents at the 75th percentile of the income distribution had almost three times as much influence as those at the 25th percentile on their senators' general voting patterns, and even more disproportional influence on specific salient roll call votes on the minimum wage, civil rights, government spending, and abortion. The preferences of constituents in the bottom fifth of the income distribution had little or no effect on their senators' votes.

* * * * *

MISSED OPPORTUNITIES FOR DEMOCRATIC GOVERNMENT

What government does not do is just as important as what it does.[39] . . . Numerous studies by scholars and independent researchers document that public education, Social Security and Medicare, the GI Bill, home-mortgage programs, and many other efforts have enhanced the quality of life for millions of regular Americans. . . . These broadly inclusive government programs have also encouraged ordinary citizens to become more active participants in our democracy.

* * * * *

But what are the equivalents of such broadly responsive programs today? The educational and training benefits for America's all-volunteer military are modest compared with those in the original GI Bill and, consequently, they have been less effective in boosting the schooling of veterans to the level of nonveterans.[42] Moreover, rising tuition, the declining value of individual Pell Grants, and state budget cuts have made higher education less affordable to nonveterans at a time when its economic value has risen and its contribution to counteracting the bias in political participation is invaluable.[43]

While Social Security protects and engages seniors, few government programs ensure opportunity and security and encourage political engagement for Americans who are not elderly. This situation reinforces the preoccupation of political leaders with improving the programs of the aged rather than assisting young and old alike . . .

NEW BARRIERS TO EQUAL CITIZENSHIP

One of the great stories of the past century in the United States has been the reduction of overt discrimination that once excluded millions of Americans from the core of political, economic, and social life. . . . America's extension of basic citizenship rights expanded the political participation of minorities and women and improved their living conditions. . . .

Yet the historic accomplishments of the 1960s "rights revolution" may now be jeopardized by continuing economic and political inequalities. . . . There were significant economic improvements in the 1990s. Minorities saw their absolute economic positions get better. The progress of the 1990s did not, however, close the income gap between whites and other racial and ethnic groups.[47] . . .

＊ ＊ ＊ ＊ ＊

As the relative economic conditions for many in the ranks of America's minorities have stagnated, improvements in minority participation and political influence have also faced challenges. The political playing field remains highly unequal, and the immediate gains of the rights revolution have not yielded sustained equalization of political voice.

Renewing American Democracy and the Tradition of Political Science

＊ ＊ ＊ ＊ ＊

The Declaration of Independence promised that all American citizens would enjoy equal political rights. Nearly every generation has returned to this promise and struggled to elevate the performance of American democracy to its high ideals. The promise of American democracy is threatened again. The threat is less overt than the barriers of law or social custom conquered by earlier generations. Today, the risk is that rising economic inequality will solidify longstanding disparities in political voice and influence, and perhaps exacerbate such disparities. Our government is becoming less democratic, responsive mainly to the privileged and not a powerful instrument to correct disadvantages and look out for the majority. If disparities of participation and influence become further entrenched—and if average citizens give up on democratic government—unequal citizenship could take on a life of its own, weakening American democracy for a long time to come.

Notes

2. Skrentny 2002.

3. Smeeding 2004.

4. Frankenberg, Lee, and Orfield 2002.

7. Although the Federal Reserve's Survey was conducted near the stock market's peak (1999), the value of the stock market remained at or near record levels even after its sharp decline (1999 to 2001), with the wealthiest households enjoying much of the gain.

16. Freeman 2004.

17. Uggen and Manza 2002; Manza and Uggen 2004.

18. Campaign Finance Institute Task Force on Presidential Nomination Financing 2003.

26. Schier 2000.

27. Rosenstone and Hansen 1993; Gerber and Green 2000.

29. Fiorina 1999; Skocpol 2003.

31. Gopoian 1984; Hall and Wayman 1990; Kroszner and Stratmann 1998; Langbein 1986.

34. Jacobs and Shapiro 2000. Erikson, MacKuen, and Stimson (2002) offer an alternative interpretation. Our research review, "Inequality and American Governance," discusses this alternative account, noting, in part, that the empirical analysis of the full political system in Erikson, MacKuen, and Stimson is not inconsistent with the account offered here.

35. Bartels 2002.

39. This point is developed in Hacker 2004.

42. Cohen, Warner, and Segal 1995.

43. National Center for Public Policy and Higher Education 2002.

47. Shapiro 2004.

References

Bartels, Larry M. 2002. Economic inequality and political representation. Paper presented at the 2002 Annual Meeting of the American Political Science Association, Boston. www.princeton.edu/[similar]bartels/papers.

Campaign Finance Institute Task Force on Presidential Nomination Financing. 2003. Participation, competition, and engagement: How to revive and improve public funding for presidential nomination politics. Washington, DC: Campaign Finance Institute.

Cohen, Jere, Rebecca Warner, and David Segal. 1995. Military service and educational attainment in the all-volunteer force. *Social Science Quarterly* 76 (1): 88–104.

Erikson, Robert S., Michael B. MacKuen, and James A. Stimson. 2002. The macro polity. New York: Cambridge University Press.

Fiorina, Morris P. 1999. Extreme voices: A dark side of civic engagement. In Civic engagement in American democracy, ed. Theda Skocpol and Morris P. Fiorina, 396–425. Washington, DC, and New York: Brookings Institution Press and Russell Sage Foundation.

Frankenberg, Erica, Chumgmei Lee, and Gary Orfield. 2002. A multiracial society with segregated schools: Are we losing the dream? Cambridge, MA: Harvard Civil Rights Project.

Freeman, Richard. 2004. What, me vote? In Social inequality, ed. Kathryn Neckerman, 703–28. New York: Russell Sage Foundation.

Gerber, Alan S., and Donald P. Green. 2000. The effects of canvassing, telephone calls, and direct mail on voter turnout: A field experiment. *American Political Science Review* 94 (3): 653–63.

Gopoian, J. David. 1984. What makes PACs tick? An analysis of the allocation patterns of economic interest groups. *American Journal of Political Science* 28 (2): 259–81.

Hacker, Jacob S. 2002. The divided welfare state: The battle over public and private social benefits in the United States. New York: Cambridge University Press.

Hall, Richard L., and Frank W. Wayman. 1990. Buying time: Moneyed interests and the mobilization of bias in congressional committees. *American Political Science Review* 84 (3): 797–820.

Jacobs, Lawrence R., and Robert Y. Shapiro. 1994. Issues, candidate image and priming: The use of private polls in Kennedy's 1960 presidential campaign. *American Political Science Review* 88 (3): 527–40.

Kroszner, Randall S., and Thomas Stratmann. 1998. Interest group competition and the organization of Congress: Theory and evidence from financial services political action committees. *American Economic Review* 88 (5): 1163–87.

Langbein, Laura. 1986. Money and access: Some empirical evidence. *Journal of Politics* 48 (4): 1052–62.

Manza, Jeff, and Christopher Uggen. 2004. Punishment and democracy: Disenfranchisement of nonincarcerated felons in the United States. *Perspectives on Politics* 2 (3): 491–505.

Mettler, Suzanne. 2002. Bringing the state back in to civic engagement: Policy feedback effects of the G.I. Bill for World War II veterans. *American Political Science Review* 96 (2): 351–65.

National Center for Public Policy, and Higher Education. 2002. Losing ground: A national status report on the affordability of American higher education. San Jose, CA. www.highereducation.org/reports/losing_ground/ar.shtml.

Rosenstone, Steven J., and John Mark Hansen. 1993. Mobilization, participation, and democracy in America. New York: Macmillan.

Schier, Steven E. 2000. By invitation only: The rise of exclusive politics in the United States. Pittsburgh, PA: University of Pittsburgh Press.

Shapiro, Thomas M. 2004. The hidden cost of being African American: How wealth perpetuates inequality. New York: Oxford University Press.

Skocpol, Theda. 2003. Diminished democracy: From membership to management in American civic life. Norman: University of Oklahoma Press.

Skrentny, John D. 2002. The minority rights revolution. Cambridge: Belknap Press of Harvard University Press.

Smeeding, Timothy M. 2004. Public policy and economic inequality: The United States in comparative perspective. Paper prepared for Campbell Institute Seminar, Inequality and American Democracy, February 20. www.maxwell.syr.edu/campbell/Events/Smeeding.pdf.

Uggen, Christopher, and Jeff Manza. 2002. Democratic contraction? Political Consequences of felon disenfranchisement in the United States. *American Sociological Review* 67 (6): 777–803.

*T*his selection focuses attention on one form of political participation—social protest—and takes a long-term view of who participates. In it, Erin E. O'Brien finds that the successes of women's organizing in the late 1960s and 1970s came with a price: white women enjoyed a disproportionate share of the material goods won and, today, this makes it harder for women of color and white women (as well as women across economic strata) to unite for collective political action. She argues that this unintended consequence of mobilization must be considered so that movement "success" cannot be evaluated by just looking at legal and social changes won. One must also consider the distribution of material benefits won.

O'Brien's analysis encourages us to consider how successful mobilization by a group in the past (women) can exacerbate differentiating characteristics among this group (racial, ethnic, social class) making collective mobilization today difficult. It also provides an example of the concept of intersectionality. Those who take an intersectional perspective examine how one's various group memberships (race, gender, social class, sexual orientation, etc.) interact to influence patterns of political participation and political behavior. Individuals are simultaneously members of multiple groups and these group memberships come together to form unique experiences and perspectives that impact political participation.

The Double-Edged Sword of Women's Organizing: Poverty and the Emergence of Racial and Class Differences in Women's Political Priorities

ERIN E. O'BRIEN

End Poverty

Corporate Father's Blame Welfare Mothers

Put a Time Limit on Poverty Not Welfare

People Before Profits

Erin O'Brien, "The Double-Edged Sword of Women's Organizing: Poverty and the Emergence of Racial and Class Differences in Women's Policy Priorities," *Women and Politics*, vol. 26, no. 3/4 (2004), pp. 25–56. Reprinted by permission of the publisher (Taylor & Francis, www.informaworld.com).

If you spot a car with one of the above bumper stickers it is a safe bet—as far as bets go—that the car's primary driver is a woman who considers poverty an important political issue. This is because women prioritize social issues in politics more than men (Sigel 1996; Mansbridge 1985),[1] poverty is a social issue (Albelda and Tilly 1996), and slapping one of these slogans on your car's rear bumper is a pretty good indicator of where your political priorities lie. But is a woman driving a SUV as likely as the one driving a Hyundai to consider poverty an important political issue? What about women forced to take the bus? Said differently, are certain women more or less likely to rank poverty among the top issues facing the nation?

Perhaps the answer to these questions has changed over time. So, for example, are women driving SUVs and the women driving Hyundais separated by social class in ways women driving Cadillac El Dorados and Chevy Vegas were not?

This article addresses these and related issues. The case of poverty is used to examine whether women's political priorities are conditioned by their class and/or race *over time*. How, if at all, the intervention of feminist identification influences these relationships also receives empirical attention. . . .

Existing literature suggests three ways women's social class and race may influence how likely they are to prioritize poverty over time. The first hypothesis comes primarily from literature on women's movements and critical history in the United States. Scholars in these fields indicate that race, class, and ethnicity regularly drive women apart (Gordon 1994; Costain 1992). . . .

Group cleavages challenged second-wave feminist organizing [of the late 1960s and 1970s]. Many poor women, women of color, lesbian women, and bi-sexual women felt that the mainstream movement was dominated by affluent women (who were disproportionately white) who neither shared their political concerns nor acknowledged how gender interacts with other group cleavages to produce subjugation (Ferree and Hess 1985; Pharr 1988). These feelings contributed to divisions within the movement and, ultimately, its demise.

Racial and class divisions among women are not just the domain of first- and second-wave organizing. In third-wave feminist organizing, differentiated identities like Latina-lesbian feminist often take center stage.[2] Commonalties across all women are rarely the political or social focus (King 1993; Ryan 2001). . . .

✽ ✽ ✽ ✽ ✽

. . . [T]he *constant differences hypothesis* suggests that class and race always divide women. As a result, poor women and women of color should consistently cite poverty at proportions above more affluent women and women of color. . . .

The *more-similar-than-different* hypothesis challenges this prediction. It does not call the conclusions of the literatures just reviewed into question. It does challenge their representativeness and applicability over time. For example, while there is little doubt that class, race, and other cleavages have been divisive for women's organizing, their disruptive effect may be overstated. Women of different races and social classes have always mobilized around poverty and social welfare issues—they simply do not always organize across their group boundaries when doing so (Abramovitz 1999, 2000). Just as tellingly, women of different social classes, races, and ethnicities came together through political concerns derived from their gender (Evans 1980). . . . It was not until these mobilization efforts achieved some level of legitimacy and success that class, race, sexual orientation, and other cleavages become more divisive. The *more-similar-than-different hypothesis* builds from these findings. It suggests the emphasis on group-based divisions among women obscures the amount of agreement between them. According to this view, similar political visions may be the norm—not exception—among women.

. . . [T]he *more-similar-than-different hypothesis* recognizes class and racial cleavages do sometimes produce different political priorities among women. But, it argues these divisions are relatively rare and are more likely to occur during the 1960s and early 1970s.

* * * * *

The *non-random fluctuation hypothesis* challenges both of these hypotheses. It focuses on how macro-level conditions alter women's lives and policy priorities. It is difficult to overstate the amount of economic, social, and political changes that women—and society as a whole—experienced from the 1960s through the year 2000. . . . These changes empowered women and can be traced, in part, to second-wave organizing (McGlen et al. 2002).

However, the material benefits won by this organizing went disproportionately to affluent women and white women (Brenner 2000). Over this same time period, wealth inequality has hit dramatic new heights and these wealthy individuals are disproportionately white (Wolff 1995; Phillips 2002). Combined these two factors produce a situation where women share fewer life experiences and material concerns across class and racial groups (Ehrenreich 1999).

According to social critic Barbara Ehrenreich, this change occurred over the time frame examined in this study. Prior to second-wave organizing, material differences between women of different races and social classes certainly existed. Nonetheless, the vast majority of these women were similarly subjugated in their intimate relationships with men. As a result, they rarely had access to their own economic resources. When women did work outside the home, they shared similar experiences of subjugation and power differentials with male superiors. Regardless of whether they worked outside the home, all women shared near sole responsibility for household duties (Ehrenreich 1999; Shelton and John 1996). In short, before the benefits of second-wave feminist organizing began to roll-in so unevenly, mid-twentieth century American women had more in common. Their economic fortunes were insecure and they were usually dependent upon men. . . . [3]

Based on this analysis, the *non-random fluctuation hypothesis* indicates all women should mention poverty at near equal rates in the 1960s and early 1970s. Social class and race should not significantly predict prioritizing poverty. But, as the 1970s progress and the material benefits of second-wave organizing are disproportionately enjoyed by affluent women and white women, these women should care less about poverty. They should mention poverty less frequently than poor women and African American women.

This article thus tests three distinct hypotheses for how, if at all, class and racial cleavages influenced how likely women were to consider poverty an important political issue over time. The first indicates constant differences among women. The second suggests periods of prolonged similarities among women punctuated by rare years where race and class influence whether or not they prioritize poverty. The third indicates that women will cite poverty at equal rates regardless of racial or class memberships through the early 1970s but that these commonalties will dissipate as the decade progresses. Once white women and more affluent women begin to enjoy the material benefits of second-wave women's organizing, they should prioritize poverty less frequently.

*****

WOMEN'S POLITICAL PRIORITIES OVER TIME: POVERTY AND THE ROLE OF SOCIAL CLASS

*****

Together the [data] . . . indicate that class is not always a significant predictor of whether or not women consider poverty a pressing national issue. Class becomes significant over time. Upper-middle-class women are the first to distinguish themselves from poor women in the period from 1974 through 1986. Their distinctiveness from poor women remains from 1988 through 2000 and, during this later time period, middle-class women follow suit.

The *non-random fluctuation hypothesis* predicted this exact empirical pattern. It indicated that second wave's uneven benefit distribution would undo commonalities in women's day-to-day experiences. Because of this, poverty would gradually fall off affluent women's political radar in favor of issues more consummate with their new social, economic, and political situation. The empirical results show exactly this—initially among upper-middle-class women who were the first to enjoy the material rewards of organizing and then among middle-class women. In short, social class does not inevitably shape women's policy priorities. Social class differences are absent from 1960 to 1972. They only emerge and solidify as affluent women disproportionately reap the benefits of second-wave feminist organizing.

 . . . [T]he empirical evidence thus far indicates that class polarization among women is neither as inevitable as the *constant differences hypothesis* suggests, nor as unusual as the *more-similar-than-different hypothesis* predicts. Instead, the fluctuating significance of class is predicted by the *non-random fluctuation hypothesis*. Precisely when upper-middle-class women and middle-class women experienced the economic security won by second-wave feminist movements, they became less likely to think that poverty was a national priority. These differences were not anomalies of one or two years. Once evidenced, they remained across years. Thus, to return to our opening example, it did not matter if women took the bus, drove a clunker, or rode in style from 1960 to 1972: they were indistinguishable when it came to prioritizing poverty issues. From 1974 to 1986, upper-middle-class women hit the brakes. Middle-class women did the same in 1988 to 2000. These results indicate class differences may not be inevitable, but they now condition poverty's salience among women.

WOMEN'S POLITICAL PRIORITIES OVER TIME: POVERTY AND THE ROLE OF RACE AND ETHNICITY

Similarly revealing patterns emerge when analysis turns to race. . . .

 . . . [F]igure 5.1 . . . compares the proportion of African-American women and

**Figure 5.1: Proportions of African-American Women and
White Women Citing Poverty as a Major National Issue 1960–2000**

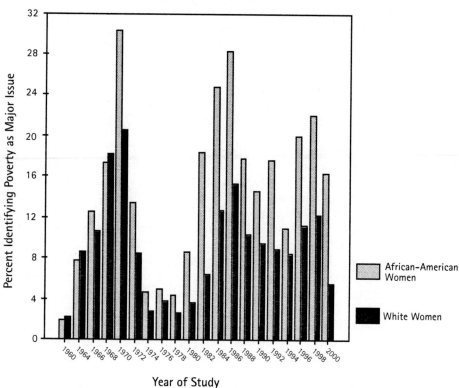

Year of Study

white women who identified poverty as a top national issue from 1960 through 2000. The figure illustrates how excepting one spike in 1968, African-American and white women self-identified poverty at almost identical levels until 1978.[6] Following 1978, the differences between black and white women are constant, and statistically significant, in . . . every year but 1994. Even in 1994 though, white women cite poverty less frequently than African-American women.

. . . Controlling for the effect of factors like social class, political party, religion, area of residence, age, education, and marital status, African-American women and white women are statistically indistinguishable in referencing poverty between 1960 and 1972. Racial differences emerge—and remain—in the . . . analysis conducted with female respondents between 1974 and 1986 as well as the one conducted with female respondents from 1988 through 2000.

This pattern indicates that racial differences are not as inevitable as the *constant differences hypothesis* suggests. Neither are they the anomalies predicted by the *more-similar-than-different hypothesis*. Instead, the . . . effect of racial group membership is felt precisely when white women began to reap disproportionate benefits from second-wave organizing. Once realized, these differences remain constant and significant over time. The *non-random fluctuation hypothesis* predicts this exact pattern. It does not romanticize the commonalities that existed among black and white women prior to second-wave organizing. Nonetheless, the empirical results seem clear: successful mobilization had the unintended consequence of exacerbating political differences among black and white women. These differences proceeded along the familiar fault lines of race and class.

AN ALTERNATIVE EXPLANATION: THE RISE OF FEMINIST IDENTIFICATION

A competing explanation for the onset and maintenance of racial and class divisions among women is that the rise of feminist identifiers, not second-wave's disproportionate resource share, are to blame. Perhaps affluent women and white women identified more frequently as feminists. As a result, they cited poverty less frequently because issues like equal pay or the Equal Rights Amendment took center stage (Mink 1998). Alternatively, feminism may be linked to caring more about poverty. If this is the case, and feminism drives the emerging significance of racial and class differences among women, we would expect feminist women to be disproportionately poor and African-American. Their feminist beliefs—not second-wave's uneven payout—would lead poor women and African-American women to cite poverty more frequently after the mid-1970s.

These challenges to the *non-random fluctuation hypothesis* are tested . . . If feminism propels the emergence and sustenance of group differences among women, then controlling for feminist identification should eliminate the statistical significance of the race and class variables.

The analysis . . . indicates otherwise. . . . Even with the feminist identifier variable included . . . upper-middle-class women become less likely than poor women to prioritize poverty during 1972–1984. These differences remain over time—although the level of significance drops somewhat for upper-middle-class women. Middle-class women also become similarly less inclined to mention poverty when compared to poor women from 1988–2000. The distance between African-American women and white women also remains after controlling for the effect of holding feminist beliefs. Class and racial differences therefore emerge as significant precisely when the *non-random fluctuation hypothesis* predicts. . . .

* * * * *

CONCLUSION

This article examined how social class and race influenced women's prioritization of poverty from 1960 through 2000. Analysis indicates racial and class differences among women are not inevitable. From 1960–1972, black women and white women were statistically indistinguishable from one other. Women of all social classes were similarly indistinguishable from one another. . . . However, as the 1970s progressed, white women diverged from African-American women. They regarded poverty a national priority less frequently. Compared to poor women, upper-middle-class women emerged as unique from 1974–1986. They were less likely to rank poverty among the top issues facing the nation. As the 1980s became the 1990s, middle-class women followed suit. Compared to poor women they too were less likely to mention poverty from 1988–2000. Racial differences remained during this period. The timing of these changes, as well as their sustained effect, is consistent with the *non-random fluctuation hypothesis*. Once the material benefits of second-wave organizing were enjoyed disproportionately by affluent women (who were mostly white) these women prioritized poverty less frequently than poor women. With these benefits in hand, their characteristic experiences and struggles overlapped less with poor women and women of color. As a result, their political priorities had more to do with their new, though imperfect, economic and social realities. Poverty was likely to fall off the radar screen.

. . . The good news is that racial and class divisions are not political inevitabilities. The era from 1960 through 1972 is certainly not ancient history. During this time frame, neither class nor race significantly predicted mentioning poverty as a top issue facing the nation. Sizeable percentages of women identified poverty from 1960–1972 and they did so regardless of their race. Yes, these cleavages condition women's policy priorities today. But a mere 35 years ago they were not so important. This offers real possibility for activists, organizers, and women's interest groups.

It is not all good news—especially if linking women for political and social change is a goal. Second-wave benefits lessened poverty's personal relevance for affluent women and many white women. Today then, women voicing concern over poverty are disproportionately poor and of color. Linking women across racial and class lines is complicated by these disparate concerns. Past movement successes therefore threaten women's ability to unite across class and racial lines today.

＊＊＊＊＊

The moral of this story is *not* to stop organizing. Clearly the social changes won by . . . mobilization improved women's lives. Culture changed. Instead, the findings push us to recognize the unintended consequences of organizing . . . Organizing per se is not problematic. The uneven distribution of organizing's benefits is problematic. If second-wave successes were distributed equitably across different categories of women, there is no reason to suspect that group cleavages would come to predict women's policy priorities.

. . . The story then is to organize but make two changes. First, movement success can not be solely conceptualized as securing legal and social change. These may be necessary components, but movements must constantly look at how the rewards they secure are distributed. . . . Second, existing women's campaigns and policy think tanks that want to attract women from diverse backgrounds would do well to alter their policy priorities. Issues like abortion and electing female candidates certainly matter for women's lives. They are appropriate priorities but, on average, they are issues that white women and more affluent women consider most important. To draw in other women, truly *prioritizing* issues like poverty is necessary. Poor women and African-American women are more likely to respond to this issue. Women's groups have long taken action on poverty but the vast majority do so infrequently . . . If an aim is mobilizing and improving the lives of women from all social strata, this is a mistake. Today, poor women and African-American women are the least likely to consider the mainstream women's groups relevant to their lives. This analysis indicates this stems partly from the issues that these groups currently prioritize. Analysis also indicates a relatively easy solution: truly emphasizing issues like poverty and economic justice that are more likely to draw in a more diverse pool of women.

* * * * *

Notes

1. There is more opinion congruence between men and women than in the past (Jenson and Christiansen 1994). However, offering the same general answer to a close-ended survey question is not the same as prioritizing similar political issues. Prioritizing involves personal issue salience and perceived importance. Women and men differ on the issues they prioritize (Sigel 1996).

2. Temporally, second-wave organizing got its start in the consciousness raising activities of the mid- to late-1960s (Ferree and Hess 1985; Ehrenreich 1999). Third-wave organizing first emerged in the late seventies to early eighties (Ryan 2001).

3. Affluent women certainly enjoyed more material possessions but, like poor women, their economic fortunes were usually dependent on men as husbands, fathers, and/or bosses. These dependencies made for economic insecurity.

6. Chi-square analysis confirms this. Until 1978, the only year where there was a statistical difference between African American and white women in citing poverty was 1968.

References

Abramovitz, Mimi. 1999. "Toward a Framework for Understanding Activism among Poor and Working-Class Women in Twentieth Century America." In *Whose Welfare*. Gwendolyn Mink, ed. Ithaca: Cornell University Press. 214–248.

_____. 2000. *Under Attack, Fighting Back: Women and Welfare in the United States*. New York: Monthly Review Press.

Albeda, Randy and Chris Tilly. 1997. *Glass Ceilings and Bottomless Pits; Women's Work, Women's Poverty*. Boston, MA: South End Press.

Brenner, Johanna. 2000. *Women and the Politics of Class*. New York: Monthly Review Press.

Costain, Anne. 1992. *Inviting Women's Rebellion: A Political Process Interpretation of the Women's Movement*. Baltimore, MD: John Hopkins University Press.

Davis, Angela. 1983. *Women, Race, and Class*. New York: Random House.

Evans, Sara. 1980. *Personal Politics: The Roots of Women's Liberation in the Civil Rights Movement and the New Left*. New York: Vintage Books.

Ehrenreich, Barbara. 1999. "Doing It for Ourselves: Can Feminism Survive Class Polarization?" *In These Times*. 23(26): 28 November. 10–12.

Ferree, Myra Marx and Beth Hess. 1985. *Controversy and Coalitions: The New Feminist Movement*. Boston: Twayne Publishers.

Gordon, Linda. 1994. *Pitied But Not Entitled: Single Mothers and the History of Welfare*. New York: Free Press.

Jenson, Larry and Robert Christiansen. 1994. "Finding Agreement Among Women on Gender Issues." *Psychological Reports*. 75: 35–44.

King, Deborah. 1993. "Multiple Jeopardy: the Context of Black Feminist Ideology." In *Feminist Frameworks: Alternative Theoretical Accounts of the Relations Between Women and Men*. Alison Jaggar and Paula Rothenberg eds. New York: McGraw-Hill. 220–236.

Mansbridge, Jane. 1985. "The ERA and the Gender Gap in the 1980 Election." *Public Opinion Quarterly*. 49: 164–179.

McGlen, Nancy, Karen O'Connor, Laura van Assendelft, and Wendy Gunther-Canada. 2002. *Women, Politics, and American Society*. New York: Longman.

Pharr, Suzanne 1988. *Homophobia: A Weapon of Sexism*. Little Rock: Chardon Press.

Phillips, Kevin. 2002. "The New Face of Another Gilded Age." *The Washington Post*. May 26. Page B2.

Ryan, Barbara. 2001. *Identity Politics in the Women's Movement*. New York: New York University Press.

Reingold, Beth. 1992. "Concepts of Representation Among Female and Male State Legislators." *Legislative Studies Quarterly*. 17: 509–537.

Shelton, Beth Anne and Daphne John. 1996. "The Division of Household Labor." *Annual Review of Sociology*. 22: 299–322.

Sigel, Roberta. 1996. *Ambition and Accommodation: How Women View Gender Relations*. Chicago: University of Chicago Press.

Wolff, Edward. 1995. "How the Pie Is Sliced." *The American Prospect*. 22 (Summer): 58–64.

*I*n this selection, Marc Mauer turns our attention to structural barriers to political participation and how these barriers impact communities of color. Mauer focuses on voter eligibility rules that systematically disenfranchise over 5 million felons and ex-felons in the United States. He demonstrates how as criminal justice policy became a "Drug War," penalties for certain types of drugs escalated dramatically—this produced a situation where people of color became disproportionately impacted by tough drug laws and, thus, disproportionately impacted by felony disenfranchisement laws. Indeed, 2 percent of the American population can not vote because of felony disenfranchisement laws as well as 13 percent of African-American men. Mauer discusses research showing how these patterns of disenfranchisement have influenced several elections, advantaging the Republican Party.

Mass Imprisonment and the Disappearing Voters

Marc Mauer

On Election Day 2000 in Florida, in the midst of all the dimpled ballots and hanging chads, Thomas Johnson stayed home. Johnson, the African-American director of a Christian residential program for ex-offenders, wanted to vote for George W. Bush, but was prevented by Florida law from doing so. In 1992, Johnson had been convicted of selling cocaine and carrying a firearm without a license in New York. After serving his sentence and moving to Florida in 1996, Johnson found that as an ex-felon he was barred from the voting booth. He was hardly alone in this situation, as an estimated 600,000 others in Florida who had theoretically "paid their debt to society" were also frozen out of the electoral process.

Nationwide, 5.3 million Americans either serving a felony sentence or having previously been convicted of a felony are forced out of the ballot box.[1] The laws that keep these citizens home can be traced back to the founding of the nation. With the founding "fathers" having granted the vote only to wealthy white male property holders, political participation in the new democracy was extended to just 120,000 of the 2 million free Americans (not counting the more than 1 million slaves and indentured servants) at the time, about 6 percent of the population.[2] The excluded population incorporated women, African Americans, convicted felons, illiterates, and the landless. Except for convicted felons, of course, all these other exclusions have been removed over a period of two hundred years, and we now look back on those barriers with a great deal of national embarrassment.

. . . [T]oday every state but Maine and Vermont (which allow prisoners to vote) has a set of laws that restrict the voting rights of felons and former felons. Forty-eight states and the District of Columbia do not permit prison inmates to vote; thirty-five states disenfranchise felons on parole; and thirty disenfranchise felons on probation. In addition, in eleven states a felony conviction can result in disenfranchisement, often for life, even after an offender has completed his or her sentence. Thus, for example, an eighteen-year-old convicted of a one-time drug sale in Virginia who successfully completes a court-ordered treatment program and is never arrested again has permanently lost his voting rights unless he receives a gubernatorial pardon.

Although the issue of disenfranchisement would raise questions about democratic inclusion at any point in history, the dramatic escalation of the criminal justice system in the past thirty years has swelled the number of persons subject to these provisions to unprecedented levels. Currently, 2 percent of the adult population cannot vote as a result of a current or previous felony conviction. Given the vast racial disparities in the criminal justice system it is hardly surprising, but shocking nonetheless, to find that an estimated 13 percent of African-American males are now disenfranchised.

The coalescence of disenfranchisement laws and racial exclusion began to be cemented in the post-Reconstruction era following the Civil War. . . .

The disenfranchisement laws adopted in a number of Southern states were not at all subtle, often requiring the loss of voting rights only for those offenses believed to be committed primarily by blacks. In Mississippi, for example, the 1890 constitutional convention called for disenfranchisement for such crimes as burglary, theft, arson, and obtaining money under false pretenses, but not for robbery or murder. In the words of a Mississippi Supreme Court decision several years later, blacks engaged in crime were "given rather to furtive offenses than to the robust crimes of the whites."[3]

* * * * *

While one might debate whether the *intended* effect of disenfranchisement policies today is to reduce minority voting power, it is inescapable that this impact could have been predicted as a logical consequence of the nation's wars on crime and drugs. The sixfold increase in the nation's inmate population since the early 1970s brought about both an absolute increase in numbers as well as a disproportionately greater impact on persons of color. Much of this was because of the inception of the modern-day "war on drugs" in the 1980s, whereby the number of persons incarcerated for a drug offense rose from 40,000 in 1980 to half a million today. Blacks and Latinos now constitute four of every five drug offenders in state prison. A considerable body of research documents that these figures are not necessarily a result of greater drug use in minority communities but rather drug policies that have employed a law enforcement approach in communities of color and a treatment orientation in white and suburban neighborhoods.[4] And the greater the number of minority offenders in the system, the greater the rate of disenfranchisement.

At modest rates of disenfranchisement such a policy is one that is clearly of concern to an individual felon but is unlikely to affect electoral outcomes in any significant number of cases. But at the historic levels that have been achieved in recent decades the issue is no longer one of merely academic interest but is likely to have a profound impact on actual electoral results.

Sociologists Christopher Uggen and Jeff Manza have produced a sophisticated model for estimating the number of disenfranchised voters in each state and the effect of their absence on elections for national office.[5] Uggen and Manza assume that felons and former felons would vote at lower rates than the (already low) national rate but that they would be more likely to vote Democratic, given that they are disproportionately comprised of minorities (an estimated 38 percent African American) and poor and working-class whites. Even with a projected lower turnout, they conclude that disenfranchisement policies have affected the outcome of seven U.S. Senate races from 1970 to 1998, generally in states with close elections and a substantial number of disenfranchised voters. In each case the Democratic candidate would have won rather than the Republican victor. Projecting the impact of these races over time leads them to conclude that disenfranchisement prevented Democratic control of the Senate from 1986 to 2000. While these projections are based on the inclusion of both current and former felons, even permitting just ex-felons to vote would likely have a significant impact as well since they represent more than a third of the disenfranchised population.

Supporters of felon disenfranchisement contend that regardless of their outcome these policies are important . . .

. . . [T]his rationale has been presented within the context of the "law and order" political climate, being expressed as a fear that convicted felons would presumably cast their vote in such a way as to weaken law enforcement institutions. . . . [I]n the words of one modern-day proponent, "criminal disenfranchisement allows citizens to decide law enforcement issues without the dilution of voters who are deemed . . . to be less trustworthy."[6] In other words, ex-felons would presumably vote for policies that help criminals and thwart the legitimate interests of otherwise law-abiding members of the community. If so, this might set up a conflict between the principle of democratic inclusion and the need for public safety.

But it is clear that in at least some cases, individuals subjected to criminal justice policies that may be overly harsh would be natural and legitimate advocates of political change. An example relates to drug policy. As the "war on drugs" has swelled prison populations and taken a disproportionate toll on minority communities, considerable opposition has developed to mandatory sentencing and related policies. In some neighborhoods, substantial numbers of people are returning home after serving five-year prison terms for low-level drug offenses. Arguably, their voices and votes, along with those of their neighbors, might be successful in electing candidates who support scaling back harsh drug laws. Is there a policy rationale that justifies excluding persons who have experienced the impact of such laws from deliberating about their wisdom?

The prospect of electoral fraud is also sometimes raised as a legitimate concern in regard to felon voting. Although there might be some validity to this argument for felons convicted of electoral fraud, it is hard to imagine why a car thief or a drug seller would be more likely than another citizen to commit such an offense. Since more than 99 percent of felons have not been convicted of electoral offenses, this seems to be a rather overbroad concern. And when electoral fraud occurs, it rarely manifests itself in the presence of a voter in the voting booth, but rather through improper counting of ballots or outright bribery. One does not need to be a registered voter to commit these offenses. Ironically, in some states, electoral offenses are classified only as misdemeanors, and therefore persons convicted of these crimes are not subject to disenfranchisement.

Disenfranchisement is sometimes premised on being a legitimate aspect of punishment for a criminal offense, but this is curious in several respects. While all other aspects of sentencing are expected to be proportional to the offense involved and are imposed by a judge on an individual basis, disenfranchisement is a penalty imposed, across the board, on mass murderers and larcenists alike. Further, criminal convictions do not otherwise result in the loss of basic rights. Convicted felons maintain the right to divorce, own property, or file lawsuits . . .

Proponents of disenfranchisement suggest that even in the most extreme cases the loss of the right to vote is never truly for a lifetime, since all states maintain a process whereby ex-felons can seek restoration of their rights from the governor. Although this is true in theory, in practice it is often illusory. A number of states impose a waiting period of five or ten years before an ex-felon can even petition to have his or her rights restored. The process of seeking restoration is also often cumbersome and expensive. . . . In Mississippi, ex-felons must either secure an executive order from the governor or convince a state legislator to introduce a bill on his or her behalf, obtain a two-thirds vote in the legislature, and have the bill signed by the governor.[7]

Data on the number of former felons who have had their rights restored are difficult to come by, but in one recent two-year period, a total of 404 persons in Virginia regained their voting rights at a time when there were more that 200,000 ex-felons in the state.[8] . . .

Although the case for disenfranchisement is hardly compelling, two primary arguments suggest that felon disenfranchisement laws are both counterproductive and out of line with evolving international norms. First, disenfranchisement policies are in sharp conflict with the goal of promoting public safety. . . . [A] primary goal of the criminal justice system and the community should be to reduce the likelihood that the person will reoffend. One means by which this can be accomplished is through installing a sense of obligation and responsibility to the community. Those persons who feel some connection to their fellow citizens are less likely to victimize others. As former Supreme Court Justice Thurgood Marshall stated " . . . the denial of a right to vote to [ex-offenders] is hindrance to the efforts of society to rehabilitate former felons and convert them into law-abiding and productive citizens."[9]

American disenfranchisement policies are also extreme by the standards of other industrialized nations. In no other democracy are convicted offenders who have completed their sentences disenfranchised for life, as is the case in more than a dozen states.[10] . . .

In recent years the increased attention devoted to this issue has resulted in a reconsideration of some of the more extreme policies within the states. . . . [I]n August 2001, the bi-partisan National Commission on Federal Election Reform, cochaired by former presidents Ford and Carter, recommended that states allow for the restoration of voting rights for felons who have completed their sentences. . . .

The irony of the combined impact of American disenfranchisement policies along with the massive expansion of the prison system is that a half century after the beginnings of the civil rights movement, increasing numbers of African Americans and others are losing their voting rights each day. It is long past time for the United States, as the Western democracy with the lowest rate of voter participation, to consider means of bringing more Americans into the electoral process rather than excluding large groups of citizens.

Notes

1. Jeff Manza and Christopher Uggen, *Locked Out: Felon Disenfranchisement and American Democracy*, (New York: Oxford University Press, 2006).

2. Alec C. Ewald, "Civil Death: The Ideological Paradox of Criminal Disenfranchisement Laws in the United States," Master of Arts Thesis, The University of North Carolina, 2000, p. 1.

3. Shapiro, p. 541.

4. See for example, Michael Tonry, *Malign Neglect* (New York: Oxford University Press, 1995).

5. Christopher Uggen and Jeff Manza, "The Political Consequences of Felon Disenfranchisement Laws in the United States." Paper presented at the annual meeting of the American Sociological Association, Washington, D.C., August 16, 2000.

6. Todd F. Gaziano, Testimony before the House Judiciary Committee Subcommittee on the Constitution Regarding HR 906, October 21, 1999, p. 2.

7. Jamie Fellner and Marc Mauer, "Losing the Vote: The Impact of Felony Disenfranchisement Laws in the United States." Human Rights Watch and the Sentencing Project, October 1998, p. 6.

8. Ibid., pp. 5–6.

9. *Richardson v. Ramirez*, 418 U.S. at 78 (Marshall, J., dissenting) (citations omitted).

10. Fellner and Mauer, p. 18.

*L*ike the APSA report and Marc Mauer's previous selection, Michael Powell and Peter Slevin examine a classic form of political participation: voting. They, however, consider the "almost" voter and the "not counted" or "lost" voter. Focusing primarily on the battleground state of Ohio in the 2004 Presidential election, Powell and Slevin report that the precincts most apt to have poorly trained poll workers, faulty voting machines, too few machines, and other problems were the same precincts that leaned Democratic. Said differently, when a machine failed or produced an irregularity, that machine was more apt to be in a poorer district. The authors indicate that while legal barriers may be removed to voting, electoral laws/practices can still systematically disenfranchise along racial and class lines and influence electoral outcomes.

Several Factors Contributed to "Lost" Voters in Ohio

MICHAEL POWELL AND PETER SLEVIN

Tanya Thivener's is a tale of two voting precincts in Franklin County. In her city neighborhood, which is vastly Democratic and majority black, the 38-year-old mortgage broker found a line snaking out of the precinct door.

She stood in line for four hours—one hour in the rain—and watched dozens of potential voters mutter in disgust and walk away without casting a ballot. Afterward, Thivener hopped in her car and drove to her mother's house, in the vastly Republican and majority white suburb of Harrisburg. How long, she asked, did it take her to vote?

Fifteen minutes, her mother replied.

"It was . . . poor planning," Thivener said. "County officials knew they had this huge increase in registrations, and yet there weren't enough machines in the city. You really hope this wasn't intentional."

Electoral problems prevented many thousands of Ohioans from voting on Nov. 2. In Columbus, bipartisan estimates say that 5,000 to 15,000 frustrated voters turned away without casting ballots. It is unlikely that such "lost" voters would have changed the election result—Ohio tipped to President Bush by a 118,000-vote margin and cemented his electoral college majority.

But similar problems occurred across the state and fueled protest marches and demands for a recount. The foul-ups appeared particularly acute in Democratic-leaning districts, according to interviews with voters, poll workers, election observers and election board and party officials, as well as an examination of precinct voting patterns in several cities.

In Cleveland, poorly trained poll workers apparently gave faulty instructions to voters that led to the disqualification of thousands of provisional ballots and misdirected several hundred votes to third-party candidates. In Youngstown, 25 electronic machines transferred an unknown number of votes for Sen. John F. Kerry (D-Mass.) to the Bush column.

In Columbus, Cincinnati and Toledo, and on college campuses, election officials allocated far too few voting machines to busy precincts, with the result that voters stood on line as long as 10 hours—many leaving without voting. Some longtime voters discovered their registrations had been purged.

"There isn't enough to prove fraud, but there have been very significant problems in running elections in Ohio this year that demand reform," said Edward B. Foley, who is director of the election law program at the Ohio State University law school and a former Ohio state solicitor. "We clearly ended up disenfranchising people, and I don't want to minimize that."

Franklin County election officials—evenly split between Republicans and Democrats—say they allocated machines based on past voting patterns and their best estimate of where more were needed. But they acknowledge having too few machines to cope with an additional 102,000 registered voters.

Ohio is not particularly unusual. After the 2000 election debacle, which ended with a 36-day partisan standoff in Florida and an election decided by the U.S. Supreme Court, Congress passed the Help America Vote Act in 2002. The intent was to help states upgrade aging voting machines and ensure that eligible voters are not turned away. To a point, it has had the desired effect.

"Viewed dispassionately, the national elections ran much more smoothly than in 2000," said Charles Stewart III, a professor at the Massachusetts Institute of Technology and a specialist in voting behavior and methodology. Because of improved technology "nationwide, we counted perhaps 1 million votes that we would have lost four years ago."

But much work remains. Congress imposed only the minimal national standards and included too few dollars. Tens of thousands of machines—including 70 percent of

Ohio's machines—still use punch-card ballots, which have a high error rate. A patchwork quilt of state rules governs voter registration and provisional ballots. (Provisional ballots are given to voters whose names do not appear on registration rolls—studies show that minorities and poor voters cast a disproportionate number of such ballots.) Ohio recorded 153,000 provisional ballots. But in Georgia, one-third of the election districts did not record a single provisional ballot in 2004.

In Florida, ground zero for 2000's election meltdown, professors and graduate students from the University of California at Berkeley studied this year's voting results, contrasting counties that had electronic voting machines with those that used traditional voting methods. They concluded, based on voting and population trends and other indicators, that irregularities associated with machines in three traditionally Democratic counties in southern Florida may have delivered at least 130,000 excess votes for Bush in a state the president won by about 381,000 votes. The study prompted heated critiques from some polling experts.

Stewart of MIT was skeptical, too. But he ran the numbers and came up with the same result. "You can't break it; I've tried," Stewart said. "There's something funky in the results from the electronic-machine Democratic counties."

Berkeley sociologist Michael Hout, who directed the study, said the problem in Florida probably lies with the technology. (Florida's touch-screen machines lack paper records.) "I've always viewed this as a software problem, not a corruption problem," he said. "We'd never tolerate this level of errors with an ATM. The problem is that we continue to do democracy on the cheap."

A HEATED RUN-UP

By October, the Bush and Kerry campaigns knew that this midwestern state was a crucial battleground. Each side assembled armies of 3,000 lawyers and paralegals, and unaffiliated organizations poured in thousands more volunteers. Both parties filed lawsuits challenging rules and registrations.

❊ ❊ ❊ ❊ ❊

AFTERMATH OF NOV. 2

After the election, local political activists seeking a recount analyzed how Franklin County officials distributed voting machines. They found that 27 of the 30 wards with the most machines per registered voter showed majorities for Bush. At the other end of the spectrum, six of the seven wards with the fewest machines delivered large margins for Kerry.

Voters in most Democratic wards experienced five-hour waits, and turnout was lower than expected. "I don't know if it's by accident or design, but I counted a dozen people walking away from the line in my precinct in Columbus," said Robert Fitrakis, a professor at Columbus State Community College and a lawyer involved in a legal challenge to certifying the vote.

Franklin County officials say they allocated machines according to instinct and science. But Hackett, the deputy director, acknowledged the need to examine the issue more carefully. "When the dust settles, we'll have to look more closely at this," he said.

In Knox County, some Kenyon College students waited 10 hours to vote. "They had to skip classes and skip work," said Matthew Segal, a 19-year-old student.

In northeastern Ohio, in the fading industrial city of Youngstown, Jeanne White, a veteran voter and manager at the *Buckeye Review,* an African American newspaper, stepped into the booth, pushed the button for Kerry—and watched her vote jump to the Bush column. "I saw what happened; I started screaming: 'They're cheating again and they're starting early!'"

It was not her imagination. Twenty-five machines in Youngstown experienced what election officials called "calibration problems." "It happens every election," said Thomas McCabe, deputy director of elections for Mahoning County, which includes Youngstown. "It's something we have to live with, and we can fix it."

As expected, there were more provisional ballots, and officials disqualified about 23 percent. In Hamilton County, which encompasses Cincinnati and its Ohio suburbs, 1,110 provisional ballots got tossed out because people voted in the wrong precinct. In about 40 percent of those cases, voters found the right polling place—which contained multiple precincts—but workers directed them to the wrong table.

In Cleveland, officials disqualified about one-third of the provisional ballots. Vu, the election board chief, said that some poll workers may have also mixed up their punch-card styluses—that would account for why a few overwhelmingly Democratic precincts recorded large numbers of votes for conservative third-party candidates.

Still, state officials saw little to apologize for, particularly in the case of provisional ballots. A recent count of provisional ballots sliced 18,000 votes off Bush's margin in Ohio. "In Washington, D.C., a voter who casts a ballot in the wrong precinct cannot have that ballot counted," said Carlo LoParo, a spokesman for Blackwell. "Yet in Ohio, it was 'voter suppression' and 'voter disenfranchisement.'"

In the days after the election, as voters swapped stories, anger and talk of Republican conspiracies mounted. "A lot of folks who, having put an enormous amount of energy into this campaign and having believed in the righteousness of their cause, can't believe that we lost," said Tim Burke, chairman of the Hamilton County election board.

Most senior state officials, Republican and Democratic alike, tend to play down the anger. National Democrats—including the chief counsel for Kerry's campaign in Ohio—say they expect the recount to confirm Bush's victory.

But that official view contrasts sharply with the bubbling anger heard among rank-and-file Democrats. While some promote conspiratorial theories, most have a straightforward bottom line. "A lot of people left in the four hours I waited," recalled Thivener, the mortgage broker from Columbus. "A lot of them were young black men who were saying over and over: 'We knew this would happen.'

"How," she asked, "is that good for democracy?"

Slevin reported from Cincinnati. Special correspondents Michelle Garcia in New York and Kari Lydersen in Chicago contributed to this report.

❧ DISCUSSION QUESTIONS ❧

1. Suppose you wanted to substantially lessen the inequities in American political participation. What specific policy changes would you make? List at least three. Why do you think it is that the United States has not adopted these changes?

2. What does it mean for representative democracy when elected officials are more likely to hear from the affluent? Does it mean that the policies produced will maintain current conditions and further advantage the affluent as the APSA report suggests? Alternatively, does relative silence from below mean that the less affluent are satisfied *or* do not view government as a place to press their claims?

3. Should felons or ex-felons be allowed to vote? Make arguments for and against the notions that felons and then ex-felons should have the franchise taken from them. What evidence do you find most convincing and why?

4. The O'Brien piece raises the concept of *intersectionality*—how various group memberships interact with one another to form potentially unique political outlooks. What if the other three readings had taken a more intersectional approach to their study of political participation? How, if at all, would this change what they have to say?

5. Both the Mauer and APSA Task Force Report note that the right to vote and hold elected office has expanded overtime in American politics. Yet, they also note increasing levels of class-, gender-, and race-based inequities. How is it that both trends can be occurring? Where do you think the United States is headed when it comes to equity and political participation? Cite specific evidence to support your conclusion.

Additional Resources

A Day's Work, A Day's Pay (2002) is a film that documents the challenges and triumphs of welfare rights organizing in New York City following passage of dramatic, punitive changes to welfare policy in 1996.

http://www.cawp.rutgers.edu
The Center for American Women and Politics (CAWP) at Rutgers University conducts research on American women and politics. Data and reports on this web site regularly investigate the gender gap and investigate voting patterns from a gender perspective (http://www.cawp.rutgers.edu/Facts5.html).

http://www.glaad.org
The Gay and Lesbian Advocates and Defenders (GLAAD) tracks the major legislative initiatives, court cases, and other actions involving gays and lesbians in the United States. It is "dedicated to ending discrimination based on sexual orientation, HIV status and gender identity and expression."

http://www.seiu.org
The Service Employees International Union (SEIU) has recently been instrumental in organizing low-wage workers for union membership and larger political engagement, participation, and activism.

http://www.hrc.org
The Human Rights Campaign (HRC) "seeks to improve the lives of GLBT Americans by advocating for equal rights and benefits in the workplace, ensuring families are treated equally under the law and increasing public support among all Americans through innovative advocacy, education and outreach programs. HRC works to secure equal rights for GLBT individuals and families at the federal and state levels by lobbying elected officials, mobilizing grassroots supporters, educating Americans, investing strategically to elect fair-minded officials and partnering with other GLBT organizations."

Iron Jawed Angels (2004) is an HBO film depicting the suffragette battle. It focuses on two real-life suffragettes, Alice Paul and Lucy Burns, and how these women negotiated prevailing notions of femininity, hostility to women getting the right to vote, and the fissures within the women's movement at the time.

POLITICAL PARTIES: WHO GETS INVITED?

Political parties' most proximate goal is to win elections. This picture illustrates the connection of candidates to their party as well as the outreach that Democrats (and, although not pictured, Republicans) are doing with the Hispanic community.

There are many ways to think about diversity when it comes to political parties in the United States. In one fundamental way, the party system in the United States is not diverse at all; only two parties—Democrats and Republicans—dominate our electoral outcomes. This is not to say that there are not any other parties in the United States; in fact, myriad other collections of individuals with shared political goals come together to form parties from the Communist Party and the Socialist Workers Party to the American Nazi Party and the Constitution Party. The Green Party has even been able to break the lock that the two major parties have on elected office and have placed over 200 of their members in offices (mainly city council seats and mayor's offices in small cities and towns) across the nation; the Libertarian Party has also had limited electoral success at the local level. However, we remain a two party system for several reasons, including the rules we typically use to define who wins and who loses elections and therefore gains seats in government.

Given this fact, one might expect the two dominant parties in the United States to be very diverse in terms of both their membership and supporters. Empirical data on this question provides some conflicting evidence. Take, for instance, the electoral outcome in the 2004 presidential election. The candidates of the major parties—George W. Bush for the Republicans and John F. Kerry for the Democrats—nearly split the vote of women equally (48 percent voted for Bush and 51 percent for Kerry), while the vote was not quite as close among Latino voters—Kerry received 53 percent while Bush got 44 percent; and among those in America who are 65 years or older Bush received 52 percent of the vote, while Kerry won 47 percent. However, if one looks to other areas there are great divides between the two parties in several important demographic categories in terms of vote choice—George W. Bush won only 11 percent of African-American votes in 2004 (a slight increase from 2000), John Kerry won only about a third of votes of white men and from those who reported going to church regularly. At the same time, George W. Bush only received about a third of the vote of those Americans who make less than $15,000 per year.[1] Clearly then, there are both major divisions and places of considerable overlap when it comes to the demographic characteristics of the individuals who cast their votes for major party candidates. These patterns impact who wins elections, which is the main proximate goal of both major parties in America.

The readings in this section will illustrate the impact of identity politics as it relates to political parties and the connection between demographic diversity and American party politics.

---

1. All data were taken from exit polls reported by CNN at www.cnn.com/ELECTION/2004/pages/results/states/US/P/00/epolls.0.html [accessed January 27, 2007].

The first piece in this section provides a description of the major groups in America that tend to support the Democratic and Republican parties. Majorie Randon Hershey takes the reader through the major divisions between the parties on several important levels, including socioeconomic status, race, gender, and ethnicity. Moreover, she provides some background as to why these important groups of Americans tend to support one party over another. Hershey also explores changes in the main coalitions of the two parties and offers hints as to how they might change in the future.

Party Coalitions and Party Change

Marjorie Randon Hershey

California Governor Arnold Schwarzenegger, sometimes known as "The Governator," has a mixed marriage, politically speaking. Schwarzenegger, a wealthy, middle-aged, white man, has owned several businesses. His father was a military officer. The governor's wife, Maria Shriver, is a journalist and comes from a large Catholic family of lawyers and activists for nonprofit groups. Using just the information in this description, would you have been able to tell which member of this couple is a Democrat and which is a Republican?

Party identifications are not distributed randomly among Americans. Some social groups lean heavily toward a Republican identification—business executives and "born-again" white Protestants, for example—and other groups, such as women, African Americans, and Jews, are more likely to consider themselves Democrats. Without any knowledge of their voting history, then, and purely on the basis of their links with certain social groups, we could predict (accurately) that Schwarzenegger is the Republican and Shriver is the Democrat.

The types of people who support a party make up what is called the party's *coalition*—the social, economic, or other groups most inclined to favor that party's candidates through good times and bad. Groups may align with a party for many reasons, but once a group has become associated with a party's coalition, its interests are very likely to affect the stands the party takes on at least some issues and the strategies it follows in campaigns.

The differences between the two parties' coalitions at a particular time are a helpful clue as to which issues dominate the nation's politics at that time. The facts that African Americans have identified so overwhelmingly as Democrats in recent decades, for example, and that southern whites are now dominantly Republican remind us that racial issues continue to be powerful in American elections.[1] At various times in U.S. history, regional conflicts, ethnic and religious divisions, disputes between agriculture and industry, and differences in social class have also helped form the basis for differences between the two parties' coalitions, as they have in other western democracies.

*****

. . . Changes in the alignment of social groups with the parties are especially intriguing because they contribute so much to shaping a nation's politics and policies. In much of this literature, great and enduring changes in the parties' coalitions have been called *party realignments*.[4] The concept of realignment is a controversial one. . . . But that should not keep us from exploring the interesting patterns of group support for the Democrats and Republicans over time and the differences these alignments make.

*****

THE SOCIAL BASES OF PARTY COALITIONS

Socioeconomic Status Divisions

Most democratic party systems reflect divisions along social class lines, even if those divisions may have softened over the years.[9] James Madison, one of the most perceptive observers of human nature among the nation's founders, wrote in the

Federalist Papers that economic differences are the most common source of factions.[10] The footprints of socioeconomic status (SES) conflict are scattered throughout American history. Social and economic status differences underlay the battle between the wealthy, aristocratic Federalists and the less-privileged Democratic-Republicans. These differences were even sharper between the Jacksonian Democrats and the Whigs a few decades later, and again during the fourth and fifth party systems.

The relationship between party and SES can still be seen in American politics today (see Table 6.1, sections A and B). Read across the top row of section A, for instance. You will find that among survey respondents in the lower third of incomes, 17 percent call themselves strong Democrats, 16 percent call themselves weak Democrats, and 17 percent lean toward the Democratic party but, toward the right side of the row, only 11, 10, and 16 percent, respectively, call themselves leaning, weak, or strong Republicans. The next column, titled "Dem. minus Rep.," shows that there are 13 percent more Democrats (counting strong and weak identifiers and Democratic "leaners") than Republicans among these lower income people.

Those with less education are even more likely to call themselves Democrats than lower-income people are (section B). Here, 22 percent of those who didn't finish high school identify as strong Democrats, 16 percent are weak Democrats and 13 percent are Democratic leaners. On the Republican side of the table, there are only 10 percent Republican leaners, 8 percent weak Republicans, and 11 percent strong Republicans among those who didn't finish high school, for an overall Democratic edge ("Dem. minus Rep.") of 22 percent. Why do we see these trends if the impact of social class is diminishing in politics? The overall decline in class voting among whites since the time of the New Deal has been counterbalanced by the very high Democratic identification among blacks, who are predominantly lower income.[11]

Socioeconomic forces, then, continue to leave their mark on American party politics. In fact, some observers argue that outside the South, less affluent voters have become even more supportive of Democrats in recent decades. The substantial gulf between rich and poor in the United States and the differences between the parties' stands on issues of special concern to lower income people (such as government-provided health care and social services) help sustain the relationship between lower SES and Democratic partisanship. The result is that, especially in congressional elections, Democrats are even more likely to win in lower income districts now than they were 20 years ago.[12]

Table 6.1: Social Characteristics and Party Identification: 2004

| | Democrats | | Independents | | | Republicans | | | |
	Strong	Weak	Closer to Dem.	Closer to Neither	Closer to Rep.	Weak	Strong	Dem. Minus Rep.	Cases
A. Income									
Lower Third	17%	16	17	13	11	10	16	13	324
Middle Third	18%	15	19	7	12	16	14	10	402
Upper Third	16%	14	15	8	11	14	21	−1	322
B. Education									
No high school diploma	22%	16	13	18	10	8	11	22	89
High school grad	18%	16	16	12	13	11	14	12	315
College	15%	14	18	7	11	16	19	1	644
C. Region									
South	19%	18	15	7	10	13	17	12	367
Nonsouth	16%	13	18	10	12	14	17	4	681
D. Religion									
Jews	44%	19	16	0	3	0	3	73	32
Catholics	19%	13	17	12	8	13	19	8	232
Protestants	15%	16	14	9	12	14	19	0	616
White Protestants*	9%	11	11	8	15	18	28	−30	452
E. Race									
Blacks	31%	31	21	12	5	1	1	76	180
Whites	14%	12	16	9	13	16	20	−7	868
F. Gender									
Female	22%	16	16	9	9	12	16	17	637
Male	12%	14	19	11	14	14	16	1	563

* The survey did not ask how many of these white Protestants consider themselves to be fundamentalist or "born again."

Note: Totals add up to approximately 100 percent reading across (with slight variations due to rounding). Dem. minus Rep. is the party difference calculated by subtracting the percentage of strong, weak, and leaning Republicans from the percentage of strong, weak, and leaning Democrats. Negative numbers indicate a Republican advantage in the group.

Source: 2004 American National Election Study, Center for Political Studies, University of Michigan; data made available by the Inter-University Consortium for Political and Social Research.

Table 6.1 also shows that the current relationship between higher SES and party differs in some interesting ways from that of the New Deal coalition [Editors' Note: The New Deal coalition refers to the status of party coalitions after the last major realignment and is tied to the proposals trumpeted by President Roosevelt that drew the poor, minorities, and immigrants to the Democratic Party]. People with a college education are no longer largely Republican; as the doors of higher education open to a wider variety of students, those with college degrees now divide themselves fairly evenly between the parties. Similarly, those with service jobs (which tend to be lower paying) and blue-collar jobs remain more likely to be Democrats, but upper-income people are no longer as distinctively Republican—perhaps because this group now contains fewer business people and more professionals, many of whom are concerned with quality-of-life issues such as the environment and women's rights. The identification of many professionals with the Democratic Party is reflected in the support Democratic candidates receive from teachers' unions and trial lawyers.

The impact of SES should not be overstated. Socioeconomic status has been less important as a basis for party loyalty in the United States than in many other western democracies,[13] and even at the height of the New Deal, the SES differences between the parties were less clear than the parties' rhetoric would suggest. Some groups locate themselves in the "wrong" party from an SES point of view; for example, white fundamentalist Protestants have trended Republican in recent years even though their average income is closer to that of the average Democrat than to the average Republican.[14] Because SES divisions between the Republicans and Democrats can be fuzzy, the parties do not usually promote blatantly class-based appeals; they try to attract votes from a variety of social groups.

Sectional (Regional) Divisions

Historically, the greatest rival to SES as an explanation for American party differences has been sectionalism. Different sections of the country have often had differing political interests. When a political party has championed these distinct interests, it has sometimes united large numbers of voters who may vary in other ways.

The most enduring sectionalism in American party history was the one-party Democratic control of the South. Well before the Civil War, white southerners shared an interest in slavery and an agricultural system geared to export markets. The searing experience of that war and the Reconstruction that followed made the South into the "Solid South" and delivered it to the Democrats for most of the next century. The 11 states of the former Confederacy cast all their electoral votes for Democratic presidential candidates in every election from 1880 through 1924, except for Tennessee's defection in 1920. Al Smith's Catholicism frightened five of these states into the Republican column in 1928, but the New Deal economic programs brought the South back to the Democratic Party for the four Roosevelt elections.

As we will see later in the chapter, however, the civil rights movement was the opening wedge in the slow process that separated the South from its Democratic loyalties. Even now (Table 6.1, section C), southerners are slightly more Democratic in their basic partisan leanings than non-southerners, thanks in large part to the overwhelming Democratic partisanship of southern blacks. But this Democratic edge is much less pronounced than it was until the 1960s, and it appears to be disappearing entirely, as white southerners become more and more likely to vote Republican in federal and state elections. . . .

* * * * *

Sectional divisions in voting are still present today; Democrat John Kerry, who lost every southern state in 2004, could attest to that. The Mountain West has sometimes acted as a unified bloc in national politics on concerns that these states share, such as protecting the coal deposits and the ranchers in the western states against federal environmental laws. So in recent presidential elections, commentators have referred to the "Republican L," the substantial support for Republican candidates in the Rocky Mountain and Plains states and then across the South.

Religious Divisions

There have always been religious differences between the American party coalitions, just as there are in many other democracies. In the early days of the New Deal, Catholics and Jews were among the most loyal supporters of the Democratic Party, although Catholic support for Democrats has declined in recent years (Table 6.1, section D). Some of the relationship between religion and party loyalty is due to the SES differences among religious groups. Yet religious conviction and group identification also seem to be involved.

Internationalism and concern for social justice, rooted in the religious and ethnic traditions of Judaism, have disposed many Jews toward the Democratic Party as the party of international concern, support for Israel, and social and economic justice.[15] The long-standing ties of Catholics to the Democratic Party reflected the party's greater openness to Catholic participation and political advancement. Most of the national chairmen of the Democratic Party during the past century have been Catholics and the only Catholic presidential nominees of a major party have been Democrats.

Northern white Protestants have trended Republican ever since the party began, but the relationship is complex. In recent years, we have seen a division between mainline Protestant denominations and white evangelicals. According to the Pew Research Center, white evangelical Protestants were evenly divided between Democratic and Republican partisanship as recently as the late 1980s, but by 2003 there were almost twice as many Republicans among this group as Democrats.[16] These evangelical Christians had particular impact on the 2004 elections, when more than 26 million white evangelicals went to the polls, comprising almost a quarter of the electorate, and three-quarters of them voted for President Bush. Increasing support for the Republicans among white "born-again" Protestants, especially in the South, is due in part to the parties' stands on issues such as abortion and school prayer as well as to Republican leaders' social conservatism and emphasis on traditional values.[17]

More generally, voters who consider themselves very religious are now substantially more Republican than Democratic. In fact, the greatest religious difference in voting preferences in the early 2000s, and arguably the best predictor of partisanship more generally, is not the difference between Catholics and Protestants but between those who attend church or other houses of worship regularly and those who attend only rarely or not at all.

Racial Divisions

Decades ago, the Republican Party, which was founded to abolish slavery, was associated with racial equality in the minds of both black and white Americans. Between 1930 and 1960, however, the partisan direction of racial politics turned 180 degrees. It is now the Democratic Party that is viewed as standing for racial equality. As a result, blacks identify as Democrats in overwhelming numbers today, as they have since at least the 1960s, regardless of their SES, region, or other social characteristics (Table 6.1, section E). In a recent poll, two-thirds of blacks interviewed agreed that the Democratic Party is committed to equal opportunity; only three in ten blacks said that about the Republican Party.[18] In 2004, 88 percent of blacks reported voting for Kerry, compared with only 41 percent of whites.[19] There is no closer tie between a social group and a party than that between blacks and the Democrats.[20]

Ethnic Divisions

Latinos are the fastest-growing segment of the United States population. The 2000 U.S. Census showed that the Latino population grew by nearly 60 percent in the previous decade to more than 35 million, and then to 41 million by mid-2004. Latinos have surpassed non-Hispanic blacks as the nation's largest minority group. Latinos have long exercised voting strength in states such as California, Texas, and Florida. As their numbers shoot up nationwide, both parties work harder to attract Latino voter support, just as Latinos seek to gain political influence to the same degree achieved by blacks. In fact, a White House pollster warned that unless Republicans steadily increased their share of the Latino vote in 2004 and beyond, Republican candidates would lose those elections.[21]

Yet winning the Latino vote is easier said than done, mainly because Latinos include many different nationalities with differing interests. The Cuban émigrés who settled in Miami after Fidel Castro took power in the 1950s tend to be conservative, strongly anti-Communist, and inclined to vote Republican, whereas the larger Mexican-American population in California leans Democratic. Surveys show that most Latino voters identify themselves as Democrats, but Republican strategists see Latinos as potentially responsive to a socially conservative message.[22] Republican strategists worked hard to deliver that message in the 2004 elections, with efforts ranging from advertising on Spanish-language TV stations to President Bush's proposal to give temporary legal status to undocumented (and often Mexican or Central American) workers. They seem to have succeeded; Latinos divided more evenly between the parties in 2004 than they had in previous elections.

Gender Divisions

For more than two decades, the votes and stands of women have diverged from those of men (see Table 6.1, section F). In 1980, about 6 percent more women voted for Jimmy Carter than men did. The so-called gender gap grew after that. Men rated President Reagan much more positively than women did, and by the mid-1980s, the gender difference had extended to partisanship; men were less likely than women to identify as Democrats. This partisan gender gap increased in the 1990s. It closed a bit in 2004, when President Bush increased his support among women. But the gap opened again in early 2005 as economic concerns replaced war and terrorism on the political agenda.[23] The gender gap has not developed as a result of women becoming more Democratic. Instead, both men and women have become more Republican, but men have done so at a faster pace and to a greater degree.[24]

Why should gender be related to partisanship? Studies of the gender gap suggest that there are differences between men's and women's attitudes on some major issues; on average, women express greater support for social programs and less support for defense spending. These differences correspond with the two parties' issue agendas; the Democratic Party emphasizes education, health care, and other social programs, whereas the Republicans put a priority on military strength and tax cuts. People's attitudes toward gender equality and abortion, in particular, have become more closely correlated with their party identification during the past three decades, and when these and other "women's issues" are stressed by candidates, a gender gap is more likely to appear.[25] The national parties also project some lifestyle differences that may affect men's and women's partisanship. Among members of the U.S. House and Senate first elected in 2002, for instance, 80 percent of those who list their spouse as sharing their last name were Republicans, and almost 70 percent of those whose spouse had a different last name were Democrats.[26]

Single women have become a particularly distinctive Democratic constituency. According to a *Los Angeles Times* national exit poll in 2004, 64 percent of single women (comprising almost one in five voters) supported John Kerry.[27] Single women, and especially single mothers, are probably more economically insecure on average than married women are, and thus could be more likely to see government social programs as an ally.

* * * * *

MAJOR CHANGES IN THE PARTIES' SUPPORTING COALITIONS

Liberal northern Democrats in the late 1940s pressed their party to deliver on the long-delayed promise of civil rights for blacks. When Democratic administrations responded, and began to use federal power to end the racial segregation of schools and public accommodations such as restaurants and hotels, some conservative white southerners felt betrayed by their national party. They found an alternative in 1964 when Republican presidential candidate Barry Goldwater opposed the Civil Rights Act. Goldwater argued that no matter how much Republicans supported civil rights, the party's commitment to smaller government and states' rights precluded the federal government from forcing integration on reluctant state governments.

Soon after, when the Voting Rights Act restored southern blacks' right to vote, their overwhelmingly Democratic voting patterns led the national Democratic Party to become even more liberal on race and other issues closely linked with race. Both national parties, then, had markedly changed their positions on this issue. The Democrats moved from an acceptance of segregation in the South to a commitment to use government as the means to secure rights for black Americans. The Republicans, with roots in the abolitionist movement, reacted against the big-government programs of the New Deal with a commitment to states' rights and small government, even at the cost of the party's traditional pro–civil rights stand.[33]

These changes in the parties' positions on race led to a slow reformation of their constituencies. . . . [C]hanges between the 1950s and 2000 in the representation of various groups within the Democratic and Republican parties in the electorate [have been important]. [Consider] first . . . the dramatic changes with regard to race. Blacks were only 6 percent of the Democratic party in the electorate, on average, between 1952 and 1960; at this time, of course, very few southern blacks were permitted to vote. By the 1992–2000 period, blacks constituted almost 20 percent of all Democrats, and Latinos, Asian Americans, and Native Americans added another 10 percent. The change was especially profound in the South; exit polls in 2000 showed that blacks made up a majority (52 percent) of the Democratic voters in the Deep South states of Alabama, Georgia, Louisiana, Mississippi, and South Carolina.[34]

At the same time, southern whites, who were a quarter of the Democratic partisans in the 1950s, dropped to just 16 percent in the 1990s (and this is probably an exaggeration of Democratic strength in the South, because change in people's party ID often lags behind changes in their voting behavior). Surveys show that in 1956, 87 percent of white southerners called themselves Democrats, but in 2000 only 24 percent did so.[35] The Democratic Party's loss was the Republican Party's gain; by the 1990s, southern whites had increased from a mere 8 percent to more than a quarter of the Republican party in the electorate, and northern whites had dropped from 89 percent to 66 percent of Republican partisans.

There have been other important changes in the parties' coalitions since Roosevelt's time. One has been an almost complete regional shift. The Northeast used to be a Republican stronghold, though dominated mainly by liberal and moderate Republicans. Now it is predominantly Democratic, as is the formerly Republican West Coast. The Mountain West used to be a Democratic region in the 1950s, but a relatively conservative one; now, like the South, it is strongly Republican. Another has been an even greater income difference between the two parties . . . By 2000, upper-income people had become a smaller part of the Democratic coalition and lower-income people were even less prominent among Republicans. In addition . . . there are new fault lines that divide the parties now, involving religiosity, gender, sexual orientation, and marital status.

So the current Democratic party in the electorate differs from the New Deal coalition in several important ways. Although it continues to include big-city dwellers, lower-income and less-educated people, and a high concentration of minority races and religions, the Democrats have lost a portion of union members and Catholics and a majority of white southerners. On the other hand . . . the party has gained a lot of support among liberals, Northeast and West Coast residents, unmarried people, gays, and those who don't consider themselves religious. In contrast, although the Republican coalition is still heavily white, higher-income, and Protestant, its Protestant base has shifted from the mainline denominations to the evangelical churches. Republicans have also gained more support from Catholics, southerners, people who live in suburban and rural areas, men, and those who define themselves as conservatives.

Notes

1. See, for example, Edward G. Carmines and James A. Stimson, *Issue Evolution* (Princeton: Princeton University Press, 1989) and Paul M. Sniderman and Thomas Piazza, *The Scar of Race* (Cambridge: Harvard University Press, 1995).

4. See V. O. Key, Jr., "A Theory of Critical Elections," *Journal of Politics* 17 (1955): 3–18; Walter Dean Burnham, *Critical Elections and the Mainsprings of American Politics* (New York: Norton, 1970); and James L. Sundquist, *Dynamics of the Party System* (Washington, DC: Brookings Institution, 1973).

9. Jeff Manza and Clem Brooks, *Social Cleavages and Political Change* (Oxford: Oxford University Press, 1999).

10. James Madison, *The Federalist No. 10*. November 22, 1787.

11. See Paul R. Abramson, John H. Aldrich, and David W. Rohde, *Change and Continuity in the 2000 and 2002 Elections* (Washington, DC: CQ Press, 2003), pp. 113–115.

12. Jeffrey M. Stonecash, *Class and Party in American Politics* (Boulder, CO: Westview Press. 2000), pp. 13 and 139, and Chapter 4.

13. See Russell J. Dalton, Scott C. Flanagan, and Paul Allen Beck, eds., *Electoral Change in Advanced Industrial Democracies* (Princeton, NJ: Princeton University Press, 1984).

14. Henry E. Brady, "Trust the People: Political Party Coalitions and the 2000 Election," in Jack N. Rakove, *The Unfinished Election of 2000* (New York: Basic Books, 2001), p. 55.

15. Steven M. Cohen and Charles S. Liebman. "American Jewish Liberalism," *Public Opinion Quarterly* 61 (1997): 405–430. See also L. Sandy Maisel and Ira N. Forman, eds., *Jews in American Politics* (Lanham, MD: Rowman & Littlefield. 2003).

16. Robin Toner, "Voters Are Very Settled, Intense and Partisan, and It's Only July," *New York Times*, July 25, 2004, p. 1.

17. See David C. Leege and Lyman A. Kellstedt, eds., *Rediscovering the Religious Factor in American Politics* (Armonk, NY: M. E. Sharpe, 1993); and Russell Muirhead, Nancy L. Rosenblum, Daniel Schlozman, and Francis X. Shen, "Religion in the 2004 Presidential Election," in Larry J. Sabato, ed., *Divided States of America* (New York: Longman, 2006), pp. 221–242.

18. "Stay or Go?" *Washington Post*, December 17, 2002, p. A8.

19. CNN exit poll data at www.cnn.com/ELECTION/2004/pages/results/states/US/P/00/epolls.0.html (accessed June 29, 2005).

20. On black political behavior, see Katherine Tate, *From Protest to Politics* (Cambridge, MA: Harvard University Press, 1994). On racial differences in issue attitudes, see Donald R. Kinder and Nicholas Winter, "Exploring the Racial Divide," *American Journal of Political Science* 45 (2001): 439–453.

21. Dan Balz, "Incumbent Reaches Beyond His Base," *Washington Post*, January 8, 2004, p. A1.

22. "Most Hispanics Say They're Democrats," *Washington Post*, October 4, 2002, p. A8.

23. Brian Faler, "Women Returning to Democratic Party, Poll Finds," *Washington Post*, May 10, 2005, p. A9.

24. Janet M. Box-Steffensmeier, Suzanna De Boef, and Tse-Min Lin, "The Dynamics of the Partisan Gender Gap," *American Political Science Review* 98 (2004): 515–528; and Karen M. Kaufman and John R. Petrocik, "The Changing Politics of American Men," *American Journal of Political Science* 43 (1999): 864–887.

25. Kira Sanbonmatsu, *Democrats, Republicans, and the Politics of Women's Place* (Ann Arbor: University of Michigan Press, 2002), Chapter 3; see also Christina Wolbrecht, *The Politics of Women's Rights* (Princeton: Princeton University Press, 2000); and Brian Schaffner, "Priming Gender," *American Journal of Political Science* 49 (2005): 803–817.

26. Calculated from *CQ Weekly's* "Special Report: Election 2002: New Senators, New Representatives," November 9, 2002, pp. 2948–2970.

27. Located at www.pollingreport.com/2004.htm#Exit (accessed June 26, 2005).

33. Nicholas A. Valentino and David O. Sears, "Old Times There Are Not Forgotten," *American Journal of Political Science* 49 (2005): 673.

34. Merle Black, 'The Transformation of the Southern Democratic Party," *Journal of Politics* 66 (2004):1001–1017.

35. Valentino and Sears, "Old Times There Are Not Forgotten," p. 676.

*O*ne potentially important change in the parties' electoral coalitions relates to the increasing Latino population in the United States. As we note (in Section 9, for instance), the rising number of Hispanic Americans will be critical to many aspects of American politics, and political parties are no different. As the largest minority group in the United States, Latinos will wield great power and this community's votes will be sought after by both parties.

In this next piece, Philadelphia Inquirer *columnist Dick Polman takes the discussion from the Hershey piece one step further and considers the impact of party coalitions on electoral outcomes with a specific eye toward ethnic minorities and the potential power of (and concern both parties have for) the Latino community. As other scholars have consistently found, an individual's party identification remains the best predictor of that individual's vote choice on Election Day; in other words, if you are a Republican, you will likely vote for Republican candidates and the same is true on the Democratic side. Recent examples bear this out: 89 percent of Democrats voted for John Kerry and 93 percent of Republicans voted for Bush in 2004; and in the 2006 midterm elections, 93 percent of Democrats voted for Democratic candidates in U.S. House races while 91 percent of Republicans stuck with their party.[1]*

Assuming these trends hold, the party that can best attract Latinos will hold an important electoral advantage. As such, Polman examines how this important voting block was positioned to impact party politics and other aspects of America politics heading into the 2008 presidential election. It is clear from the title that Polman thinks the Democratic Party was in the best posit into attract votes from Hispanic Americans. Additionally, this piece illustrates how this aspect of diversity in American politics impacts not only party politics but also reaches into public policy, presidential and congressional elections, and other areas of American politics as well.

The American Debate: GOP Drops the Ball on Hispanic Vote

DICK POLMAN

Karl Rove is right.

That's not a misprint.

President Bush's career guru has long insisted that Republicans will never achieve permanent majority status unless they can connect with Hispanic voters. Since his White House departure, he has warned Republicans that their persistent immigrant-bashing is hazardous to their long-term political health. In Rove's words, "You cannot ignore the aspirations of the fastest-growing minority in America."

But the party seems to be rolling up the welcome mat, even at the risk of alienating Hispanics who have the potential to swing five crucial states in the 2008 presidential election. As conservative political activist Clint Bolick warned in an Arizona newspaper not long ago, "If Republicans continue chasing Hispanic voters away, they can kiss their national electoral prospects good-bye."

Under severe pressure from the predominantly white GOP base, most party leaders have largely renounced the Bush-Rove inclusion strategy. Rove's original idea was to enact a reform law that would clear a pathway to citizenship for an estimated 12 million illegal immigrants, thereby crafting the image of a Hispanic-friendly GOP; indeed, Bush was talking about this way back in 2001. But the party base didn't buy it, nor did the talk-radio conservatives, and the reform plan died in June on the Senate floor.

That was merely the latest blow to the inclusion strategy. Last year, when the Republicans still ran the House, they passed a bill that in essence sought to kick the illegals out of the country. The heat on Bush got so intense that he knuckled under and backed a bill to build a border fence. Sixteen months ago, a worried Republican analyst named Matthew Continetti told me, "The optimistic [GOP] message is pro-Latino and inclusive. The pessimistic message is 'Build a wall.' And one thing we know is, optimistic messages win."

Sure enough, in the congressional elections last November, the pessimistic message lost. Whereas Bush captured as much as 44 percent of the Hispanic voters when he won reelection in 2004 (a record high for a GOP presidential candidate), Republican congressional candidates drew only 30 percent in 2006. The latter figure is nine points lower than the GOP congressional share in the midterms of 2002. It also appears that '06 Hispanic voters, by dint of their growing numbers, were pivotal in helping the Democrats win four western House seats previously held by the GOP.

Hispanic Americans, of course, are not monolithic; they hail from Mexico, Puerto Rico, Cuba, Guatemala, Argentina, and many more. And even though, as a percentage of the U.S. electorate, their numbers have tripled during the past quarter-century (from 3 percent to the current 9), they are hardly dominant nationwide.

Nevertheless, despite their ethnic diversity, they share some political traits. They are generally conservative on cultural issues and wary of government handouts. (As John Raya, a Hispanic plumbing contractor in California once told me, "We're just Middle America with a tan.") On the other hand, they generally gravitate to the party that they perceive to be more tolerant and welcoming (traditionally, the Democrats). And while they are still not populous everywhere (accounting for only 2.7 percent of the Pennsylvania electorate, for instance), they now have enough numerical clout to tilt five states on the presidential election map: Florida, New Mexico, Arizona, Nevada and Colorado.

Bush won all five in 2004. But, in part because of growing evidence that Hispanics are souring on the GOP, Democrats say they believe all five are in play next year. It's no accident that the Democrats have decided to hold their '08 convention in Colorado. It's no accident that Democratic presidential candidate Bill Richardson—the first serious Hispanic to seek the White House, and ultimately a strong vice presidential possibility—is stressing his ethnicity and his record as governor of New Mexico.

But the Republicans' worst nightmare could be Florida. According to the 2006 exit polls, Florida Hispanics favored the Democratic candidates at the top of the midterm ballot for the first time in three decades. As Florida Republican congressman Lincoln Diaz-Balart, a Cuban immigrant, reportedly lamented after the '06 elections, "There has been too much of an anti-immigrant tone [from the GOP]. When people start to perceive that immigrants are being put in the same category as a threat to national security, it's hard to get your message across."

Nor does the GOP's traditional edge in Florida appear to be safe any longer. The party has long reaped the votes of the anti-communist Cuban Americans, the most dominant Hispanics in the state, who have long been focused on toppling Fidel Castro. But the younger voters in that community are increasingly registering as independents; they reportedly care more about their economic prospects than they do about Fidel. And they have been joined by an influx of new citizens from Central and South America. All told, as recently as a decade ago, at least 60 percent of Hispanics in pivotal Miami-Dade County were registered as Republicans; today, the GOP share is less than half.

* * * * *

What's most puzzling is that the Republicans seem intent on repeating a sorry chapter in their own history. Thirteen years ago, in California, Republican Gov. Pete Wilson won reelection by bashing immigrants and supporting a referendum to kick illegal immigrant kids out of the schools. Two years later, GOP presidential candidate Bob Dole decided to adopt the same tone. The '96 results speak for themselves: Hispanic voting surged, and Republicans were wiped out in the California legislature. Meanwhile, Bob Dole received only 21 percent of the Hispanic votes nationwide, the worst GOP showing since that electorate was first tracked in 1972.

Karl Rove was well aware of the California lesson. So were the Hispanic Californians who lashed out at the GOP in 1996. I spoke with many of them, and their warning at the time was no different from what Rove is saying today.

Perhaps Sal Mendoza, an insurance broker and school board member in Santa Ana, Calif., said it best: "I think Republicans are so obsessed with their traditional conservatism . . . that they've lost track of the bigger picture. They're sitting on gold"—the Hispanic electorate—"but they don't know how to mine it. And if you can't mine it, you will lose."

Notes

1. All data are again from CNN exit polls: 2004: see above; 2006: www.cnn.com/ELECTION/2006/pages/results/states/US/H/00/epolls.0.html [all accessed January 27, 2007].

*M*odern *American political party politics can be full of stereotypes and general-izations. For instance, Republicans are the party of the rich while Democrats are the poor people's party. There are many others; and from selections both in this section and throughout the book, we will come across similar statements. One of these might be that Democrats are "the gay person's party." After all, the conventional wisdom holds that the Democratic Party is a better fit for gays and lesbians because it has been more tolerant on several issues surrounding gay rights than the Republican Party.*

In the next piece, we have included a selection from Richard Tafel, a leader of the Log Cabin Republicans (a grassroots organization dedicated to working "within the Republican Party to advocate equal rights for all Americans, including gays and les-bians"*), who outlines reasons why he believes the Republican Party is a good fit ide-ologically for gay and lesbian Americans. Tafel argues that the traditional conservative values espoused by the Republican Party—including the promotion of a strong national defense, free markets, individual rights, individual responsibility, and limited government—offer an attractive home for gay Americans.

Tafel's argument encourages us to consider the degree to which demography should be destiny for political party identification and to what degree, if any, the major parties have become complacent in representing minority interests when they believe particular groups are "theirs" come election time.

* Log Cabin Republican mission statement, online.logcabin.org/about/mission.html [accessed January 27, 2007].

How Gay Republican Strategies Can Advance the Gay Equality Movement

RICHARD TAFEL

Perhaps because they do not feel they represent the bulk of gay voters, gay Republicans have been reluctant to lead within the gay movement. But that has so far denied the gay community the most powerful political idea: libertarianism. The information age is uniquely tailored to the libertarian strategy, and the signs are everywhere. Libertarian ideas of strong national defense, free markets, individual rights, individual responsibility, and limited government are gaining new acceptance, but, more to the point, these are ideas that are compatible with and conducive to happy and integrated gay lives.

STRONG NATIONAL DEFENSE

One of the issues that has attracted many gay people to the Republican Party is its traditionally vigorous support for a strong national defense. Given the choice between a candidate for president like Jesse Jackson who is supportive of gay rights and another candidate who has a weaker position on gay rights but supports a strong national defense, many gay Republicans would vote for the person who they feel will offer the greatest basic protection to all American citizens. On the face of this, it would appear that gay Republicans are voting against their own interests, but the gay Republican views his interest as an American citizen in danger of having his country invaded as outweighing the need for passage of a gay rights bill. In other words, what is the point of having a president who supports domestic partnership but at the same time would leave the country vulnerable to an invasion from an outside enemy?

I think that generations of gays who lived through the Cold War and who chose the Republican Party based on their decision on the belief that foreign policy and national defense were of paramount importance. As the fear of attack from outside forces has subsided, so has the importance of the issue lessened as a primary reason for gays to be attracted to the GOP. In fact, the Cold War allowed the GOP to pull together a diverse coalition of voters on social issues who were united against Communism and who prioritized that issue when they voted. The fall of the Soviet Union served to unveil the division within the GOP on social issues, many of which had emerged only over the previous two decades, for example, abortion and gay rights.

* * * * *

FREE MARKETS

My friend Cesar from Colombia had been in the United States for six months when the annual gay pride parade was held in Washington. I'm not a big fan of gay pride

---

parades, where some people feel the need to broadcast all of their personal preferences from the back of a flatbed truck. But my jaundiced view of the parade was ameliorated when I saw it through Cesar's eyes. He had questions about everything. We laughed at the campiness of many of the participants, and the desperation of some to reveal their specific personal sexual desires. As group after group marched by on 17th Street in Dupont Circle, the "gay strip to the fruit loop," as it's known, Cesar wanted to know more about all he'd seen that day. Coming from a country that has a gay rights law, but where being gay means sneaking out to bars and even having to maintain a spouse for public appearances, Cesar was curious about why the United States, which does not have a gay rights law, allows personal freedom for gays, while his country does not. The difference between the two countries is our free market system.

The ability to own our own businesses, spend our income where we want, and work in a free market system has allowed us to succeed in ways that have not been available to gays in other countries. The fact is, America's business community is far ahead of America's legislators in offering employees nondiscrimination. And a quick look around the globe shows that where there are free markets, there are freer gay people, and where markets are less free, gays have fewer civil rights. Free market economies, with their emphasis on the bottom-line success of companies, create a greater opportunity for employees to be judged on their performance and not on their personal lives.

One would think that this relationship between free markets and free people would be obvious to the gay and lesbian community, but that's not the case. In the last couple of years I've had the opportunity to speak before an audience of grassroots liberationist activists at "Creating Change," a conference hosted by the National Gay and Lesbian Task Force. Each year I've begun my comments by articulating Log Cabin's support for individual rights, individual responsibilities, less government, and free markets. And each year, when I've said "free markets," the audience has booed and hissed me.

I've found myself and other gay Republicans repeatedly caricatured as being wealthy. I've been told that I'm a Republican because I'm rich and want to protect my money, though in truth I come from a family of eight and we were comfortably middle-class suburbanites. Most gay Republicans I've met, especially those who are wealthy today, came from lower-income families. Their hard-won success in attaining the American dream has led them to the GOP.

Some gay Republicans come to the party from their experience with the success of the free market, while others come from their bad experiences with the politics and economics of the far left. . . .

❋ ❋ ❋ ❋ ❋

Gay individuals are already thriving in the information age, most notably in the competitive American workplace. The more competitive the industry, the more gay-supportive the companies. Already more than half of the Fortune 500 companies in America have established nondiscrimination policies for their gay employees. It is no accident that Silicon Valley leads the nation in corporate gay-friendliness. They simply don't have time to play games with what their employees do in their personal life; they must by necessity embrace diversity or lose their competitive edge. They need to make a profit, and that means they need brains, creativity, ambition, and contentment among their employees, an environment ideally suited to the openly gay person. Another example of the move toward simply accepting talent however and wherever it is found can be seen in the fact that 50 percent of employees in the technological field are immigrants.

* * * * *

The free market forces of capitalism which gay activists so deride are the very forces that have permitted us to organize and thrive and, in the case of AIDS, to live. As global markets become free markets, the gay movement's continued opposition to them hinders our advancement toward more freedom. Global market trends indicate that in the future the gay movement of the First World will be joined by gays in the developing world.

INDIVIDUAL RIGHTS

In the spring of 1997, I was in the studio of the all-news cable channel New York 1, about to join a debate on the record of Republican mayor Rudolph Giuliani. The news of that day for gay New York politics was that openly lesbian state assembly-woman Deborah Glick had been passed over in favor of a heterosexual black woman, Virginia Fields, when the Democratic mayoral candidate, Ruth Messinger, made her endorsement for Manhattan borough president.

Gay Democratic activists were furious. Ultra-left, openly gay then-City Council member Tom Duane said that he was tired of giving money and votes to the Democratic Party and getting nothing in return. A liberationist leader from ACT UP, Bill Dobbs, called it "the meltdown of the gay leadership" in New York politics.

When I was asked to comment, I said, "It was the meltdown of gay identity politics." What struck me most about that debate was that no one made any reference to the merits of either candidate. The New York Democratic machine was so mired in special-interest identity politics that all it could think about was not offending one group more than another. Identity politics has forgotten the importance of individuality—both candidates were simply symbols in the city's spoils system.

At the same time gay political leaders tell the straight society that they demand respect for diversity and demand that gays should be judged as individuals, they have punished those in the gay community who act as individuals. The wing of the Democratic Party that embraces identity politics views people not as individuals but as members of a group. This kind of identity politics too often forces members to suppress their individualism, and too often requires is groups to trade on their victim status.

* * * * *

Gay Republicans find themselves divided when it comes to support for employment bills that protect gays from being fired, bills such as the Employment Non-Discrimination Act (ENDA), which is currently being pursued in Congress. They ask themselves, how can a person be in favor of passing another nondiscrimination bill and at the same time claim to be against big government? The truth is that I actually participated in the drafting of ENDA, hoping that my input would make it a less intrusive bill than it might have otherwise been. For example, I pushed for language that would ban affirmative action for gays, and while many on the drafting team support affirmative action for other minorities, they agreed to make it clear that that result was not what we were looking for.

The reasons for supporting ENDA apply on a number of important levels. On the purely political level, the fact is that in 1964 America decided on how it would deal with disenfranchised blacks by adding a new law, the Civil Rights Act. A libertarian today might argue that the decision to move forward that way was wrong, an argument Barry Goldwater put forward at the time. But that same libertarian would have to acknowledge that this is the way our country has decided to protect minorities who experience discrimination in the workplace and in housing.

Today in America, if you as a minority are not on the list of protected groups, you may have no defense against discrimination. There are numerous documented examples from around the nation of gays who have been fired from their jobs and of employers who concede that they fired them simply because they were gay. Yet, when those individuals go to court to level charges of discrimination, judges tell them that they are, in fact, not protected under the current law.

The strategic reasons that national gay organizations have chosen to push for passage of such a bill is pragmatic. Protecting gays from being fired appeals to basic American ideas of fairness—an overwhelming number of Americans support a federal law protecting gays from being fired simply because of their sexual orientation.

The less philosophical and more psychological reason for employment bills could best be described as symbolic. There are a few ironies here. The gay person who is most likely to lobby for and support ENDA is likely to be a person who doesn't live in fear of losing a job because he or she is gay. The people most likely to need protections in the workplace are those who aren't out. The other irony about nondiscrimination laws is that they usually pass only after the majority of society is comfortable with the group seeking protection.

The symbolism of this particular piece of legislation isn't lost on Capitol Hill. Both those who oppose and support ENDA do so largely as a measure of their own ideas as to whether or not it is acceptable to be gay. Yes, they will all wrap their explanations for support or opposition in philosophy, but at the end of the day their position on the bill is their way of saying they support or don't support gay people.

Gay people also tend to use bills such as ENDA to track their own progress. If it passes in Congress, gays will feel victorious, members of the religious right will feel defeated, and the country will experience a new climate of opposition to everyday discrimination in the workplace.

ENDA is a case study of the various levels at which civil rights laws play themselves out in our society. I think we all wish that gays could simply be given the same protections everyone else is given under the Constitution, but until that really happens, even gay libertarians will support legislation that guarantees that we're all judged on our merit on the job and that no American is denied the same opportunity as another in trying to make a living. And before he passed away, even Barry Goldwater supported ENDA.

Author Andrew Sullivan is one of the few gay authors who understands the trend toward the individual and less government. He advised the gay community in *Virtually Normal* to shift its focus from seeking government protection to removing government-imposed barriers to equal treatment. He argues for a new movement strategy: equal marriage rights for gays, lifting the ban on gays in the military, and the repeal of sodomy laws.

The movement away from group identity politics toward a respect for individuals in all their complexity is growing. This is the perfect opportunity to show clearly where government and society still discriminate. And while the gay leadership is slow to change, there is a grassroots movement away from big government solutions on issues such as gay marriage, gays in the military, sodomy repeal, adoption rights, and the responsibility of being a good citizen.

INDIVIDUAL RESPONSIBILITY

The AIDS epidemic brought out the gay community's best and worst impulses toward individual responsibility. No community in modern times has responded to its own needs better than gays during the early years of the AIDS epidemic. Friends and lovers suffered and supported one another through the devastation and death, while society in general was either purposely neglectful or outright discriminating. But the epidemic also took a toll on a community that had politically rejected individual responsibility and embraced victimization.

*****

A gay movement that talks only about rights and about getting rights will always be rebuffed by society if rights are not wedded to responsibilities. An AIDS movement that talks only about government solutions and funding, without demanding personal responsibility for behavior, will find it very difficult to lobby for AIDS dollars in the coming generation.

On a very personal level, taking responsibility for your life means that you have some control over your destiny. Accepting victimization, seeing yourself as oppressed, means that someone or something outside of yourself controls your destiny. This key difference runs like a huge divide between liberationists and the assimilationists who see power outside themselves and libertarians who see power within themselves. The failure of a person to accept responsibility for his behavior can be debilitating, and even self-destructive.

LIMITED GOVERNMENT

*****

. . . [F]ear of big government is not shared by many gay activists I've encountered. On the campaign trail in New Jersey for Republican governor Christie Whitman's reelection in 1997, I spoke before a gay and lesbian town hall meeting at Kean College. When I asked the audience if they believed big government could solve their problems, I got nods, smiles, and applause. The era of big government might be over for Bill Clinton, but not for that gay audience.

I then asked if they supported universal health care. Again, I got nods, smiles, and applause. Then I asked how they would feel if the health care system were under the control of Senator Jesse Helms or a Health and Human Services secretary named Pat Robertson. The audience shrieked with horror and began hissing. I replied that all the nose wrinkling in the world couldn't undo the danger of big government in the wrong hands. The big government gays build today can come back to haunt them tomorrow.

No group should be more in favor of limited government than minorities, I said, because as history shows, no group is more likely to be abused by government than those in the minority.

In the early days of the AIDS epidemic the activists got a quick crash course in government regulation and protested at the FDA headquarters. But by the early 1990s the activist community had become the chief proponent of slowing down the approval of drugs through the FDA.

In 1994, Log Cabin AIDS advisor Jim Driscoll, AIDS treatment activist Jules Levin, and I filed a citizen's petition at the Food and Drug Administration to seek accelerated approval for the new generation of AIDS drugs. Contrary to the public perception, we encountered opposition to the early approval of these drugs from every major gay and AIDS organization, on the grounds that the drugs were "rushed to market" for the sole purpose of making profits for the drug companies.

In fact, when the FDA approved 3TC, the first breakthrough drug for the new combination therapy, members of the leading elite AIDS organization, the Treatment Action Group, actually stood on their chairs in a hearing to voice their opposition to its approval. If these groups had succeeded in their goal, thousands of people who have found new life after using the breakthrough drugs in combination would have been dead by now. The antagonism toward the free market from AIDS and gay groups can have deadly consequences for those we care about. When the FDA reform legislation passed in 1997, with provisions to speed up breakthrough drug approval, Jim Driscoll was the only representative from either the AIDS community or the gay community invited to the signing ceremony at the White House.

In 1997, Log Cabin Republicans held its annual national convention in Washington. It had been almost four years since we had opened the national office there, and we gathered only a year after the Republican National Convention in San Diego, where we had successfully prohibited any anti-gay speeches like those in 1992. At the Washington convention, the highlight was the keynote address of Congressman Jim Kolbe, Republican of Arizona. He was the chairman of a House Appropriations subcommittee and a leading proponent in the Republican conference of NAFTA (the North American Free Trade Agreement) and free trade. He had also publicly come out just before we all went to San Diego in 1996, and was at the time the highest-ranking openly gay member of Congress ever to serve.

His speech at the convention, which was broadcast nationwide on C-SPAN, was for many in the room a culmination of Log Cabin's work over the years. It was his first address before a national gay audience, and he chose the occasion to assault the big government mentality of the gay left and the religious right:

> I am both fascinated and amused by the convergence in views of some Republicans on the right side of our party with the views of gay, liberal Democrats. Neither would even admit their common philosophy, but it is there, nevertheless. The so-called conservative Republican deplores big government, welfare programs, erosion of personal liberties—and then votes for constitutional amendments to ban flag burning, or to proscribe specific medical procedures for a doctor performing an abortion, or to deny gays their rights to fully participate in our society.

Liberal, gay Democrats, on the other hand, deplore the intrusion of government into the bedroom or the doctor's examining room—and then proceed to wax eloquent for programs that would nationalize the entire health care delivery system, or compel poor people to live in substandard housing operated by the liberal bureaucracy, or decry programs to give education vouchers to lower-income parents so that they might send their children to schools of their own choosing.

We might be pardoned for thinking sometimes that we are the only real Republicans around, consistently advocating smaller government and less taxes. We might be excused for excessive hubris for thinking Log Cabin Republicans are the only gays who really understand that individual liberties are for everyone.

The gay movement, which has until now focused on changing Washington, is beginning to realize the importance of limited government and the realization that real, lasting change takes place in the grass roots. This remains anathema to Washington-based groups that do their fundraising at the local level and pursue their politics in Washington.

THE CHALLENGE TO THE GOP

The Republican Party is at a crossroads. It can maintain the traditional tenets of the party of Lincoln: individual rights, individual responsibility, free markets, limited government, and a strong national defense. And it can invite anyone who believes in these core principles to join the party. If the leaders in the GOP choose this path it will become a strong, majority party that can offer true leadership to America as we fully enter the information age.

Or the GOP can pander to the religious right, which has gained some prominence in the party through its work in the local and state apparatus, not through any shared vision of the party's core principles. The Republican Party could reject its traditional tenets and adopt new core principles based on a fundamentalist Christian interpretation of the Bible. This would require new litmus tests that would cast out most elected GOP officials today. The GOP would require each Republican to be anti-gay, anti-abortion, pro-school prayer, pro-protectionism, pro-isolationism, anti-big business, anti-education, and anti-immigration. It would be a party that uses the power of a big, paternalistic government to impose an uncompromising social agenda on every American and every local community. Candidates who are divorced or who have admitted to drug use or adultery would be turned away; many who already control certain state parties, such as the party in Texas, are pressing to excommunicate any Republican who does not vocally support every comma and period of their extreme platform. If the party chooses this path, it will return to being a minority party with regional strength limited to certain communities in the Deep South and mountain West.

* * * * *

So the choice for the GOP is clear and simple, not complicated. And whatever side you are on, one thing is for sure—it is not going away any time soon. Those who just put their heads in the sand hoping it will evaporate somehow will only find themselves forced into a corner. Bob Dole learned that lesson the hard way in his final campaign for the presidency.

---◈◈◈---

O *ne view of political parties describes them as being constructed of three legs—*
party in the electorate, party as organization, and party in government. The first
three pieces of this section have dealt with party in the electorate; Section 10 covers
party in government. In the final piece of this section, we switch gears and include a
piece on party as organization.

Here, Melissa Haussman discusses how women have been represented in the
Democratic and Republican parties' national organizational structures over time.
Haussman illustrates how neither party was very inclusive until relatively recently
and that the work of a few women on each side increased the number of women as
decision makers in both parties. She includes a discussion of women's roles and impact
as leaders in their party organization as, among other roles, delegates to the national
committees. While it was arguably a slow rise, women today play an important role
in shaping the policy of both party organizations.

Can Women Enter the "Big Tents"? National Party Structures and Presidential Nominations

Melissa Haussman

In the summer of 2001, the Republican and Democratic Parties each announced women-focused initiatives that could help women get nominated for president.[1] The presence of a viable candidate pool of women who possess electoral experience in the state legislatures, statewide elective office, or Congress (13 percent in the latter and 24 percent as a state legislative average) is another hopeful sign [Editors' Note: See Section 10 for more details on this point]. In 2002, five states have women governors who were elected, at least partially, on the typical "chief executive" criterion of economic management ability.[2] With the parties' awareness of women's majority status as voters and increasing representation in electoral office, it seems reasonable to expect a woman's nomination by a major party within the next few presidential election cycles.

Some may question whether parties still matter in the presidential nominating process. To a certain degree, at least regarding presidential elections, the debate concerns different party levels.[3] Some commentators find their evidence for a declining

---

Melissa Haussman, "Can Women Enter the 'Big Tents'? National Party Structures and Presidential Nominations." From *Anticipating Madam President* edited by Robert P. Watson and Ann Gordon, pp. 59–79. Copyright © 2002 by Lynne Rienner Publishers, Inc. Used with permission of the publisher.

role in the increased importance to candidates of media, money from nonparty sources, and more evident "self-starter" routes to candidacy. Still others argue that the selection of nominees through the primary process since 1972 has all but destroyed state party leaders' control over delegate selection.

* * * * *

The argument advanced in this chapter is that political party structures remain important to a presidential nomination bid. Their importance is less overt during the invisible primary and the primary season, and sometimes scholars have to do investigative work to find out exactly when and how they matter. Party structures and networks do matter at those stages and are shown to clearly matter during the presidential general election. . . .

* * * * *

WOMEN'S POLICY AND ELECTORAL COMMITTEES IN THE NATIONAL PARTIES

This part of the discussion traces the presence of women in the national committee structure, both during and between national conventions. One of the earliest official commitments to gender equality was the "Fifty-Fifty Rule," adopted by both the Democrats and the Republicans, stating that men and women must be equally represented on all nationally appointed party committees. This mandate is carried out via the different national committee selection mechanisms of the two parties and, in certain instances, is said to trickle down to state and local party committees as well.[53] Currently, there are fifteen women Republican state committee chairs.[54] Each state committee sends one male and one female delegate to the national committee. The DNC has a rule that each state committee chair and vice chair must be of opposite sexes to achieve gender balance. Thus, the Democrats have fifteen women state committee chairs and thirty-five women state committee vice chairs.[55] These numbers constitute significant increases over their 1996 levels, especially since "in the post-reform party system, the post of state party chair now serves as a stepping stone to elective office for both men and women."[56]

In 1952, when state committee chairs were added to the RNC, it tilted the balance on the national committee even more toward a male majority. Currently, the RNC requires that one-third of its membership be female.[57] In 1960, the Republicans added the requirement that half of all convention committee members be women; this requirement does not apply to delegates because "the Republican party has traditionally regarded the selection of delegates as a state matter."[58] The Democrats added the rule requiring equal gender representation among convention delegates in 1971. Following the rise of women delegates at the Democratic National Conventions, there was a noticeable increase in women at Republican conventions from 1972 to 1980 to about one-third of the overall number of delegates.[59] It must be noted that the two parties did not simply have an epiphany at one point regarding the necessity of including women in reasonably proportional numbers at the national conventions. It was the result of hard work by the National Women's Political Caucus (NWPC) since its founding in 1971, "an important political battle . . . that succeeded in doubling and tripling women's representation in the post-party reform era."[60]

Both national parties have the rule of gender balance at the chair level; so if a woman is chair, a man will be vice chair. So far, each party has had only one woman as chair of its national committee: Jean Westwood of the Democratic Party and Mary Louise Smith of the Republican Party. It has been noted that they were figureheads, in that they were appointed before the second-wave women's movement had become institutionalized. Even more significantly, neither was treated to the same perks as all other (male) national party leaders have enjoyed, and each one was removed after the election, instead of being kept on as chair "during the crucial party-building years between conventions."[61]

The route to chairmanship of the national party depends on whether the party controls the White House or not, and so too does the number of women delegates to the Republican National Convention. Following a Republican culture described by Jo Freeman as having "whom you know" rules for advancement, "in 1984, the proportion of Republican women increased to a record 44 percent largely through the intervention of President Reagan's campaign manager, Ed Rollins, who personally called each state party." . . . After the 1984 convention, when there was a contested primary in 1988, the "proportion of women delegates" at the Republican National Convention returned to about one-third.[62] A similar comparison was made between the uncontested Republican primary in 1992 and the contested one in 1996.

Since women's presence in elected office is continually increasing, by 2002 they constituted more of the Democratic superdelegates as well. Democratic women currently comprise two of the nation's governors, fifteen chairs of state committees and thirty-five vice chairs, and fifty-four members of the U.S. Congress.[63] The addition of these unpledged delegates to the required floor of 50 percent of pledged delegates means that women constitute an important voting bloc for issues still decided at the national conventions, such as platform and rules changes. Also, the women superdelegates can be an important group to lobby on behalf of presidential contenders in the years before the convention.

The two oldest "women's divisions" within the Democratic Party structure are the "women's bureaus," begun after national suffrage was granted in 1920.[64] They are by no means activist organizations, and their emphasis for most of the twentieth century was on integrating women into the party (i.e., mobilizing the vote) to work on behalf of male candidates.

The "highest" Democratic women's policy committee within the national party structure, listed as a national committee, is the Women's Leadership Forum, begun in 1993. The WLF website states that during the 2000 election cycle, it "raised a record-breaking $7 million, and exceeded its goal of engaging over 100,000 women in electoral and grassroots activities." It also has as its stated goal the formation of a network of elected and activist women across the country and currently has "20 state and regional chapters and a membership of over 6,000 women."[65] Since 1993, the WLF has raised "nearly $30 million for the DNC," although no breakdown is given as to how much of that went to women candidates. Also within the national committee structure is the Women's Campaign Council within the Democratic Senatorial Campaign Committee (DSCC), formed in 1992. During that election cycle, it raised $1.5 million, which was distributed among ten women candidates for the Senate. Since then, it has worked to expand the membership and national visibility of the organization.[66] Current and former DNC staff consider the Women's Campaign Council to be the most important body in efforts to elect more women Democrats, including at the presidential level.

Other "allied" women's groups are the National Federation of Democratic Women and the Women's National Democratic Club (formed in 1922). Although they are usually viewed as more low-key networking organizations for women Democrats, the federation announced the creation of its PAC in December 2001. As its website states, "it has been established to provide financial support for Democratic women, Democratic candidates and other Democratic committees nationwide . . . and state and local offices" (evaluated on a case by case basis).[67]

In the Republican Party, the National Federation of Republican Women (NFRW) is the oldest women's group that has conducted sustained activity on behalf of women. It was given official RNC status in 1988 by being granted a voting seat on the twenty-eight-member council governing the party between national conventions (and therefore RNC meetings).[68] The NFRW describes itself as "the education arm" of the national party. Its website describes it as a "grassroots organization with nearly 95,000 women and 1800 unit clubs nationwide."[69] The NFRW lists its interests as policy development within the party, including issues related to children, women, work, healthcare, and so on. Another interesting activity the group mentions is its ability to generate a "Comprehensive Advocacy Alert," in which a national hotline is quickly set up "by the NFRW president to generate support or opposition for an issue that concerns the members of the Federation." It can also be done in response to a request by a member of Congress, a member of the Executive Committee, or a state federation president. First, the NFRW president contacts the Executive Committee members, who start the chain, as the website states—"until *every Federation member has been reached*" (emphasis in the original).[70] Members are requested to follow up a call to the relevant officials (the phone numbers, addresses, and websites for the White House and Congress are provided) with a fax or email. Another step suggested is to "call a local and then a national radio show," with Rush Limbaugh's show given as the example. This strategy of mass phonebanking, faxing, and emailing has been used by high-profile interest groups, such as the National Rifle Association, since the 1980s, as well as by Republican campaign committees. . . . Another important function of the women's federations in both parties is conducting and arranging campaign schools with well-known consultants. This has been a growth industry in both parties, for the Republicans since the 1980s, and for the Democrats, a bit later.

* * * * *

A final word on the question of whether the two national parties now acknowledge that women's candidacies are potential winners is that many legislative studies of women have shown that, at least for the U.S. Congress, when similar types of races are compared—for example, a race for an open seat or a race against an incumbent—men and women win at similar rates. Most accounts weight the unusual number of open seat races as the main factor for the Year of the Woman in 1992. It would have been interesting if the two parties had been ready for women to run in the last major sweeping out of incumbents, in 1974–1976. Also, the two parties have given women congressional candidates more money, on average, than men in similar races (with the exception of Republican women incumbents in 1994). It was also true that throughout the 1980s, women candidates received a higher average amount from the Republican Party than from the Democratic Party, both because the Republicans had much more money at the time and because the party had an official strategy during the 1980s of trying to counter the gender gap by electing more female candidates.[75]

Therefore, it is clear with regard to the national parties that "where there is a will, there is a way." It is true with regard to recruiting women candidates, supporting them with technology and money, and supporting a particular issue stance. One can only wonder when the will to put the resources that have been used for Congress since 1992 will be used to nominate and elect the first woman president.

THE NATIONAL PARTIES AND WOMEN VOTERS

Within a few weeks of each other in the summer of 2001, both parties announced initiatives to work on getting out women's votes in future elections and educating voters on party issues affecting women. The Democratic Party calls its effort the "Women's Vote Center," and it is coordinated with and by the Women's Leadership Forum at the national committee level. The new project was described as being based in the political and communications wings of the DNC and was designed to get the word out to active and potential women voters. It would thus "educate, engage, and mobilize women voters throughout the nation." As the newly appointed DNC chair, Terry McAuliffe, noted, "we know that when women vote, Democrats win—and with their help, we will make a difference in the lives of American working families."[76] . . .

The project of encouraging women's turnout is called "Winning Women" in the Republican Party and is being coordinated by the vice chair of the national committee, Ann Wagner. It appears that the RNC vice chair, a woman, is allocated special responsibility for women's programs. The Republican Party instituted a similar effort a decade ago.[77]

Although these initiatives are helpful in that they mobilize more women to vote, thus helping the two national parties, they also gloss over a key problem. Study after study has shown that women voters do not necessarily tend to vote for women candidates more than men, so that mobilizing more women voters may help women candidates, but there is no confirmed statistical relationship. That is why, for example, any studies of the "gender gap" show that women and men have voted for different parties (women favor the Democratic Party and men the Republican Party) since 1980. Similarly, more women than men supported Republicans during the 1940s and 1950s.[78] In short, the gender gap is primarily about the different nature of support for the two parties. It may or may not involve the candidate's gender in a particular election. This "party support gap" is based on which of the two parties manages to frame its issues so as to appeal to women, whether it be the pro-ERA stance or "strong leadership of Eisenhower" through the 1950s or the fight to keep social and education programs funded that created the Democratic-leaning gap among men since the 1980s. Both national parties seem to be weighting this strategy very heavily, probably with an eye toward congressional and future presidential elections.

WOMEN AS PARTY OUTSIDERS?

An excellent scholar of women's relationship to the parties, Denise Baer, believes that in the postreform party system operative since the 1970s, the rules for gaining influence for women are harder to interpret. For example, in the "prereform" days, she notes that women were able to become party activists through their previous work in women's organizations. Although official rules in both parties have opened up the organizations to women's participation, Baer warns that women's roads still traverse many minefields. For example, "informal associations" have become more important within the parties, and when they are linked to lines drawn among hardened factions, as they increasingly are, women are likely to be drawn into these battlegrounds. Thus, "the more active women are within the party, the more opportunity they have to be recruited via party-linked factions and groups—a fundamentally decentralized and 'privatized' process beyond the reach of party rules."[79] The result is that to gain more influence within the party organizations, women must demonstrate that they represent the organized women's movement, which is an increasingly difficult task in these purportedly "post-second-wave women's movement times."[80]

Partially because of the ever-shifting nature of alliances within the party structures, women's organizations have quite often used a bipartisan strategy, similar to that of many corporate PACs, in the desire not to shut out any potential ally.[81] Both parties have demonstrated since women received the national vote in 1920 that sometimes women are more important to them than at other times; no party has held a monopoly on being either the "good" or the "bad" guy. One example is that in 1985, the "DNC under Paul Kirk disestablished the [National] Women's [Political] Caucus."[82] It has since been reestablished.

*****

CONCLUSION

*****

Many eminent parties and elections scholars point to party organizations as the "intervening variable," or linkage point, between society (voters) and political institutions. They have noted, as has been noted here as well, that parties exist in a "feedback" loop with other political and social changes. For example, in the wake of great social change, such as the civil rights movement, the Vietnam War, or the loss of a presidency because of a scandal-based resignation, the two parties have undertaken reforms. Similarly, the context within which and the means by which one party undertakes change often drives a convergence toward a new norm; such examples can include changed primary seasons, adoption of a service-based model of party organization, new fundraising tactics, or an interest in representing more women on state and national party committees. These new norms continue the feedback loop toward more change; women candidates work to raise ever more money for their campaigns and seek, via party committees, to have more platform influence, for example. Although some have stated that "conventional wisdom" holds that the first woman president will come from the Republican Party, since she will supposedly be viewed as less "liberal" by the U.S. electorate, that remains to be seen. If there is still an assumption within either of the two parties that women are "not yet ready for prime time" exposure as presidential candidates, it is time to root out that assumption as archaic. Women candidates win at equal rates to men.

The discussion about when the party organizations, both state and national, appear to be most important to the presidential nomination and election process also contributes to this outlined framework for electing a woman president. For example, in the prenomination period of the invisible primary and the visible primary season, party activists and organizers relay, either formally or informally, their opinions about various candidates' chances for a win to crucial opinion shapers in the media, which then affects the candidate's ability to gain money and votes during the primaries. The parties are now in the position to do this for a woman candidate in the early stages of her presidential campaign. Also, during the election campaign, the parties can throw their considerable weight behind women candidates to ensure their election. If the right combination of party issue stances and the gender of the candidate lines up in the right way, the United States will soon be able to proudly claim its first woman president.

Notes

1. They are, respectively, "Winning Women" in the RNC and the "Women's Vote Center" in the DNC.

2. Green, National Women's Political Caucus study; to access the report, see www.nwpc.org/news_weekly.cfm; Burrell, "Campaign Finance."

3. Party decline theorists are discussed in Herrnson, *Party Campaigning in the 1980s*.

53. Jennings, "Women in Party Politics," p. 223.

54. Information provided by the Information Division of the Republican National Committee on May 8, 2002.

55. Information provided by the RNC and DNC on May 8, 2002.

56. Baer, "The Political Interests of Women," p. 115; Baer notes that in 1996 women had ten of the state Democratic committee chairmanships (meaning that they were vice chairs in forty states) and Republican women held six party chairs.

57. Ibid., p. 109.

58. Ibid., p. 111.

59. Ibid., pp. 109, 111.

60. Ibid., p. 110.

61. Ibid., p. 115.

62. Ibid., p. 111; Freeman, "Whom You Know vs. Whom You Represent," pp. 215–244.

63. Some of this information was obtained through analyses available from the DNC Women's Vote Center, May 8, 2002.

64. Cott, "Across the Great Divide," p. 162.

65. Women's Leadership Forum, www.wlf-online.org.

66. Burrell, "Women's Political Leadership," p. 170.

67. National Federation of Democratic Women, www.nfdw.org.

68. Baer, "The Political Interests of Women," p. 111.

69. National Federation of Republican Women, www.nfrw.org.

70. Ibid.

75. B. Burrell, "Campaign Finance," pp. 30–37.

76. Democratic National Committee chair Terry McAuliffe cited in *Democratic News,* June 8, 2001.

77. Burrell, "Women's Political Leadership," p. 171.

78. Mueller, "The Empowerment of Women," pp. 16–36.

79. Baer, "The Political Interests of Women," p. 113.

80. Ibid.

81. Ibid., p. 112.

82. Ibid., p. 111.

References

Baer, D. "The Political Interests of Women." In Lois Duke Whitaker, ed., *Women in Politics: Outsiders or Insiders?* 3rd ed. Upper Saddle River, NJ: Prentice Hall, 1999, pp. 99–118.

Burrell, Barbara C. "Campaign Finance: Women's Experience in the Modern Era." In Sue Thomas and Clyde Wilcox eds., *Women and Elective Office.* Oxford: Oxford University Press, 1998: 30–37.

_____. "Women's Political Leadership and the State of the Parties." In Daniel Shea and John Green eds., *The State of the Parties: The Changing Role of Contemporary American Parties.* Lanham, MD: Rowman and Littlefield, 1994.

Cott, Nancy. "Across the Great Divide: Women in Politics Before and After 1920." In Louise Tilly and Patricia Gurin, eds., *Women, Politics, and Change.* New York, Russel Sage, 1992.

Freeman, Jo. "Whom You Know vs. Whom You Represent." In Mary Katzenstein and Carol M. Mueller, eds., *The Women's Movements of the United States and Western Europe.* Philadelphia: Temple University Press.

Herrnson, Paul. *Party Campaigning in the 1980s.* Cambridge, MA: Harvard University Press, 1988.

Jennings, Kent. "Women in Party Politics." In Louise Tilly and Patricia Gurin, eds., *Women, Politics, and Change.* New York, Russel Sage, 1992.

Mueller, M. "The Empowerment of Women." In M. Mueller ed., *The Politics of the Gender Gap.* Newbury Park, CA: Sage, 1988.

✦ DISCUSSION QUESTIONS ✦

1. As the selection from Marjorie Randon Hershey indicates, the party coalitions of both the Democrats and Republicans are changing. Given the gains that George W. Bush made with the Latino community in 2004 but also the GOP's difficulties in 2006 (as seen in the Polman piece), what might happen with the party coalitions as we move past 2008 and the election cycles that follow?

2. What effect might issues such as immigration reform, affirmative action, and the governmental response to Hurricane Katrina have on the party coalitions?

3. Think about your own background characteristics (race, gender, ethnicity, socioeconomic status, sexual orientation, etc.). According to the "conventional wis-

dom," what party *should* you support? What party (if any) do you actually support? Why?

4. As the proportion of individuals who identify as Latino/a or Hispanic continues to increase in the United States, there is potential for this group to become an even more formidable force in U.S. electoral politics. What factors, if any, work *against* Latinos becoming a dominant voting bloc in the United States? How might these be overcome?

5. Third parties rarely get a high percentage of the vote. Many argue, however, that both the Democratic and Republican parties are deaf to the concerns of many disadvantaged social groups. Has two-party dominance made it more or less difficult for disadvantaged groups to have their political interests translate into policy outputs?

Additional Resources

http://www.logcabin.org
The Log Cabin Republicans are the nation's largest organization of Republicans who, according to their website, "support fairness, freedom, and equality for gay and lesbian Americans." The site contains information the group's agenda, local and state chapters, and events.

http://www.dnc.org and http://www.rnc.org
The Democratic and Republican national party committees, respectively, each contain links to their party platforms, or statements of the party's principles, many of which are impacted by diversity themes.

Dylan's Run (2002) is a documentary film about Dylan Glenn's run for a congressional seat in Southwest Georgia, aiming to unseat incumbent Democrat Sanford Bishop. The film chronicles Glenn's effort to become the first African-American Republican elected to Congress from the deep South since Reconstruction. The documentary offers a unique perspective on racial, ideological, and regional intersections.

http://www.nbra.info
The National Black Republican Association is a national group of African-Americans seeking to expand the reach of Republican principles and policy ideals into the black community.

7

ORGANIZED INTEREST GROUPS: WHAT ARE INTERESTS AND WHO ORGANIZES THEM?

Nancy Pelosi, Speaker of the United States House of Representatives, speaks at an event sponsored by EMILY's List, a political action committee that focuses on electing pro-choice women to the Congress, and is one of the most powerful in the United States.

There may be no more diverse group of political actors in the United States than interest groups. One estimate has the number of organized interests operating in the United States today approaching 25,000;* moreover, estimates place the number of lobbyists—those who carry the water for these groups and other organizations, corporations and unions—in Washington, D.C. at nearly 30,000 and the number of political action committees (PACs) is estimated at over 4,000. While the overall goal of each interest group, lobbyist, or PAC is generally the same—that is, to influence government to act favorably on its policy agenda, the specific goals of the groups that exist are nearly as vast as their numbers. Whether it is a group that is well known, such as the National Association for the Advancement of Colored People (NAACP), the National Organization for Women (NOW), the U.S. Chamber of Commerce, or the American Association of Retired Persons (AARP), or is a lesser-known group like the National Beer Wholesalers Association, the Log Cabin Republicans, or the Alpaca Owners and Breeders Association, each seeks to promote its own interest.

---

* This estimate is taken from Frank R. Baumgartner, "The Growth and Diversity of U.S. Associations, 1956–2004 Analyzing Trends Using the *Encyclopedia of Associations*." Working paper, March 29, 2005.

Interest groups, because of their often-narrow focus on issues, have also become known as "special interests," which carries with it a negative connotation in American politics today. Americans are distrustful of lobbyists and interest groups, in part, because of this (for example, some of the most recent scandals emanating from Washington D.C. involved former lobbyist Jack Abramoff who was convicted of bribing members of Congress), yet nearly one in five Americans have voluntarily joined four or more separate organized interest groups. Moreover, some estimate that the average American, whether he or she knows it or not, has his or her interests represented by at least two separate special interest groups. Thus, while there is considerable mistrust and skepticism toward interest groups, many (though not all) Americans associate with them. Advocates of interest groups regularly cite this fact and stress that the interest groups are only practicing a constitutionally guaranteed right found in the First Amendment: the right "to petition the government for a redress of grievances." What is not to like? The defining issue for the politics of diversity, however, is whether or not all interest groups and all Americans can equally apply the right to petition government and join organized interests groups.

In this section we examine the contributions and challenges of interest groups focusing on the interests of women, African-Americans, and Latinos, as they attempt to influence the governmental process. Interest groups generally have three strategies for trying to affect public policy: an electoral strategy where they try to impact the makeup of government with the hopes that with more elected officials friendly to their position, the easier it will be to pursue their agenda; a legislative strategy where they try to impact the policy-making process by advocating for or against legislation, or by helping to shape the content of legislation; and a post-legislative strategy that includes resolving disputes through the courts or administrative rule-making system. We deal with the first two of these strategies in this section, as the third is covered in Sections 12 (the courts) and 13 (civil rights).

Interest groups are a dominant force in the electoral process in America today. As we also noted above, there are over 4,000 PACs that exist mainly to raise and spend money in the hopes of affecting the outcome of elections; they also donate significant sums money to candidates for office. In this first article, Margaret Talev explores one of the leading and most successful PACs in American elections—EMILY's List, an organization that was born with the goal of seeing more women elected to Congress. As Talev reports, EMILY's List is considered to be the nation's largest PAC, given its spending and contributions to candidates in recent years. Not only has EMILY's List made significant strides toward its goal (see Section 10 for the number of women serving in the House and Senate), but it has created ripples that have been felt throughout

the interest group community, inspiring others to create similar (and competing) groups as well as being a leader in the strategies and tactics of modern campaigning.

EMILY's List: a Force for 20 Years

Margaret Talev

When a group of Democratic, abortion-rights feminists founded EMILY's List in 1985, its goal was to elect women to the U.S. Senate.

As EMILY's List celebrates its 20th anniversary today, that goal seems downright unambitious.

Consider: Women now hold 14 of 100 Senate seats and 67 of 435 House seats in Congress [Editors' Note: see the Legislative Branch section for updated figures after the 2006 elections]. Eight of the nation's governors are women. And polling shows Democratic Sen. Hillary Clinton and Republican Secretary of State Condoleezza Rice among the most popular prospective candidates for the presidency in 2008.

But in no small way, EMILY's List fueled those women's political advancements by building the machine that boosted pro-choice female Democrats—and also by inspiring the creation of dozens of like-minded and different-minded groups at the local, state and national levels.

The Susan B. Anthony List supports anti-abortion candidates, which translates largely to Republican women but also includes Democrats, and, sometimes, men running against female abortion-rights supporters.

The WISH [Women In the Senate and House] List aims to elect pro-choice, moderate Republican women to local, state and national office.

"We gave women credibility in politics like they'd never had before," EMILY's List president and co-founder Ellen Malcolm said. "The members of EMILY's List can take great pride in the fact they have changed the direction of this country. Their contributions have changed the face of power in America."

"What they did, they were very effective at doing—and it was the diametric opposite of all the things I believed were good for women," said Marjorie Dannenfelser, president of the Susan B. Anthony List. Dannenfelser's group was formed in response to the 1992 elections, in which EMILY's List–backed women picked up four more seats in the Senate and 20 in the House.

"I can definitely say, what was dubbed the 'Year of the Woman' motivated me," Dannenfelser said.

EMILY's List gets its name not from a woman but from an acronym for a slogan Malcolm was playing around with at the time: "Early money is like yeast" [it makes the dough rise . . .].

"I never bake," Malcolm, now 58, said in a telephone interview this week. "I dunno, I just thought it up. It was much more the growth and the expansion, that you used yeast to make dough. We knew we wanted to raise early money because it was the early barrier to women putting together campaigns."

For its logo, the group used a red and yellow-orange rectangle that resembled the look of a packet of Fleischmann's yeast. It was an attention-getting theme.

"If we'd called it the Democratic Women's Political Network," Malcolm said, "we would have raised $1.98 by now."

Fifteen women had served before in the Senate, but most had been appointed or elected because of their fathers' or late husbands' political credentials. A couple of Republican women with previous political experience had been elected. But as EMILY's List saw it, no Democratic woman had won a Senate seat completely on her own merits.

In 1986, the newly formed EMILY's List backed two female Democrats for the Senate—Harriett Woods of Missouri, who lost, and Barbara Mikulski of Maryland, who won, made history and remains in office.

EMILY's List saw its membership swell in 1991, when allegations of sexual harassment against Clarence Thomas in his Supreme Court confirmation hearings energized some Democratic female voters.

What made EMILY's List such a force, campaign experts say, was its techniques for bundling, getting donors to give in a coordinated fashion to candidates it recommended. PACs are capped at $5,000 per candidate per election; but last year, EMILY's List had 101,000 affiliates who wrote 106,000 checks to candidates it recommended.

Today, EMILY's List is ranked as the nation's largest political action committee, according to the Political Money Line campaign finance database. It raised $33 million in the 2004 election cycle and has taken in more than $10 million this year, putting it ahead of Moveon.org, various unions and the National Rifle Association.

It served as a model for groups beyond those promoting women, such as Club for Growth, which focuses on supporting candidates in Republican primaries who promote economic growth.

"We certainly picked up on the concept of bundling from EMILY's List," said the group's executive director, David Keating.

Marie C. Wilson is president of a nonpartisan group, the White House Project, which aims to elect the first woman president.

"We have attitudes now that are shifting, not only about people who feel comfortable with a woman president but who think a woman could do as well as a man. That's a sea change. Once people trust women in those nontraditional areas—homeland security, foreign policy and the economy—that allows people to actually trust women in the presidency."

Wilson said women's groups need to do better at recruiting new talent at lower levels of government, however. The percentage of state legislative seats held nationally by women has been stuck at about 22 percent over the past decade, she said. Also, while women's congressional representation has risen, men's experience shows that may not translate to the Oval Office.

"Four of the last five presidents have been a governor," she said.

*T*his next piece is the first to address a common theme of the last three readings on interest groups: what they do after Election Day in a legislative strategy to affect policy and pursue their goals. The first article that hits on this theme, by Ronnee Schreiber, takes a broad view of interest groups and considers how two women's organizations define policy preferences and how they bring this "woman's perspective" to policy-making. However, in her article, Schreiber examines two groups that do not fit some common assumptions about women's groups and she challenges the conventional wisdom as it relates to the policy preferences of these "women's groups." Schreiber examines two conservative women's organizations—the Concerned Women for America (CWA) and the Independent Women's Forum (IWF)—and examines how these groups challenge the assumption that all women's groups are feminist groups as well.*

In this piece, Schreiber illustrates how both organizations define their policy goals, how they arrive at the positions they take (pro-life, for example), and how these policy preferences are born out of gender consciousness, even if they do not fit the current notions of what constitute "women's groups" in American politics. The groups Schreiber examines certainly fit the definition of a special interest group—they have a narrow agenda to deal with issues that affect particular interests (women and families)—but are not the groups that typically spring to today's American mind when asked about the prototypical women's organization.

---

* Schreiber's attention to what constitutes "women's issues" or "women's consciousness" are reminiscent, in part, of readings in the Legislative Branch section on "black interests."

Injecting a Woman's Voice: Conservative Women's Organizations, Gender Consciousness, and the Expression of Women's Policy Preferences

RONNEE SCHREIBER[1, 2]

✳ ✳ ✳ ✳ ✳

A question that has consistently motivated women and politics research is: which women support the "women's movement" and its policy goals?[3] Explorations of this

Ronnee Schreiber, "Injecting a Woman's Voice: Conservative Women's Organizations, Gender Consciousness, and the Expression of Women's Policy Preferences," *Sex Roles*, vol. 47, no. 7–8 (October 2002), pp. 331–342. © 2002 Plenum Publishing Corporation. With kind permission from Springer Science+Business Media.

question have come from scholars examining "gender consciousness" (Conover, 1988; Gurin, 1985; Hildreth & Dran, 1994; Klein, 1984; Miller, Hildreth, & Simmons, 1988; Rhodebeck, 1996; Tolleson-Rinehart, 1992). Their analyses suggest that gender conscious women, that is, those who identify with women as a group and feel affected by the social conditions under which that group lives (Tolleson-Rinehart, 1992), are the ones who support the women's movement and will express a "woman's perspective" on policy issues (Conover, 1988). This literature frequently conflates *women's* activism and policy issues with *feminism;* and it fails to explain the behavior of conservative women. As such, it not only forecloses understanding of conservative women's activism, but leads to mistaken conclusions and assumptions in feminist explanations of women's policy preferences and activism.

In this article I examine two national conservative women's organizations—the Concerned Women for America (CWA) and the Independent Women's Forum (IWF)—to show how conservative women leaders link gender identity and policy preferences. I describe these organizations below. Like feminists, these women, through their organizations, not only act collectively as women, but also bring a "woman's perspective" to policy issues. Although some scholars have not denied the impact of right-wing movements on feminist goals and activities (Conover & Gray, 1983; Klatch, 1987; Marshall, 1995), others have characterized conservative women as victims of false consciousness, pawns of conservative men or right-wing funders (Dworkin, 1983; Hammer, 2002), or "women's auxillar[ies] of the conservative elite" (Kaminer, 1996), thus diminishing the attention and serious consideration appropriate to such a political force. Although we get some sense of the relationships among gender identity, political activism, and policy preferences among feminist women from gender consciousness research, there is little beyond the small number of studies of women's activism on abortion and the Equal Rights Amendment (ERA) (Brady & Tedin, 1976; Ginsburg, 1989; Luker, 1984; Mansbridge, 1986) to explain the link between gender identity and policy preferences among conservative women (see Klatch, 2001, for a discussion of the formation of gender consciousness among conservative women). And, in studies of women's organizations and women's collective policy activism (Boneparth & Stoper, 1988; Bookman & Morgen, 1988; Costain, 1988; Ferree & Martin, 1995; Freeman, 1976; Gelb & Palley, 1987), almost no research exists on how conservative women's organizations act in the policymaking process (for an exception see Marshall, 1995; 1996). As the CWA and IWF are prominent national organizations, these omissions are significant ones.

With its 500,000 members,[4] the CWA is one of the largest grassroots women's organizations in the country and has been described as "a key Christian-Right organization of the post-Reagan era" (Moen, 1992, p. 53). Now 23 years old, it actively participates in national debates on a range of significant political issues. Since the recent weakening of the Christian Coalition, the organization is well-positioned and likely to become an even stronger leader in the conservative movement (Schwartz, 2001). For its part, the high-profile IWF was featured in a *Washington Post* story that emphasized its keen ability to get its leaders on the public airwaves and detailed the number of its associates who have positions in, or strong ties to, the current Republican administration (Morin & Deane, 2001). These political powerhouses include "Second Lady" Lynne Cheney and U.S. Secretary of Labor Elaine Chao. And, in the spring of 2002, the

IWF's President, Nancy Pfotenhauer, was appointed by U.S. President George W. Bush to be a delegate to the United Nations Commission on the Status of Women. She has also been selected to sit on the U.S. Secretary of Energy's Advisory Board.

The CWA and IWF are not "just" conservative organizations; they are national conservative *women's* organizations. Their status as such shapes policy debates and influences political outcomes. They are well positioned to exert influence as counter-movement organizations—to take on the feminist movement, mobilize women, and vie for the right to make claims about women's policy preferences and goals. In the following section I discuss in more depth how the gender consciousness literature portrays the relationship between gender consciousness and policy preferences, and indicate how it fails to account for, or explain, the actions of conservative women leaders and organizations.

GENDER CONSCIOUSNESS AND POLICY PREFERENCES

Although a survey of the gender consciousness literature shows some lack of consistency across the studies (Jenkins, 2002), generally scholars argue that gender consciousness is an important link between gender identity and political action and policy preferences (Conover, 1988; Gurin, 1985; Klein, 1984; Miller et al., 1988; Tolleson-Rinehart, 1992). Measures of gender consciousness include some sense of discontentment with women's social and political status, such as views about gender roles, feelings of relative deprivation, and/or support for the women's movement. In this context, gender identity is politicized and, mostly, feminist. It is the basis for gender consciousness and guides women's political ideologies and policy goals. It appears from this body of work, therefore, that only feminist policy preferences are motivated by gender consciousness. This finding is incongruent with the fact that these same researchers note an increase in the number of women who do identify with their gender and do not support feminist goals (Miller et al., 1988; Tolleson-Rinehart, 1992). Consequently, conservative women's unique, but gendered, perspectives on public policies are never fully evaluated. Indeed, one often gets the impression from these studies that conservative women are either motivated by something other than gender consciousness, or are not really considered to be "acting as women" in the political process.

* * * * *

. . . My concern with the gender consciousness literature is not only its lack of attention to conservative women but its conflation of feminist interests with women's interests.[6] Conover (1988), for example, argued that the "expression of a *woman's* perspective" with regard to policy preferences (p. 1005), is facilitated, in part, by a *"feminist identity"* (p. 1005, emphasis added). Additionally, Tolleson-Rinehart (1992) asserted that gender conscious women are the ones who create gender gaps, even though conservative women, many of whom are gender conscious, do not align themselves with the women who sway public opinion and voting outcomes in more liberal and feminist directions. . . .

* * * * *

In these studies, gender consciousness research, therefore, is more revelatory of feminist beliefs than it is of women's self-awareness as a demographic cohort (Jenkins,

2002). The end result is a clustering of conservative women with men, erasing the potential for, and thus the understanding of, the distinctively gender conscious policy preferences among conservative women. And, even when scholars are attentive to the differences between feminist and nonfeminist women, conservative women are eventually left out of analyses because they are not feminist and presumably act like men. But conservative women are changing public discourse about women's interests; indeed one of the main goals of the IWF is to transform debates about "women's" issues by offering the viewpoints of conservative women. Similarly, the CWA refers to itself as the "nation's largest public policy women's organization." As these interest groups lay claim to representing women, they also have the potential to mobilize women and link them to conservative causes (Marshall, 1996; Schreiber, 2000). In addition, when conservative women leaders act as women to make claims for women, they undermine feminist claims to knowing and representing women's interests.

My corrective to the omission of conservative women from the gender consciousness literature is to study conservative women collectively organized, that is, in women's organizations. Although the gender consciousness literature mostly focuses on women at the mass level, it can also be used to explain women active at the elite level and those organized into interest groups. We know, for example, that feminist women's organizations can be gender conscious in that they have organized collectively as women and speak for women from a woman's perspective (Costain, 1988; Ferree & Martin, 1995; Gelb & Palley, 1987). Building on the knowledge we have about feminist organizations and their policy advocacy, but using concepts from the gender consciousness literature, I show that conservative women collectively organized are gender conscious in their expression of women's policy interests. That is, I apply insights about the relationship between gender consciousness and policy preferences among women at the mass level to women organized at the elite institutional level. . . .

The CWA and IWF are clearly gender conscious in one sense: they are women's organizations and identify themselves as such (Schreiber, 2002). But, without seeing or understanding the relationship between gender consciousness and policy preferences for conservative women, we cannot adequately explain the terrain of political debates on a range of important political issues. Thus, I ask if and how collectively organized conservative women are gender conscious in their expression of public policies. That is, do they, like, feminist activists and organizations, articulate a "woman's perspective" on policy issues?

※ ※ ※ ※

THE ORGANIZATIONS

Both the CWA and IWF represent conservative women, though each speaks for a slightly different constituency. Like feminists, conservative women are not monolithic. Klatch (1987) categorized them as either social conservatives or laissez-faire conservatives, with each expressing a different worldview about gender, religion, economics, and the role of government. *Social conservatives* are deeply religious, see the traditional heterosexual family as the core of society, and root social problems in the moral realm. *Laissez-faire conservatives* point to the economic realm as the source of problems, and emphasize individuality and the desire for freedom from government intrusion (Klatch, 1987). Klatch (1987) also argued that socially conservative women tend to be gender identified, whereas laissez-faire conservative women do not recognize their "collective interests as women" (p. 10) and are not necessarily antifeminist. Although the organizations I study generally conform to Klatch's distinctions, with the CWA being composed of socially conservative women and the IWF of laissez-faire conservatives, the laissez-faire conservatives of the IWF also express the need to act collectively as women and thus have formed into a women's organization. Unlike the laissez-faire women that Klatch interviewed, this group of laissez-faire conservatives does believe that feminism is, at least partly, to blame for many social and economic problems. Thus, both organizations are explicitly antifeminist and both believe that feminists have undervalued the need for attention to gender differences between women and men. Despite these variations from Klatch's ideal types, these two organizations nicely represent the range of conservative women in the United States.

Concerned Women for America (CWA)

The CWA was founded in 1979 by Beverly LaHaye. Its formation and subsequent growth coincided with the politicization of the Christian Right in the late 1970s and early 1980s (Green, Guth, Smidt, & Kellstedt, 1996).[8] Originally located in San Diego, California, the CWA began with local prayer chapters that mobilized women around issues such as opposition to the equal rights amendment (ERA) and legalized abortion. In 1987, the CWA relocated to Washington, D.C., establishing a national office and a national presence. Today the CWA has a professionally staffed office in Washington, D.C., and members in all 50 states, and claims to be the largest women's organization in the United States.[9] Through e-mail, a monthly magazine, a website, and phone calls, its national staff work closely with local members, updating them on legislative affairs and training them to be effective activists. CWA's socially conservative mission, according to its website, is to "protect and promote Biblical values among all citizens—first through prayer, then education and finally by influencing our society—thereby reversing the decline in moral values in our nation" (www.cwfa.org/about). Its multi-issue policy agenda includes opposition to homosexuality, abortion, pornography, and funding the United Nations. Through advocacy on its issues, the CWA works in coalition with such conservative organizations as the Christian Coalition, the American Family Association, the Family Research Council, and several antiabortion groups.

Independent Women's Forum

In comparison to the CWA, the IWF is a much younger and smaller organization. Although it only claims about 1,600 paid subscribers to its publications, this media-savvy group has garnered considerable attention and clout since its founding. Established in 1992, it grew out of a group of women who worked for the George H. W. Bush administration and who met regularly to hear speakers and network. These conservative women leaders are well connected to, or are themselves, key policy and opinion makers (Morin & Deane, 2001). Resembling more of a think tank than a grassroots organization, the IWF was founded to take on the "old feminist establishment" (Independent Women's Forum [IWF], 1996). As a group of laissez-faire conservatives (Klatch, 1987), it describes itself as an organization that promotes "common sense" and provides "a voice for American women who believe in individual freedom and personal responsibility . . . the voice of reasonable women with important ideas who embrace common sense over divisive ideology" (IWF, 1996). Unlike the CWA, it does not have a grassroots membership, but like the CWA, it employs professional staff.

The IWF delights in caricaturing feminists[10] and "debunking" supposed myths about issues such as the need for an equal rights amendment and pay equity policies. To advocate for its issues, the IWF has collaborated with other conservative organizations such as the American Enterprise Institute, the Center for Equal Opportunity, and the Foundation for Academic Standards and Tradition.

The CWA and IWF as Gender Conscious Policy Advocates

The CWA's and IWF's expression of a "woman's perspective" on policy issues reflects a complex interplay between ideology and strategy. First, both groups believe that women bring gendered and unique perspectives to policy concerns. In this sense, their gender consciousness has ideological roots emanating from the belief systems of the women who lead the organizations. But, as countermovement organizations, vying with feminists over who legitimately represents women, the CWA and IWF also recognize the value of having conservative women as policy advocates. It is more difficult for conservatives to be attacked as "antiwoman" if conservative women are making political claims as and for women (Schreiber, 2002). Thus, the framing of policy goals from a "woman's perspective" both reflects their conservative ideology about gender differences and stems from a desire to establish credibility as women's organizations. In this latter sense, it is a strategic choice—one that exemplifies the power and salience of identity politics in the United States (Schreiber, 2002). The purpose of this study is not to disentangle the ideological effects from the strategic ones, but rather to show the results of both.

In the sections below I discuss one of the primary missions of the CWA and IWF—to offer women's, but not feminist, voices in debates on a range of public policies. Second, I provide in-depth analyses of two policy issues that have been central to the feminist movement for decades—reproductive health and Title IX—to show how the CWA and IWF, like feminists, articulate "women's perspectives" in these cases. Here I offer evidence that challenges the prevailing notion that only feminist women express women's perspectives on policy issues.

JUST "MAINSTREAM" WOMEN SPEAKING OUT

The CWA and IWF chastise feminists for making universalist claims on behalf of women. Nonetheless, both the CWA and IWF also make broad-based claims for women.

In much of its publicity information, the IWF proclaims itself to be the "voice of *reasonable* women with important ideas who embrace common sense over divisive ideology" (IWF, 1996, emphasis added). Here the word "reasonable" is loose and unspecific, suggesting that its constituency of women can be construed quite broadly. In addition, showing that it thinks of itself as speaking to and for a majority of women, the IWF declares: "Who represents the *real* interests of American women? The IWF does, and here's how" (www.iwf.org). The CWA offers analogous reasoning about its representation of women. Although the organization clearly talks about being composed of, and speaking for, "Christian"[11] women, it also frequently asserts that it is "mainstream" (Franceski, 1998). Indeed, in speaking of which women the CWA's goals appeal to, group founder LaHaye claims that "the *vast majority* of women, thank God, want to raise children with integrity and strong character" (LaHaye, 1993, p. 138, emphasis added).

Interviews with organizational leaders also produced narratives about the organizations' perception of the relationship between gender identity and policy preferences. Respondents expressed strong commitments to helping women and examining issues as they affect women. And, according to these organizations, women's interests are not just those associated with traditional women's issues, but also those that arise in the context of dealing with a range of public policies. Although IWF board member Wendy Gramm (Interview: January 20, 1999) initially qualified that "the main mission [of IWF] is simply . . . to educate others about how *this* group of women thinks," she emphatically added that the IWF also seeks to show "how issues affect women, what is the impact on women of different policy issues. So it really is an educational role, injecting *a woman's* voice into the policy debate" (interview, emphasis added). Her colleague Kimberly Schuld (Special Projects Manager, IWF. Interview: November 24, 1998) also expressed how the organization is gender conscious in its expression of women's policy interests: "We talk about the impact on women, not women's issues. That is the way I see it. For instance, we could take a tax issue and say 'how does this impact women' and 'where are you missing that in your communications to women'" (interview).

* * * * *

Similarly, the CWA's former President Carmen Pate (interview: August 18, 1998) noted how the organization seeks to speak for women.

> With every issue, we can bring in why it should be of concern to women, and that is what we try to do: why mom should be concerned, why wives should be concerned, why you should be concerned about your daughters. That is the connection that we try to make. How will this impact women long term? (interview)

Although these organizations are critical of feminists for making universal interest claims as and for "women," both groups link their identities as women's organizations with their stances on public policies. The CWA and IWF also incorporate narratives about men's, children's, and familial interests into their rhetoric. This enables them to link women's interests with conservative rhetoric about families, and to build bridges between women and the broader conservative movement (see Marshall, 1996, for a related argument). From the standpoint of the CWA and IWF, it also helps to mark them as different from feminist organizations, because both the CWA and IWF contend that feminists care little about the interests of men and families. For example, the IWF's Anita Blair (Vice President and Counsel, IWF. Interview: October 30, 1998) told me:

> [W]e don't simply look at what is good for women, because that obviously puts you in opposition to men and children. So our principles are to try and get the

facts, to use common sense, and then to make public policy decisions based on what's best for everybody, for a society, as a whole, not just women.

She added, "I believe that men and children are just as important in the world as women are."

The CWA makes similar claims about men and children, but, consistent with many socially conservative organizations, emphasizes the word "family" to do so. For example, in contrasting the CWA's policy agenda with that of its feminist counterparts, Seriah Rein (New Jersey Area Representative, CWA. Interview: August 6, 1998) noted that the CWA's issues were "family issues . . . [w]omen impacting family issues. They are not all women's issues." Finally, the CWA's LaHaye critiques feminists for not recognizing that women's lives are intertwined with men. LaHaye considers this to be a result of feminists' self-centeredness and an affront to "family values." On this issue LaHaye (1993) wrote,

> The pitfall of the feminist is the belief that the interests of men and women can be severed; that what brings suffering to the one can leave the other unscathed. (p. 186)

Although these organizations formed because they were critical of feminists for claiming to represent the majority of women, both groups talk about their missions in ways similar to feminists. These conservative organizations speak on behalf of women, demonstrating that the expression of a woman's perspective with regard to public policies may not necessarily be feminist. In addition, the CWA and IWF have the potential to transform the meaning of women's interests to be more consistent with conservative values about gender roles and families. In so doing, they effectively compete with feminists over the construction of women's interests.

THE CWA'S OPPOSITION TO ABORTION: IT'S A WOMAN THING

The CWA challenges the feminist assertion that when it comes to abortion rights, it is in the interest of women to be pro-choice. For the socially conservative CWA, opposition to abortion and most forms of birth control is central to its agenda.[12] The organization lobbies for legislation to limit and/or make abortion illegal and opposes federal funding of most domestic and international family planning programs. Although its position on reproductive health issues is consistent with many other socially conservative organizations that oppose abortion because of beliefs about the "sanctity of life" (e.g., the Christian Coalition, the National Right to Life Committee), the CWA also strongly holds that support for abortion and family planning programs hurts women. That is, they are gender conscious in their explication of why they oppose abortion. Women are, according to the CWA, "abortion's second victim" (Wadkins, 1999, p. 2). Talking as women, about women's interests in this case, not only reflects the CWA's gendered perspective on the issue, but also enables it to tackle pro-choice advocates who have long argued for attention to women's bodies and lives in reproductive health care debates.

Another example of how the CWA articulates a "woman's perspective" about abortion policy is found in its discussions about "Post Abortion Syndrome" (PAS). In effect, PAS is shorthand for what the organization believes are negative consequences women face after having abortions. The CWA argues,

Post-abortive women may: require psychological treatment/therapy, suffer post-traumatic stress disorder, experience sexual dysfunction, engage in suicidal thoughts or attempt suicide, become heavy or habitual smokers, abuse alcohol and illegal drugs, acquire eating disorders, neglect or abuse other children, have relationship problems, have repeat abortions, re-experience the abortion through flashbacks, be preoccupied with becoming pregnant to replace the aborted child [and] experience anxiety and guilt. (Wadkins, 1999, pp. 6–7)

In linking specific women's health concerns to its antiabortion platform, the CWA also claims that "abortion can significantly increase a woman's risk of getting breast cancer";[13] therefore, "abortion is deadly—not only for unborn children, but also for the women who abort them" (Wallace, 1997, p. 11). The group urges lawmakers to require reproductive health professionals to inform women of this link and recently touted the case of a woman who sued a North Dakota clinic for false advertising when it claimed in a pamphlet that no correlation has been found between abortion and breast cancer (Green, 2002). Much to the dismay of the CWA, a judge found for the clinic. At the time of this writing, the case was being appealed.

* * * * *

The CWA also raises similar concerns about the abortifacient RU-486, "partial birth abortion" (PBA),[14] unlicensed abortion clinics, and the contraceptive pill. For example, in a Family Voice article entitled "RU-486: Killer Pills," one author warned women of the "dangerous" side effects of RU-486.

Women who took RU-486 in clinical trials experienced firsthand just how "easy" the abortion pill is. Common side effects included: painful contractions, nausea, vomiting, diarrhea, pelvic pain and spasms, and headaches—as well as the trauma of seeing their aborted baby . . . Chemical abortions like RU-486 will *not* advance women's health. (Wallace, 1997, p. 6, emphasis in original)

And, on the subject of PBA, the CWA wrote that not only is the end result of a "purely elective" abortion a "dead child," but,

[F]ew people realize the *danger to the mother.* Dr. Joseph DeCook of the American College of Obstetrics and Gynecology declares *PBA is riskier for the mother than any other type of abortion:* the opening of the cervix for a pro-longed time involves a greater risk of infection. (Wallace, 1997, p. 6, emphasis in original)

Finally, in a pamphlet detailing the negative side effects of most forms of birth control, the CWA cautioned women that,

In the past 30 years, various chemicals and devices that manipulate women's reproductive systems have come on the medical scene. Women need to know precisely what they do and what risks they present. (CWA, nd)

Clearly, these reproductive health narratives promote the CWA's socially conservative antiabortion stance. Of course, this is not without intention on the part of the CWA. As feminists have long argued for redirecting attention from fetal rights to women's health concerns in abortion debates (Daniels, 1993), using gender conscious arguments enables the CWA to counter feminist claims about women's interests. In doing so, the CWA demonstrates how a group of "gender conscious" women can be antiabortion and do so from a "woman's perspective." Although its position on abortion is hardly consistent with that of most feminist organizations, its speaking as and for women indicates coherence between identity and policy preferences for these conservative political actors.

IWF ON TITLE IX: DEMEANING TO WOMEN

Through a program entitled Play Fair, the IWF takes on a prominent feminist policy achievement Title IX. Title IX, part of a 1972 law that outlaws gender discrimination in federally funded educational institutions, has been used successfully to increase attention to, and funding for, women's sports in colleges and universities. The Office for Civil Rights (OCR), a division of the U.S. Department of Education, is the agency in charge of enforcing Title IX. To do so, the OCR developed a three-pronged test to determine if schools were in compliance. Schools could show that the ratio of male and female athletes closely parallels the ratio of male and female students—this is sometimes known as proportionality; a history of expanding opportunities for athletes of the underrepresented sex; or, that the interests of the underrepresented sex had been fully and effectively accommodated. A school only needs to meet one of these three criteria, but in 1996, the OCR issued a clarification stating that the first option, proportionality, was the surest way for schools to demonstrate that they were in compliance. The IWF likens this proportionality option to a quota system and is therefore highly critical of Title IX. It claims that too many schools opt for this test, thereby strangling men's sports and demeaning women's athletic accomplishments.

From the point of view of the IWF, Title IX regulations are akin to affirmative action, a policy the IWF opposes and contends hurts women. Speaking from a "woman's perspective," the organization argues that it is women's relative lack of interest in sports, not discrimination, that creates discrepancies in the numbers of female and male college athletes. The IWF charges that feminists have misinterpreted the meaning of gender differences and women's interests in this case, because feminists are prone to antimale biases. Feminists, it argues, are quick to blame men for women's relative lack of involvement in collegiate athletics and are eager to cut resources for men's sports.[15] As IWF founder Anita Blair said about the enforcement of Title IX through proportionality, "This is mean-spirited, dog-in-the-manger feminism at its worst. Why deny men sports opportunities just because relatively fewer women are interested in athletics?" (IWF, 1997, p. 15)

* * * * *

Finally, the IWF also suggests that enforcing Title IX through proportionality damages women's sports. It contends that it has a responsibility as a woman's organization to care about the issue and inform women about the dangers of implementing Title IX in this way. In an extensive, 35-page policy brief the IWF alleged:

> By allowing, and even encouraging, schools to set high minimums for women's teams, coaches are finding themselves taking on some sub-standard players to beef up the roster. This affects the competitiveness of women's teams, as well as

their morale. It cannot be good for women's sports markets in the long term to field non-competitive teams. (Schuld, 2000, p. 21)

Title IX is one of the most profound legislative achievements of the feminist movement in the past three decades. Certainly it is a "women's issue" from the standpoint of those who fought for it and benefited from it. But the IWF, critical of how the law has been interpreted and enforced over the years, sees it as an affront to women's abilities to make decisions about their interests free of government involvement and ideological persuasion. And, like the CWA, the IWF articulates its concerns from a woman's perspective, indicating that these organizations are indeed gender conscious as they make policy claims.

CONCLUSION

My foray into conservative women's organizations' framing of policy goals does not only highlight the limitations of current research on gender consciousness. It also elucidates the very real and significant consequences of having conservative women's voices reverberating through legislatures and in the media. The presence of the CWA and IWF means clashes will occur among women about the meaning of women's status in politics and the family and about the nature and origins of gender differences and the role of government in women's lives. As gender conscious political institutions, feminist and conservative women's organizations battle over whose stories about women are most representative. And, given that their narratives about women's lives have concrete policy implications, this battle over authenticity is meaningful . . .

* * * * *

Notes

1. Department of Political Science, San Diego State University, San Diego, California.

2. To whom correspondence should be addressed at Department of Political Science, San Diego State University, 5500 Campanile Drive, San Diego, California 92182; e-mail: rschreib@mail.sdsu.edu.

3. Here I use the phrase "women's movement" to mean the *feminist* women's movement as it reflects how the gender consciousness scholars cited in this article have defined and measured the term.

4. According to the CWA, this figure represents the number of people who have contributed money to the organization within the 24-month period preceding the count.

6. There are several other aspects of the gender consciousness literature that fail to explain conservative women's activism. For example, some assert such a narrow interpretation of politicization that they suggest "traditional women" are not likely to seek government assistance in dealing with "privatized" women's issues (Hildreth & Dran, 1994). Others use an "equal roles" measure as one proxy for feminism (Tolleson-Rinehart, 1992). But as Sapiro and Conover noted, an "equal roles" measure may not be an accurate indicator of feminism. As they argued, "the majority of men and women believe that men and women can have different

roles and still be equal" (2001, p. 10). This is certainly the case for both the CWA and IWF, organizations that believe gender differences are natural, but should not be the basis for gender discrimination. For a broader critique of the gender consciousness literature see Jenkins (2002).

8. Most of the members of the CWA identify as evangelical or fundamentalist Protestants (Guth, Green, Kellstedt, & Smidt, 1995).

9. On its website, www.now.org, the National Organization for Women (NOW) also claims to have 500,000 members, but the CWA contends that NOW really has less than 100,000.

10. The feminist movement in the United States is diverse and includes national organizations, community groups, direct service providers, campus-based groups, websites, and list serves (Blee, 1998; Bookman & Morgen, 1988; Brownmiller, 1999; Cohen, Jones, & Tronto, 1997; Echols, 1989; Ferree & Martin, 1995; Katzenstein & Mueller, 1987; Martin, 1990). When the CWA and IWF talk about the feminist movement, however, they are usually referring to nationally organized interest groups, especially the National Organization for Women (NOW), NARAL, the Planned Parenthood Federation of American (PPFA), the American Association of University Women (AAUW), and the Feminist Majority Foundation (FMF). CWA and IWF name these feminist groups as proxies for the entire feminist movement.

11. Although the CWA just uses the term "Christians," it is specifically referring to evangelical Protestant and fundamentalist Christians, the religious group that comprises most of its membership (Guth et al., 1995).

12. The CWA refers to the intra-uterine device (IUD), Norplant, Depo-Provera, and the "pill" as "abortifacients" on the grounds that each of these forms of birth control can prevent a fertilized egg, or embryo, from becoming implanted in a woman's uterus. The CWA recognizes the term "human embryo" to be the same as "unborn child"; intentionally making the uterus "hostile" to the embryo is considered equivalent to having an abortion (Concerned Women for America [CWA], 1998).

13. Its argument is based on a meta-analysis conducted by Brind, Chinchilli, Severs, and Summy-Long (1996). As summarized by the CWA, Brind et al. argued that "early in her pregnancy, a woman experiences a major surge of estrogen that causes immature breast cells to multiply. These cells are allegedly more susceptible to carcinogens, but are protected when a woman begins to lactate. If her pregnancy is aborted, however, the woman's breast cells are left in the vulnerable state, because they do not receive the benefit of lactation that comes from full-term pregnancies" (Wallace, 1997, p. 10). The pro-choice PPFA notes, however, that in an analysis of the approximately 25 studies examining the link between breast cancer and abortion, cancer researchers at the National Cancer Institute and the American Cancer Society found no conclusive relationship. It also asserts that Brind and his colleagues analyzed studies that contained faulty methods and inconclusive findings (Planned Parenthood Federation of America [PPFA], 2000b).

14. This refers to an abortion procedure known as a "D and X" or dilation and extraction in which a fetus is removed whole from a woman. The procedure is most common in second and third trimester abortions (after 24 weeks) and usually performed when the fetus or woman's life is endangered. According to the Planned Parenthood Federation of America (which cites the Centers for Disease Control), in the United States 1.5% of abortions are performed after 20 weeks of pregnancy. (PPFA, 2000a)

15. For detailed arguments against IWF's position on Title IX see the websites of the Women's Sports Foundation (www.womenssportsfoundation.org), and the Feminist Majority Foundation (www.feminist.org).

References

Bacchetta, P., & Power, M. (2002). *Right-wing women: From conservatives to extremists around the world.* New York: Routledge.

Blee, K. (1998). *No Middleground: Women and radical protest.* New York: New York University Press.

Boneparth, E., & Stoper, E. (1988). *Women, power and policy: Toward the year 2000.* New York: Pergamon Press.

Bookman, A., & Morgen, S. (1988). *Women and the politics of empowerment.* Philadelphia: Temple University Press.

Brady, D. W., & Tedin, K. L. (1976, March). Ladies in pink: Religion and political ideology in the anti-ERA movement. *Social Science Quarterly, 56,* 564–575.

Brind, J., Chinchilli, V. M., Severs, W. B., & Summy-Long, J. (1996, October). Induced abortion as an independent risk factor for breast cancer: A comprehensive review and meta-analysis. *Journal of Epidemiology and Community Health, 50,* 481–496.

Brownmiller, S. (1999). *In our time: A memoir of a revolution.* New York: Dial Press.

Cohen, C., Jones, K., & Tronto, J. (1997). *Women transforming politics: An alternative reader.* New York: New York University Press.

Concerned Women for America. (1998, July). Glossary of abortifacients. In Library [Online]. Retrieved July 21, 2000, from www.cwfa.org/library/life/1998-07-pp-glossary.shtmi

Concerned Women for America. (nd). *High-tech "birth control": Health care or health risk?* [Pamphlet]. Washington, DC: Concerned Women for America.

Concerned Women for America. Retrieved September 5, 2002, from http//:www.cwfa.org

Conover, P. (1988). Feminists and the gender gap. *Journal of Politics, 50,* 985–1009.

Conover, P. J., & Gray, V. (1983). *Feminism and the new right: Conflict over the American family.* New York: Praeger.

Costain, A. N. (1988). Representing women: The transition from social movement to interest group. In E. Boneparth & E. Stoper (Eds.), *Women, power and policy: Toward the year 2000* (pp. 26–47). New York: Pergamon Press.

Daniels, C. (1993). *At women's expense: State power and the politics of fetal rights.* Cambridge, MA: Harvard University Press.

Dworkin, A. (1983). *Right-wing women.* New York: Perigree Books.

Echols, A. (1989). *Daring to be bad: Radical feminism in America, 1967–1975.* Minneapolis: University of Minnesota Press. Feminist Majority Foundation. Retrieved June 5, 2002, from http//:www.feminist.org

Ferree, M. M., & Martin, P. Y. (1995). *Feminist organizations: Harvest of the new women's movement.* Philadelphia: Temple University Press.

Freeman, J. (1976). *The politics of women's liberation.* New York: McKay.

Franceski (1998). Interview with the director of broadcast and media, CWA. October 29, 1998.

Gelb, J., & Palley, M. L. (1987). *Women and public policies.* Princeton: Princeton University Press.

Ginsburg, F. (1989). *Contested lives: The abortion debate in an American community.* Berkeley: University of California Press.

Green, J. C., Guth, J. L., Smidt, C. E., & Kellstedt, L. A. (1996). *Religion and the culture wars: Dispatches from the front.* Lanham, MD: Rowman and Littlefield.

Green, T. L. (2002, April 1). Bad day for pro-lifers in North Dakota. In cwfa.org/library/ life [Online]. Retrieved May 5, 2002, from cwfa.org/library/life/2002-04-01-abc-link.shtml

Gurin, P (1985). Women's gender consciousness. *Public Opinion Quarterly,* 49, 143–163.

Guth, J. L., Green, J. C., Kellstedt, L. A., & Smidt, C. E. (1995). Onward Christian soldiers: Religious activist groups in American politics. In A. J. Cigler & B. A. Loomis (Eds.), *Interest group politics* (pp. 55–76). Washington, DC: Congressional Quarterly Press.

Hammer, R. (2002). *Antifeminism and family terrorism.* Lanham, MD: Rowman and Littlefield.

Hildreth, A., & Dran, E. M. (1994). Explaining women's differences in abortion opinion: The role of gender consciousness. *Women & Politics,* 14, 35–51.

Independent Women's Forum. Retrieved September 5, 2002, from http//:www.iwf.org

Independent Women's Forum. (1996). *Who are we? The future* [Recruitment Pamphlet]. Washington, DC: Independent Women's Forum.

Independent Women's Forum. (1997, June). Bad sports: The quota team scores a touchdown. *Ex Femina,* p. 1.

Jenkins, K. (2002). *The paradox of feminist consciousness and political participation.* Paper presented at the annual meeting of the American Political Science Association, Boston, MA.

Kaminer, W. (1996, November–December). Will class trump gender? *The American Prospect,* pp. 44–52.

Katzenstein, M. R, & Mueller, C. M. (1987). *The women's movement of the United States and Western Europe: consciousness, political opportunity and public policy.* Philadelphia: Temple University Press.

Klatch, R. (1987). *Women of the new right.* Philadelphia: Temple University Press.

Klatch, R. (2001). The formation of feminist consciousness among left- and right-wing activists of the 1960s. *Gender and Society,* 15, 791–815.

Klein, E. (1984). *Gender politics: From consciousness to mass politics.* Cambridge, MA: Harvard University Press.

LaHaye, B. (1993). *The desires of a woman's heart.* Wheaton, IL: Tyndale House.

Luker, K. (1984). *Abortion and the politics of motherhood.* Berkeley: University of California Press.

MacLeod, L. A. (1997, October). Mexico City revisited. *Family Voice,* pp. 16–20.

Mansbridge, J. (1986). *Why we lost the ERA.* Chicago: University of Chicago Press.

Marshall, S. E. (1995). Confrontation and co-optation in antifeminist organizations. In M. M. Ferree & P. Y. Martin (Eds.), *Feminist organizations: Harvest of the new women's movement* (pp. 323–338). Philadelphia: Temple University Press.

Marshall, S. E. (1996). Marilyn vs. Hillary: Women's place in new right politics. *Women & Politics,* 16.1, 55–75.

Martin, P. Y. (1990, June). Rethinking feminist organizations. *Gender and Society,* 4, 182–206.

Miller, A. H., Hildreth, A., & Simmons, G. L. (1988). The mobilization of gender group consciousness. In K. B. Jones & A. G. Jonasdottir (Eds.), *The political interests of gender* (pp. 106–134). London: Sage.

Moen, M. (1992). *The transformation of the Christian right.* Tuscaloosa, AL: The University of Alabama Press.

Morin, R., & Deane, C. (2001, May 1). Women's forum challenges feminists, gains influence. *Washington Post,* p. A06.

National Organization for Women. Retrieved September 5, 2002, from http//:www.now.org

Phelan, S. (1993). (Be)Coming out: Lesbian identity and politics. *Signs: Journal of Women in Culture and Society, 18,* 765–790.

Planned Parenthood Federation of America. (2000a). Abortions after the first trimester. In Fact Sheets [Online]. Retrieved April 27, from www.plannedparenthood.org/library/facts/abotaftlst_010600.html

Planned Parenthood Federation of America. (2000b). Anti-choice claims about abortion and breast cancer. In Fact Sheets [Online]. Retrieved April 26, 2000, from www.plannedparent-hood. org/library/facts/factcancer_022800.html

Rhodebeck, L. A. (1996, August). The structure of men's and women's feminist orientations. *Gender and Society, 10,* 386–403.

Sapiro, V., & Conover, P. (2001). Gender equality in the public mind. *Women & Politics, 22,* 1–36.

Schreiber, R. (2000). *"But perhaps we speak for you:" Antifeminist women's organizations and the representation of political interests.* Unpublished doctoral dissertation, Rutgers University.

Schreiber, R. (2002). Playing "femball": Conservative women's organizations and political representation in the United States. In P. Bacchetta & M. Power (Eds.), *Right-wing women: From conservatives to extremists around the world* (pp. 211–223). New York: Routledge.

Schuld, K. (2000, September 2). National girls and women in sport day. In News [Online]. Retrieved April 2, 2002, from www.iwf.org/news/000209.shtml

Schuld, K. (1998). *Why would a woman's group complain about Title IX?* Washington, DC: Independent Women's Forum. Schwartz (2001). Interview with the vice president for government relations, CWA. December 10, 2001.

Tolleson-Rinehart, S. (1992). *Gender consciousness and politics.* New York: Routledge.

Wadkins, J. (1999, January). Reaching abortion's second victims. *Family Voice,* pp. 3–8.

Wallace, M. (1997, January). The hidden link: Abortion and breast cancer. *Family Voice,* pp. 10–11.

Women's Sports and Fitness Foundation. Retrieved June 5, 2002, from http//:womensports-foundation.org

Wuthnow, R. (1998). *The restructuring of American religion.* Princeton: Princeton University Press.

The groups discussed in the Schreiber piece—the Concerned Women for America (CWA) and the Independent Women's Forum (IWF)—are organizations that draw on their membership to help achieve their goals—they write letters and make phone calls to elected officials, as well as engage in other tactics to get the grassroots involved. The two groups also seek out other organized interest groups to work with on important issues; in other words, the build coalitions to make their presence even stronger. This is the specific topic of the next piece by Janita Poe.

Poe takes the reader back to 2002 when, for the first time, the leader of the League of United Latin American Citizens (LULAC), the leading Latino civil rights organization, addressed the NAACP. This piece raises important questions for both the

NAACP and LULAC (and about coalition building in general). Latinos are now the largest minority group in the United States. To what degree, if any, does the NAACP want to maintain its singular focus on the plight and advancement of black Americans? What efficacy is there in "black-brown" alliances? In addition, the article raises a point that can be extended to all interest groups who operate in an open process to petition government—LULAC is only one of many Latino civil rights groups. To what degree then can LULAC claim to represent the interests of Latinos when there is sometimes disagreement among Latino interest groups about what Latino interests are and which interests should be prioritized? Creating a unified message in this context is difficult but the lack of a unified message can also be detrimental to LULAC's (and other Latino/a interest group) goals.

African-Americans, Latinos Seek to Build Coalition

JANITA POE

Standing at the podium before some 3,000 NAACP members at their national convention last week, Hector Flores, president of LULAC, the nation's oldest Latino civil rights organization, suddenly seemed inspired.

"Viva NAACP!" he chanted repeatedly at the end of his speech.

Soon, the audience was on its feet, in enthusiastic applause.

"Viva LULAC! Viva America!"

It was the first time in memory that a LULAC leader had spoken before the NAACP convention. As such, Flores' appearance symbolized the relationship between the main civil rights organizations representing the two largest minority groups in the country—there were emotional feelings of unity, but they were based on a particular speech on a particular day, not a full-fledged alliance.

"So much of our work in our communities depends upon the partnership we celebrate today," said Flores, who was elected president of the League of United Latin American Citizens last month. "As long as we continue to work together, our communities will continue to reap great rewards."

According to the 2000 U.S. Census, Latinos have surpassed African-Americans as the largest ethnic group in the country. Buoyed by immigration, the Latino population increased 58 percent in the '90s, to 35.3 million in 2000. During that same period, the black population rose 16 percent, to 34.7 million.

As the Latino population continues to grow, the role of the NAACP—an organization established to serve "colored people"—is in question. Who is "colored," just African-Americans or others too?

Meanwhile, the existence of several Latino civil rights groups—including LULAC, the National Council of La Raza and the Mexican-American Legal Defense and Education Fund—makes creating a unified voice for minority ethnic groups more difficult.

At the core of the problem, members of these groups say, is the perception that the civil rights groups are too divided and competing for limited resources. Indeed, the battle for jobs, housing, social services and government funding has intensified with the economic downturn over the past two years. In addition, political differences have created some tensions between blacks, who vote overwhelmingly Democratic, and Latinos, who have a more diverse voting record.

THE LARGEST GROUPS

The NAACP—whose defined mission is "the protection and enhancement of the civil rights of African-Americans and other minorities"—is the largest and oldest of the groups. Founded in 1909, the NAACP has 500,000 members and a staff of more than 220 people.

The two largest Latino groups are LULAC and La Raza. Established in 1929 in Corpus Christi, Texas, LULAC has 115,000 members and a staff of about 100. LULAC seeks "to advance the economic condition, educational attainment, political influence, health and civil rights of the Hispanic population of the United States."

La Raza was created in 1968 in Phoenix and has a membership of 30,000 and a 100-member staff. Its mission is "to reduce poverty and discrimination, and improve life opportunities for Hispanic-Americans."

NAACP board Chairman Julian Bond said his organization is eager to strengthen ties with Latino civil rights groups. "It is obvious that there is a growing population of Hispanics in the United States and they have been and will be important allies and partners in the fight for civil rights," said Bond, a former Georgia legislator.

Latino leaders say they, too, want to build coalitions and create a united voice on common issues.

La Raza Senior Vice President Charles Kamasaki said the primary missions of the NAACP and La Raza are "quite similar." "Both of us seek to address poverty and discrimination in our respective communities," Kamasaki said. But Kamasaki said he thinks political and cultural differences—and lack of knowledge about discrimination against Latinos and other nonblack minorities—may keep African-Americans and Latinos from coming together more quickly.

"I hope for rapid progress towards strengthened coalitions and activity," said Kamasaki, who is Japanese-American and was born in Texas. "But we have prejudice, stereotypes and barriers to overcome first."

BARRIERS REMAIN

Among the barriers is a feeling among some African-Americans that blacks are less accepted into the mainstream than other ethnic groups. In addition, despite decades of political activism and get-out-the-vote campaigns, some NAACP members feel their organization is not taken seriously by political candidates. Bond pointed out that some NAACP members felt snubbed by Texas Gov. Rick Perry because he spoke at the LULAC convention in Houston last month but declined to speak before the NAACP.

But Bond said division and debate over individual issues could only weaken the potential power base of black and brown America. "We can't allow outsiders to divide coalitions," Bond said. "There is no profit in competing for who suffered most."

Among Latinos, some say competition for power is a barrier to the growth of their civil rights movement. In addition to LULAC and La Raza, there are at least 50 national and 500 local Latino and professional and civil rights groups. Also, some Latinos have affiliated with the NAACP.

"We have so many distinct groups in the Latino community and they have different cultural perspectives and orientations," said Josie Valdez, vice president of the Salt Lake City NAACP and a third generation Mexican-American. "Even though we are all Latinos, we just don't always agree."

One organization that works to unite civil rights groups is the Leadership Conference on Civil Rights. Established in 1950, the conference brings together some 100 groups representing minorities, women, unions, gays and others.

The Leadership Conference plays a critical role in some regions of the country with large numbers of Latino residents. In Texas, for example, Latinos made up 32 percent of the population in 2000, and blacks accounted for 12 percent. (In Georgia, despite fast growth in the Latino population, blacks were still the dominant minority, making up 29 percent of the population as opposed to 5 percent for Latinos.)

Also, in some largely white areas, civil rights groups have become very integrated, with a strong emphasis on general human rights. Membership in the NAACP chapter in Salt Lake City, for example, is divided equally between blacks, whites and Latinos, with a few Native Americans as well. Among the officers are a black president, a Latino vice president, a Native American vice president and a white treasurer.

Valdez said she thinks people of various backgrounds are open to working for another group's civil rights if they feel welcome and sense common goals.

"I don't think LULAC or La Raza or the NAACP has made it a priority to build coalitions," said Valdez. "It's not that they aren't interested; there just hasn't yet been a burning critical issue to really bring us together. Everyone has been caught up in their own fight."

*T*he final selection on interest groups turns directly to those individuals hired to do interest group's most direct legislative work: lobbyists. Like it or not, lobbyists are *integral to the policy-making process today. Among other things, they share information with lawmakers and are experts on the particular issue on which their group focuses.*

In his piece, Jeffrey Birnbaum describes the status of diversity in lobbying today. African-Americans are significantly underrepresented among these political professionals. Birnbaum goes beyond just documenting these patterns, though, as he identifies some of the hurdles that pose barriers to minority entry into this profession. This final reading points to a real political irony: The array of interests groups provides one of the most diverse aspects of American politics, but the actors hired to forward these groups' interests in the legislative arena are markedly homogeneous.

Number of Black Lobbyists Remains Shockingly Low

JEFFREY H. BIRNBAUM

Robert G. Drummer has been a lobbyist for a long time. He represents the American Moving and Storage Association and the City of Atlanta. But one thing has not changed since he first left Capitol Hill as an aide in 1995: the number of African American lobbyists like himself has remained remarkably small.

"The number has risen, but it's been a slow growth," he said. As president of the Washington Government Relations Group (WGRG), a trade association of black lobbyists, Drummer should know. The organization has about 100 members and a database of black federal lobbyists that tops 200.

The database probably doesn't capture every African American registered to lobby in the District. But even if it includes only half of the real total—or even a quarter—the number is still minuscule. According to the nonpartisan PoliticalMoneyLine.com, the total number of currently registered federal lobbyists is 29,702.

How is it possible that any profession—let alone a profession that deals with the government—has such a tiny representation of African Americans?

Lobbyists suggest a few reasons. One is that blacks are underrepresented in Congress, especially in the Senate, and the result is that relatively few African Americans get the experience they need to become professional lobbyists. Another explanation is that because black lobbyists have been so rare for so long, the network of predominantly white people who do the hiring for lobby groups doesn't routinely reach out to blacks.

And then there's the K Street Project excuse. Pressure on lobbying groups from the Republican Congress over the past decade to hire Republicans only has limited the market for blacks, since very few tend to belong to the GOP.

But none of these analyses account for the basic, embarrassing fact of the shockingly low number of African American lobbyists.

At a recent luncheon meeting of the WGRG, everyone agreed there was a problem. "There's something broken," said Paul N.D. Thornell, the senior lobbyist for United Way of America. "Rarely in a room of other lobbyists do many people look like me."

"Lobbying in health care is a little bit better," said Stefanie J. Reeves of the American Speech-Language-Hearing Association. "But it's not that good."

In an earlier column I wrote that the number of women and minority lobbyists has been growing in recent years, but that was only partly true. Women lobbyists have become commonplace while African American lobbyists remain exceptional. I did a disservice by not pointing that out.

There will be people who will think it's wonderful that blacks have been able to stay away from so tainted a vocation. I disagree. Lobbyists are integral to the process that produces our nation's laws and regulations. When any group is not at the bargaining table, everyone suffers. And like it or not, lobbyists are among the most important folks at that table.

The pool of black congressional aides—from which lobbyists are often drawn—is pretty shallow, especially in the Senate. The June issue of *DiversityInc* magazine reports that of the approximately 1,000 most senior staff jobs in the Senate, only 2.9 percent are held by blacks.

Nonetheless, African American lobbyists have banded together in both loose and formal ways for 25 years. According to the WGRG's new Web site, www.WGRGInc.org, a group of 20 regulars who represented DuPont, Mobil and Westinghouse (among other big companies) began meeting consistently in 1981. In the mid-80s, the lobbyists named themselves the Second Wednesday Group because they tended to gather on the second Wednesday of each month.

In the mid-90s, the group went dormant. But it was revived in its current form in 1997 by John Chambers of the law firm Arent Fox. These days, the nonpartisan WGRG helps lobbyists network with congressional staffers and each other. It also promotes charitable works and educational activities with an eye toward promoting lobbying as a career for African Americans.

There are so few black lobbyists in town that some of them try to take a jocular view of the situation. "Ain't but two of us," joked Fred McClure of Sonnenschein Nath & Rosenthal LLP, when asked how many African American lobbyists there are—"one Democrat, one Republican." McClure would be the Republican in that formulation, and that can be lonely, he said.

Patrice Webb, a lobbyist for Free Press, a nonprofit media reform organization, has noted with regret that blacks often are directed into social policy rather than corporate-type lobbying roles. Michael J. Frazier, an independent lobbyist and former Transportation Department official, agrees. "I can't figure out why the Fortune 500, which generally has been good on diversity in other areas, isn't as good at having diversity in their government affairs offices," Frazier said.

But Drummer, the WGRG's president, believes that the situation will gradually improve. "That's our hope and expectation," he said. We'll see.

DISCUSSION QUESTIONS

1. To be a "woman's issue" must it also be a "feminist" issue? In addition, are "women's issues" limited to policy questions such as abortion, gender equity, child care, affirmative action and education, or do they expand into other policy areas as well? What is a woman's issue and to what degree must there be overlap between women and between women and men for those to be the case? By taking the positions on issues such as Title IX and abortion that they do, are CWA and IWF really working to benefit all women?

2. What is the result of African-Americans and women being underrepresented among lobbyists? Does this mean that these groups are not represented in government as well as they should be? After reading the selections in Section 10 on the legislative branch, is your answer different?

3. Why do you think interest groups are less apt to hire individuals of color and/or women? Is it purposeful? Is it racism or sexism on the part of the interest group? The perception is that legislators are lobbied more effectively by people "like them." Is it a pipeline issue? Something else?

4. Is EMILY's List a sexist organization if it is only trying to help female candidates who are pro-choice get elected to office? Will women who benefit from EMILY's List contributions and campaign assistance be beholden to them and their donors and only represent "women's issues?" Alternatively, is EMILY's List only getting unique attention because they are a woman's group? After all, do not all interest groups try to capture the ear of elected officials?

5. As the United States evolves and sees the number of Latinos rise, what are the challenges of other groups that work on behalf of minority groups? Does this call for more coalition building across interest groups? Does the increasing diversification of minority organized interests in Washington, D.C., represent a challenge or unique opportunity? How might these opportunities or challenges be capitalized upon?

Additional Resources

http://www.naacp.org
The National Association for the Advancement of Colored People is the country's oldest civil rights interest group. Its stated mission is to "ensure the political, educational, social, and economic equality of rights of all persons and to eliminate racial hatred and racial discrimination."

http://www.now.org

The National Organization for Women "is the largest organization of feminist activists in the United States. Since its founding in 1966, NOW's goal has been to take action to bring about equality for all women. NOW works to eliminate discrimination and harassment in the workplace, schools, the justice system, and all other sectors of society; secure abortion, birth control and reproductive rights for all women; end all forms of violence against women; eradicate racism, sexism and homophobia; and promote equality and justice in our society."

http://www.lulac.org

The League of United Latin American Citizens (LULAC) "is the largest and oldest Hispanic Organization in the United States." This interest group's goal is to advance the economic condition, educational attainment, political influence, health and civil rights of Hispanic Americans through community-based programs across the country.

http://www.aarp.org

The American Association of Retired Persons (AARP) is one of the most powerful and influential organized interest groups in the United States because of its size and members' regular voting habits. It champions issues important to senior citizens.

http://emilyslist.org

This is the web site of the group, EMILY's List, profiled in Margaret Talev's piece.

http://www.cwfa.org and http://www.iwf.org

These are the web sites for the groups, Concerned Women for America and the Independent Women's Forum, profiled in Ronnee Schreiber's article.

http://www.lwv.org

The League of Women Voters is a non-partisan organization dedicated to more civic participation. Their web site includes informant on the group's projects and events, issue priorities, leadership, and state and local chapters.

8   MEDIA SOURCES AND THE POLITICS OF USE AND REPRESENTATION

Katie Couric's ascendancy to anchor at CBS News is notable both for the relative absence of females running nightly news programs and the amount of scrutiny her performance has received.

When one thinks about American politics, it is difficult *not* to think about the media. Politics and the media are intimately intertwined whether in the form of seemingly endless political advertisements during the election season, the "blogosphere," "podcasts," C-SPAN, or even *The Daily Show with John Stewart*. Using the term *media* as though it were in the singular rather than plural form is a bit misleading though, as there are so many different media sources that can potentially affect American politics. Television media, for example, can include political talk shows on cable networks such as the Fox News Channel (*The O'Reilly Factor*), CNN (*The Situation Room*), or MSNBC (*Countdown with Keith Olberman*) as well as the Sunday morning public affairs shows such as *Meet the Press* and *Face the Nation*. Television also carries many of our national candidate debates, the bulk of political advertisements during campaign season, and the nightly news. Additionally, talk radio has become a popular and influential source of political discourse and debate. The same is true of the Internet. Individuals not only obtain political information over the Internet, they can register for some government programs, and a limited number of state parties have even experimented with online voting in their presidential caucuses. Even though some of the most prominent newspapers in the nation have seen a slide in their circulation, print media also remains an important source of political information.

The readings that follow in this section reflect this wide area of sources that constitute "the political media." They also directly engage the intersection of demographic diversity, American politics, and these various media sources. This area of American politics, at first, might not appear to affect or be affected by diversity issues. However, as the readings below clearly illustrate, the demographic diversity of the United States is not only intertwined with questions of how the media handle political stories, but it can affect how those stories are told. In particular, we see different media sources intersect with diversity and American politics in terms of key concepts including representation and access. Indeed, the diversity lens conjures up important debates about the ways the media can either heighten or mitigate existing inequalities in the United States. The next time you see a story on the evening broadcast news, cable news channel, posted on a web site, or in a newspaper or news magazine, think about how the different diversity angles explored below affect not only the content of the story, but how that story is told.

*T*he first selection comes from The White House Project (an advocacy organization established for the advancement of women in public life) and turns our attention to TV. Their report, "Who's Talking Now," builds upon earlier research into gender differences in appearances on Sunday morning political talk shows. The report's findings indicate that the five major networks' Sunday morning shows largely fail in terms of gender equity when it comes to guest appearances—and have done so over time. When females are present, they are more likely to be in later segments of the show and less apt to be repeat commentators. The White House Project Report thus concludes that these shows fail to offer a full debate with all sides represented. Women's voices are far too marginalized in this arena and this influences the range of opinions to which Americans are exposed, painting an inaccurate picture that there are only a few female political experts. Here again we see issues of representation and equity appear.

The report contends that gender balance is particularly important on these programs for two reasons. One, the individuals on these shows serve as "opinion leaders," meaning that the views and points they express tend to become the ones that define the larger debate on an issue—both in elite circles and among everyday citizens. While most Americans may not watch these shows, the views expressed on Sunday morning talk shows concerning, for example, tax cuts, influence the way others end up talking and thinking about tax policy. Media scholars call this "agenda setting" and the White House Project report contends that the voices of women should regularly be a part of setting the agenda for debate on key political issues. The report also argues that the gender balance of guests on Sunday morning talk shows is important for a second reason. Individuals who appear on the Sunday morning shows gain prestige. After an appear-

ance, their word or opinion goes even further. They are considered more credible. This is the "authority conferring" effect of Sunday morning shows and the White House Project suggests women should enjoy this as frequently as men. Combined, the opinions expressed on Sunday shows can set the tenor of larger political debate and send messages about who is, and is not, an "expert." For these reasons, the White House Project sees it as important that women's voices are equally present in this forum.

Who's Talking Now: A Follow-Up Analysis of Guest Appearances by Women on the Sunday Morning Talk Shows

THE WHITE HOUSE PROJECT

The White House Project has been tracking the presence of women on the Sunday morning talk shows since January 2000. *Who's Talking Now: A Follow-Up Analysis of Guest Appearances by Women on the Sunday Morning Talk Shows,* is the third in a series of studies that examines the five major broadcast networks' Sunday talk shows for the number of female guest appearances, their placement on the show, and their topics of conversation.[1] This research is the most comprehensive analysis to date of women's participation on the Sunday morning talk shows.

Since the publication of the first study in 2001, the networks' combined record on the inclusion of women has remained largely unchanged. Our research indicates an overall increase of 3% in female guest appearances on the five major broadcast networks' Sunday morning talk shows. In our initial study, conducted between January 1, 2000 and June 30, 2001, women comprised 11% of guest appearances. In our second study from January 2002 to June 2002, women's appearances increased to 13%. In our most recent research, conducted between November 7, 2004 and July 10, 2005, that number has risen to 14% (see Figure 8.1).

Some networks, however, have shown a much greater increase than the five-network average of 3%. CBS, for example, doubled their percentage of female guests, from 9% in 2001 to 18% in 2005. NBC also showed a sizeable increase, up from 9% in 2001 to 16% in 2005. FOX improved their percentage from 9% to 12%. ABC remained steady at just under 15%. But CNN declined from 14% in 2001 to only 11% in 2005.

In short, our findings continue to show that women are vastly under-represented in this popular forum for debate, and therefore, remain largely invisible to the greater public. Despite progress in the number of female leaders over the past few decades, women who hold positions of power are still too often unseen and unheard.

In the aftermath of the 2004 presidential election, for example, efforts to under-stand and explain the outcome were greatly influenced by the Sunday talk shows, which steered post-election analysis in two main directions, suggesting that the elec-tion was the product of "bad campaign strategies" by the Kerry campaign and/or the desire for a "new moral imperative" by Bush voters. **Right or wrong, the post-election analysis on the Sunday talk shows was not the product of a democratic debate since it largely excluded the opinions of female pundits and politicians.** Women may have played prominent roles in the campaigns of both parties and may have made a criti-cal difference in the election's outcome, but their voices were rarely heard on the Sunday talk show circuit.

Like our initial study, our most recent research illustrates the need to widen the scope of political debate in this country so that it becomes more democratic and bet-ter reflects the views of all of its citizens. The sooner we have a more representative offering of female leaders speaking on behalf of their constituencies, the closer we will be to having a true democracy. As it stands, women comprise more than 50% of this country's population but are only about 15% of elected officials nationwide. Moreover, the United States ranks 63rd in the world with respect to women's politi-cal representation.

Because the Sunday morning talk shows play an important role in shaping our nations political agenda and have the power to confer expert status on their guests, we believe that an increase in the number and frequency of appearances by women on these shows would improve the public perception of women. And, more specifically, it would provide a more accurate reflection of their present status as experts, leaders and authority figures. The gains made, though modest, in women's leadership are not accurately reflected in one of the most popular venues of public deliberation—the Sunday morning talks shows. As a result, progress continues to be slow in improving the numbers of female leaders and in making this country more democratic.

* * * * *

WHY SUNDAY MORNING SHOWS?

The Sunday morning talk shows are a critical forum for our nations political debates, and a crucible where leaders are forged. Research has shown that the shows have an "agenda-setting effect" and an "authority-setting effect." The selection of topics by the network shows influences the priorities of citizens across the country as well as the priorities of those inside the beltway. This comes as little surprise since comments from the shows are often quoted in Monday morning newspapers, and program snippets are often replayed or alluded to on Monday morning news programs (as well as on late night talk shows—from which a majority of Americans get their news). In addi-tion to influencing the nations political agenda, the shows also establish the profiles and visibility of leaders by conferring expert status on the guests who appear on the shows. And, they are an important testing ground for would-be Presidents. The shows provide prominent public figures an opportunity to showcase their policy positions, and demonstrate their expertise on issues of the day. Unfortunately, as our findings indicate, the line-up of guests does not mirror the current level of women in leadership positions across this country or accurately represent the pool of experts available . . .

METHODOLOGY

This study . . . looked at Sunday morning political talk shows on the five major broadcast networks: *This Week* (ABC), *Face the Nation (CBS)*, *Late Edition with Wolf Blitzer* (CNN), *Fox News Sunday* (FOX), and *Meet the Press* (NBC). In the period studied—November 7, 2004 through July 10, 2005—there were 179 shows in total—36 episodes for each network except CNN, which had 35.[2] In addition, a combined total of 787 guests appeared on the shows.

In our analysis, the transcript of each show was reviewed, catalogued, coded and analyzed. Each guest was classified by gender, and type of guest (occupation)—elected officials; government officials; former elected and/or government officials; private professionals; media representatives; foreign officials; campaign officials; party officials; and religious leaders. Secondly, the issues about which each guest spoke were classified according to the following categories: domestic politics, international politics, social issues, economic issues, cultural issues, religious issues and other. Finally, an analysis was conducted of (1) the overall representation of female and male guests; (2) type of guest according to gender; (3) location of guest appearance within show (first segment or later); (4) shows where women made no guest appearances; (5) the relation of gender to specific subject areas; and (6) the percentage of male and female guests who made repeat appearances.

* * * * *

FINDINGS AND ANALYSIS

As shown in Figure 8.1, the total percentage of female guest appearances on the five major broadcast networks' Sunday talk shows increased slightly from 11% in 2000–2001 to 14% in 2004–2005. While the trend is heading in the right direction, the overall line-up of guests on the Sunday shows still fails to reflect the diversity of opinion and the range of key players available to speak on major political, social and economic issues. Clearly, there is much room for improvement.

Figure 8.1:

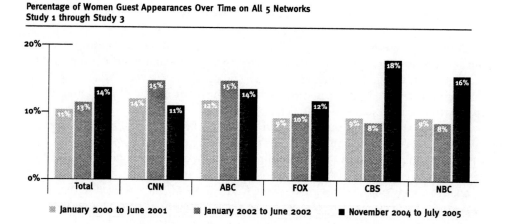

Percentage of Women Guest Appearances Over Time on All 5 Networks
Study 1 through Study 3

While the overall increase in guest appearances since our initial study is a modest 3%, some networks have made much more impressive gains. CBS, for example, doubled their percentage of female guest appearances from 9% in 2000–2001 to 18% in 2004–2005. And NBC doubled their percentage of female guest appearances from 8% in 2002 to 16% in 2004–2005. CNN, on the other hand, decreased their percentage of female guest appearances from 15% in 2002 to 11% in 2004–2005.

STILL NOT TALKING

... As evident in Figure 8.2, our research indicates an alarming number of Sunday talk shows with no female guest appearances—nearly six out of ten shows in 2004–2005 do not include a single female guest appearance. In 2002, 57% of shows had no women guest appearances. The overall gain since 2002 was slight, but some of the networks have showed significant improvement. CBS not only increased its numbers of female guest appearances, but continues to produce the most gender diverse Sunday show, and has the lowest percentage of shows with no women guests—47%. NBC has also made significant progress in this area, decreasing their number of shows with no female guest appearances from 73% in 2002 to 50% in 2004–2005.

Figure 8.2:

Shows Where Women Made No Guest Appearances — 2002 and 2004/5

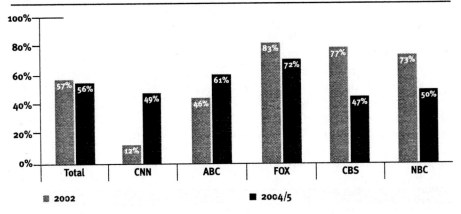

Although there have been overall improvements in women's appearances since our initial study, the disparity between men's appearances and women's appearances is still glaring, as evident in Figure 8.3. Men still comprise between 82% and 89% of the appearances on all five networks, which means that nearly all news and debate comes from male voices and male perspectives.

Over the course of the three time periods studied between 2000 and 2005, female guest appearances on the Sunday shows increased by only 3 percentage points from 11% in our initial research to 13% in our 2002 study, and up one more point to 14% in our most recent study [see Figure 8.4].[4] ... CBS, NBC, and (to a lesser extent) FOX, can claim some real progress, while CNN and ABC have moved in the wrong direction. The disparity between networks suggests that low percentages of female guest appearances are a reflection of network choices rather than a lack of qualified women as possible guests.

Figure 8.3:

**Guest Appearances by Gender
Nov. 2004 to July 2005**

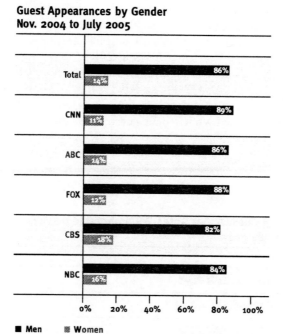

■ Men   ▓ Women

Figure 8.4:

**Women Guest Appearances over Time on Each Network
From 2000-2001 to 2004-2005**

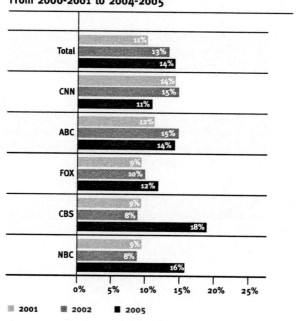

▓ 2001   ▓ 2002   ■ 2005

To compound the evidence that women are not equally represented on network Sunday shows, our research also indicates that when women do appear as guests, they are significantly less likely to reappear on that same show than men. For the five major networks' Sunday talk shows, only 14% of female guests made repeat appearances in 2002 and a somewhat better 17% in 2004–2005.[5] As evident during the 2004–2005 study, as indicated in Figure 8.5, the frequency of female repeat guest appearances was highest at CBS (27%) and NBC (24%) and only half that (12–13%) at the three other networks. In the eight month time period we examined, male guests made 186 repeat appearances while female guests made only 37.

Figure 8.5:

Women Repeat Guest Appearances Within Specific Network Nov. 2004 to July 2005

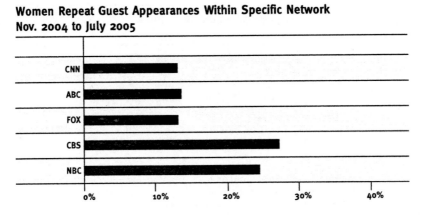

NOR HEARD . . .

* * * * *

The data reveals slow but steady progress on the topic of domestic politics (see Figure 8.6). In 2000–2001, 8% of female guests spoke about domestic politics; by 2002 the number had risen to 13%, and by 2004–2005 it increased to 16%. There has been less progress on the international front. The percentage of female guests speaking on international issues dropped from 14% in 2001 to 11% in 2002, though the percentage increased to 14% in 2005. In our initial study, women appeared more often in discussions of cultural, economic and social issues, but these categories generally represent a much smaller portion of a show's discussion. In addition, even in these categories, women lost ground—decreasing from a high of 33% in 2002 to 9% in 2004–2005 on cultural issues; from a high of 18% in 2002 to 13% in 2004–2005 on economic issues; and from a high of 19% in 2001 to only 8% in 2004–2005 on social issues.

Figure 8.6:

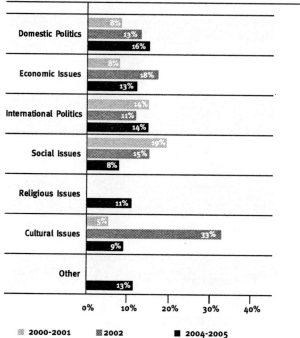

Women and the Topics they Spoke About Across All Networks 2000-2005

Domestic Politics — 8%, 13%, 16%
Economic Issues — 8%, 18%, 13%
International Politics — 14%, 17%, 14%
Social Issues — 19%, 15%, 8%
Religious Issues — 11%
Cultural Issues — 5%, 35%, 9%
Other — 13%

0% 10% 20% 30% 40%

▓ 2000-2001   ▨ 2002   ■ 2004-2005

WHO'S TALKING?

When we examined the occupations of the women who appeared on the Sunday talk shows, we found that they were most likely to be media representatives or elected officials . . . Out of a total of 107 appearances by women, 35 were made by media representatives and 29 were made by elected officials. When appearances by female media representatives were compared to appearances by male media representatives, we found that women made up 29% of the field. But, when we compared the number of appearances by female elected officials to the number of male elected officials who appeared, women made up only 10% of the category.

Women fared much better in the "campaign official" category, where they made up 67% of the field when compared to appearances by men. However, because the campaign official category only includes six total appearances, this category finding is not as compelling.

The third and fourth largest occupational categories in which women were represented were private professional and government official. There were no female party officials on the shows, and very few religious leaders, foreign officials, and former elected/government officials.[7] . . .

Comparing the 2004–2005 results with those from 2002 (Figure 8.7), we see that the largest increase by occupation was for female campaign officials. In the 2002 time period, there were no female campaign officials on the Sunday talk shows, whereas in the 2004–2005 period there were four. There was also an increase in the number of female private professionals—up 6 percentage points from 13% in the 2002 time period to 19% in the 2004–2005 period. However, the number of female elected officials appearing on the Sunday shows declined from 24% to 11%, and female government officials declined from 20% to 17%.

Figure 8.7:

Women's Occupation and Gender Across All Networks
2002 to 2005

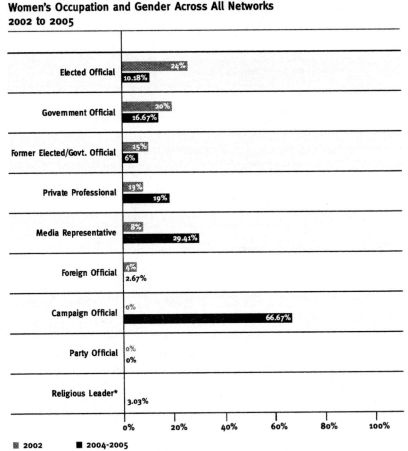

■ 2002   ■ 2004-2005

*Due to the large number of religious leaders who appeared
as guests on 2004/5 shows, a category has been added.

The most disturbing findings to come from this part of our research is that the percentage of female elected officials in the 2004–2005 period dropped markedly since our 2002 study. Moreover, only 1 in 10 elected officials to appear on the Sunday shows were women in 2004–2005. This suggests that the women whose job it is to represent this country's citizens are not given the same opportunities as their male counterparts to be visible in a popular forum for political debate and to have their voices heard.

SECONDARY BILLING

Women continue to bring up the rear when it comes to guest placement. On the Sunday morning talk shows, the most important segments are aired at the beginning of the show and the least important toward the end. As our research demonstrates, men are much more likely than women to be seen in the first segment.

*****

When comparing women's placements in the first segment over time and across all networks, little progress has been made. In 2000–2001, 12% of appearances in the first segment were made by women (Figure 8.8). In our 2005 study, that number barely increased one percentage point to 13%.

Figure 8.8:

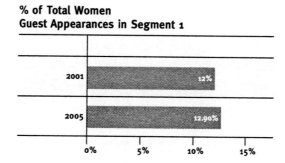

% of Total Women Guest Appearances in Segment 1

CONCLUSION

As stated previously, there has been an overall increase in female presence on the Sunday morning talk shows, since our initial study. However, our research demonstrates that the increase in women's visibility has primarily occurred in the segments toward the end of the shows rather than in the more frequently watched opening segment. Women, it seems, tend to be relegated to the less important and less frequently watched portions of the show.

In addition, when women do appear on Sunday morning shows, they do not reappear on the same shows with a frequency on par with men. Is this due to scheduling difficulties? Are producers less inclined to rebook women for a particular reason? The numbers don't tell us why women are making repeat appearances less often—but the numbers do indicate that there is room for improvement.

Looking across the entire study, it is clear that progress, albeit slow, is being made in some areas. However, in a number of instances, it appears the networks are taking one step forward and two steps back. Maintaining vigilance is warranted to ensure that women's expertise and leadership is increasingly showcased on these national Sunday talk shows. In the future, The White House Project will endeavor to continue our research into the guest appearances of women on Sunday morning talk shows so that, one day, our news and debate.

Notes

1. The White House Project's research examined the following shows from November 7, 2004 through July 10, 2005: *This Week* (ABC), *Face the Nation* (CBS), *Late Edition with Wolf Blitzer* (CNN). *Fox News Sunday* (FOX), and *Meet the Press* (NBC).

2. On July 10, 2005 CNN broadcast a hurricane special in place of its usual program, *Late Edition with Wolf Blitzer.*

4. All comparisons to out initial study reference the Study 1 data that excluded Presidential candidates.

5. This figure represents the percentage of female guests on a specific network show that appeared more than once during the study period.

7. Due to the large number of religious leaders who appeared as guests on 2004/5 shows a category has been added.

*I*n this second reading, Martin Gilens turns attention to how the print media depicts political news. Like the White House Project, Gilens stresses that all political issues and stories have multiple angles or ways they can be depicted. We call these "media frames." Gilens looks at how the major newsweeklies (Time, Newsweek, and U.S. News and World Report) framed or covered poverty from 1950–1992 and the racial composition of those photographed in the stories. In looking at stories beginning from 1965, Gilens finds that the news media dramatically over-represent the numbers of poor people who are African-American. He argues that this overrepresentation is far from random. Stories that took a negative frame about poverty—perhaps emphasizing how irresponsible behavior can lead to poverty—were much more apt to depict a black face. White faces, however, were more apt to appear when the story took a positive or neutral frame. Here, a diversity lens makes this contrast salient.*

Gilens indicates that both the striking overrepresentation of African-Americans in print media depictions of poverty over time, and the strong correlation between negatively framed stories and pictures of African-Americans, influences public perceptions on poverty and welfare. Americans dramatically exaggerate the percentage of poor people who are African-American—regardless of where they live. Those who do so are most apt to have negative views on welfare policy and believe that individuals claiming welfare lack the work ethic.

Correlational Framing: Media Portrayals of Race and Poverty

MARTIN GILENS

Among it's many and various applications, the concept of "framing" has been used to describe the alternative ways in which a news story can be packaged and presented by journalists . . .

＊＊＊＊＊

. . . [A] frame is a characteristic of an individual story. A body of news stories can be characterized by the frequency with which particular frames appear, and the ebb and flow of alternative frames can be traced over time. But these aggregate characterizations of news coverage simply reflect the prevalence of media frames which exist as attributes of the individual news stories. In contrast, my analysis of the news media's coverage of poverty suggests that media frames also exist as emergent properties that characterize a body of stories. In particular, "correlational frames" can reflect the association among story elements across a set of news stories.

In my examination of poverty stories in magazine and television news, I found that for most of the past four decades African Americans have been dramatically overrepresented in pictures of the poor. This in itself constitutes a media frame in which poverty is portrayed as a "black problem." But perhaps more significantly, I found that the racial representation of the poor varied over time and across poverty subgroups. Black faces were most prominent during periods when the media discourse on poverty was most negative and least likely to be found during periods when the content of media poverty stories became more sympathetic. Similarly, I found that news stories about the least sympathetic subgroups of the poor were the most likely to feature African Americans. In other words, the media frame that associates African Americans with the most negative aspects of poverty exists as a *correlation* between the "moral valence" of a story on poverty and the race of the poor people chosen as examples.

RACE AND POVERTY IN THE NEWS

In my recent book, *Why Americans Hate Welfare: Race, Media and the Politics of Antipoverty Policy*, I examined news coverage of poverty between 1950 and 1992. For my data I drew primarily on the country's three most prominent weekly newsmagazines, *Time, Newsweek*, and *U.S. News and World Report*. I chose these magazines because they are widely read, national in scope and distribution, and have been published continuously for many decades. They also contain large numbers of pictures, an especially important consideration in studying the racial portrayal of the poor . . .

Martin Gilens, "Correlational Framing: Media Portrayals of Race and Poverty." Originally published in *Political Psychology Newsletter*, Political Psychology Section of the American Political Science Association, 1999. Reprinted with permission.

Figure 8.9: Racial Makeup of the Poor in Newsmagazines

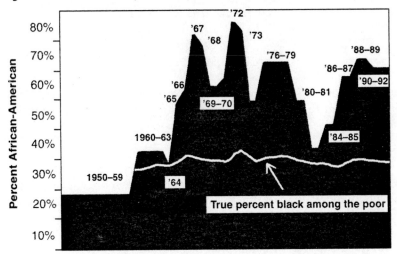

Based on the 6,117 poor people pictured in *Time, Newsweek,* and *U.S. News and World Report* between 1950 and 1992.

To assess media portrayals of poverty, I first identified every poverty-related story in these three magazines published during the period of interest. To determine the racial content of news magazine coverage of poverty, each poor person pictured in each of these stories was identified as black, nonblack, or undeterminable. In all, I found pictures of 6,117 individual poor people in 1,256 poverty stories, and I was able to determine the race for 72% of those pictured (the remaining 28% are excluded from the analyses discussed below). Over the entire four-and-a-half decades studied, 53% of all poor people pictured were African American; in reality, the percentage of African Americans among the poor during this period averaged 29%.

CHANGING IMAGES OF THE POOR

Magazine portrayals over-represent African Americans in pictures of the poor, but the degree of overrepresentation of blacks has not been constant throughout this period. Images of poverty in these magazines changed quite dramatically in the mid-1960s. From the beginning of this study through 1964, poor people were portrayed as predominantly white. For example, only 18% of the poor pictured in newsmagazines in the 1950s were black. But starting in 1965 the complexion of the poor turned decidedly darker. From only 27% in 1964, the proportion of African Americans in pictures of the poor increased to about 50% in 1965 and 1966, and then to 72% black in 1967 (see Figure 8.9).

In *Why Americans Hate Welfare* I discuss a number of reasons for the dramatic changes in the racial portrayals of poverty in the mid-1960s including black migration to northern cities, urban riots, and changes in the focus of the civil rights movement. Two factors which clearly do not help to explain these changes are any real shifts in the racial composition of America's poor, which has remained remarkably constant throughout this period (see Figure 8.9), and the birth of the War on Poverty, which was associated with images of poor whites rather than poor blacks.

In fact, news coverage of the War on Poverty nicely illustrates the correlational framing that characterized poverty coverage over the four decades I examined. President Johnson's announcement of the War on Poverty in January of 1964 led to a huge increase in attention to poverty in the news. But this early coverage did not associate the War on Poverty with African Americans; only one-quarter of the poor pictured in stories about the War on Poverty during 1964 were black. These early news stories on the War on Poverty were not only light in complexion, they were also overwhelmingly positive or neutral in tone, focusing on the problem of poverty in America and the antipoverty efforts of the president and the congress. Starting in 1965 however, coverage of the War on Poverty became much more critical, and only then did black faces start to appear in large numbers.

Three lines of criticism were prominent in coverage of the War on Poverty during 1965. First, many stories questioned Sargent Shriver's leadership of the antipoverty effort. Second, considerable attention was devoted to local disputes between city government and community groups over control of War on Poverty resources. Finally, substantial coverage focused on difficulties within the Job Corps program, one of the first War on Poverty programs to get off the ground. Fifty percent of the poor pictured in War on Poverty stories during this period were black, as were 55% of those in stories on the Job Corps.

This same tendency to associate positive or neutral stories with white faces and negative stories with black faces is evident as poverty coverage shifts in tone over the following decades. For example, after a slight decline in the proportion of blacks in poverty stories during the late 1960s, the election year of 1972 found the highest proportion of African Americans of any year studied (at 76%). This year also saw some of the most negative coverage of poverty and welfare, with calls for welfare reform coming from both sides of the political spectrum and both presidential candidates. The media reflected (and reinforced) the widespread concern that welfare was "out of control," and published dozens of stories on welfare abuse, "runaway costs," and mismanagement in state welfare bureaucracies. The true proportion of blacks among welfare recipients had hardly changed from a few years earlier, but as the media discourse on welfare became more critical, the percentage of black faces in stories on welfare grew from 52% in 1969–70 to 75% in 1972–73.

The unusually high proportion of African Americans in negative stories about the poor represents one pole of the media's correlational framing of race and poverty. The other side of this relationship consists of sympathetic poverty stories which tend to be illustrated with far fewer blacks. Of the four decades examined, I found the lowest proportion of African Americans during the early 1980s, a period of economic decline and cutbacks in government antipoverty efforts. In stark contrast to the way poverty was portrayed in the early 1970s, the media's coverage of poverty during the "Reagan recession" of the early 1980s was extremely sympathetic toward the poor.

The two most common themes of poverty stories during this period concerned the growth of poverty and the debates over government cutbacks. Although a few of these stories sought to convince readers that "The Safety Net Remains" (as a *Time* magazine story from this period was titled), most of this coverage was highly critical of the Reagan administration's efforts to trim government programs for the poor. A good example is *Newsweek's* prominent story titled "The Hard-Luck Christmas of '82" which proclaimed "With 12 million unemployed and 2 million homeless, private charity cannot make up for federal cutbacks." The story went on to describe the desperate condition of poor families living in camp tents or in automobiles, portraying them as the noble victims "who are paying the price of America's failure of nerve in the war on poverty." Reflecting the general lack of black faces in these sympathetic poverty stories, "The Hard Luck Christmas of '82" included only 3 African Americans among the 18 poor people pictured. As a whole, blacks made up only 30% of the poor people pictured in stories on poverty and anti-poverty programs from 1982–83, the lowest proportion of any point in the 43 years I examined.

Another theme in poverty stories from this period concerned the "newly poor," that is, formerly middle-class Americans who fell into poverty during the recession of the early 1980s. Typical of this coverage is a (white) family of four profiled in a *U.S. News and World Report* story from August of 1982. This story describes how the Telehowski family was "plunged into the ranks of the newly poor" when the father lost his job as a machinist with an auto-parts company. No longer able to afford a car or even an apartment, the Telehowski's reluctantly applied for welfare and became squatters in an abandoned house in inner-city Detroit. The Telehowski family, with their two small children and their determined struggle to support themselves, indicate the extraordinary sympathy that the "newly poor" received in news coverage from the early 1980s. Time magazine went even farther in proclaiming the virtues of the newly poor, writing "The only aspect of American life that has been uplifted by the continuing recession: a much better class of poor person, better educated, accustomed to working, with strong family ties."

It is not surprising, of course, that poverty is portrayed in a more sympathetic light during economic hard times. What is noteworthy, however, is that along with shifts in the tone of news reporting on the poor come shifts in the racial mix of the poor people in news stories. The true proportion of blacks among America's poor varied only slightly over the four decades examined, but the racial portrayals of the poor in newsmagazines shifted dramatically as media attention tamed from highly critical coverage of welfare during 1972–73 to highly sympathetic stories on poverty during the recession of the early 1980s.

* * * * *

THE IMPACT OF NEWS FRAMING ON THE PUBLIC

It is clear that news framing can affect readers' and viewers' perceptions of the topics covered and the political judgments they make (to cite but a few of the relevant studies, see Capella & Jamieson 1997; Iyengar 1991; Nelson, Clawson, and Oxley, 1997; Nelson and Kinder 1996; Neuman, Just, and Crigler 1992; Price, Tewksbury, and Powers 1997). Equally clear is that the specific examples used to illustrate a story can have a profound impact on the conclusions that readers draw (e.g., Brosius and Bathelt 1994; Hamill, Wilson, and Nisbett 1980; Zillmann, et al. 1996).

The news media's exaggerated association of poverty with African Americans also appears to have influenced the public. Surveys show that Americans dramatically exaggerate the extent to which blacks compose the poor. Moreover, perceptions of the extent to which blacks make up the poor are virtually identical in states with large numbers of poor blacks and states with minuscule numbers of blacks among their poor. This geographic constancy of perceptions suggests that it is not personal experience that shapes Americans' perceptions of the race of the poor, but the images they consume in the media.

It also appears that the public's perceptions (or misperceptions) of the racial nature of poverty influence their judgments of the poor. For example, white Americans who think most welfare recipients are black express much more negative views about the work ethic of those on welfare than do whites who think most welfare recipients are white. (These differences remain virtually unchanged when political ideology and demographic characteristics are held constant.)

If the general overrepresentation of blacks in media images of the poor does impact the public's views about poverty and welfare, what about the correlational framing that associates poor blacks with the *undeserving* poor? The perception of poor blacks as lazy is a centuries old stereotype dating at least to the efforts of southern slave holders to justify their "peculiar institution." But as other aspects of racial attitudes became more liberal during the 1960s and 1970s, the perception that African Americans are to blame for their economic problems grew. In part this was due to the dismantling of the most obvious legal barriers to black economic progress and the achievement of important legal tools in the Civil Rights Act of 1964 and the Voting Rights Act of 1965. At the same time, however, the existing stereotype of blacks as lazy, and the association of black faces with the negative media discourse on poverty that emerged during the later 1960s and early 1970s helped to cement the association between African Americans and the undeserving poor.

It is unrealistic to expect news images to mirror reality. But as our primary source of information about politics and society, news organizations must make a conscious effort to avoid destructive and inaccurate stereotypes. Correlation framing suggests that this effort cannot be conducted on a story by story basis. Instead, attention must be paid to the body of news stories that collectively convey information or misinformation about the social world. This task is not as imposing as might be imagined. Reacting to concerns about the images of minorities in the news, some news organizations have instituted "photo audits" to systematically track the way minorities (or women) are portrayed. For example, in 1988 the *Seattle Times* began to count photographs of minorities appearing in positive, neutral, and negative contexts, and found that negative images of minorities outnumbered positive images by four to one. In response to this dismal portrayal of minorities, and to the discussion and "consciousness raising" that ensued among the news staff, coverage changed. In the following year, positive images of minorities outnumbered negative images. By 1990, the *Times* published twice as many photographs depicting minorities positively as negatively (a ratio that closely approximated the portrayal of whites in the *Times'* coverage). As the *Seattle Times'* experience shows, when a news organization makes the fair representation of different social groups a priority and takes concrete steps to monitor its own news content, substantial change can be accomplished in a short time.

Through studies of the nature and impact of news framing, academics can both strengthen our understanding of how the media influence public perceptions and provide a firmer foundation for media practitioners to resist the kinds of stereotypical coverage I found so prominent in news stories on American poverty.

* * * * *

References

Brosius, Hans-Bemd, and Anke Bathelt. 1994. "The Utility of Exemplars in Persuasive Communications." *Communication Research* 21(1, February): 48–78.

Capella, Joseph N., and Kathleen Hall Jamison. 1997. *Spiral of Cynicism: The Press and the Public Good.* New York: Oxford University Press.

Hamill, Ruth, Timothy Decamp Wilson, and Richard E. Nisbett. 1980. "Insensitivity to Sample Bias: Generalizing from Atypical Cases." *Journal of Personality and Social Psychology* 39: 578–589.

Iyengar, Shanto. 1991. Is *Anyone Responsible: How Television Frames Political Issues.* Chicago: University of Chicago Press.

Nelson, Thomas E, R. A. Clawson, and Z. M. Oxley. 1997. "Media Framing of a Civil Liberties Conflict and Its Effect on Tolerance." *American Political Science Review* 91(3, September): 567–583.

Nelson, Thomas E., and Donald R. Kinder. 1996. "Issue Frames and Group-Centrism in American Public Opinion." *The Journal of Politics* 58(4, November): 1055–1078.

Neuman, W. Russell, Marion R. Just, and Ann N. Crigler. 1992. *Common Knowledge; News and the Construction of Political Meaning.* Chicago: University of Chicago Press.

Price, Vincent, David Tewksbury, and Elizabeth Powers. 1997. "Switching Trains of Thought: The Impact of News Frames on Readers' Cognitive Responses." *Communication Research* 24(5, October): 481–506.

Zillmann, Dolf, et al. 1996. "Effects of Exemplification in News Reports on the Perception of Social Issues." *Journalism and Mass Communication Quarterly*, 73(2), 427–444.

*L*ike Gilens in the previous selection, Stephanie Greco Larson examines how the media frames its stories and depicts the individuals it covers. She offers a brief essay summarizing the scholarly research on American women and politics in the media. When it comes to covering feminist organizing or women's organizations, scholarship indicates mainstream media largely ignored these groups until 1970. When these groups began to receive attention it was often stigmatized. Today, however, women's groups generally find that their press releases and policy work is covered by the media. Turning to coverage of modern first ladies, Larson finds that these women—regardless of political party—get the most negative coverage when they involve themselves in "political" activities rather than more traditional activities. Similarly pigeonholed coverage is sometimes witnessed with women in the electorate.

On this subject, terms such as gender gap or soccer mom are often misunderstood by the media and ignore the nuanced ways in which women think and behave politically. Research also suggests that women candidates find it more difficult than male candidates to direct or lead their news coverage and receive more "Can she win?" coverage rather than coverage of her issue positions.

Readers interested in these topics will be intrigued to know that Larson concludes that there is much to be learned about women, politics, and media but that the evidence thus far suggests the media often treats men and women differently. This piece captures and utilizes several themes which run throughout other selections in this volume.

American Women and Politics in the Media: A Review Essay

STEPHANIE GRECO LARSON

---

* * * *

Most of the research on women and politics in the media is divisible into the topics of advertising, and news coverage of the women's movement and feminist organizations, first ladies, women candidates, women politicians, and women in the electorate. . . .

THE WOMEN'S MOVEMENT, FEMINIST ORGANIZATIONS, AND THE MEDIA

Research on the content of news coverage during the feminist movement of the 1970s illustrates both the achievements and frustrations of the movement's efforts

to receive favorable attention for itself and feminist issues. Susan Douglas (1994) provides telling examples of how the mass media demonized, trivialized, and sexualized feminists. More systematic analyses of mainstream coverage of the women's movement (Costain, Braunstein, and Berggren 1997), the National Organization of Women (Barker-Plummer 2000), and feminists and feminism (Ruddy 1997), reveal that the media either ignored or stigmatized feminism prior to 1970. Eventually, the movement brought certain women's issues to the media's attention (Barker-Plummer 2000; Costain, Braunstein, and Berggren 1997; Huddy 1997). NOW's active press relations efforts effectively publicized sexual equality issues (Barker-Plummer 2000) although the media provided relatively little coverage for the abortion rights debate because it lacked drama and simplicity (Terkildsen, Schnell, and Lang 1998).

Stephanie Greco Larson, "American Women and Politics in the Media: A Review Essay," *PS: Political Science and Politics*, vol. 34, no. 2 (June 2001), pp. 227–230. Copyright © 2001 American Political Science Association. Reprinted with the permission of Cambridge University Press.

FIRST LADIES AND THE MEDIA

. . . Although some scholars examine campaign coverage of presidential candidates' wives (Bystrom, McKinnon, and Chaney 1999), news about first ladies receives the most attention. For example, Scharrer and Bissell (2000) compared coverage of the political and nonpolitical activities of three first ladies: Nancy Reagan, Barbara Bush, and Hillary Clinton. They found that all three received negative coverage when they were politically active.

Perhaps because of Hillary Clinton's redefinition of the role of first lady, scholars have taken a closer look at the narrative themes that dominated her coverage (Gardetto 1997) and the strategic mistakes made by the White House press office when managing her image (Winfield 1997). Research on first lady coverage has begun to theorize about the cultural contradictions of the role and the problematic coverage this ambivalence generates (Brown 1997; Brown and Gardetto 2000). A focus group study explored the impact of the media's Hillary Clinton coverage, and found that audiences interpreted her coverage differently based upon their political ideologies (Brown 1997).

MEDIA COVERAGE OF WOMEN IN THE ELECTORATE

. . . The media exaggerates the gender gap (Ladd 1997), focusing only on which candidate is winning rather than relevant women's issues (Borquez, Goldenberg, and Kahn 1988). In fact, journalists often misunderstand the gap (Norrander 1999). In 1984 the gender gap and the simplistic notion that women as a whole form a single voting bloc were virtually sold to the press by women's groups who wanted deference from politicians (specifically to have Walter Mondale pick a female vice-presidential running mate) (Book 1988; Frankovic 1988). In 1996, media attention to the gender gap resulted from: the parties' promoting women at their conventions; the marked difference of opinions between the sexes on political issues; and journalists who had for some time been sensitized to the gap (Frankovic 1999).

Another way that the media characterized the female electorate in 1996 was as "soccer moms." . . . Not only did the media portray soccer moms as alienated (Poole and Mueller 1998), it exaggerated their importance to the outcome of the election (Carroll 1999). Both Carroll (1999) and Vavrus (2000) criticized the media for grossly generalizing women and reducing them to depoliticized stereotypes whose only concerns were motherhood and consumerism (Vavrus 2000).

WOMEN CANDIDATES IN THE NEWS

Kim Fridkin Kahn has extensively studied how the news media covers women candidates relative to men, and the consequences of this coverage (1992, 1993, 1994a, 1994b, 1996). Her findings indicate that women have a harder time controlling the media's agenda than do their male counterparts. Women candidates receive less issue coverage and more negative comments on their viability (Kahn 1996). Although some recent research challenges the extent of women candidates' disadvantages (Rausch, Rozelt, and Wilson 1999; Smith 1997), these studies lack the extensiveness and rigor of Kahn's work. In addition, even these studies bring bad news for female candidates: the studies' female subjects received more negative coverage than their male opponents (Rausch, Rozell, and Wilson 1999) and less coverage in open races (Smith 1997). . . .

WOMEN CANDIDATES' CAMPAIGN ADVERTISING

. . . The research that both surpasses simple analysis of content and studies the effects of advertising in experimental settings shows that women's ads are less effective if the candidate is emoting (Hitchon, Chang, and Harris 1997), and work best if they emphasize stereotypical female issues (Iyengar et al. 1997).

MEDIA COVERAGE OF FEMALE POLITICIANS

Given the lack of research on media coverage of female politicians, it seems as though scholars lose interest in female candidates if they win their elections. *Women Politicians in the Media,* by Maria Braden (1996), is full of examples of news stories that trivialize and stereotype women officeholders, from Jeannette Rankin to current politicians who are quoted complaining about sexist coverage. However, a systematic content analysis of newspaper coverage of women in the 103rd Congress finds few examples of these (Carroll and Schreiber 1997). Instead, their coverage contained frequent references to women as the agents of change and to women's issues (Carroll and Schreiber 1997).

* * * * *

References

Barker-Plummet, Bernadette. 2000. "News as a Feminist Resource? A Case Study of the Media Strategies and Media Representation of the National Organization of Women, 1966–1980." In *Gender Politics, and Communication*, ed. Annabelle Sreberny and Liesbet van Zoonen. Cresskill, NJ: Hampton Press, Inc.

Bonk, Kathy. 1988. "The Selling of the 'Gender Gap': The Role of Organized Feminism." In *The Politics of the Gender Gap: The Social Construction of Political Influence*, ed. Carol M. Mueller. Newbury Park, CA: Sage Publications.

Borquez, Julio, Edie N. Goldenberg, and Kim Fridkin Kahn. 1988. "Press Portrayals of the Gender Gap." In *The Politics of the Gender Gap: The Social Construction of Political Influence*, ed. Carol M. Mueller. Newbury Park, CA: Sage Publications.

Braden, Maria. 1996. *Women Politicians in the Media*. Lexington, KY: University of Kentucky Press.

Brown, Mary Ellen. 1997. "Feminism and Cultural Politics: Television Audiences and Hillary Rodham Clinton." *Political Communication* 14:255–70.

Brown, Mary Ellen, and Darlaine C. Gardetto. 2000. "Representing Hillary Rodham Clinton: Gender, Meaning, and News Media." In *Gender, Politics, and Communication*, ed. Annabelle Sreberny and Liesbet van Zoonen. Cresskill, NJ: Hampton Press, Inc.

Bystrom, Dianne G., Lori Melton McKinnon, and Carole Chaney. 1999. "First Ladies and the Fourth Estate: Media Coverage of Hillary Clinton and Elizabeth Dole in the 1996 Presidential Campaign." In *The Electronic Election*, ed. Lynda Lee Kaid and Dianne G. Bystrom. Mahwah, NJ: Lawrence Erlbaum Associates Publishers.

Carroll, Susan J. 1999. "The Disempowerment of the Gender Gap: Soccer Moms and the 1996 Elections." *PS* 32:7–11.

Carroll Susan J., and Ronnee Schreiber. 1997. "Media Coverage of Women in the 103rd Congress." In *Women, Media, and Politics*, ed. Pippa Norris. New York: Oxford University Press.

Costain, Anne N., Richard Braunstein, and Heidi Berggren. 1997. "Framing the Women's Movement." In *Women, Media, and Politics*, ed. Pippa Norris. New York: Oxford University Press.

Douglas, Susan 1994. *Where the Girls Are: Growing Up Female with the Mass Media*. New York: Times Books.

Frankovic, Kathleen C. 1988. "The Ferraro Factor: The Women's Movement, the Polls, and the Press." In *The Politics of the Gender Gap: The Social Construction of Political Influence*, ed. Carol M. Mueller. Newbury Park, CA: Sage Publications.

Gardetto, Darlaine C. 1997. "Hillary Rodham Clinton, Symbolic Gender Politics, and the *New York Times*: January-November 1992." *Political Communication* 14:225–40.

Hitchon, Jacqueline C., Chingching Chang, and Rhonda Harris. 1997. "Should Women Emote? Perceptual Bias and Opinion Change in Response to Political Ads for Candidates of Different Genders." *Political Communication* 14:49–69.

Huddy, Leonie. 1997. "Feminists and Feminism in the News." In *Women, Media, and Politics*, ed. Pippa Norris. New York: Oxford University Press.

Iyengar, Shanto, Nicholas A. Valentino, Stephen Ansolabehere, and Adam F. Simon. 1997. "Running as a Woman: Gender Stereotyping in Political Campaigns." In *Women, Media, and Politics*, ed. Pippa Norris. Oxford: Oxford University Press.

Kahn, Kim Fridkin. 1992. "Does Being Male Help? An Investigation of the Effects of Candidate Gender and Campaign Coverage on Evaluations of U.S. Senate Campaigns." *Journal of Politics* 54:497–512.

_____. 1993. "Gender Differences in Campaign Messages: The Political Advertisements of Men and Women Candidates for U.S. Senate." *Political Research Quarterly* 46:4812.

_____. 1994a. "The Distorted Mirror: Press Coverage of Women Candidates for Statewide Office." *Journal of Politics* 56:154–73.

_____. 1994b. "Does Gender Make a Difference? An Experimental Examination of Sex Stereotypes and Press Patterns in Statewide Campaigns." *American Journal of Political Science* 38:162–95.

_____. 1996. *The Political Consequences of Being a Woman*. New York: Columbia University Press.

Ladd, Carl Everett. 1997. "Media Framing of the Gender Gap." In *Women, Media, and Politics*, ed. Pippa Norris. New York: Oxford University Press.

Norrander, Barbara. 1999. "Is the Gender Gap Growing?" *In Reelection 1996: How Americans Voted*, ed. Herbert F. Weisberrg and Janet M. Box-Steffensmeier. New York: Chatham House Publishers.

Poole, Barbara L., and Melinda Mueller. 1998. "Alienation and the Soccer Mom: A Media Creation or a New Trend in Voting Behavior?" In *Engaging the Public: How Government and the Media Can Reinvigorate American Democracy*, ed. Thomas J. Johnson, Carol E. Hayes, and Scott P. Hayes. Lanham, MD: Rowman & Littlefield Publishers.

Rausch, John David, Mark Rozell, and Harry L. Wilson. 1999. "When Women Lose: A Study of Media Coverage of Two Gubernatorial Campaigns." *Women & Politics* 20(4): 1–22.

Scharrer, Erica, and Kim Bissell. 2000. "Overcoming Traditional Boundaries: The Role of Political Activity in Media Coverage of First Ladies." *Women & Politics* 21(1): 55–84.

Terkildsen, Nayda, Frauke I. Schnell, and Cristina Ling. 1998. "Interest Groups, the Media, and Policy Debate Formulation: An Analysis of Message Structure, Rhetoric, and Source Cues." *Political Communication* 15:45–61.

Vavrus, Mary Douglas.1998. "Working the Senate from the Outside in the Mediated Construction of a Feminist Political Campaign." *Critical Studies in Mass Communication* 15:213–35.

Winfield, Betty Houchin. 1997. "The Making of an Image: Hillary Rodham Clinton and American Journalists." *Political Communication* 14:241–53.

*T*his *final piece directs attention to how Americans use the media to achieve their political objectives. Karen Mossberger and her colleagues examine the issue of access to the Internet across social groups. Government agencies are increasingly posting information about their programs on the web, many programs require online application, and considerable amounts of political information from both traditional and non-traditional sources are housed on the web. But, building on prior work, Mossberger and colleagues report that there are substantial "access divides" in terms of who has Internet access at home, an e-mail address, and a home computer. The poor, less educated, elderly, Latinos, and African-Americans come out on the losing end on each of these indicators. Mossberger and her colleagues conclude that the Internet access divide is still very real and remains firmly intact. This is problematic for representative democracy as politics moves increasingly to electronic-based communication and participation.*

The Access Divide

KAREN MOSSBERGER, CAROLINE J. TOLBERT, AND MARY STANSBURY
WITH RAMONA MCNEAL

When public officials talk about policy with regard to the digital divide, the topic usually centers on access. During the Clinton administration, policies implemented to address disparities in information technology usage were expressly designed to increase Internet access. Programs such as the Technology Opportunities Program (TOP) under the Department of Commerce and the Community Technology Center (CTC) initiative and the E-Rate administered by the Department of Education were put into place to increase access to disadvantaged groups. When President Bush released his budget proposal for the fiscal year 2003, it called for the termination of both the TOP and CTC initiatives.[1] The reasoning for ending these programs, like the justification for creating them, is based on access. The 2002 Department of Commerce report *A Nation Online: How Americans Are Expanding Their Use of the Internet* argued that these programs had met their goals and that the American public is coming online at a satisfactory rate.[2]

Whereas the Bush administration predicts sunny skies in its digital divide forecasts, others see darker clouds on the information technology horizon. More than 100 groups, including the National Urban League, the National Congress of American Indians, and the American Council of the Blind, came together on Capitol Hill in May 2002 to launch the Digital Empowerment Campaign to oppose Bush's decision to cut the CTC and TOP programs. Joining these groups was a number of lawmakers, including Senator Barbara Mikulski (D-Md.) and Representative Ted Strickland (D-Ohio).

They argue that, although it is true that Americans are getting connected in increasing numbers, there are still gaps in online use based on race, ethnicity, and income. For example, whereas 60 percent of the white households had Internet access in 2001, only 34 percent of African American and 38 percent of Latino households did. In addition, whereas nearly 78 percent of households with income between $50,000 and $75,000 have Internet access, only 40 percent of those with household incomes between $20,000 and $25,000 have web access. Groups protesting proposed cuts in the federal budget fear that elimination of these programs will make it more difficult to address inequalities related to technology access.[3]

This chapter presents the findings on access from our low-income survey and subjects our results to more rigorous analysis than the methods used in previous studies. We therefore provide more decisive evidence that an access divide in fact exists and is not fading over time.

＊＊＊＊＊

. . . [T]his chapter will use two different surveys to explore the influence of a variety of factors on information technology access. First, we examine broad trends in our own 2001 survey data, using simple percentages. Second, we analyze data on Internet access using information drawn from the 1996, 1998, and 2000 ANES [American National Election Studies][4] survey. The ANES is a nationwide, large-scale study that conducts in-person and telephone surveys using randomly selected respondents. The ANES allows us to examine Internet access over time, while our survey includes more specific questions about access to varying forms of information technology and also includes a representative sample of low-income respondents. In addition to using complementary data sources, we employ a more accurate methodology to analyze the data. Simple percentages are supplemented by multivariate regression procedures and a Monte Carlo simulation technique that estimates probabilities and predicts the likelihood of information technology access.[25]

LOW-INCOME SURVEY: PATTERNS OF ACCESS AND USE

Frequencies provide descriptive trends and a first cut at the data in terms of understanding who does and does not have access to information technology. Sixty-one percent of our respondents reported having access to a home computer, and 54 percent reported having home Internet access. This closely tracks the figures on Internet use for the U.S. Department of Commerce study conducted in September 2001.[26] Compared to the 61 percent of respondents who have home computer access, 58 percent had an e-mail address through which they can send or receive e-mail. Only a small percentage of respondents (14 percent) said they had high-speed Internet access. We also included more detailed questions on alternative ways to access information technology. This is especially important for low-income respondents who do not have a computer or Internet access at home.

The survey allowed respondents the opportunity to identify multiple locations for access to computers and the Internet. Almost equal percentages of respondents used a computer at home (54 percent) and at work (49 percent). Of employed respondents, however, 65 percent used the computer at work. Relatively small percentages of respondents (15 percent) used the computer at a school or a public library. Yet more than a quarter of those surveyed used the computer at a friend or relative's house (26 percent). This suggests the interpersonal potential of information technology use, perhaps for entertainment, information search, or informal instruction.

A parallel story emerges when examining venues for Internet access. Compared to the 51 percent of respondents who actually used the Internet at home, 34 percent used the Internet at work (45 percent of employed respondents used the Internet at work), while close to the same number use the Internet at a school (11 percent) or a public library (10 percent). Twenty percent used the Internet at a friend or relative's house, which is double the rate of Internet use at libraries and schools. For the general population, usage of information technology at home, however, far outweighed usage at other locations, even work. This finding demonstrates the importance of measuring home Internet access rather than lumping together Internet access at home and other locations. Home access allows more privacy and greater flexibility in terms of length of use and round-the-dock availability.

How do these figures change if we examine the answers given by people who do not have a computer at home? Do more of these individuals use computers at other places? Of the 710 respondents without a home computer, 30 percent use the computer at work, 9 percent at school, and 13 percent at the library. Twenty-four percent used a computer at a friend's house. These frequencies are comparable to those for the overall population. The data suggest that patterns of computer use outside the home do not differ significantly among those with and without a home computer. Individuals without a home computer are not using public access more than those with home access. The Internet is used even less outside the home by those without a home Internet connection. Of the 841 respondents without Internet access at home, 17.5 percent indicated they use the Internet at work, 7 percent at school, 9 percent at the library and 16 percent at a friend's house. These figures are lower than the percentages for the overall population. The data show that work or the homes of friends and relatives are the most common venues to access information technology outside of the home, regardless of home access.

Home and work are clearly associated with more frequent access to information technology than a friend or relative's house, schools, or public libraries. We asked respondents about the number of tunes they used computers and the Internet at varying locations. When asked, "Last month, how often did you use a computer at home," 14 percent reported low usage (1–10 times), 20 percent moderate usage (11–30 times), and 17 percent high usage (31–100 times), while 5 percent reported very high usage (more than 100 times). Very high frequency of computer use was more likely to take place at work rather than at home: 8 percent reported low use at work (1–10 times), 12 percent moderate use (11–30 times), 17 percent high use (31–100 times), and 12 percent very high use of over 100 times. In contrast, frequency of access was much lower at a friend or relative's house: 22 percent reported low use (1–10 times), 2 percent moderate use (11–30 times), and less than 1 percent of the respondents high or very high use at a friend or relative's house. Frequency of access at public libraries was even lower. Only 12 percent reported low usage, 1.5 percent moderate usage, and less than 1 percent high or very high usage. Although friends, relatives, and libraries may provide exposure to information technology, work or home access is associated with consistent use.

EXPLORING PATTERNS OF ACCESS . . .

The descriptive statistics presented in the last section give us a picture of current access and use but tell us little about the causes of disparities or the development of trends . . . [T]o understand changes over time, we analyze access to information technology drawing on the 1996, 1998, and 2000 ANES . . . Beginning in 1996, the ANES also began collecting data on Internet access and use. For the remainder of this chapter, we use multivariate statistics to ascertain which factors are statistically significant when we control for other possible explanations.

Before presenting our findings, a few words are necessary to describe our model. The dependent variable—the result that we want to explain—is Internet access.[27] The independent variables—the factors that potentially influence Internet access—are individual-level attitudinal and demographic factors suggested by the findings of previous studies and the fifth report (2002) of the U.S. Department of Commerce series, *A Nation Online: How Americans Are Expanding Their Use of the Internet*.[28] This most recent installment of the Department of Commerce's digital divide series indicates that, although Internet access has been increasing for all groups, there are still significant gaps based on race, ethnicity, age, and, in particular, income and education.

＊ ＊ ＊ ＊ ＊

THE FINDINGS: ANES DATA

By examining Internet access over time using statistical controls, we discover some unexpected patterns. One of the most stable findings . . . is that the young are significantly more likely to have access to the Internet, when we control for other factors. Although the young are more likely to have Internet access, they also tend to have lower incomes. . . .

Because young people were the first to embrace the Internet, regardless of income, when going online was a relatively new phenomenon, low-income individuals were actually more likely to have Internet access in 1996 and 1998. Thus, in 1996 and 1998 the low-income groups (which often included the young and students) and upper-income groups tended to have the highest access to the Internet. By 2000 the number of Internet users had expanded sufficiently that the expected relationship of increased income is associated with more Internet access.[31] . . .

Across the years, individuals with more education are more likely to have access to the Internet, holding other factors constant. In 1998, females are less likely to have Internet access than males, but this relationship does not hold in 1996 and 2000. There is evidence that strong Republicans are more likely to have Internet access and strong Democrats significantly less, confirming previous research.[32] . . . The other notable finding is that African Americans have significantly lower access to the Internet in both 1998 and 2000 compared to whites.[33] Our analysis of the ANES survey is fairly consistent with government reports that are not based on multivariate statistics and earlier studies based on e-mail access alone.[34] The main difference we discovered was that relationship between income and access was complex at the beginning of the Internet's diffusion, because of the number of students and other young people who adopted the technology early on. A more straightforward relationship between income and access has developed over time.

LOW-INCOME SURVEY DATA

The ANES survey data, however, do not include a representative sample of the poor or of African American and Latino populations. Accurately measuring the experiences of these important populations is necessary to sufficiently define the access divide. The ANES data also do not include measures of access such as e-mail. Do the same demographic patterns associated with Internet access using the ANES data appear in our national representative sample?

*****

As in previous research, the poor, the less educated, and the old were significantly less likely to have a home computer, an e-mail address, or Internet access. Unlike the ANES data, which include small samples of racial and ethnic minorities, our data indicate that *both* African Americans and Latinos were significantly less likely to have home computers, e-mail addresses, or Internet access than whites, after controlling for socioeconomic conditions. Findings from the low-income sample demonstrate that race and ethnicity clearly matter in the access divide, even after accounting for variations in income and education. Asian Americans and whites were found to have comparable access. These findings also provide evidence that partisanship is an important factor in measuring the access divide. Republicans were more likely to have an e-mail address and home computers than the reference group (independents), while Democrats were less likely to have Internet access than those without strong partisan ties.

Table 8.1: What Matters

Who Is Least Likely to Have Internet Access at Home?
Poor
Less educated
Democrats
Latinos
African Americans

Table 8.1: What Matters (continued)

Who Is Least Likely to Have an E-mail Address?[a]

    Poor

    Less educated

    Old

    Females

    Latinos

    African Americans

Who Is Least Likely to Have a Home Computer?[b]

    Poor

    Less educated

    Latinos

    African Americans

Note: The only statistically significant differences are the ones reported above. . . . When multivariate regression is used, these are the variables that matter, holding other factors constant.

a. Republicans are statistically more likely to have an e-mail address than independents, but Democrats are not statistically less likely to have an e-mail address.

b. Republicans are statistically more likely than independents to have a home computer, but Democrats are not.

* * * * *

   . . . [I]ncome plays an important role in determining home Internet access, controlling for other factors, including education, age, race, ethnicity, gender, and partisanship. All else equal, individuals in the lower income category had a 39 percent probability of having Internet access, compared to those in the highest income group, who had a 63 percent probability of enjoying home Internet access, a difference of 24 percentage points.

   Education was important as well. Holding other factors constant, college graduates were 21 percent more likely to have home Internet access than those with only a high school diploma; those with some graduate education were 35 percent more likely to have Internet access than those without a high school degree. Of respondents with some graduate education, 71 percent had access to the Internet at home, compared to 65 percent of college graduates, 54 percent of individuals with some college, 44 percent of high school graduates and 36 percent of respondents without a high school degree. Education and income emerged as important factors in the access divide, consistent with other studies, even in multivariate statistical analyses.

   As the earlier analysis of the ANES data showed, age continues to be an important factor. The simulations show a 24 percent increased probability of having access for twenty-eight-year-olds . . . in comparison to individuals who are sixty-one years of age . . . For the young, the likelihood of having Internet access from home was 67 percent, all else equal, compared to older respondents, for whom there was a 43 percent likelihood of having home Internet access. Holding other demographic and attitudinal factors constant, differences based on gender were not statistically significant.

Table 8.2: What Matters

Who Is Least Likely to Have Internet Access at Home?

Poor (39% for low income vs. 63% for high income)—24 point difference

Old (43% for 61-year-olds vs. 67% for 28-year-olds)—24 point difference

Less educated (44% for high school graduates vs. 65% for college graduates—21 point difference)

African Americans (37% vs. 54% for whites)—17 point difference

Latinos (41% vs. 54% for whites)—13 point difference

Democrats (54% vs. 64% for Republicans)—10 point difference

Note: Estimates are based on a hypothetical respondent who is female, white, and independent with values for education, age, and income set at their mean. The only statistically significant differences are the ones reported above.... We have calculated the probability of access, holding other factors constant.

Contradicting other reports that find only education and age matter in the digital divide, we find that race and ethnicity clearly do matter, though somewhat less than education and income.[37] Asian Americans had the highest predicted probability of Internet access (72 percent), with whites significantly behind (54 percent). Latinos trail whites (41 percent), and the probability of having home Internet access is lowest for African Americans (37 percent). The difference in the probability of home Internet access between Asian Americans and African Americans is 35 percent. Even after holding constant socioeconomic status, some racial and ethnic minorities (African Americans and Latinos) are significantly less likely to have access to the Internet at home than whites and Asian Americans.

The findings for partisanship were mixed. Democrats were less likely to have Internet access (54 percent) than Republicans (64 percent) and independents (58 percent). Because individuals with Republican partisanship are 10 percentage points more likely to have access to the Internet at home than Democrats, this may have some influence on policy. Republicans may be less concerned about issues such as the access divide, for example, or may be more interested in issues such as e-government, given their more wired constituency.

CONCLUSION

The aims of this chapter have been both descriptive and analytical. Our low-income sample offers a detailed picture of computer and Internet access for disadvantaged groups. Several trends are visible. Most Americans use computers and the Internet at home or work, and a quarter use computers at a friend or relative's house. A much smaller percentage (about 15 percent) use public access services at libraries. The percentage of people who use computers in places outside the home is similar for both those with and without home access, and in fact those lacking a home connection are less likely to use the Internet in other places such as libraries. This suggests a lack of interest or a dearth of knowledge and skill regarding the Internet. Frequent use of computers and the Internet occurs at work or at home. Information technology use in other places tends to be sporadic. These simple percentages demonstrate the significance of home access but can tell us little about what influences access.

. . . [W]e find unequal access to the Internet over a period of years and continuing inequities for the Internet, e-mail, and computer ownership. Our analysis of the ANES data over time demonstrates that gender disparities for computer and Internet access have faded. Statistically significant differences still exist in e-mail access, and perhaps this can be explained by differences in jobs. The complex relationship between income and age that existed when young people were among the earliest adopters of the Internet has given way as income has increased in importance. The ANES data show that African Americans are statistically less likely to have access, but the more representative sample in our survey shows that this is true for Latinos as well.

Table 1 compares the reported gaps in access to the Internet based on race, ethnicity, education, and income from the NTIA 2000 survey[39], Pew Research 2000 survey[40], and analysis of our low-income survey (Tolbert, Stansbury and Mossberger 2001). While Pew and the NTIA report only simple percentages, our analysis reports expected probabilities based on a multivariate regression analysis that controls for correlation, or overlap, between factors such as race, education, and income.

Table 8.3: Measuring the Access Divide

Internet Access	Department of Commerces/ NTIA Survey[a]	Pew Research Survey[b]	Low-Income Survey[c]
Race gap (African American vs. whites)	22.6	14	17
Ethnicity gap (Latino vs. white)	22.5	6	13
Eduction gap (high school diploma vs. college degree)	34.1	41	21
Income gap (below $30,000 vs. above $30,000)	39	34	24

[a] U.S. Department of Commerce 2000b

[b] Pew Research Center 2000

[c] Tolbert, Stansbury, and Mossberger 2001

Notes: For the low-income survey, data are predicted probabilities based on multivariate regression. Data reported on income gaps for NTIA and Pew are estimates because income is not measured in exactly the same intervals in the three surveys.

Although the NTIA survey overestimates racial disparities in Internet access between African Americans and whites, Pew underestimates the racial divide. Our data and analysis suggest that, after controlling for other factors, whites are 17 percentage points more likely to have Internet access than African Americans. In measuring the ethnicity gap, we again estimate a middle position, lower than the NTIA survey and higher than the Pew Research survey. All else equal, we find that whites are 13 percentage points more likely to have Internet access than Latinos.

Because simple percentages tend to exaggerate, or overestimate, the true relationships, our analysis reveals that the education gap is smaller than that reported by Pew and NTIA, but is still substantial and larger than disparities in access based on ethnicity or race. Individuals with a college degree are 21 percentage points more likely to have Internet access than those with only a high school diploma. Finally, all three studies report enduring gaps between the affluent and poor. Holding other demographic factors constant, we estimate that individuals with incomes above $30,000 are 24 percentage points more likely to have Internet access than those with incomes below $30,000. Our findings are consistent with those reported by the other studies.

The striking result is that all three studies based on different survey data and statistical methods report persistent gaps in access to the Internet based on race, ethnicity, education, and income. This is even so for the most recent data, which have been heralded by the Bush administration as evidence that the digital divide is vanishing and insignificant. The data reveal that a "digital divide" in terms of information technology access is an undeniable reality. Even as more Americans purchase computers and flock online, most of the disparities that emerged during the latter half of the 1990s remain.

Notes

1. Benner 2002, 1.

2. U.S. Department of Commerce 2002. 3. Wright 2002, 1–2.

3. Wrights 2002, 1–2.

4. Editor Note: Authors included this description elsewhere in the original.

25. King, Tomz, and Wittenberg 2000.

26. Our figures fall near the data for September 2001 cited by the NTIA. The NTIA reported 66 percent and 54 percent for computer and Internet use by individuals, and 57 and 51 percent for household ownership of computers and home Internet access, respectively. Our data for individual home computer and Internet access are within the standard margin of error of +/– 4 points in comparison to the NTINs reported household data (U.S. Department of Commerce 2002).

27. Because Internet access is measured by a dummy variable, with Internet access coded 1 and 0 otherwise, logistic regression coefficients are reported in Table A2.2.

28. U.S. Department of Commerce 2002. 29. Chew 1994.

31. We measure income by including an additional squared term (income multiplied by income) to model a quadratic equation.

32. For similar findings, see Bucy 2000. This does not, however, match the prediction that all strong partisans are likely to have access, as Chew's (1994) findings on other media suggest.

33. Recent research based on the CPS suggests that Asian Americans have higher Internet access than whites (U.S. Department of Commerce 2002).

34. Neu, Anderson, and Bikson 1999.

37. Nie and Ebring 2000.

39. U.S. Department of Commerce 2006.

40. Pew Research Center 2000.

References

Benner, J. 2002. Bush plan "digital distortion." *Wired News* (February 7). Available [online]: www.wired.com/news/print-10,1294,50279,00.html 15 May 20021.

King, G., M. Tomz, and Jason Wittenberg. 2000. Making the most of statistical analysis: Improving interpretation and presentation. *American Journal of Political Science* 44: 347–361.

Neu, C. R., R. H. Anderson, and T. K. Bikson. 1999. *Sending your government a message. E-mail communication between citizens and government.* Santa Monica, Calif:: RAND.

Nie, N., and L. Erbring. 2000. *Internet and society: A preliminary report.* Stanford, Calif: Stanford Institute for the Quantitative Study of Society, Stanford University. Available [online]: wwwscanford.edu/

Pew Research Center. 2000. Campaign and Internet survey. October 10–November 25. Available [online]: www.pewinternet.org/dacasets/ index.asp (5 January 2002).

U.S. Department of Commerce. 2000b. National Telecommunications and Information Administration. *Falling through the net. Toward digital inclusion.* Available [online]: www.esa.doc.gov/ftmOO.htm (18 March 2002).

_____. 2002. National Telecommunication and Information Administration. *A nation online. How Americans are expanding their use of the Internet.* Available [online]: www.ntia.doc.gov/ndahome/dn/ anationonline2.pdf (18 March 2002).

Wright, G. 2002. Groups, lawmakers protest Bush plan to cut programs to bridge digital divide. Gannett News Service (May 26). Available [online]: www.demews.com12002/technology/0205/15/technology-489537.htm (10 June 2002).

DISCUSSION QUESTIONS

1. Are some media sources more or less likely to enlarge the voice of poor Americans? If so, which sources?

2. The White House Project report, Gilens's piece, and Larson's reading each point out places where particular social groups are over- or under-represented in American politics with problematic ramifications. How does this occur? Are those who produce the shows and stories the authors discuss doing this on purpose? Does intent matter?

3. Many have heralded the Internet as a democratizing force in American politics. The selection by Mossberger and colleagues dampers this claim. What is your view? From the perspective of diversity in American politics, what role does the Internet currently play? What role might it play?

4. Gilens examined how major newsweeklies depicted race and poverty over time. His was a diversity-themed analysis of how a particular policy issue, poverty, was covered. What about issues that receive relatively little media attention? Make a list of at least five important national issues that receive relatively little attention. Do these "off-agenda" issues disproportionately impact certain demographic groups in the United States?

5. What if The White House Project had analyzed the morning talk shows for something other than gender? What do you think the findings would have looked like if they had assessed the racial, ethnic, social class, and/or sexual identity of those invited on the Sunday morning political talk shows? How, if at all, does this matter for democratic debate?

Additional Resources

HIP-HOP: Beyond Beats and Rhymes (2006) is a documentary that examines how women are depicted in hip-hop culture and what this means for protest and gender politics amongst African-Americans. Particular attention is given to hip-hop videos.

Bulworth (1998) is a controversial film that works at the nexus of race, politics, hip-hop, and social class.

http://commondreams.org
Common Dream provides a collection of progressive media articles on current events garnered from a variety of media sources.

http://www.accuracy.org
The Institute for Public Accuracy (IPA) "promotes the inclusion of perspectives that widen the bounds of media discussion and enhance democratic debate."

http://www.mediaresearch.org
The Media Research Center seeks works to ensure that conservative opinions are voiced in the mainstream media.

CAMPAIGNS AND ELECTIONS:
SEARCHING FOR VOTERS

New Mexico Governor Bill Richardson had appeal as a candidate for president as a Latino who also had both executive and foreign policy experience. However, he dropped out of the Democratic primary in early 2008 and later began campaigning for Senator Barack Obama.

As a foundation of our representative democracy, fair and competitive elections are crucial to both the theory and practice of our political system. We elect our political leaders at all levels of government regularly. Moreover, those whom we elect as our leaders can be an important measure of how "representative" our system is.

For example, some people would argue that a political system isn't truly democratic unless the significant segments of the overall society are represented in its governmental institutions. We have seen this perspective in each of the sections of this volume that cover our governmental institutions—the Executive Branch, the Legislative Branch, and the Courts. To some, the idea of representativeness has meant that there should be a physical presence of major minority group members in the three branches of government.

Of course, representativeness may be measured in more than one way, but people often relate to politics in general through the diversity considerations. It is quite possible that the social background of a candidate may be more important to some voters than the candidate's position on policies. For those voters, the significance of symbolic representation is greater than factors related to substantive representation.

When considering how campaigns and elections interact with diversity, it becomes apparent how the range of conflict and cleavages within the political system are expressed. Prior to the 1960s, such cleavages often took the form of loyalty to a political party by voters. More recently, these cleavages have been expressed through "identity politics" by increasing numbers of voters. For example, decreasing party identification in some voters has been replaced in some cases by an increased voter connection to their race, gender, religion, ethnicity, or sexual orientation. Evaluations of candidates and public policies may be made through a voter's perceptions regarding their own political identity, rather than a loyalty to a political party label.

As the central means for forming our governments at all levels, elections—and the campaigns that are mounted prior to those elections—continuously intersect with issues of diversity. Discussions of candidate qualifications often include such "credentials" as whether a candidate is a woman, Latino, or African-American, especially if the make-up of the district's voters encourages those discussions. The demographic background of candidates can be important because the demographic background of *elected officials* is considered important by many voters and groups. Both political party and campaign organizations often think of voters in terms of race, gender, or ethnicity because voters of the same demographic background have similar voting preferences and behaviors (i.e., they are considered "voting blocs").

The readings in this section address several important topics related to diversity in American campaigns and elections. These include how candidates, party organizations, and interest groups seek to mobilize minority voters, as well as how women are perceived as candidates. Our last article in this section provides a broad overview regarding the levels of participation and typical vote choices that have been made by minorities and other groups in the United States.

These articles cover both the process of campaigns and elections as well as the results. Because elections are held frequently and are an important part of the ongoing democratic process, how our population has changed and how electoral politics is responding to those changes will continue to be an important topic for students and practitioners of politics.

*I*n *"Looking for Voters in All the New Places,"* Ari Pinkus *notes the trend of the Latino population growth in states that one might not necessarily associate with such a trend, including Washington, Oregon, and North Carolina. This population will play a vital role in both parties' electoral fortunes in both the short and long term. Pinkus demonstrates how electoral alignments are changing and the role of minority groups in this contested terrain. This perspective highlights how demographic changes in the electorate can influence both the campaign process and the resulting electoral outcomes.*

Finding and persuading Latino voters is a particular challenge in the United States, but an increasingly critical challenge to overcome for those interested in winning elections: candidates, political parties, and even interest groups. As described in the Introduction, the 2000 Census has shown that Hispanics are now the largest minority population in the United States. They are by far the largest minority group in California, with an estimated 13.1 million Latinos living in California in 2006. Because of this fact, candidates and parties have begun to focus on attracting the support of Latino voters. As this article notes, voter registration drives that target Latino voters can make a substantial difference in the outcome of many elections in the United States.

Looking for Voters in All the New Places: Hispanic Immigrants Are Settling in Unexpected Spots, and Pols Scramble to Enlist Their Support

ARI PINKUS

A voter registration drive for Hispanics wouldn't be a surprise in states close to the U.S.-Mexican border. After all, one would expect to find large numbers of Hispanic voters there. But such a drive in North Carolina might be more surprising. North Carolina is one of eight states in the country where the Hispanic population grew by more than 200 percent between 1980 and 2000, according to the Pew Hispanic Center in Washington, D.C. The others are Florida, Virginia, Washington, Nevada, Georgia, Oregon and Massachusetts.

"What we're seeing is that the majority of the growth in the Hispanic community is in non-traditional Hispanic areas," said Maria Cardona, a principal at the Dewey Square Group in Washington, D.C. "We're not going to see the political implications of this growth for another 10 years, because a lot of these people are undocumented. Many are legal residents, but they're not quite yet voters. . . .

They are ready and willing to receive a political message right now, so they're ripe basically for the picking. Five to 10 years from now might be too late."

In North Carolina, the Hispanic advocacy group El Pueblo works on picking those ripe voters. The Raleigh-based nonprofit registered more than 1,300 people in 2004; for 2006, the goal is to add 1,000 more to the rolls, said Marisol Jimenez-McGee, director of the group's advocacy programs. But the possible number is far larger; before 2003, North Carolina's voter registration form did not include

Ari Pinkus, "Looking for Voters in All the New Places: Hispanic Immigrants Are Settling in Unexpected Spots, and Pols Scramble to Enlist Their Support," *Campaigns and Elections*, July 2005, pp. 26–27. Reprinted with permission.

"Hispanic" on its ethnic checklist. So in addition to recruiting new voters, El Pueblo tries to get Hispanics to re-register.

Statistically, the Old North State's Hispanic community reflects the national one, she said. The median age is 26, a third are younger than 18, and 60 percent are in elementary school. Part of Jimenez-McGee's task—and that of the Democratic and Republican parties—is to convince these people that they have a stake in the outcome of elections.

"I travel all around the state talking about the personal, the political," she said. "I talk about the personal experience of being an immigrant and assimilating into this country, and the challenges of that assimilation all within this political context. It creates an environment in which Spanish families are learning what it means to be American." She also knows what motivates her audience.

"What we found is that Latinos don't vote for a party; they vote on the issues. . . .

Issues of economy, job security, education, health. They tend to be more conservative, much more religious, and they tend not to support things like gay marriage."

That conservatism has helped the Republicans make some inroads with the Hispanic community, which had been more inclined toward the Democrats in the past. The GOP's opposition to abortion and gay marriage is in sync with many Hispanics. And to remind them of those philosophical similarities, the party dispatches operatives to Hispanic pastors and congregations.

The Democratic National Committee—a client of Cardona's—has had to adjust to the fact that it can no longer depend on getting broad support from Hispanics. That's partly because new immigrants from Central and South America do not understand the ties the party had with second- and third-generation Hispanic Americans, she said.

"The Republicans have understood these demographic changes that have occurred," she said, "and they are spending millions of dollars in changing the way they communicate with this electorate. The Democrats have not kept pace." To recruit Hispanic Democrats in North Carolina and elsewhere, Cardona tells her client to get on the ground now.

"Don't just talk about immigration, don't just talk to discrimination and civil rights. We want to hear about how you're going to ensure that the public schools are safe and effective, and that there are teachers and books.

"In immigrant families," she continued, "the mother is becoming a lot more involved in the kinds of decisions a family makes from a political standpoint. . . .

She's watching the television, she's listening to the radio, so she's the one who's going to get a lot of the news. Going to her is going to be just as important as going to the father."

El Pueblo's Jimenez-McGee has more advice for those hoping to reach her constituency "I don't care if you can say, 'Hola, mi nombre es.' I don't care if you can say, 'Buenos dias.' What I want to know is what do you think about education," she said. "Latinos are Republicans, Democrats, we're conservatives, we're liberals, we're progressives. . . .

A lot of it depends on what generation we are, if we're born here, if we're naturalized. You can't make assumptions based on ethnicity about what's going to sell us, and that's what's been the most challenging thing for campaigns."

In this next piece, The Economist magazine continues to explore the importance of Latino voters in U.S. elections. Because Latino voters have the potential to affect close elections, this group is considered to be a crucial voting bloc in current and future elections. From a campaign perspective, this often means that loyal supporters of one party or the other (African-American voters, for example) are more likely to be taken for granted as general election candidates and campaigns search for—and tailor their messages to—voters who could change an election outcome in a tight race. In close elections, candidates often tend to focus their attention on swing voters, on independents, and on undecided voters.

With this background in mind, New Mexico Governor Bill Richardson is profiled in this article. He is considered to be well-qualified in both domestic and foreign policy, and his experience includes serving as Secretary of Energy in the Clinton administration. As a Latino, Richardson has the potential to capture a considerable bloc of Hispanic votes. However, at the time this article was written, Richardson was not considered a front-runner for the Democratic nomination. Coupled with the article above, this reading shines a light on the increasing significance of Latino voters and the influence this may have on who wins elections, how campaigns are waged, and what kinds of public policies are ultimately made.

The Man from New Mexico; The Candidates: Bill Richardson and the Latino Vote

THE ECONOMIST

Bill Richardson is the strongest second-tier contender for the Democratic nomination, and the only one with any hope of challenging the big three—Hillary Clinton, Barack Obama and John Edwards. He has two main selling points. One is his résumé—which includes an incident in which he offended Saddam Hussein by showing him the sole of his shoe. The other is that, despite his name, he is Hispanic. (His mother is Mexican and, though he was born in California, he lived in Mexico until he was a teenager.)

Mr. Richardson's résumé certainly sounds presidential. After 14 years in Congress, he was America's ambassador to the United Nations. He has run a large federal bureaucracy (as Bill Clinton's energy secretary), and a state (he is currently the governor of New Mexico). The contrast with the big three is striking. Neither Mr. Obama nor Mr. Edwards has ever run anything much, and Mrs. Clinton's main qualification—eight years as the unofficial chief adviser to a president—is marred for some voters by the fact that she was married to him. One of Mr. Richardson's more amusing campaign ads shows him at a job interview where the interviewer shrugs: "For what we're looking for, you might be a little over-qualified."

Mr. Richardson's foreign-policy experience is a plus, especially when compared with beginners such as Mr. Edwards and Mr. Obama. He has won a reputation for troubleshooting in horrible places, having secured the release of American prisoners in North Korea and Sudan as well as Baghdad. And he proposes a swifter and more complete withdrawal from Iraq than any of his big rivals, which should please Democratic primary voters. On the downside, some of his more ambitious foreign ventures have flopped. A ceasefire he helped broker in Darfur this year, for instance, was instantly broken.

Mr. Richardson's domestic experience lends him credibility in crucial areas. A former energy secretary, voters may assume, will know how to tackle climate change. And he is reckoned to be a pretty good governor. He has cut taxes and balanced budgets, buoyed by an oil windfall. He raised teachers' salaries and extended benefits to gay partners of state employees. No one would mistake him for a stereotypical Democrat, though: he favours both the death penalty and gun rights.

He has weaknesses. He is a back-slapping, deal-making kind of politician, which is fine, but he often sounds fuzzy when talking about policy minutiae. And while hardly a slave to Democratic Party fashion, he is not immune to it either. In the 1990s, he supported the North American Free-Trade Agreement; now he says he is "disillusioned" with free trade.

Mr. Richardson's Latino heritage will probably help him. Hispanics make up about 15% of the population. Many are not yet citizens and so cannot vote, but the Hispanic electorate will have nearly doubled between 2000 and 2008, from 7.5 million to 14 million, by one estimate. Hispanics are both the largest and the fastest-growing minority, and their votes are up for grabs. Whereas African-Americans vote monolithically for the same party (the Democrats), Latinos switch back and forth a bit.

George Bush wooed them assiduously and won 40% of the Latino vote in 2004—twice the share his fellow Republican Bob Dole had managed eight years previously. But then nativist Republicans derailed Mr. Bush's plan for a more welcoming immigration system. Some of them, such as Congressman Tom Tancredo of Colorado, used alarmist rhetoric that sounded hostile to Hispanics in general. Hispanics duly dumped the Republicans—the Democrats' 19 percentage point lead in 2004 swelled to 39 points in 2006.

Democratic strategists confidently predict that they will maintain their lead among Latinos in 2008. Immigration reform is still stalled, and the top Republican presidential candidates, with the conspicuous exception of John McCain, are pandering to nativist voters. The line-up at Republican presidential debates was all-white until a few days ago, and includes both Mr. Tancredo and Duncan Hunter, who boasts he will build not one but two fences along the Mexican border. Neither has a chance of winning, but the contrast with the Democrats is nonetheless stark. Two of their candidates speak fluent Spanish (the other is Christopher Dodd). All attended a debate on Univision, a Spanish-language channel, on September 9th; the Republicans have yet to follow suit.

It is pointless to make long-term predictions about how a group as diverse as Latinos will vote—it depends how each party treats them. But one can wager that Republican raging about illegal immigration will boost the Democrats next year. If they take Florida, a big swing state where 11% of those who voted in 2006 were Latino, it will be hard for a Republican to win the White House. That is also true if they capture Arizona, New Mexico, Nevada and Colorado, which are all heavily Hispanic.

A Latino preference for Democrats, however, does not translate easily into a ticket with Mr. Richardson on top. At a recent campaign stop in Las Vegas, he stroked the crowds competently and bilingually, but without displaying much of his rivals' star power. And thanks to his name, many Latinos do not even realise he is one of them. Hillary Clinton, who is better-known and better-organised, is far more popular among Latino Democrats—a poll in March showed her beating him by 60% to 9%. But Mr. Richardson is bullish about catching up. He did well in the Univision debate with quips such as: "If you build a 12-foot wall, people will get 13-foot ladders." He is vying for third place in New Hampshire.

But still, his most realistic shot may be at the vice-presidency. The Democratic nominee is likely to be a white female senator from the north-east. A male Latino governor from the south-west would balance the ticket nicely. One snag, though, is that Mrs. Clinton is said not to be a huge fan. It is not clear why, but a joke Mr. Richardson told in 2005 cannot have helped.

In a speech at the Gridiron dinner, a Washington event where hacks and politicians traditionally mock themselves and each other, Mr. Richardson spoke about Democratic presidential candidates. "We've got a lot of good ones," he said. "There's Governor [Tom] Vilsack of Iowa—he'd bring back the Midwest. There's [Senator] Joe Biden—he'd bring back the national-security voter. And there's Hillary Clinton—she'd bring back the White House furniture."

In this article, we turn to difficulties that female candidates may face in securing votes. For example, one year before the 2008 presidential election, Hillary Clinton was considered a front-runner for the Democratic presidential nomination. She and Barack Obama fought a highly competitive presidential primary race throughout most of the primary campaign season.

The 2007 Washington Post *article selected for this section argues that female presidential candidates face particular challenges when running for our highest political office. The article notes that females must be seen as tough enough for the job, but still appear feminine. Previous studies have indicated that voters expect a president to be strong and decisive. Unlike male presidential candidates, female candidates must find a balance between appearing to be strong enough for the job, but not so strong that they are regarded as angry or unfeminine. Is it possible that there are different "rules" for female candidates?*

The Rules for Female Candidates

LIBBY COPELAND

BE TOUGH, TOUGH, TOUGH

Project strength, ladies! Set that jaw! If there is a single rule for female politicians—especially those seeking an executive office such as governor or president—it's that they must work harder than male candidates to appear strong and decisive. When voters don't know the candidates well, they are more likely to fall back on stereotypes of women as nicer, more conflict-averse and more emotional, says Leonie Huddy, who directs the Center for Survey Research at the State University of New York at Stony Brook.

Georgia Duerst-Lahti, a political science professor at Beloit College, says the phrase she sees most often in media reports to represent concern about female weakness is whether the candidate can handle "crisis decision-making." (None of that looking into another leader's eyes and just trusting him!)

You, Geraldine Ferraro, you remember! You were running for vice president in 1984 and got the question about whether you were tough enough to push The Button.

"They would never ask that and they never did ask that of a man," Ferraro says.

Duerst-Lahti suggests that the importance of toughness may help explain Hillary Clinton's relative hawkishness.

"She came out and she was the toughest of all of them in the Democratic field, at least on what to do in Iraq," Duerst-Lahti says. "She had to out-masculine all her male counterparts."

BUT NOT TOO TOUGH

In the 2002 Massachusetts gubernatorial race, Mitt Romney described his opponent Shannon O'Brien's attacks on him as "unbecoming"—after she questioned him sharply about his position on abortion during a debate. Unbecoming: antonym of ladylike? Discuss.

Former Washington mayor Sharon Pratt (formerly Sharon Pratt Kelly) was criticized for being cold. Clinton has been described by Karl Rove as "brittle" and by the head of New York's Republican Party as "an angry woman."

It's the same old story. A strong man is admired. A strong woman is—well, with due deference to a line Barbara Bush once used about Ferraro—it "rhymes with rich."

Female candidates traverse a narrow path, avoiding behaviors that might give rise to stereotypes. Be firm, but not angry. Be compassionate, but not weepy. Too much emotion: dangerous.

(See: September 1987. Patricia Schroeder cries when announcing she isn't running for president. AP headline: "She Says Crying Not Sign of Weakness.")

MANAGING THE CLOTHES

"Women are more likely to appear in business clothing in ads, whereas guys often roll up their sleeves and appear in work shirts," says Huddy. That's because women need to reinforce the image of themselves as competent and professional.

Republican strategist Kellyanne Conway says she tells all of her female candidates: "You need to figure out what to do with your gender and then you need to stick with it." That means one hairstyle and one look. The less written about appearance, she says, the more space for stances. In her 2000 Senate race, Clinton turned to dark pantsuits. "She basically put herself in what I call a campaign uniform," Conway says.

With that uniform and a relatively consistent hairstyle, Clinton blunted the impact of two of those female candidate bugaboos. There's a trifecta, you see.

"Hair, husbands and hemlines," says Duerst-Lahti.

Which leads us to . . .

MANAGING THE HUSBAND

This is a particular issue for Clinton, of course. But prominent spouses can be an issue for any political candidate because they tend to draw the spotlight away from the person running for office. (See: Teresa Heinz.) It just so happens that, as Joan Hoff, former president of the Center for the Study of the Presidency, points out, female candidates are more likely to have spouses who are at least as successful and prominent as they are.

And then there's the larger cultural discomfort of a man subordinated. Pratt says when she served as mayor, people tended to assume her husband had a larger role in the decision-making of her office than he did.

Cut to the academic: "It's because we think of men as autonomous and we think of women as heteronomous. Women are always connected; men stand alone," Duerst-Lahti says.

In a best-case scenario, the spouse himself recognizes the need to maintain a supporting role. Bill Orr, who once described himself as "a former male chauvinist pig," has said he had to come around to the idea of his wife, Kay, running for governor of Nebraska. But she ran and won—serving from 1987 to 1991—and he decided he needed to raise money to redecorate the mansion.

He put out a "First Gentleman's Cookbook."

BE PREPARED TO BE A SYMBOL

In the same way that a smaller statistical sample means that each person polled carries more weight, women on the national stage are made to stand in for other women. They are studied for what they tell us about the state of contemporary womanhood.

During her husband's first term, Clinton told the *Wall Street Journal*: "A friend told me I've turned into a gender Rorschach test. People are not really often reacting to me so much as they are reacting to their own lives and the transitions they are going through."

Everything is symbolic. Everything is closely studied for its intent and its implications. Which is why women can get offended if a male candidate calls his female opponent "ma'am" a lot, as Bob Ehrlich did to Kathleen Kennedy Townsend in a 2002 gubernatorial debate in Maryland.

Which is why some people looked at the Democratic debate last week and saw a front-runner being scrutinized, and others saw a whole bunch of men ganging up on a woman. A tough woman, but still.

"What was she—a pinata for two hours?" asks Ferraro, who is supporting Clinton and says she objects only to the nature and extent of the attacks, which she perceived as "personal."

"I can't remember when a front-runner was attacked for two hours like that."

"The tone was probably *less* personal than if she'd been a man," argues Democratic strategist Anita Dunn. "I think the candidates are being relatively careful."

Former congresswoman Pat Schroeder, who is supporting Clinton, believes the former first lady is scrutinized to a degree male candidates are not. She cites the recent interest in Clinton's hearty laugh.

"Have you ever heard the president's laugh?" Schroeder asks. She demonstrates with a breathy little chuckle. "'He-he-he-he.' It's like Woody Woodpecker."

Actually, people have been making fun of his laugh for years.

So much is about what you see in these inkblots.

*T*he final piece in this section helps us to understand which citizens pull the lever in the ballot box, as well as who skips the process completely. This selection by political science scholars, asks and tries to answer the question, "Who voted?" Over time, political scientists have created a variety of models to help understand voter turnout. The models seek to understand the relative influences of legal or structural factors and individual characteristics such as gender, race, ethnicity, religion, income level, and educational status. The Abramson et al. reading summarizes the record of voter turnout by major social groups in the 2004 election. Turnout is just as important as understanding how different groups tend to vote (voter preference for party or candidate). The Abramson et al. analysis confirms the findings of many other scholars—

those with higher incomes and education vote more than those with lower incomes and less formal education.

Who Voted?

PAUL R. ABRAMSON, JOHN H. ALDRICH, AND DAVID W. ROHDE

Before discovering how people voted in the 2004 presidential election, we must answer a more basic question. Who voted? Turnout is lower in the United States than in any other industrialized democracy, with the possible exception of Switzerland. . . .

In 2004 George W. Bush won 62 million votes, while John F. Kerry won 59 million, so the approximately 80 million Americans who did not vote could easily have elected any presidential candidate.[3] Both parties did a good job of turning out their supporters, although there is some evidence that the Republicans did a better job.

* * * * *

In 2004, George W. Bush received more votes than any presidential candidate in American history, and John F. Kerry received the second largest number. But these numbers are less impressive once one considers that the voting-age population was 221 million and that only 55.3 percent of the voting-age population voted. According to our calculations, only 28.0 percent of the voting-age population voted for Bush. . . .

. . . [T]urnout among the voting-age population increased in seven of the ten election intervals between 1920 and 1960. Two of the exceptions—1944 and 1948—resulted from the dislocations during and after World War II. Specific political conditions account for increases in turnout in certain elections. The jump in turnout between 1924 and 1928 resulted from the candidacy of Alfred E. Smith, the first Catholic candidate to receive a major-party nomination, and the increase between 1932 and 1936 resulted from Franklin D. Roosevelt's efforts to mobilize the lower social classes, especially the industrial working class. The extremely close contest between Nixon and the second Catholic candidate, John F. Kennedy, partly accounts for the high turnout in 1960, when turnout rose to 62.8 percent of the voting-age population and was slightly higher among the politically eligible population and the voting eligible population.[13] This was far below the percentage of eligible Americans that voted between 1840 and 1900, although it was the highest level of the voting-age population that had ever voted in a presidential election. Nonetheless, U.S. turnout in 1960 was still well below the average turnout attained in most advanced democracies. . . .

* * * * *

Between 1960 and the century's end, changes that tended to increase turnout occurred. After the passage of the Voting Rights Act of 1965, turnout rose dramatically among African Americans in the South, and their return to the voting booth spurred voting among southern whites. Less-restrictive registration laws introduced during the past three decades have made it easier to vote. The National Voter Registration Act, better known as the "motor-voter" law, which went into effect in January 1995, may have added nine million additional registrants to the rolls.[15]

* * * * *

TURNOUT AMONG SOCIAL GROUPS

Although turnout was relatively low in 2004, especially when compared with other advanced democracies, it was not equally low among all social groups. To compare turnout among social groups, we rely on the National Election Study (NES) survey conducted by the Survey Research Center and the Center for Political Studies of the University of Michigan.[18] The NES survey is based exclusively on whether or not respondents said that they voted.[19] In 2004, actual votes counted showed a turnout among the politically eligible population of about 60 percent, whereas in the 2004 NES, 76 percent said that they had voted.

* * * * *

Race, Gender, and Age

Table 9.1 compares reported turnout among social groups, using the NES survey. Our analysis begins by comparing African Americans with whites.[23] As the table shows, whites were nine percentage points more likely to report voting than blacks. . . .

[A]ll eight vote validation studies showed that blacks were more likely to overreport voting than whites, so it seems likely that these differences are greater than the NES surveys suggest.[24] Of course, racial differences in turnout are far smaller than they were before the Voting Rights Act of 1965. The first Current Population Survey of U.S. turnout, conducted in 1964, found that whites were 12.5 percentage points more likely to vote than nonwhites.[25] Racial differences in turnout may have been smallest in 1984, when Jesse Jackson's first presidential candidacy mobilized African Americans to vote.[26]

But racial differences were relatively small in 2004. According to the Current Population Survey, 67.2 percent of white non-Hispanic citizens and 60.0 percent of black citizens reported voting.[27] Given the relatively small number of black respondents in the NES survey, we cannot make many comparisons among blacks. Southern blacks were less likely to vote than blacks outside the South.[28] African Americans who had not graduated from high school had lower turnout than those who had graduated. Finally, as in most surveys, black women were more likely to report voting than black men. All of these differences were found in the Current Population Survey.

The NES studies include only citizens. As our table shows, Hispanic citizens were less likely to vote than non-Hispanic citizens.[29] The Current Population Surveys include noncitizens, but their recent publications allow analysts to calculate turnout for both the voting-age population and the voting-age-citizen population. In 2004, according to the Current Population Survey, only 28.0 percent of voting age Hispanics voted; among voting-age Hispanic citizens, however, 47.2 percent said that they voted. Even this latter figure, however, is far below the percentages of non-Hispanic white citizens and of black citizens who reported voting.[30]

Table 9.1 shows that white women were somewhat more likely to vote than white men. In all presidential elections through 1976, surveys consistently showed men more likely to vote than women. The 1980 presidential election seems to mark a historical turning point at which the participation advantage of men was eliminated. In recent Current Population Surveys, women have been slightly more likely to vote than men. In 2004, for example, among voting-age citizens, women were 3.3 percentage points more likely to vote than men; among non-Hispanic white citizens, women were 2.5 percentage points more likely to vote; and among black citizens, women were 7.5 percentage points more likely to vote.[31]

Table 9.1: Percentage of the Electorate Who Reported Voting for President, by Social Group, 2004

Social group	Voted	Did not vote	Total	(N)[a]
Total electorate	76	24	100	(1,066)
Electorate, by race				
African American	70	30	100	(169)
White	79	21	100	(769)
Hispanic (of any race)	63	37	100	(76)
Whites, by gender				
Female	81	19	100	(397)
Male	77	23	100	(371)
Whites, by region				
New England and Mid-Atlantic	78	22	100	(153)
North Central	80	20	100	(233)
South	76	24	100	(181)
Border	79	21	100	(42)
Mountain and Pacific	82	18	100	(161)
Whites, by urbanicity				
Inner city or large city	76	24	100	(156)
Suburb	80	20	100	(227)
Small town	83	17	100	(189)
Rural area	79	21	100	(146)

Table 9.1: Percentage of the Electorate
Who Reported Voting for President, by Social Group, 2004 (continued)

Social group	Voted	Did not vote	Total	(N)[a]
Whites, by birth cohort				
Before 1939	82	18	100	(147)
1940–1954	86	14	100	(203)
1955–1962	86	14	100	(129)
1963–1970	77	23	100	(98)
1971–1978	76	24	100	(95)
1979–1986	57	43	100	(94)
Whites, by social class				
Working class	66	34	100	(230)
Middle class	85	15	100	(456)
Whites, by occupation				
Unskilled manual	61	39	100	(87)
Skilled manual	69	31	100	(142)
Clerical, sales, other white collar	82	18	100	(193)
Managerial	85	15	100	(93)
Professional and semi-professional	89	11	100	(170)
Whites, by level of education				
Not high school graduate	58	42	100	(90)
High school graduate	74	26	100	(248)
Some college	80	20	100	(215)
College graduate	93	7	100	(131)
Advanced degree	94	6	100	(86)
Whites, by annual family income				
Less than $15,000	62	38	100	(72)
$15,000–$24,999	74	26	100	(77)
$25,000–$34,999	70	30	100	(81)
$35,000–$49,999	84	16	100	(111)
$50,000–$69,999	80	20	100	(123)
$70,000–$89,999	91	9	100	(102)
$90,000–119,999	88	12	100	(83)
$120,000 and over	88	12	100	(81)
Whites, by union membership[b]				
Member	85	15	100	(158)
Nonmember	78	22	100	(609)

Table 9.1: Percentage of the Electorate
Who Reported Voting for President, by Social Group, 2004 (continued)

Social group	Voted	Did not vote	Total	(N)[a]
Whites, by religion				
Jewish	95	5	100	(22)
Catholic	81	19	100	(208)
Protestant	79	21	100	(399)
No preference	76	24	100	(124)
White Protestants, by religious commitment				
Medium to low	81	19	100	(123)
High	77	23	100	(127)
Very high	90	10	100	(61)
White Protestants, by religious tradition				
Mainline	79	21	100	(134)
Evangelical	79	21	100	(170)
Whites, by social class and religion				
Working-class Catholics	68	32	100	(60)
Middle-class Catholics	85	15	100	(131)
Working-class Protestants	67	33	100	(119)
Middle-class Protestants	83	17	100	(229)

[a]Numbers are weighted.

[b]Respondent or a family member in a union.

* * * * *

Official election statistics do not present results according to race, and so we need surveys to compare turnout among blacks and whites in each region. As we have already noted, southern blacks were less likely to vote than blacks elsewhere. As Table 9.1 shows, white turnout, too, was lower in the South. Seventy-six percent of southern whites reported voting; among whites elsewhere, 81 percent did. The relatively low level of turnout in the South results partly from the lower level of education in that region.[34] Though regional turnout differences still exist, they have declined dramatically during the past three decades. According to the 1964 Current Population Survey, southern whites were fifteen percentage points less likely to vote than whites outside the South, and nonwhite southerners were twenty-eight percentage points less likely to vote than nonwhites outside the South. But regional differences were small in 2004. White non-Hispanic citizens living in the South were as likely to report voting as whites outside the South, and southern black citizens were only 2.5 percentage points less likely to say that they voted than blacks outside the South.

* * * * *

As in previous surveys, the 2004 NES survey found that turnout was very low among the young. Among the cohort born after 1978 (aged 18 to 26), fewer than three out of five claimed to have voted, and even the cohorts born between 1963 and 1970 and between 1971 and 1978 had relatively low levels of turnout. In the 2004 Current Population Survey, reported turnout among the entire citizen population was 63.8 percent; among citizens between the ages of 18 and 24, only 46.7 percent said that they voted. Older Americans do not disengage from politics as once was thought. Even in surveys that find older Americans less likely to vote, the lower turnout results from their lower levels of formal education.[36]

* * * * *

Social Class, Income, and Union Membership

As Table 9.1 shows, there were clear differences between the working class (manually employed workers) and the middle class (nonmanually employed workers). Middle-class whites were nineteen percentage points more likely to report voting than working-class whites.[38] Although this distinction between the working class and the middle class is crude, it appears to capture a politically meaningful division because when we further divide respondents according to occupation, we find that clerical, sales, and other white-collar workers (the lowest level of the middle class) are more likely to vote than skilled manual workers.

Family income is also related to electoral participation, with reported voting very low among whites with annual family incomes of less than $15,000.[39] Reported turnout was very high among whites with annual family incomes of $70,000 and above. Americans with higher levels of income are more likely to have higher levels of education, and both income and education contribute to voting. The 2004 Current Population Survey also revealed a strong relationship between income and reported turnout. However, education has a greater effect on turnout than income does.[40]

Surveys over the years have found a weak and inconsistent relationship between union membership and turnout. Being in a household with a union member may create organizational ties that encourage voting, and in 2004 union leaders made a concerted effort to mobilize their members to support Democratic candidates. As Table 9.1 reveals, in 2004 whites in union households were more likely to report voting than whites in households with no union members.

Religion

In the postwar years Catholics have been more likely to vote than Protestants, although the difference has declined. As Table 9.1 reveals, in 2004 white Catholics had only marginally higher levels of reported turnout than white Protestants. Jews have a higher level of education than gentiles, and postwar surveys show they have higher levels of turnout. The 2004 NES survey shows Jews to have the highest level of turnout among the three basic religious groups, although the number of Jews sampled is too small to reach reliable conclusions. Whites with no religious preference are somewhat less likely to vote than any of the basic religious groups.

In recent elections, fundamentalist Protestants have launched get-out-the-vote efforts to mobilize their supporters, and we examined turnout among white Protestants in some detail.[41] . . . We classified white Protestants according to their level of commitment. To receive a score of "very high" on this measure respondents had to report praying several times a day and attending church at least once a week, to say that religion provided "a great deal" of guidance in their lives, and to believe that the Bible is literally true or the "word of God."[43] White Protestants with "very high" levels of religious commitment were very likely to report voting.

Beginning in 1990 the NES has asked detailed questions that allow us to distinguish among Protestant denominations and thus to conduct analyses of religious differences that could not be conducted earlier. We can now divide Protestants into four groups: evangelical, mainline, ambiguous affiliation, and nontraditional. Most white Protestants can be classified into the first two categories which, according to Kenneth D. Wald, make up over two-fifths of the total U.S. adult population.[44] According to R. Stephen Warner, "The root of the [mainline] liberal position is the interpretation of Christ as a moral teacher who told his disciples that they could best honor him by helping those in need." In contrast, Warner writes, "the evangelical position sees Jesus (as they prefer to call him) as one who offers salvation to anyone who confesses in his name." Liberal, or mainline, Protestants stress the importance of sharing their abundance with the needy, whereas evangelicals see the Bible as a source of revelation about Jesus, "treasure it and credit even its implausible stories. Liberals argue that these stories are timebound, and they seek the deeper truths that are obscured by myths and use the Bible as a source of wisdom."[45]

In classifying Protestants as mainline or evangelical, we rely on their denomination. For example, Anglicans, Congregationalists, and most Methodists and Presbyterians are classified as mainline, whereas Baptists, Pentecostals, and many small denominations are classified as evangelicals.[46] In 1992, 1996, and 2000 white mainline Protestants were more likely to report voting than evangelicals. . . .

[I]n 2004 fundamentalist churches launched a massive get-out-the-vote effort, and in 2004 white evangelicals were as likely to report voting as white mainline Protestants. Given the relatively low levels of education among evangelicals, turning out at the same rate as mainline Protestants is an impressive achievement.

In Table 9.1 we can note the differences between white Protestants and white Catholics by looking at the combined effect of class and religion. The table reveals no differences between working-class Catholics and working-class Protestants or between middle-class Catholics and middle-class Protestants. But among both Catholics and Protestants, middle-class whites are more likely to vote than working-class whites.

Education

We found a strong relationship between education and reported electoral participation. Reported participation is very high among whites who have graduated from college, and low among whites who have not graduated from high school. Strong differences were also discovered by the 2004 Current Population Survey. Among white non-Hispanic citizens who have graduated from college, 82.7 percent voted; of those who had not graduated from high school, only 40.3 percent did. As Raymond E. Wolfinger and Steven J. Rosenstone demonstrate, formal education is the most important variable in explaining turnout in the United States.[47] Better-educated Americans have skills that reduce the information costs of voting and can acquire information about how to vote more easily than less-educated Americans; the better-educated are also more likely to develop attitudes that contribute to political participation, especially the view that citizens have a duty to vote and that they can influence the political process.

As Table 9.1 shows, among whites who did not graduate from high school,[48] fewer than three out of five claimed to have voted, whereas among college graduates (including those with advanced degrees) over nine out of ten said that they voted. Even though surveys may somewhat exaggerate the relationship between formal education and electoral participation, the tendency of better-educated Americans to be more likely to vote is one of the most extensively documented relationships in voting research.[49]

* * * * *

Notes

3. According to Walter Dean Burnham there were 201,541,000 politically eligible Americans in 2004 (personal communication, May 31, 2005), and his results suggest there were 79 million nonvoters. Michael P McDonald estimates that the voting-eligible population in 2004 was 202,674,771. See Michael P McDonald, "2004 Voting-Age and Voting-Eligible Population Estimates and Voter Turnout," at elections.gmu.edu[Voter Turnout 2004.htm (accessed July 25, 2005). Using his numbers, we would conclude that there were 82 million nonvoters.

13. According to Burnham's estimate, turnout was 64.5 percent, while according to the McDonald and Popkin estimate it was 63.8 percent. See Burnham, "The Turnout Problem," 114; and McDonald and Popkin, "The Myth of the Vanishing Voter," 966.

15. Robert Toner, "Parties Pressing to Raise Turnout as Election Nears," *New York Times*, October 20, 1996, Y1, Y4. For estimates of the effect of this reform on turnout, see Raymond E. Wolfinger and Jonathan Hoffman, "Registering and Voting with Motor Voter," *PS: Political Science and Politics* 34 (March 2001): 85–92.

18. In our analyses of the 1980, 1984, 1988, and 1992 elections, we made extensive use of published reports using the Current Population Surveys conducted by the U.S. Bureau of the Census. In our analysis of the 1996 election, only a preliminary report was available, but we used it where we could to compare these findings with those of the NES survey. However, in our analysis of turnout in 2000, not even a preliminary version of the Current Population Survey report was available. Fortunately, the Census Bureau published a detailed report of the 2004 CPS in May 2005. See *Voting and Registration in the Election of November 2004* (U.S. Department of Commerce, U.S. Bureau of the Census, 2005), available at www.census.gov/population/www/socdemo/voting/ cps2004.html (accessed June 21, 2005).

19. We classified one respondent who said that she voted, but who said she did not vote for president, as a nonvoter.

23. In 2004 race was classified according to the respondent's response to the following question: "Which racial or ethnic group best describes you?" In our analysis, we classify respondents who answered "Black," "Black and Asian," "Black and Native American," and "Black and White" as black. Respondents who answered "White" and mentioned no other race were classified as white. . . .

24. The vote validation studies are not free from error, for some true voters may be classified

as validated nonvoters if no record can be found of their registration or if the records inaccurately fail to show that they voted. The voting records where African Americans live are not as well maintained as the records where whites are likely to live. . . .

25. The Current Population Surveys are much larger than the NES surveys and report information about registration and voting for over 60,000 people. About two out of five of these reports are proxy reports provided by the respondent about other members of his or her household. A recent study by Benjamin Highton suggests that relying on these proxy reports does not create significant biases in analyzing the correlates of turnout. See Benjamin Highton, "Self Reported Versus Proxy-Reported Voter Turnout in the Current Population Surveys," *Public Opinion Quarterly* 69 (Spring 2005): 113–123.

26. See Katherine Tate, "Black Political Participation in the 1984 and 1988 Presidential Election," *American Political Science Review* 85 (December 1991): 1159–1176. For a more extensive discussion, see Katherine Tate, *From Protest to Politics. The New Black Voters in American Elections,* enl. ed. (Cambridge: Harvard University Press, 1994).

27. U.S. Bureau of the Census, Voting and Registration in the Election of November 2004.

28. . . . [W]e consider the South to include the eleven states of the old Confederacy. In our analysis of NES surveys, however, we do not classify residents of Tennessee as southern because the University of Michigan Survey Research Center conducts samples in Tennessee to represent the border states. In this analysis . . . we classify the following ten states as southern: Alabama, Arkansas, Florida, Georgia, Louisiana, Mississippi, North Carolina, South Carolina, Texas, and Virginia.

29. Our classification was based on the same question used to classify the respondent's race: "What racial or ethnic group best describes you?" The following categories were classified as Hispanic: "Black and Hispanic," "Asian and Hispanic," "Native American and Hispanic," "Hispanic," and "Hispanic and White."

30. U.S. Bureau of the Census, Voting and Registration in the Election of November 2004.

31. Ibid.

34. See Raymond E. Wolfinger and Steven J. Rosenstone, *Who Votes?* (New Haven: Yale University Press, 1980), 93–94.

36. Wolfinger and Rosenstone, *Who Votes?* 46–50.

38. We use this distinction because it allows us to make comparisons over time and is especially interesting for studying change over the entire postwar period. . . .

39. Our measure of family income is based upon the respondent's estimate of his or her family income in 2003 before taxes. For those cases where the respondent refused to reveal his or her family income or where the interviewer thought the respondent was answering dishonestly, we relied on the interviewer's assessment.

40. See Wolfinger and Rosenstone, *Who Votes?* 13–36.

41. A question asking Christians whether they were a "born-again Christian" was not included in the 2004 NES survey.

42. David C. Leege, Lyman A. Kellstedt, and others, Rediscovering the Religious Factor in American Politics (Armonk, NY: M. E. Sharpe, 1993).

43. We are grateful to David C. Leege for providing us with the detailed information used to construct this measure. . . .

44. Kenneth D. Wald, *Religion and Politics in the United States,* 4th ed. (Lanham, Md.: Rowman and Littlefield, 2003), 161.

45. R. Stephen Warner, *New Wine in Old Wineskins: Evangelicals and Liberals in a Small-Town Church* (Berkeley: University of California Press, 1977), 173.

47. Wolfinger and Rosenstone, *Who Votes?* 13–36.

48. Because there were only 31 whites who had not attended high school, we combined whites with eight grades of education or less with whites who had not graduated from high school.

49. Silver, Anderson, and Abramson's analysis of the 1964, 1968, and 1968 vote validation studies shows that respondents with higher levels of education do have very high levels of turnout. . . .

DISCUSSION QUESTIONS

1. Why are there differences in voting turnout among different groups of U.S. citizens? Do you support reforms such as same-day registration, multiple-day voting, mandatory voting, or automatic registration? What about the practice of printing ballots in multiple languages?

2. Historically some groups have tended to support one major party or another. Some of these patterns have not been as reliable over the past 20 years. What changes (political, partisan, economic, or social) have occurred since the 1980s that have influenced some of the voting behavior among Latinos, African-Americans, women, and Catholics? What issues of importance today will continue to change voters' preferences? Why?

3. Are there "different rules" for female political candidates—especially Presidential candidates? How must female Presidential candidates present themselves to voters that is different from male candidates?

4. Does a presidential candidate's ethnicity, race, or gender help or hurt his or her chances for a major party's nomination? It has been argued that early presidential primary and caucus states—New Hampshire and Iowa, for example—are not representative of the U.S. voting population and therefore unfairly influence the nomination process and possibly the outcome. Do you agree? Why? Can these states *positively* affect the democratic process? If so, how?

5. Traditionally, we have thought of the emergence of Hispanics to be restricted to a few states in the Southwest, in Florida, and in New York. This does not seem to be the case anymore. Why? What is drawing Hispanics to states such as North Carolina and Washington?

Additional Resources

http://www.cawp.rutgers.edu
Center for American Women and Politics (CAWP) at Rutgers University provides research and education on matters relating to women and politics, as well as training programs designed to increase the number of women in elected office at all levels of government. A related program is specifically designed to help elect Latinas to public office.

http://www.mccormacktmp.umb.edu/cwppp/index.jsp
The Center for Women in Politics and Public Policy at the University of Massachusetts, Boston, conducts gender-related research on female candidates, elected and appointed officials, and public policy issues related to gender.

http://www.chci.org
The Congressional Hispanic Caucus Institute offers leadership development opportunities, as well as scholarships and internships for young people that are designed to improve representation of Hispanics in higher education, government, and business. Programs specifically related to campaigns and elections include "Go Vote," "Go Run," "Lead a Political Life," and "Women Helping Women Win."

http://www.emilyslist.org
EMILY's List is an organization created to "help elect pro-choice Democratic women to office." Provides financial support through its PAC, as well as information and advocacy resources. EMILY is an acronym for "Early Money Is Like Yeast—it makes the dough rise."

http://www.ncbcp.org
The National Coalition on Black Civic Participation seeks to promote civic engagement and leadership for African-Americans. Among their many programs include voter registration advocacy and a specific goal of increasing participation among African-Americans under 35 (the Black Youth Vote program).

http://www.latino-alliance.org
The Latino Alliance PAC is a Republican-oriented political action committee that seeks to promote Latino interests within a Republican Party vision. In recent elections, it has been one of the most active PACs representing Latino interests.

http://www.now.org
The National Organization for Women (NOW) web site provides information on political issues, candidates, and campaigns, and offers opportunities to become politically active or make campaign contributions to a NOW Political Action Committee (PAC).

The Latino Vote 2008 (2008) is a PBS *NOW* program that investigates the increasing Latino voting population, its importance in the 2008 election, and Republican Party tactics in Florida that sought to win Latino voter support in the face of anti-immigrant rhetoric elsewhere.

Bulworth (1998) is a film that follows a disillusioned and suicidal white liberal politician running for the U.S. Senate. The character falls in love with an African-American woman and decides to be totally honest during his campaign by using hip-hop music and culture to tell the truth.

10

THE LEGISLATIVE BRANCH: HOW REPRESENTATIVE IS IT?

Members of the Congressional Black Caucus (CBC) hold a press conference on Capitol Hill. The CBC is one of the most well organized and cohesive Congressional caucuses.

The basics of our modern Congress were formed in 1787 at the Constitutional Convention. The make up of the delegates to that meeting was not very diverse, as the founding fathers were mainly affluent, white landowners. Looking at our representatives in today's Congress, one may not think that much has changed. The 110th Congress that took office in January 2007 includes a membership of the United States Senate that is 84 percent male and 95 percent white; in the House of Representatives those figures are 84 percent and 83 percent respectively. In addition, many members of Congress are trained as attorneys or business people and report that they have to take a pay *cut* when they serve in Congress and receive a salary that exceeds $160,000 a year.

As we noted in the introduction to Section 9, elections are fundamental to our representative democracy because they are the mechanism through which we choose our leaders. Some of the diversity issues discussed there (as well as others such as racial gerrymandering) along with those in Sections 11 and 12 are also important in this section on Congress because we confront similar issues in the House and Senate. For instance, does it matter whether the membership of our national legislature mirrors our population? What is the impact of a small percentage of women and minorities in the halls of Congress? This section builds on these themes and looks at what has and has not changed when it comes to diversity in the U.S. Congress.

249

The following selections encourage us to think of diversity in terms of numerical representation as well as the ways in which representatives may, or may not, represent the interests of those outside their own demographic confines. They consider whether it is best, from the standpoint of democracy, if elected officials feel beholden to the constituents who elected them as well as those who look like them but live outside their district. The articles examine and the role and place of diversity (or lack thereof) on Capitol Hill in Washington, D.C. While much of the discussion in this section is focused on representation and specifically the debate between substantive versus symbolic representation, the readings also illustrate the politics of identity, as well as conflicts and contributions brought about by demographic cleavages.

Overall, the readings consider congressional representation from the vantage point of those represented and those doing the representing. Questions of legitimacy and voice in a democratic polity tie them together.

*I*n the first piece Lois Romano provides a brief description of how women and minorities are currently represented in both chambers of Congress in the wake of the 2006 midterm elections. While the number of representatives who are minority group members or belong to an underrepresented group in Congress has increased in the last several decades, there was little change in the gender and racial breakdown of the Congress that assembled after the 2006 elections. One continues to be hard-pressed to say that the collection of officials we elect to our highest representative body looks like America. That said, strides have been made, and to go along with the returning members who include a former welfare recipient, a Cuban exile, and the son of a goat herder who went to Harvard, the 110th Congress includes some groundbreaking members—including the first Muslim American, Keith Ellison (D–MN)—as well as some additional "every day" Americans including a football coach, a social worker, and a chemist. With 86 women currently in the 110th Congress, there are more women serving in our national legislature now than at any other time in its history. For the first time in history, the Speaker of the House, Nancy Pelosi, is female (making her second in line for the presidency behind Vice President Dick Cheney). Finally, the numbers of African-Americans, Hispanic-Americans, and Asian-Americans also have increased over time—though not necessarily at a steady rate and, again, the 110th Congress saw no dramatic gains.

Hill Demographic Goes Slightly More Female

Lois Romano

The House and Senate elections this week added at least five women to the next Congress, the only notable demographic shift in an otherwise dramatic political upheaval.

For the most part, Congress will remain dominated by white men. In terms of racial demographics, neither body will see a change in numbers, but the influence of minority leaders could increase: Five blacks and one Hispanic are in line for House committee chairmanships.

On the religious front, Democrats in Minnesota elected the House's first Muslim member.

The congressional black population will remain unchanged at 43, with three members leaving the House and three elected to the next Congress, all Democrats—Yvette Clarke of New York, Keith Ellison of Minnesota and Henry "Hank" Johnson Jr. of Georgia. In Senate races, black candidates did not do well. Rep. Harold E. Ford Jr. (D-Tenn.) was defeated in his Senate bid, as was Maryland's Lt. Gov. Michael S. Steele. Sen. Barack Obama (D-Ill.) remains the only black Senate member.

Although for years Democrats and the black community pushed to recruit more African American candidates, there were no complaints yesterday about the status quo.

Myra L. Dandridge, a spokeswoman for the Congressional Black Caucus, said the elections had particular historical significance because "five members stand to chair five very powerful, prominent House committees." In addition, another member, Rep. James E. Clyburn (D-S.C.), is a contender for majority whip, the No. 3 position in the House.

"This demonstrates diversity among the ranks of the House leadership and mirrors how America looks," Dandridge said.

The number of Hispanic legislators remains unchanged, with 23 in the House and three in the Senate. Rep. Nydia M. Valazquez (D-N.Y.) is in line to be chairman of the House Small Business Committee.

"Of course, we're disappointed," said Arturo Vargas, executive director of the National Association of Latino Elected and Appointed Officials.

"The real issue for us is the need to field Latino candidates in non-majority Latino districts," he said. "We need to see that crossover, and we need the party to recognize viable Latinos. . . . For the most part Latinos in Congress are representing Latino majority districts. But the three senators show they can get elected statewide."

The elections added one Asian American member to the House, bringing the total to six, in addition to the two senators from Hawaii.

The elections also yielded several armed services veterans and an unusually large group of non-career politicians. Twenty of the new Democratic lawmakers come from a variety of professions—including a sheriff, a college professor, a high school teacher, a football coach, a social worker and a chemist.

Women in Congress made a net gain of five seats, three in the House and two in the Senate, bringing the total to 86. At least eight new Democratic women and two Republican women were elected to the House, with the possibility of a few more in still unresolved races. Two female Senate victors—Democrats Claire McCaskill of Missouri and Amy Klobuchar of Minnesota—will bring the number in that body to 16.

Women's advocates were hoping for larger gains but were hampered by the loss of four Republican House seats held by women. Nonetheless, the Democratic victories showed that women generally run well as agents of change "because they are viewed as outsiders," said Deborah L. Walsh, director of the Center for American Women and Politics at Rutgers University.

As far as having a legislative impact, Walsh said, "women do bring a different set of life experiences to policymaking. Women in both parties are more likely than men to focus on issues affecting women, families and children."

*R*epresentation is key in a body such as the Congress. But this concept is not so straightforward—especially when we add the lenses of race, gender, ethnicity, sexual orientation, social class, and other demographic cleavages. Indeed, we can think of representation in both "descriptive" and "substantive" terms. Descriptive representation (also called symbolic representation) focuses on the demographic characteristics of a representative. With descriptive representation, we look at a member of Congress and describe what social or demographic groups he or she fits into. In this model, the addition of more African-American representatives, for instance, helps legitimize the political status of African-Americans and brings the issues of concern to African-Americans to the fore. Some observers argue that descriptive representation also sends the message to all Americans that our society and political system are open and accessible to everyone. In other words, Congress becomes more legitimate as it approximates the demographic profile of the United States.

Substantive representation *focuses less on demographic numbers. Rather, it concentrates on the needs of a representative's constituents and whether that representative gives voice to these concerns regardless of whether they have a similar "bundle of demographics." The notion of substantive representation begs some intriguing questions you should think about: Can a member of Congress who is white effectively represent African-Americans? Should he or she? Is this optimal? The other side of that question is just as intriguing: Can an African-American member represent the interests of their white constituents? Similarly, are men able to represent "women's" issues and vice versa? Just as importantly, how do we determine how this occurs and how much is sufficient for us to be satisfied that true representation is taking place?*

Carol Swain's article builds on these themes. In the second half of Swain's piece she pushes us to another level, asking what, exactly, are "black interests" anyway? The same can be asked of "women's interests," "Latina interests," or "lower-class interests." Considering this issue requires us to think about how much of one's political perspective comes from one's demographic group memberships; how various groups' interests may overlap; and whether or not it is unduly confining to define interests, even in part, by demography. These questions are difficult but demand answers if we are to truly engage the issue of whether Congress is, or can be, a truly representative body.

The Representation of Black Interests in Congress

CAROL SWAIN

The political interests of African Americans are varied and complex.[1] Although the black middle class is increasing in size and some of its members are politically conservative, an alarming proportion of blacks remain at the bottom of the economic ladder, in need of the type of assistance likely to be offered by a liberal government and yet deeply distrustful of all government. The ability of the political system to address the needs of its black citizens is a test of representative democracy. More than two decades after the passage of civil rights legislation, African Americans are still underrepresented in political office, particularly at the federal level. They have sought to increase their congressional representation by challenging white incumbents in majority-black districts and by demanding that courts and state legislatures create new districts with black majorities. But often this way of proceeding has limited black politicians to two choices: to wait in the wings for retirement, death, or crippling scandal to remove white incumbents, or to fight among themselves for those seats made available in newly created black districts. And in recent years, the prospects for getting more blacks into Congress by using these two strategies have decreased dramatically. The retirement in 1990 of Louisiana's Lindy Boggs left no white politicians representing majority-black congressional districts, and 1990 census data initially revealed few areas where new districts with black majorities could be drawn. This situation occurred at a time when the percentage of blacks in Congress, although greater than it had ever been before, was far smaller than the percentage of blacks nationally. In 1991, when blacks held 25 of the 435 seats in the House of Representatives and

Carol Swain, "The Representation of Black Interests in Congress" from *Black Faces, Black Interests.* Cambridge, MA: Harvard University Press, 1995, pp. 3–19. Reprinted by permission of the author.

constituted roughly 6 percent of the House, African Americans made up 12 percent of the U.S. population.

The magnitude of the unsolved problems facing black communities throughout America raises troubling questions for people who equate black representation with more black faces in Congress. What will happen to black representation when courts and state legislatures can no longer draw new majority-black congressional districts? Do blacks have any alternatives for increasing their congressional representation? Can more black politicians be elected in majority-white congressional districts? Can white politicians represent black interests?

* * * * *

WHAT IS REPRESENTATION?

What, indeed is representation? And what is so special about black representation? Of the many analyses of the concept, Hanna Pitkin's is the most useful. Pitkin distinguishes between "descriptive representation," the statistical correspondence of the demographic characteristics of representatives with those of the constituents, and more "substantive representation," the correspondence between representatives' goals and those of their constituents.[2]

Descriptive representation can be examined by comparing the incidence of particular demographic characteristics in the population—for example, race, gender, religion, occupation, or age—with those of the representative. I define descriptive representation for African Americans as representation by black officeholders; that is, for this kind of representation the match between the race of the representative and his or her constituents is paramount. But a shared racial or ethnic heritage is not necessary for substantive representation and says little about a politician's actual performance. Bernard Grofman notes: "Being typical may be roughly synonymous with being representative, but it is neither a sufficient nor necessary condition for effective representation."[3] The extent and quality of substantive representation can be determined by examining the responsiveness of the representative to his or her constituency.

More black faces in political office (that is, more descriptive representation for African Americans) will not necessarily lead to more representation of the tangible interests of blacks. Robert Smith, Dianne Pinderhughes, and Mack Jones have used the term "symbolic representation" to refer to the failure of black (and, by extension, any) elected officials to advance the policy interests of the constituency.[4] In effect, they refer to descriptive representation that is *not* accompanied by substantive representation. Whenever we consider the descriptive representation of blacks in Congress, we must always ask whether substantive representation is also present.

WHAT ARE BLACK INTERESTS?

Because representation involves a relationship between constituents and elected officials, the question of interests immediately arises. What is it that is being represented? W. B. Gallie describes "interest" as an essentially contested concept—one that is used differently by different writers and that can obscure real issues.[5] But here it is sufficient to note that interest can have both objective and subjective components, which can at times conflict with each other for a given individual or group.[6] We may assume, for example, that two-parent families are "better" than one-parent families, that employment is better than unemployment, and that good health is preferable to poor health; but some individuals and groups may not share the values of, or agree with, those who attempt to define what their objective interests are. Thus what certain researchers consider "deviant" in some black families may only appear so because of the tendency of American society to judge black behavior by the cultural norms of whites.

Subjective interests are less observable because they are so closely connected with the feelings, emotions, and temperaments of the people involved. Usually subjective interests are, in fact, related to objective conditions and circumstances—but they do not have to be. The perception of subjective interests may be influence by cultural and psychological needs that lie outside the range of normal political activity—for example, the need of African Americans to feel that their contributions as a group are valued by society at large. Whenever an individual or a group defines an issue or concern as an interest, then that interest becomes at least to some extent legitimized as a worthwhile pursuit and should be taken seriously by anyone who purports to represent that individual or group on the issue in question.

If one accepts both objective and subjective indicators of interests as valid, what happens when these interests diverge? The conclusion is often that the individual or group is a victim of a false consciousness or, perhaps, of a consciousness that has not been raised. Those who seek to advance their own notion of the interests of a particular group commonly reach this conclusion. Having defined what is in the group's objective interest, they argue that it should be in its subjective interest as well, and, if it is not, they claim that the group is (for whatever reason) unaware of its "true" interests. The question of whether or not a group or individual is evincing a false consciousness is a normative one—it cannot be resolved empirically. For the present purposes, therefore, it is sufficient to identify objective and subjective indicators of the interests of American blacks and then to ask whether and to what extent these are represented in Congress.

No one can argue that African Americans are monolithic. Some are capitalists; others are socialists. Most live in the South, but some reside in the Northeast, Midwest, and other sections of the country. Some are doctors, lawyers, and engineers; others are sanitation workers, street cleaners, and domestics. Owing to these differences the interests of blacks must vary in important ways; still, it would be a mistake to place more emphasis on the variations within American black society than on the commonalities. Broad patterns of objective circumstances and subjective orientations characterize American blacks, and striking differences continue to exist between black and white Americans well over a century after abolition and a quarter of a century after the enactment of civil rights legislation.

*****

Black interests on Capitol Hill, at least as measured by the policy congruence between the representative and his or her black population, are better looked after by the Democratic congressional party. On every indicator, Republicans are less responsive to black interests than are Democrats. Black representatives are thus not the only source of black representation in Congress—white Democrats also appear to represent blacks well. If the Democrats continue to be the more responsive of the two major parties, black interests will be best served by the election of more Democrats. On the one hand, that the Democrats represent black interests, or at least the policy preferences of a large number of blacks, should be reassuring for most African Americans. It suggests that black interests will certainly be represented in Congress, even if the number of black faces remains low. On the other hand, black influence would be substantially reduced if the Republicans were to win control of the House. This is not to say that voting on issues is the only way members of Congress can represent their constituents. . . . Black representation means more than policy congruence between black interests and roll-call votes.

Notes

1. I am using the terms "black" and "African American" interchangeably to refer to people of African descent.

2. Hanna F. Pitkin, *The Concept of Representation* (Berkeley: University of California Press, 1967); J. Roland Pennock and John W. Chapman, eds., *NOMOS X: Representation* (New York: Atherton Press, 1968); Ronald Rogowski, "Representation in Political Theory and in Law," *Ethics*, 91 (April 1981), 395–430; Robert Weissberg, "Collective vs. Dyadic Representation in Congress," *American Political Science Review*, 72 (1978), 535–548.

3. Bernard Grofman, "Should Representatives Be Typical of Their Constituents?" in Bernard Grofman, Arend Lijphart, Rbert Mckay, and Howard Scarrow, eds., *Representation and Redistricting Issues* (Lexington, Mass.: Lexington Books, 1982), p. 99.

4. Their usage differs from Pitkin's use of "symbolic representation" as a phenomenon that occurs when constituents believe in the legitimacy of the representative because of what he or she is perceived to be, rather than what he or she actually achieves in office. Unlike descriptive representation, which can be discerned by the presence of shared demographic characteristics, or substantive representation, which can be identified through activities, symbolic representation is more ambiguous and less useful for characterizing black members of Congress. See Robert C. Smith, "Recent Elections and Black Politics: The Maturation or Death of Black Politics," *PS*, 22 (June 1990), 160–162; Dianne Pinderhughes, *Race and Ethnicity in Chicago Politics* (Chicago: University of Illinois Press, 1987), p. xix; Mack H. Jones, "Black Office-Holding and Political Development in the Rural South," *Review of Black Political Economy* (Summer 1976).

5. W. B. Gallie, "Essentially Contested Concepts," in Max Black, ed., *The Importance of Language* (Englewood Cliffs, N.J.: Prentice Hall, 1962).

6. William E. Connolly, *The Terms of Political Discourse*, 2nd ed. (Princeton: Princeton University Press, 1983); Isaac D. Balbus, "The Concept of Interest in Pluralist and Marxian Analysis," *Politics and Society*, 1, no. 2 (February 1971), 151–177; Brian Barry, *Political Argument* (London: Routledge & Kegan Paul, 1965), chap. 3; Andrew Reeve and Alan Ware, "Interests in Political Theory," *British Journal of Political Science*, 13 (October 1983), 379–400.

*T*hinking about how members of Congress from different genders, races, and ethnicities approach representation in the abstract, as we do in the first two readings, can only take us so far. It is entirely another matter when we consider how they put these ideas into practice. In other words, how do representatives use their understanding of representation to actually influence congressional policymaking? From a diversity perspective, do members from underrepresented groups negotiate day-to-day policymaking differently from white, male officeholders? In the next piece, Debra Dobson turns our attention to the real, material impact that minority members of Congress can have. Her interviews with female members of Congress demonstrate the decision-making processes these women go through and how they believe their gender affects their ability to get an issue on the agenda and decided in line with their own beliefs. She uncovers a variety of views reminding us that there is considerable diversity in perspective among women.

Representing Women's Interests in the U.S. House of Representatives

Debra L. Dodson

The all-male Senate Judiciary Committee's performance in the Hill-Thomas hearings raised questions about the ability of a predominantly male Congress to represent women. Those 1991 hearings angered women across the nation and inspired them to open their checkbooks as never before to support women (particularly Democratic women) candidates during the 1992 campaign. Increased resources of women's PACs, unprecedented enthusiasm of women voters for women candidates in key races, greater tendencies of women candidates to "run as women," and the election of record numbers of women to the U.S. Congress in the 1992 elections seemed destined to create a new political era (Cook, Thomas, and Wilcox, 1994; see also Baruch and McCormick, 1993). With 54 women serving the newly elected 103rd Congress, compared with only 31 in the 102nd, it seemed likely that more members of Congress would "act for" women because more of them would be women whose life experiences provided somewhat different lenses through which to view problems, policies, and legislative alternatives.

A critical question, however, was whether these record numbers of women who wanted to make a difference could do so in an institution like the U.S. Congress—a predominantly male institution whose members had come under fire for "just not getting it." The 103rd Congress seemed an ideal laboratory for exploring what would happen when the desire to make a difference on a whole range of policy issues collided with institutional norms, structures, processes, and realities. After all, even though record numbers of women were serving, they were still a small minority of members (initially 6 percent, then ultimately 7 percent in the Senate and 10.8 percent in the U.S. House) and they would be relative newcomers with less seniority, power, and knowledge that comes through experience.

The generous support of the Charles H. Revson Foundation enabled the Center for the American Woman and Politics (CAWP) to take full advantage of this laboratory, conducting interviews about women's roles and their impact on selected policies during the 103rd Congress (January 1993—January 1995). This chapter compares and contrasts the ways women made a difference in the abortion rights policies (Dodson, 1995a), women's health policies (Schreiber, 1995), and health care reform (Dodson, 1995b) in the U.S. House of Representatives. . . .

CAWP followed women members of the 103rd Congress from January 1993 through December 1994. CAWP conducted more than 250 in-depth, unstructured interviews with women members of Congress, congressional staff (working for members or committees), and lobbyists closely involved in at least one of seven policy areas (women's health, abortion, health care reform, the crime bill, NAFTA, internal congressional reform, and campaign finance reform).

* * * * *

THE BASIS FOR DIFFERENCE

Not surprisingly, most women members of Congress saw women as having some common concerns, and the vast majority of women members interviewed—Republicans and Democrats alike—acknowledged feeling a responsibility to represent those special concerns of women, in addition to representing the concerns of their districts. Differences in the events and experiences that touch women's and men's lives contributed to gender differences in what they recognized as problems and what they defined as important.

Many respondents traced women's common concerns to the sexual division of labor, with women members quite often speaking of women's role as caregivers. For example, when asked what women have in common, Representative Lynn Woolsey (D-Calif.) replied, "The need to take care of . . . our parents, our children, each other, our husbands if we have them. We're the caretakers. It isn't that men don't care about these things. . . . It's just that it's more important to us."

Other types of personal experiences contributed to a recognition of both common concerns and the relevance of politics to those concerns. Representatives Marilyn Lloyd (D-Tenn.) and Barbara Vucanovich (R-Nev.), both breast cancer survivors, and Representative Rosa DeLauro (D-Conn.), an ovarian cancer survivor, brought unique personal experiences to the public debate about women's health issues. These close calls in their own lives raised their awareness of and commitment to women's health as a political issue. While there were some differences among them, Representative DeLauro explained her views this way,

> I had an interest in women's health issues . . . because I'm a survivor of ovarian cancer. I was stunned when I came here to find out that . . . research on women's health concerns was almost nonexistent, that women were not part of the clinical trials and the NIH [National Institutes of Health], there was no Office of Women's Research at the NIH. So the whole focus on women's health was important to me.

Yet the impact of the personal went beyond women's health issues and caregiving, with numerous women members directly or indirectly alluding to sex discrimination. As District of Columbia delegate Eleanor Holmes Norton, a civil rights attorney, explained,

> Much of my view of women comes out of the life I've lived and the commitments I've made long before even thinking about running for Congress. Growing up in a segregated city and going to a segregated school raised my consciousness very early about [racial] discrimination. . . . The transfer of that from blacks to women was almost automatic. . . . By the time I got to Congress, my view on women and my feeling of responsibility for pressing forward their demands was very well formed. . . . This was just another place, another forum, to act on them.

Having for whatever reason recognized shared concerns among women, the vast majority of women members felt a responsibility to bring those matters to the table. As Representative Deborah Pryce (R-Ohio) explained, "Women have to speak up for things that affect women, because the men don't—not out of malice but because it's just not of interest to them." Nor is it in their realm of experience, as Representative Nancy Johnson (R-Conn.) told us:

> We automatically think, "How will this affect the environment? How will this affect people at the work site?" But we really don't think, "How will this affect women who work at home? Women in the workplace with home responsibilities? Women who are single parents?" I know a lot more about the shape of women's lives and the pattern of women's lives, so I need to look and see how public policy will affect those patterns and who it will help or hurt.

Although some of the women had come to Congress to focus on women's issues, others initially had been reluctant to do so. However, what these women encountered when they arrived left at least some of them feeling they had no choice but to speak for women. As Representative Marge Roukema (R-N.J.), a leader in the Family and Medical Leave effort, explained,

> When I first came to Congress . . . I really didn't want to be stereotyped as the woman legislator. I wanted to deal with . . . things like banking and finance. But I learned very quickly that if the women like me in Congress were not going to attend to some of these family concerns—whether it was jobs or children or . . . pension equity or whatever—then they weren't going to be attended to. So I quickly shed those biases.

A few of the women who felt a responsibility to act on behalf of women—even a few elected as recently as the 1990s—recalled their struggle with the legitimacy of acting on such concerns. Representative Patsy Mink (D-Hawaii) ultimately became one of the Congress's most consistent and tireless advocates for women, but she struggled with this concern as well, as she recalled,

> When I first came to Congress in 1965, I had a notion that my basic responsibility was to my constituents and my state. And gradually . . . I . . . realized that I had a far greater role to play. . . . It extended far beyond just caring for the constituents' needs. I had to speak for all the women in America. It was *not* something that I came to Congress understanding, but certainly it hit me very quickly after I arrived.

The acknowledgement by most women members of Congress that women's and men's lives give them different perspectives, combined with the sense of responsibility they felt to represent these different perspectives, provided a foundation for women to have a distinctive, collective, gender-related impact on public policy.

The question remained, however, of whether and how this potential for difference could be realized within Congress in any of these policy areas. At first glance, one might conclude that little was different because of women's presence. Women's health would seem to be a likely area where women might make a difference; however, in those few instances during the 103rd when up or down recoded floor votes were taken on women's health provisions, women and men were about equally supportive. Similarly, gender's relevance for health care reform was unclear, since women and men divided along partisan lines over the best plan, with little evidence of intraparty gender difference in cosponsorship of the major bills (Dodson, 1995b). Only on abortion rights did women cast consistently more feminist floor votes than their male colleagues (see Dodson, 1995a), but ironically it is an area where some have concluded that women are prevented by institutional factors from having any substantial influence on the shape of those policies prior to the floor vote (Norton, 1995). Yet, as the discussion in this chapter will show, women managed to make a difference in all three policy areas, albeit in different ways along the path from introduction to passage and in ways that can often be missed by reliance on traditional quantitative measures (like roll call votes or cosponsorship) used in legislative studies.

EVIDENCE OF DIFFERENCE: DEFINING THE AGENDA

In each of the three policy areas—women's health, abortion rights, and health care reform—the women members of the Congressional Caucus for Women's Issues (CCWI) seemed to reach some degree of consensus on a (formal or informal) agenda. With 41 of the 47 female U.S. House members plus the D.C. delegate being members of the CCWI, the bipartisan agreements forged within the Caucus reasonably can be considered the agenda of women members. The staff resources and structure of the Caucus went a long way toward fostering a collective voice among the women; without the Caucus women might well have supported similar policies, but coming together to work for those policies would have been far more difficult. As this section shows, however, the ease with which women could unite around a shared agenda varied across policy areas, as did the likelihood that the women members' agenda would be embraced by the entire chamber.

Women's Health

Women continued to do in the 103rd Congress what they had begun in previous Congresses: they defined women's health as a political problem, and they crafted and advanced a bipartisan legislative agenda to address it. One longtime Capitol Hill lobbyist explained, "If the women had not been there, there would be no women's health agenda. There never would have been. I think they are wholly and completely responsible. . . . I will go even a step further and say that the Caucus [Congressional Caucus for Women's Issues] is almost really the one that was responsible."

The Caucus initially introduced its bipartisan agenda for women's health, the Women's Health Equity Act (WHEA), in the 101st Congress. It was an 18-item omnibus bill to address gender inequalities in the treatment of women's health issues, with a particular focus on taxpayer-funded medical research. Women members continued to define the women's health agenda through WHEA, subsequently updating, revising, expanding, and reintroducing versions in both the 102nd and 103rd Congresses. By the 103rd, WHEA had increased to 32 provisions, 23 of which were sponsored solely by women (Congressional Caucus for Women's Issues, 1993). As in the past, sponsors of these measures included women from both parties.

These omnibus WHEA bills provided a variety of women's health provisions that could either stand alone or be attached to other pieces of legislation. WHEA was not only the women's health agenda for women members, but also the agenda for the entire Congress. Virtually every women's health provision that passed or came close to passing in the 103rd Congress had its roots in the Caucus' WHEA bills. The influence of the Caucus was apparent in some measures sponsored by men. For example, when asked about women's influence on women's health provisions included in the NIH Revitalization Act, the Minority Health Improvement Act, and the Preventative Health Amendments—all sponsored by Representative Henry Waxman (D-Calif.)—one staffer explained:

> The input from the women members of Congress, specifically the Women's Caucus, was absolutely the fundamental principal in getting these provisions in these bills. In every case . . . the initiative came from the Women's Caucus. . . . They [women members of the Caucus] were always wiling to negotiate on these points, but I would say that they were the springboard for all of the [women's health] provisions that were incorporated into these bills.

Three factors were central to the women's success in reaching agreement on a women's health agenda and in turn influencing the Congressional agenda. First, by focusing more heavily on the allocation of the federal dollars for health research, WHEA managed to avoid partisan conflict within the Caucus and within the Congress as a whole. Second, the rise of a grass-roots political movement to fight breast cancer increased constituent pressure on members both to support women's health measures and to take the problem seriously. Third, momentum created by these two factors was magnified by the absence of an organized political opposition to women's health.

Abortion Rights

If women's health is a case study in how women members forged a shared agenda that influenced the congressional agenda, abortion rights is a case study in how women can have at least some impact on the agenda when confronted by ideological and institutional obstacles. The pro-choice effort had been largely led in previous congresses by the predominantly male leadership of the Pro-choice Task Force. However, record gains for women in the 1992 elections brought into the 103rd Congress an infusion of members who cared passionately about reproductive rights. As a result, the CCWI adopted a pro-choice stand for the first time in its history, signaling women members' intention to shape congressional policy on abortion rights. The changes were summed up by one House staffer in the following way:

> Before [the 103rd Congress] the head of the abortion rights group was [Representative] Les AuCoin [(D-Ore.)], which I think kind of irritated a lot of women members. Not that he was ineffective, or that he didn't have good people working for him. . . . [But] Mr. AuCoin left, and someone else took that leadership spot, and it happens to be women. . . . I think the women have taken over more.

Nevertheless, this power shift was not effortless, and it was not as complete as one might assume given the success women had in shaping the women's health agenda.

Women members first had to agree among themselves on priorities, for a well-organized opposition to abortion rights meant that any pro-choice victory would be hard fought and require much in the way of political capital. When they began the session, the top priority was the Freedom of Choice Act (FOCA). But the increased presence of African-American women in the Congress caused the CCWI to reexamine its priorities and push funding to the top of its agenda instead. As one staffer explained:

> The area where you very strongly felt the increased diversity is in . . . what the focus on abortion was going to be. At the beginning of the 103rd Congress, the incumbent [veteran] congresswomen . . . were talking primarily about the Freedom of Choice Act and what the strategy should be around that, and [saying] we'll have it passed by the House in the summer. And primarily the African-American congresswomen said, "Wait a minute. That's not our priority. Our priority is funding and removing the restrictions on poor women's funding under Medicaid. It really means nothing for women to have this right to choose if they can't afford to pay for it and there isn't any funding."

The conflict among women over FOCA reflected to some degree the differences in the needs and concerns of their constituents. As one lobbyist noted,

> You have to remember that . . . people have different constituencies. For example, [Representative] Barbara Kennelly's [D-Conn.] district is not the same as [Representative] Maxine Waters's [D-Calif.] district. I mean Maxine Waters represents Compton, which is a very poor, almost 100 percent black district, and Barbara Kennelly's is probably the opposite. So I'm reluctant to say that the same amount of divisiveness that exists within the pro-choice movement exists between the Women's Caucus, because I'm not sitting in on those meetings, but . . .

Ultimately, the working consensus of the CCWI became that funding should be given priority over FOCA, and once that decision was made, the Caucus never took up FOCA again. There were no guarantees that women's priorities would sway their male colleagues. For one thing, women members were still a small proportion of the membership. Second, women had been ignored by longtime FOCA sponsor Representative Don Edwards (D-Calif.) despite the fact they had been a solid core of support for FOCA in Congress. Edwards, chair of the House Civil and Constitutional Rights Subcommittee, failed to consult them prior to introducing a version of FOCA some Caucus members found objectionable. A staffer explained:

> You've probably heard people talk about the first meeting of the Women's Caucus in 1993, when everything sort of hit the fan. That's when Pat Schroeder said, "They're introducing a bill [FOCA] that is weak on parental notice and funding." . . . It got people agitated, and that's when they said, "Let's form a task force." . . . You know, it seems unbelievable to me . . . that FOCA would have been introduced without the senior woman on the committee, Pat Schroeder, the senior woman in the House, having looked at the bill. It just seems surprising to me.

The Caucus failed to get the changes in FOCA that would have addressed concerns about funding for poor women or minors' access to abortion. Nevertheless, in an indirect—albeit negative—way their agenda did affect FOCA's fate. Even with unity among pro-choice supporters FOCA would have had a difficult time passing, because the antiabortion forces both inside and outside Congress were well organized. However, the erosion of enthusiasm for FOCA among the women and the redirection of women's efforts elsewhere (e.g., lifting the Hyde ban, Freedom of Clinic Access [FACE], health care reform) deprived Representative Edwards of some of the energy he needed to launch a full battle. As a result, FOCA never made it through the rules committee and to the floor for a vote.

* * * * *

EVIDENCE OF DIFFERENCE: INCORPORATING THE WOMEN'S AGENDA INTO LEGISLATION

Raising awareness of problems, developing agendas with solutions to those problems, and getting male colleagues to buy into those agendas are important first steps—but they are only first steps. The next step is to incorporate that agenda into legislation. Just how successful women were in doing this varied depending on their positioning within the institution—and the level of opposition to their agenda. Waiting until the bill gets to the House floor might be for naught, since the rule governing debate may limit amendments and lobbying the full chamber rather than simply a committee or subcommittee may take a great deal more effort.

Women's Health

Committee assignments were important in determining whether the agendas that women coalesced around would be reflected in legislation. This was true even in the case of women's health—an issue no member wanted to be seen as opposing. (As one women's health advocate put it, "When those guys come out of committee, they don't want to be seen as voting against breast cancer [research]—that doesn't look good. There's a certain amount of bipartisanship based on the sort of 'mom and apple pie' issues that women's health now represents.") Although the momentum behind women's health remained strong and stable across the 102nd and 103rd Congresses, one major change between the two Congresses (in addition to the shift from a Bush to a Clinton administration) was that women members were added to the Appropriations' Labor, Health and Human Services subcommittee (Labor/HHS) during the 103rd Congress. No longer would women have to lobby the panel as outsiders, as one Democratic staffer explained:

> We got . . . women [on] a committee that had not had women on it since 1974. But when you added . . . [four] women onto an entity that had not had women on it before, . . . it . . . accelerated and increased an influence [support for women's health] that was already felt because of the involvement of people outside the subcommittee itself with the issues that we handle. But it was a very significant change.

In the absence of women members, there almost certainly would have been some appropriations for women's health. However, it is significant that in an era of cutbacks, the addition of women to the Labor, Health and Human Services (Labor/HHS) subcommittee was accompanied by some substantial increases in women's health funding during the 103rd Congress: the National Cancer Institute's appropriation for breast cancer research increased 75 percent; Breast and Cervical Cancer Mortality Prevention Act appropriations increased by approximately a third; and the NIH Women's Health Initiative appropriations increased substantially (Congressional Caucus for Women's Issues, 1994c). In addition, language in the Labor/HHS committee report targeted monies for breast, cervical, and ovarian cancers; osteoporosis; lupus; and problems disproportionately affecting aging women. Getting this language into the report was significant because it meant that agencies could be held accountable in the next appropriations cycle for activities on these medical concerns.

Not surprisingly, the general consensus in interviews was that having women on that subcommittee played a critical role in increases for women's health programs. As one lobbyist recalled:

> Women on the Appropriations Committee . . . really went to bat for us. . . . It's very easy to get members of Congress to say they're *for* more money for breast cancer research, or they of course want to see the breast cancer epidemic ended. And of course they believe it's an important issue. But it's not so easy to find members of Congress who are willing to actually pick up the banner and go into battle on the issue. Nita Lowey did that. And Nancy Pelosi did it. Rosa DeLauro. The women members who were on the Appropriations Committee really went into battle on this issue.

With money limited, Representative Pelosi (D-Calif.) summed up the impact of women on that subcommittee in the 103rd: "It helps a great deal to have women at the table when the pie is being carved up. . . . Our presence there made a tremendous difference in the breast cancer money."

*****

Abortion Rights

If it was important to have women on a committee to advocate for universally popular programs like finding a cure for breast cancer, their presence was even more critical on Labor/HHS Appropriations when it came to the ever-controversial issue of Medicaid funding of abortion. It is probably true that abortion rights legislation of some type would have been on the agenda regardless of whether women served on key committees; but without women on the Labor/HHS Appropriations subcommittee, the Caucus's priority of overturning the Hyde ban on Medicaid funding of abortions probably would not have been pursued as vigorously. The success Representatives Rosa DeLauro (D-Conn.), Nancy Pelosi (D-Calif.), and Nita Lowey (D-N.Y.) had in lifting the Hyde Amendment from the Labor/HHS Appropriations bill in subcommittee was a reflection of their commitment to choice and their willingness to challenge business as usual. As one staffer recounted:

> When I say the women were critical to this [removing the Hyde Amendment in the subcommittee], it has to do with the composition of the subcommittee, fundamentally, which changed by their presence. . . . We probably had a majority for years on rape and incest. But as a courtesy to Mr. Natcher [the subcommittee chair], in fact, people did not raise that as a subcommittee issue. It was always dealt with in full committee or on the floor. . . . So you had a change in the composition, and the votes were just different in subcommittee. And women were part of that.

Nevertheless, having women in key committee positions committed to pursuing the CCWI's priorities could not ensure victory—it could only ensure that the issue was placed on the agenda. In a 31–18 vote, the full committee reversed the subcommittee action and restored the Hyde Amendment. Some blamed women for the loss, citing poor strategy on their part; others chalked up the win for Hyde to the ideological composition of the committee. The reasons for their loss in committee (and later their crushing defeat on the floor) remain a matter of debate. However, the commitment of a minority of members, particularly in the face of an organized opposition, could not ensure victory.

Health Care Reform

The politics of health care reform and abortion rights were alike in two respects: (1) both would have been on the agenda of the 103rd Congress regardless of whether women served; and (2) having women who supported the CCWI's agenda on relevant committees increased the likelihood that their shared agenda would be included in bills, for the Caucus members were limited in what they could accomplish as outsiders.

The Ways and Means Committee is a case in point. After much highly publicized criticism by women members about the inadequate women's health provisions in the Clinton health plan (e.g., biennial, rather than annual, mammography coverage for women 50 and older), the chair's markup (or amendments) in Ways and Means altered coverage to bring it closer to current medical standards. It provided biennial mammography coverage for women in their forties and annual coverage for women 50–64. However, in a cost-saving move, coverage then reverted to biennial coverage for women 65 and older. Both female members of the panel, Representatives Nancy Johnson (R-Conn.) and Barbara Kennelly (D-Conn.), offered amendments to strengthen mammography coverage and these were the only such amendments that come to a vote. But it was Kennelly who succeeded in improving the bill for women.

Representative Kennelly found the $40 million needed to cover the cost of annual mammograms for seniors, offered the amendment, and got it passed on a voice vote in the committee. Whether a male member of the committee would have offered the same amendment in the absence of women is unclear (although it is noteworthy that Representative Nancy Johnson offered the only other mammography provision that was brought to a vote in that committee). What is clear is that having an advocate for women's health needs on the committee was important, as this Republican staffer noted:

> She [Mrs. Kennelly] was able to offer that amendment at the Ways and Means Committee [stage] and find the revenue to pay for it. An amendment like that would almost certainly have never passed on the floor. . . . For all practical purposes, the tax portions of it are locked off . . . any bill that comes out of the Ways and Means Committee. They are not subject to amendment [on the floor].

* * * * *

CONCLUSION

In each of the three policy areas, women members of the 103rd Congress made a difference. The scope of that difference and how it manifested itself varied across the policy areas; but with methodological tools sufficiently flexible, their distinctive gender-related impact could be observed. Some policy areas are easier for women to reach bipartisan agreement on than others; concerns of race, class, and ideology seemed less relevant to women members' interactions on women's health, for example, than on abortion or health care reform. Women were better able to get the Caucus's consensus incorporated into legislation on health issues than in other areas, and this difference was partially due to committee assignments, the extent to which the membership of committees or the House would support them, and the degree of organized opposition to their efforts. As a small minority of members (and a minority that is lower in seniority, status, and committee power than men), women needed sympathetic male colleagues who would support their agenda and help them work to advance it. And, as almost any newly emerging group finds, the decision to attempt to take control of an area where many political battles have been fought previously places the group in the position of treading on territory already staked out by others, as happened with reproductive rights and FOCA in particular.

* * * * *

Finally, two cautionary notes. First, when women members of Congress talk enthusiastically about women's shared concerns and the responsibility they feel to represent those concerns, they may convey an image of unity and consensus that fails to reflect the diversity among women. Women differ in the solutions they see to the problems that women face, they differ in the kinds of women they represent, and they differ in the extent to which these concerns are salient. As clichéd as it has become, women are not monolithic . . . Second, men have played important roles in supporting women's agendas. Until women are chairs of powerful and key committees, hold half the leadership positions, and have the expertise that comes through years of experience, they will have to continue to build the strong ties to male colleagues that enable them to accomplish goals they would not otherwise accomplish.

References

Baruch, L., and K. McCormick. 1993. "Women's PACs Dramatically Increase Their Support in 1992: An Overview." *CAWP News and Notes* (Winter): 10.

Congressional Caucus for Women's Issues. 1993. "Women's Caucus Calls for Equitable Treatment of Women in Health Care Reform." Press release, September 14.

Congressional Caucus for Women's Issues. 1994c. "Summary of Health Care Reform Proposals." *Update* (June): 10.

Cook, Elizabeth Adell, Sue Thomas, and Clyde Wilcox, eds. 1994. *The Year of the Woman: Myths and Realities.* Boulder, Colo.: Westview Press.

Dodson, Debra L. 1995a. "The Impact of Congresswomen on Reproductive Rights Policies in the 103rd Congress." Paper presented at the Annual Meeting of the Midwest Political Science Association, April 6–8.

Dodson, Debra L. 1995b. "The Impact of Women on Health Care Reform" The Case of the 103rd Congress." Paper presented at the Annual Meeting of the American Political Science Association.

Norton, Noelle. 1995. "Women, It's Not Enough to Be Elected: Committee Position Makes a Difference." In *Gender Power, Leadership and Governance*, ed. Georgia Duerst-Lahti and Rita Mae Kelly. Ann Arbor: University of Michigan Press.

Schreiber, R. 1995. "'To Vote Against Breast Cancer Research Is to Vote Against Women': The Rise of Women's Health on the National Agenda." Paper presented at the annual meeting of the Midwest Political Science Association, April 6–8.

*T*he final piece in this section makes us consider members of underrepresented groups from perspectives beyond demography while simultaneously recognizing demography matters. The piece chronicles the important role U.S. Senator Susan Collins (R-ME) played in implementing the recommendations to reform the intelligence community provided by the 9/11 Commission in the wake of the attacks of 2001. Martin Kaddy II's article documents how Collins was the handpicked chair of both the Democratic and Republican leadership to lead the Senate Governmental Affairs Committee. This recounting of a female senator at the center of a critical and delicate governmental reform is a clear example of the contributions that women *have made in the halls of Congress. As the Collins case suggests, members of under-represented groups do not just weigh in on "their" issues. Collins was chosen to lead the important committee on governmental responses to terrorism because of her moderate nature and her ability to work with senators on both sides of the aisle. In this manner, she corresponds to classic views of women as "bridge builders" but also departs from these views about women in Congress in that she is a member of the Republican Party and was working at the epicenter of national security issues.*

In the Eye of the Overhaul Storm

Martin Kady II

Late at night on July 22, as the Senate prepared to close up shop for its August recess, Republican and Democratic leaders huddled together to decide who would lead the Senate's effort to put the recommendations of the independent Sept. 11 commission into a bill.

There was no argument, according to leadership aides familiar with the decision.

Majority Leader Bill Frist and Minority Leader Tom Daschle agreed: Susan Collins, a moderate Republican from Maine and chairwoman of the Governmental Affairs Committee, would guide the chamber through the creation of a national intelligence director and a centralized counterterrorism operation.

It was not just a matter of committee jurisdiction that put Collins at the helm of the proposed overhaul. Her soft-spoken, deliberate public speaking style belies a tenacity and investigative focus she has shown with top national security officials, whether as committee chairwoman or as a lower-ranking member of Armed Services, where she grilled Army generals about the Abu Ghraib prison scandal.

Collins is at the center of this intelligence overhaul because she runs a committee that has already taken on major government reorganization with the creation of the Department of Homeland Security, and because she appears to hold no parochial allegiances to the intelligence agencies that have been targeted for a shake-up. As a moderate voice in a very divided Senate, she has friends on both sides of the aisle, and her position on very tight votes is always closely watched. Legislation that comes out of Governmental Affairs should have a strong head of steam because it has the firm imprint of Collins and the panel's ranking Democrat, moderate Joseph I. Lieberman of Connecticut.

* * * * *

Collins is venturing into a political and bureaucratic swamp, bogged down by the institutional resistance of the intelligence community, turf wars among committee

Martin Kady II, "In the Eye of the Overhaul Storm," *CQ Weekly*, vol. 62, no. 32 (August 7, 2004), pp. 1906-1911. Copyright 2004 by Congressional Quarterly Inc. Reproduced with permission of Congressional Quarterly Inc. in the format Textbook via Copyright Clearance Center.

chairmen and a White House that is hesitant to make sweeping changes that would create a truly powerful intelligence chief.

"The stakes are very high, the issues are complicated, and people resist reorganization," Collins said in an interview. "I do not discount in any way how very difficult this is going to be. . . . These are individuals who fiercely resist having their authority taken away, but we can't just let it doom any reform."

* * * * *

On Capitol Hill, a total of nine committees have scheduled a dozen hearings throughout the month—a sign that members are politically sensitive to the Sept. 11 commission's call for change. But the number of panels involved underscores another problem highlighted by the independent commission: Too many committees claim jurisdiction over the intelligence community, resulting in shoddy oversight. The commission has urged Congress to reorganize itself by giving intelligence committees more powers and creating permanent Homeland Security committees in both chambers. That is a tall order in that it would involve forcing powerful chairmen to give up coveted oversight and budgetary prerogatives.

History does not favor Collins' prospect for changing how the closely guarded spy world conducts its business. A look at the past 50 years of efforts to overhaul the intelligence structure reveals a trail of failed and forgotten initiatives. Her colleagues say the challenge she faces is matched only by the urgent need to fix the intelligence community.

"This is a situation that cries out for acting in the national interest," said Lieberman. Referring to the task that has fallen on Collins' shoulders, he said, "This is a test."

GROOMED FOR THE JOB?

Collins is the least senior head of a standing Senate committee and has not had as high a profile in national security issues as lawmakers such as John W. Warner, R-Va., chairman of Armed Services, or Pat Roberts, R-Kan., head of Select Intelligence. In many ways, however, Collins has been groomed for the job of overhauling the intelligence structure for nearly 30 years, dating back to her days as an intern for then-Rep. William S. Cohen of Main (House, 1973–79; Senate, 1979–97) during the summer Watergate hearings in 1974.

Cohen "was a freshman Republican standing in judgment of his party's president," Collins recalls.

Collins also carries with her the spirit of a long line of savvy yet independent Maine politicos. Her father and mother were both mayors of the down-eastern town of Caribou, and four generations of ancestors served in the Maine Legislature.

Maine politicians tend to see themselves as outsiders—hearty individuals who distrust big government and the national party line. That explains Collins' two role models, former Main Republican Sen. Margaret Chase Smith (House, 1940–49; Senate, 1949–73), who was among the first to question the anti-communist investigations of Republican Sen. Joseph R. McCarthy of Wisconsin (1947–57); and Cohen, a moderate Republican who served as Secretary of Defense in the Clinton administration.

Collins' tenure as staff director of the Governmental Affairs Subcommittee on Oversight of Government Management in the 1980s whetted her appetite for investigations and for holding the bureaucracy accountable, according to associates and friends. According to Robert Tyrer, a long-time associate who ran Collins' 1996 Senate campaign and is now president of the Cohen Group, a consulting firm run by Cohen, Collins spent many hours investigating the painstaking details of Social Security disability laws.

After years of working in non-elected positions, she ran for office for the first time at age 41, becoming a candidate for governor of Maine in 1994. She lost to Angus King, an independent, in a close three-way race, but the statewide name recognition from the gubernatorial race paved the way for her 1996 run for the Senate. One of her few critics, Democratic activist L. Sandy Maisel, said she is a "show horse" who makes politically savvy moves to gain power.

"She is very good at getting publicity and being the front person," said Maisel, who directs the Goldfarb Center for Public Affairs and Civic Engagement at Colby College, in Waterville, Maine.

As a moderate Republican willing to oppose her party's conservative wing, Collins is often wooed by both sides in the evenly divided Senate. Collins opposed her party 22 percent of the time on party line votes in 2003, and voted against the Bush administration 14 percent of the time last year, according to CQ vote studies. In 2002, she voted with her party 57 percent of the time.

She was a swing vote on the bill that created the Department of Homeland Security in 2002 (PL 107-296), as she held out for greater protections for government union workers in the legislation. She won some concessions from the Bush administration but did not get the labor rules that she and many Democrats had wanted. Collins voted in favor of the final bill.

Collin's tenacity and independence were on display late last year, when she demanded extra information from administration officials about what type of intelligence was flowing to the Terrorist Threat Integration Center, a newly formed intelligence analysis unit. The officials eventually provided the information six months later—but only after Collins prodded them with several letters. She became the first lawmaker to visit the center, known as TTIC, so she could see first-hand how the unit was working.

At a May hearing in Senate Armed Services on the Abu Ghraib prisoner abuse scandal, Collins demonstrated her ability to zero in on the heart of a question. In an exchange with Gen. John P. Abizaid, Collins got the commander of all U.S. forces in the Middle East to acknowledge that there were several contradictory doctrines for prisoner interrogations in Iraq that had opened the way for mistreatment of prisoners.

Collins also has shown that she does not let bureaucrats off the hook under questioning. At the Aug. 3 hearing on intelligence changes, Collins asked a CIA official: "Who makes the final call in an intelligence dispute" between agencies? The official, Philip Mudd, deputy director of the CIA's Counterterrorist Center, gave a lengthy answer about agencies working together, concluding that they are "quite cooperative." Collins interrupted, demanding once again, "Who makes the call? Who decides?" She never got a firm answer, which fed her conclusion that there should be a top intelligence chief with real powers to referee intelligence disputes.

Supporters say she will be no pushover when it comes to mandating real change in intelligence, despite opposition from high-ranking military and CIA officials. Any thoughts that Collins' committee might be the place to soft-pedal intelligence legislation are quickly dismissed by those who know her.

"When Susan gets interested in something, you can abandon the idea that the issue will go away," said Tyrer. "People who don't know her do not understand how tenacious she is."

King, her former opponent, believes that Collins' independent streak makes her a natural in such a complicated and controversial policy area as an intelligence overhaul.

"Those chairmen [of other committees] have vested interests," said King, who served as governor from 1995 to 2003. "They were there when there were no problems [with intelligence]. She's the right person in the right place at the right time."

ORDER OF BATTLE

Still, Collins cannot control what happens outside her committee. And in a Senate filled with larger-than-life, battle-tested figures, Collins will be challenged as never before on the intelligence shake-up.

The opinions of the Senate Armed Services and Intelligence Committee members—whose constituencies have the most to lose in an overhaul—will carry enormous influence once the debate reaches the Senate floor.

"We must stay clear of political pressure and resist the urge to move boxes around when in fact there are complicated issues," warned Sen. Chuck Hagle, R-Neb., a member of Senate Intelligence. "We have to be careful not to push up against some artificial deadline, like the end of the year."

Roberts, who, as Senate Intelligence chairman may yet produce his own restructuring legislation, also sounds a note of caution. "I need to know exactly what kind of authority the [director of national intelligence] would have over the budget, and over hiring and firing," he said.

Meanwhile, a wide range of officials from the intelligence community also have picked apart the various proposals laid out by the Sept. 11 commission.

John McLaughlin, the acting CIA director, opposes the creation of a national intelligence director. And John O. Brennan, the director of the Terrorist Threat Integration Center, has called some of the Sept. 11 commission recommendations for a new intelligence hierarchy "unworkable."

Under the current system, the director of central intelligence is head of the CIA and serves as the titular head of the entire 15-agency intelligence community. In practice, however, the CIA director cannot command operations at organizations like the Defense Intelligence Agency or the National Security Agency, both of which are under the Pentagon. And he does not have much budgetary power: Requests to reprogram money within the intelligence community can take months to be approved.

As things now stand, the Defense Department commands at least 80 percent of the intelligence budget—an authority the Pentagon will be loath to relinquish to a national intelligence director.

Amid such strong institutional resistance, some officials have come before Collins' committee to support the idea of giving an intelligence czar real budgetary power. "A central authority and control over some of the budget process is vital," said retired Army Lt. Gen. Patrick Hughes, now assistant secretary for information analysis at the Department of Homeland Security. "I think the national intelligence director can have budget authority, and the intelligence organizations . . . can effectively operate."

Collins and Lieberman, after listening to these mixed reactions from intelligence officials at the Aug. 3 hearing, agreed that the national intelligence director should have strong budgetary powers as well as operational control over intelligence collection and analysis, whether it is happening in Langley or at the Pentagon.

SEIZING OPPORTUNITIES

After a restless August of politically charged hearings, the real work will begin in committees some time after Labor Day. While House panels may continue work on legislation, the spotlight will remain on Collins' panel. Her task is to produce a measure that wins over enough Democrats and Republicans to create overwhelming support on the Senate floor, rather than a bill that just squeaks by without a strong political mandate.

With so much at stake, Collins is already being pressured both publicly and privately about restructuring the intelligence world. Witnesses at her hearings have warned her that recommendations that sound good in a commission report or in legislative language may not automatically translate into better intelligence gathering and analysis.

"It's one thing to sketch [intelligence management changes] on a board; it's another thing to implement it on a day-to-day basis," said Brennan, the director of the Terrorist Threat Integration Center, which will be absorbed into the new National Counterterrorism Center, if it is created. "The system today is working much better than it ever was before."

Brennan's comments underscore the challenge that any intelligence overhaul faces. The officials who have testified before Congress universally agree that better human intelligence, better analysis and better information sharing are necessary to prevent another terrorist attack. But they worry about giving an outsider too much operational or budget control.

"We need to keep structures that allow us to operate with speed," said the CIA's Mudd.

Since she decided to scrap her August recess and start hearings July 30, Collins says she also has received calls from several senators and top intelligence officials—and not all of them have been supportive of the plan to create a national intelligence director with significant budget powers.

She would not say exactly who had called, but she says she is not intimidated by the resistance to change in a community that cherishes its privileged standing on Capitol Hill, its considerable budget and, perhaps most importantly, its secrecy.

"Some believe the commission's findings are ill-founded and don't want legislation. And some want a minor tweak" to existing law, Collins said.

"My hope is to produce a bill by Oct. 1."

DISCUSSION QUESTIONS

1. Must Congress be a mirror image of the diversity within the general population to work effectively as a representative body for all Americans? If the answer is yes, what categories of individuals must be represented in equal proportion to the larger citizenry? For instance, do we stop at race and gender, or do we continue into other categories, such as sexual orientation and social class, demanding that the Congress include a requisite number of individuals in these groups? At what point, if any, do we stop?

2. Would Congress do a better job—would the policy outputs of the conflict that stems from the political process more evenly distribute the benefits and burdens of policy—if the composition of Congress reflected American society?

3. Is it "fair" to ask members of Congress to represent the interests of their demographic group(s) as well as that of the constituents in the district? What if the interests of these groups clash and create conflict?

4. Does the election of individuals who do not fit the conventional wisdom about different groups in politics—like J. C. Watts, an African-American Republican—forward diversity goals or undermine them?

5. If we believe diversity among its members is important for Congress, then why is there not more of it? What barriers exist and how would you respond to the argument that a more representative body is a historical inevitability?

Additional Resources

http://www.clerk.house.gov
The Office of the Clerk of the U.S. House of Representatives includes information about current women Members, biographical profiles of women who have previously served in Congress, material on national events that shaped successive generations of women Members of Congress, and images of each woman member past and present (http://womenincongress.house.gov/).

Let's Get Frank (2004) is a documentary film about Barney Frank, the first openly gay politician on Capitol Hill, during and after the impeachment of Bill Clinton.

http://www.ncsl.org
The National Conference of State Legislatures (the organization representing all the state legislatures in the United States) devotes a section of its web site to the Women's Legislative Network whose mission is to "Promote the participation, empowerment, and leadership of women legislators" (http://www.ncsl.org/programs/wln/).

http://oversight.house.gov
The U.S. House of Representatives' Committee on Oversight and Government Reform in its Subcommittee on Federal Workforce, Postal Service, and the District of Columbia, issued a report on the representation of women and minorities in the Congressional agencies (senior executive service positions). The report details how women and minorities are represented in bureaucratic positions in Congress. http://oversight.house.gov/documents/20071113090052.pdf

http://www.nbcsl.org
The National Black Caucus of State Legislators is a group of nearly 650 African-American state legislators across the nation that is committed to opening doors, providing access, and educating its membership.

http://www.cawp.rutgers.edu
The Center for Women and Politics at Rutgers University has as its stated mission to "promote greater knowledge and understanding about women's participation in politics and government and to enhance women's influence and leadership in public life." The Center also has a number of research projects on women in Congress and women in state legislatures on its web site (http://www.cawp.rutgers.edu/Research.html).

THE EXECUTIVE BRANCH:
MORE THAN A ONE-*MAN* SHOW

The two main contenders for the Democratic Party's
nomination for president—Senators Hillary Clinton and
Barack Obama—talk at the podium during a campaign
event; both were striving to become the first president
who was not white or male.

The United States has had 43 presidents over the course of its 230-plus year history.
The presidency, and the executive branch in general, have undergone countless
changes since George Washington first took the oath of office in 1789, but one thing
that has not changed in the time between Washington and the current occupant of the
White House, George W. Bush, is that all 43 presidents have been relatively affluent,
white men. The presidency, through the course of history, is unquestionably then the
least demographically diverse office in the federal government. Certainly presidents
have come from different backgrounds and experiences, as James Madison went to
Princeton, while his near contemporary Andrew Jackson had little formal education
and hailed from the backwoods of the Carolinas; Ulysses S. Grant, while a famous
Civil War general, graduated from West Point as a mediocre student.[*] The fact
nonetheless remains that American presidents have mainly been wealthy, Protestant,
white males.[**]

Even if we expand our examination to those who have been candidates for the White House we find that the vast majority of major party candidates for president have been wealthy, white males. This is not to say there have not been notable exceptions: in 1972, Shirley Chisholm was the first African American woman to make a bid for the White House; and just in the last three decades or so, we have seen Al Sharpton, Jesse Jackson, and Alan Keyes—all African American men—run for their party's nomination for the presidency. In 2000, U.S. Senator Elizabeth Dole (NC) sought to lead the Republican Party's presidential ticket, while former senator Carol Mosley-Braun (IL) ran for the Democratic nomination.

The race for the White House in 2008 may well alter these patterns. In addition to being the most diverse battle for the White House in history, the chances that a woman, an African American, or a Latino would be elected were greater than ever before. As this book went to press, Barack Obama (D-IL) was the presumptive nominee, defeating the strongest female contender for the White House to date, Hillary Clinton (D-NY). Among the other Democratic candidates was New Mexico Governor Bill Richardson, a Latino. While the Republican Party's front-runners did not embody such diversity, they did boast former Massachusetts governor Mitt Romney, a Mormon, among their ranks. But it was certainly Clinton and Obama who dominated the discussion at the time—and showed great promise of reaching the ultimate goal in pre–general election polls when matched up against probable Republican candidates.***

The articles that follow exhibit a number of themes that run throughout this volume, such as the contributions of political actors from underrepresented groups and the challenges they face, and the political representation of underrepresented groups within government. Additionally, the readings in this section encourage us to utilize a diversity lens when considering the executive branch. When we consider the individual who holds the highest office in the land, his demographics have remained amazingly similar. But when we turn to the entire executive branch we witness an increasingly diverse bureaucracy and are reminded that these increases (and decreases) have come under both Republican and Democratic presidents. Some of the issues that remain are: (1) How does demography matter in presidential elections as we move through the 21st century? (2) What impact, if any, will demographic change have in the highest office of the land? and (3) Is a more demographically representative bureaucracy a "better" bureaucracy?

---

* More on presidential biographies can be found at www.whitehouse.gov/history/presidents/ [accessed January 13, 2007].

** President John F. Kennedy remains the only non-Protestant to ever be elected to the highest office in the land.

*** Readers might peruse www.pollingreport.com or some other public opinion source for more data on this point.

W*hile the 2008 presidential primary campaign included a great deal of demo-graphic diversity among its participants, it remains a question whether any candidate can break the affluent, white, male "lock" on the White House. Certainly the 2008 candidacies of Senators Clinton and Obama have represented the best chance to date, but is America "ready" for a female or African-American president? Benjamin Wallace-Wells addresses these questions in the reading that follows.*

The challenges and contributions of a diverse group of candidates are clear in this article. As this article's title makes clear, the issue of presidential electability is still potentially bound up in demographic diversity. Both Clinton and Obama faced great hurdles in their bid for the White House. As Wallace-Wells notes, the question is no longer whether racism will allow women and people of color to participate in politics, but whether it will allow them to lead. If one of these two individuals were able to reach the Oval Office, it would, according to Wallace-Wells, "be a particularly American achievement, [and] an affirmation of American ideals."

Is America Too Racist for Barack?
Too Sexist for Hillary?

BENJAMIN WALLACE-WELLS

The 2006 elections were for the technocrats and the operatives, pitting the Democratic tacticians against the Karl Rove machine. But the next election is already beginning to look quite different: 2008 may be one for the novelists.

Viewers of the election returns late on Tuesday [November 7, 2006], after all, got an early start on the iconography of the next presidential race. The cable networks' cameras cut between Sen. Hillary Rodham Clinton, thanking her supporters for an overwhelming victory in the New York Senate race, her husband standing pointedly behind, and a smiling Sen. Barack Obama of Illinois, giving cautious, professorial analysis to the television viewers. Nobody noted the significance, but it stared us all in the face: The two presumed leading contenders [at the time] for the Democratic presidential nomination [were] a woman and an African American.

Their candidacies—coming after elections resulting in the . . . first female speaker of the House and the second black governor since Reconstruction—suggest that the next elections may play in ways that are more cultural and symbolic than tactical and political. Are Americans ready to put a black man or a woman in charge of the country? And does the hefty symbolism that Obama and Clinton would bring help one of them more than the other—in other words, is the country more racist or more sexist?

Democracies are awkward like this. Despite incessant polling, we really get only one moment every two years, at best, to measure how Americans feel about things, and these elections must stand as imperfect proxies for a mess of subjects: what we think about religion, whether we like being included in the international conversation, whether Northeast bluebloods would tolerate a Texan as their leader.

But when it comes to race and sex, this seems a slightly more legitimate game: The question that remains for black Americans and women isn't whether prejudice has diffused to the point that they can participate in the United States, it's whether they can legitimately hope to lead it.

Today, they may have reasons to be optimistic. Poll numbers for Clinton and Obama are among the strongest of any presidential hopefuls. It now seems nearly as common for political leaders in television shows and movies to be women or racial minorities as white men. Recent polls have found that the percentages of Americans who say they would not vote for a hypothetical black or female presidential candidate, long formidable, have dwindled into the single digits. And [the 2006] elections put House Minority Leader Nancy Pelosi (D-Calif.) [into the speaker's chair] and Democrat Deval Patrick, who is black, in the Massachusetts governorship.

But as the two would-be presidential candidates grapple with how to manage the legacies of their own identities, Obama seems engaged with a more problematic political feeling. Even if race is more socially crippling than gender—even if it was less likely that Obama would make it to Harvard Law than that Clinton would make it to Yale Law—the symbolism of race can also be awfully empowering to individual politicians who learn to harness it. Most Americans want to believe that the culture has moved past its racial problems, and that the symbol of that progress would be widely cheered. Compared with Clinton, says George Lakoff, a linguistics professor and Democratic message guru, "Obama clearly has it better."

Whatever racism remains in this country, it coexists with a galloping desire to put that old race stuff behind us, to have a national Goodbye to All That moment. The most recent such occasion was Obama's much-publicized tour to promote his book of policy prescriptions, "The Audacity of Hope." The Denver Post called him a "rock star," the Seattle Times found him "electrifying," and even the Deseret News in Salt Lake City described the "raucous greeting" he received in Utah. This rapture wasn't only because of what Obama has said; most of his audiences had not heard much from him or read much of his book. It was because he symbolizes the possibility of a more modern America.

Clinton had a best-selling autobiography and a media-heavy book tour, too, but the coverage had less to do with the symbolism she carried as a woman than with her history as Bill Clinton's wife, and with the way she was positioning herself for the future. There are many reasons for this difference, but one critical one has to do with the legacies of oppression that each inherits. While many Americans have a sincere sense of sentimentality and nostalgia for what Clinton may consider outdated gender roles, a much smaller number have that kind of feeling for racial segregation. There is the sense that, by electing a female president, the nation would be meeting a standard set by other liberal democracies; the election of a black man, by contrast, would be a particularly American achievement, an affirmation of American ideals and a celebration of American circumstances.

Obama's mixed-race heritage is rarely far from his political conversation. He writes of having a Kansan mother "as white as milk," and a Kenyan father "as black as pitch." He has used his race explicitly while speaking in Africa and urging politicians there to move beyond tribalism, and implicitly while speaking in southern Illinois to punctuate an address about the challenges of globalization. In his speeches, Obama uses his simple presence as an establishment national political figure who is black to serve as a metaphorical exclamation point—a visual assurance that the country can work for everyone.

This is how he used it in his most famous speech, at the 2004 Democratic National Convention: "I stand here today, grateful for the diversity of my heritage, aware that my parents' dreams live on in my two precious daughters. I stand here knowing that my story is part of the larger American story, that I owe a debt to all of those who came before me, and that, in no other country on Earth, is my story even possible."

When Clinton gives a speech, her gender is just as evident, but she doesn't give it nearly the same kind of rhetorical prominence. She is as likely to talk about handing out buttons for Republican Barry Goldwater as a child as about what her presence as a political woman means for the country. Her most famous speech during the current political cycle dealt with a topic close to her own identity: In January 2005, she gave a widely praised talk to a group of New York state family-planning providers, telling them that the pro-choice movement had failed to acknowledge the great emotional cost involved in having an abortion. For Clinton, a hero to many women who support abortion rights, this was regarded as a particularly brave stance.

But in a speech about such a personal topic, what is most noteworthy is its impersonality. Clinton didn't mention her own experiences as a wife or a mother, but seized upon a trip she took to Romania as first lady, where she learned about the policies of the dictatorship of Nicolae Ceausescu, who tried to force every woman to have five children for the glory of the state, subjecting them to monthly roundups and reproductive exams attended by the secret police. It's a striking story, but what's even more striking is the way Clinton introduced it: "My own views of family planning and reproductive rights are heavily influenced by my travels as first lady," she said. . . . Were Clinton's views on these issues not fully formed before she began traveling as first lady?

The contrast is vivid in the two senators' autobiographies. Obama's, "Dreams From My Father," is an attempt to explain his evolving political awareness as a direct articulation of his roots. Here is the way Clinton begins her life story, "Living History": "I wasn't born a first lady or a senator. I wasn't born a Democrat. I wasn't born a lawyer or an advocate for women's rights and human rights. I wasn't born a wife or a mother."

Part of this difference is simple personal style. And there's also the matter of learned political behavior: Clinton has spent a decade and a half being beaten up, often personally and viciously, for the intersection of her gender and her politics, and it would make sense if she were trying to disconnect the two. But there is something else here.

The political progress of women and African Americans has long been intertwined; the suffragette movement gained huge momentum from the complaint that black men had received the right to vote before women of any race. But when it comes to modern political leadership, women have become more present. In January [2006], the Senate will have 16 women and one African American, while eight women and one African American will be governors. Geraldine Ferraro was a vice presidential running mate more than 20 years ago, and still no black politician has reached that plateau.

Gender, meanwhile, may have become part of the political wallpaper. When Rep. Harold E. Ford Jr. and Maryland Lt. Gov. Michael Steele ran for Senate [in 2006], their race was mentioned in virtually every story; when Sen. Debbie Stabenow and Claire McCaskill ran, their gender was barely noted. The ferocity of national feelings about race can still be threatening. . . . But if the nation feels its racial sins more clearly, it also has a more urgent desire to get past them. "I think gender has become more normal in leadership," said Marie Wilson, president of the White House Project, a New York nonprofit that works to develop female leaders with the goal of having a woman in the White House. "Race is a much more troubling, sadder, unresolved part of our history than the issue of gender, so it certainly looms larger."

Of course, the civil rights and women's rights movements of the 1960s have left vastly different legacies. No political figure would dare deny the saintliness of the Rev. Martin Luther King Jr.; Betty Friedan's name is a political dirty word. Repression of blacks was the stuff of massive state-leveraged cruelty—the police dogs and fire hoses—while repression of women in this country was made of quieter stuff: bras, aprons and constitutional amendments.

Obama is frequently called post-racial, the suggestion being that because he has an exotic background, Americans are looking at a newer model of a human. The metaphor works for Obama politically, because it contains the idea that his youth lets him create a more modern and inclusive brand of politics than the rhetoric of civil rights-era politicians such as Jesse Jackson. Clinton's Jesse Jacksons are Ferraro, who bombed, and Pelosi, who is still hanging around.

This is the ultimate imbalance between the would-be presidential contenders, and it's both rough on Clinton and helps explain why Obama's public presentation is so much more closely linked to his identity: There's a model for being post-racial, but there's no easy way to be post-gender.

Fredrick Harris, a political scientist at the University of Rochester, sees a post-gender future out there, and its name is Condoleezza Rice. The secretary of state, he notes, "is unmarried, has no children, is completely dedicated to her job, for pleasure she plays the piano and works and that's about it."

Clinton has made different choices, but they have their limits. Politically, she has done everything that Obama has done: She has become a serious policy professional, moved toward the center and renounced the excesses of 1960s-style identity politics. And yet these moves are received as the tacks of a smart politician. For Obama, they are received as the arrival of his race.

*T*he second piece in this section turns from electability to governance. Assume for a moment that either Senator Clinton or Senator Obama, or some other women or person of color did become president (either in 2008 or at some point in the future). How drastically would things change in the White House? How would the office of the presidency change? Specifically, how would the new president lead and govern?

As we introduced in the previous section, there is a difference between symbolic and substantive representation. Would things be all that different? We know from the readings in Section 10 that female legislators sometimes approach their jobs differently than their male counterparts; would this be true for a female president as well? This is a question that Lori Cox Han explores, from three important perspectives. First, women face hurdles to be seen as viable candidates by the public, hindered both by the pool from which presidential candidates are typically drawn and the stereotypes associated with the abilities of male and female candidates. Second, Cox Han examines how a female president might relate to other actors in the process (e.g., Congress) given the different approaches women sometimes bring to governing. And finally, Cox Han considers how a female president might fare in communicating with the nation in an era of the rhetorical presidency and in which the press is such a dominant force in determining the success of a president.

Presidential Leadership:
Governance from a Woman's Perspective

LORI COX HAN

The date is January 20, 2005, and another presidential inauguration has arrived. Across the nation, Americans gather in front of their television sets to witness the ritual and tradition of seeing the newly elected president place left hand on the Bible, right hand in the air, and with the help of the chief justice of the U.S. Supreme Court, take the oath of office. But today, Americans will do more than just witness the start of yet another presidential administration, with the requisite inaugural address, parade, and endless parties and celebrations throughout the nation's capital. Americans will also experience an important and historic first in this nation's politics. The final political glass ceiling has been broken—a woman has been elected president of the United States! And while the public and political pundits alike grapple with the soon-to-be-familiar term *Madam President*, it is clear that nothing about the office will ever be the same.

Or will it? What role does being a woman play in presidential leadership? Does the job of president, both defined and constrained by enumerated, implied, and inherent powers within Article II of the U.S. Constitution, change based on the sex of the occupant of the Oval Office? Would scholarship on the subject of presidential power and leadership, crafted and refined over the past several decades by political scientists, historians, and journalists, be suddenly rendered useless in its ability to explain the office because the new president is a woman? Although these questions may seem somewhat oversimplified, they are nonetheless timely and important. The likelihood of the above scenario, although optimistic, is not completely out of the realm of possibility, as women continue to make gains in the number of elected offices and other positions held within government at all levels. And although electing a woman president by the end of the first decade of the twenty-first century may still be a long shot, perhaps a more viable option would be the election of the first-ever woman vice president. Even so, the issues of presidential leadership and governance for a woman, particularly one who either inhabits the Oval Office or is a heartbeat away from the presidency, are essential to understand as the United States comes closer to the possibility.

* * * * *

GOVERNANCE, LEADERSHIP, AND THE PRESIDENCY

The terms *governance* and *leadership* have separate and distinct definitions yet are inextricably intertwined, especially within the context of the U.S. presidency. Governance is "the process of implementing modern state power, of putting the program of those who govern into place."[1] Governance within a democracy implies a relationship between a political leader and citizens and between the leader and other government officials holding positions of power. Leadership has a variety of definitions, but in general terms, it is a process that involves influence, occurs in groups, and includes attention to goals.[2] The definition of leadership can also include "individual traits, leader behavior, patterns of interacting, role relationships, relations with followers, and follower perceptions." The job of the president, then, obviously encompasses both governance and leadership—occurring through "formal aspects of government and in a multitude of ways surrounding formal governing."[3]

Based mostly on the scholarship of political scientists, the definition of presidential leadership that emerged in 1960 was Richard Neustadt's view that modern presidential power equates the ability to bargain and persuade.[4] Since then, other important works have redefined, modified, and expanded the notion of presidential leadership to encompass various views of presidents and the presidency, including the president as a transformational leader as well as the state of the postmodern presidency.[5] Other important topics shaping the definition of presidential leadership have included changes in the political environment,[6] the institutionalization of leadership within the executive branch,[7] policymaking and the president's relationship with Congress,[8] and the public presidency and changes in White House communication strategies.[9]

* * * * *

Three essential factors help to determine the extent of successful presidential leadership: vision (the ability to articulate a clear vision and purpose that inspires the American people about the direction of both government policies and the nation as a whole), skill (the ability to take advantage of opportunity and circumstance through a good sense of timing, policy skills, and political savvy), and political timing (an overall sense of power and when to use it appropriately given the circumstances and political environment).[12] Other factors must also be considered if presidents are to maximize their leadership potential, including effectiveness as a public communicator, organizational capacity (staffing and leadership style within the White House), cognitive style (intellectual curiosity coupled with either attention to detail or abstract thinking skills), and emotional intelligence.[13]

Would the necessity of these leadership qualities differ for a woman president? By constructing three general (albeit not all inclusive) categories of important traits for successful presidential leadership—political experience (viability as a candidate, knowledge of government policies), political skill (the ability to work with Congress and other political actors, effective leadership of the party, and influence over the national agenda), and political communication (mastery of the bully pulpit, successful news management)—how a woman would fare in this job and the impact of gender on the presidency can be examined.

POLITICAL EXPERIENCE: WOMEN AS VIABLE CANDIDATES

Aside from the constitutional requirements for the office of the presidency—being at least thirty-five years old, a fourteen-year U.S. resident, and a natural-born citizen— no other formal criteria exist for presidential candidates. However, several informal qualifications have limited the pool of potential candidates, including religion, race, and gender. Nearly all presidential and vice presidential candidates have been Protestant, white, and male. John F. Kennedy, a Catholic, remains the only non-Protestant to hold the office of the presidency. . . .

It is important to note that many of the issues surrounding presidential leadership and whether the candidate will succeed at the job are first addressed during the presidential campaign. The character, personality, and style of presidential candidates have become a mainstay in the evaluation process during both the primaries and the general election. The health and age of the candidate, as well as family ties and personal relationships (particularly marital status and fidelity) are also important characteristics in the public's mind.[15] Although party affiliation and policy preferences are still important factors among voters, the decline of partisan loyalty and the desire for party nominees to appeal to moderate, middle-of-the-road voters during the general election has placed more emphasis on the candidate as an individual. Certainly during the television age of politics and as political news reporting has become more cynical, sensationalized, and hypercritical, scrutinizing the character or style of a presidential candidate through the lens of the news media is common practice throughout the campaign.[16]

Given these qualifications, where do Americans find their presidential and vice presidential candidates? . . .

... The potential pool of women candidates has never been larger than following the 2000 elections. In 2001, women held seventy-two, or 13.5 percent, of the 535 seats in the 107th U.S. Congress (thirteen of the 100 seats in the Senate and fifty-nine of the 435 seats in the House of Representatives, both all-time records). At the state level, women held eighty-nine of the 323 statewide elective executive offices across the country (27.6 percent). Also, 1,663 (22.4 percent) of the 7,424 state legislators in the United States were women. The number of women serving in state legislatures has increased more than fivefold since 1969 when 301, or 4 percent, of all state legislators were women.[19]

However, there has traditionally been a dearth of women governors, both past and present, which suggests at first glance that women candidates may not benefit from the insider versus outsider phenomenon [which has been important recently] in the race for the presidency. Prior to the five women governors serving in 2001, only fourteen women had previously served as a state's top executive, beginning as early as 1925 with Democrat Nellie Tayloe Ross of Wyoming, who replaced her husband after he died in office (two other women replaced their husbands upon their death or impeachment). Ella Grasso, a Democrat from Connecticut who served from 1975 to 1980, was the first woman elected as governor in her own right. Republicans would not elect their first woman governor until 1986, with the election of Kay A. Orr of Nebraska. And although the governor's office of large states is one of the most likely stepping-stones to the White House, only one of the five-largest electoral states (California, New York, Texas, Florida, Pennsylvania) has ever elected a woman as governor—Democrat Ann Richards of Texas, elected in 1990.[20]

Taking a closer look at gender stereotyping suggests that the lack of women governors as potential presidential candidates may not be such a bad thing from the perspective of a women's viability during the campaign. Research in recent years has shown stereotypes to exist about both male and female candidates. Women, who are considered more compassionate, are seen as more competent in the traditional "female" policy areas of health care, the environment, education, poverty, and civil rights. Men, who are considered more aggressive, show stronger competencies in the traditionally "male" policy areas of military and defense matters, foreign policy, and economic and trade issues.[21] These same traditionally "male" issues are highlighted during U.S. Senate campaigns, whereas traditionally "female" issues are emphasized in gubernatorial races.[22] Therefore, women governors seeking the White House may very well be hurt by their lack of policymaking experience with traditionally "male" issues, like foreign policy and military matters, and women members of Congress may actually benefit more by the insider label from political experience at the national level. All governors running for president must overcome the perceived lack of experience in the international arena (Clinton and Bush are recent examples). Therefore, women presidential candidates coming from Congress, especially those members serving on committees dealing with economic, military, or international issues or perhaps having a cabinet-level presidential appointment, may have an easier time answering the inevitable question about their political experience and knowledge of relevant national and international issues.

* * * * *

POLITICAL SKILL: LEADERSHIP AND THE NATIONAL AGENDA

Even prior to election and inauguration, a potential president must create a strong image of leadership in the minds of U.S. voters. Appearing presidential, both during the campaign and once in office, is an essential ingredient for political success. However, how leadership is conceptualized has served as an important barrier for women in politics, particularly for those seeking elected office. Leadership has historically been defined on male, not female, terms. Whether in politics, business, or military circles within the United States, strong leadership is defined as an attempt to exert one's will over a particular situation, a societal view that "has been conditioned by the interpretation of American history as written." This, in turn, affects how the public will view other aspiring leaders, particularly women.[24] Also not helpful to women seeking the presidency is the notion of "presidential machismo," which is the image desired by many Americans to have their president exhibit tough and aggressive behavior on the international stage. . . .

✳ ✳ ✳ ✳ ✳

Studies that have looked at gendered differences in leadership show that in some areas, particularly politics and business, women often bring "a more open, democratic, and 'people-centered' approach to their leadership positions." However, it has also been suggested that a more inclusive and participatory approach to leadership is not exclusive to women and that since women have yet to reach parity with men in leadership positions, not enough evidence yet exists to categorize leadership styles based on gender alone.[27] Nonetheless, of the examples from other countries, women national leaders have exhibited diverse leadership styles—some more traditionally "male," like that of former British prime minister Margaret Thatcher, and some more traditionally "female," like that of former Philippine president Corazon Aquino.[28]

However, if any of these stereotypes about women leaders are to be believed and accepted, then a woman president may actually have an advantage in working within the federal system of shared powers. According to David Gergen, an experienced political adviser to Presidents Nixon, Gerald Ford, Reagan, and Clinton, "a president should see himself as the center of a web" and develop cooperative working relationships with six distinct groups: Congress, the press, the public, foreign powers, domestic interest groups, and domestic elites. All these groups share the expectation of being included within the decisionmaking process in the White House. . . .

. . . Again, if we assume that women leaders tend to exhibit leadership styles that focus on cooperation, and given the earlier prediction that a woman presidential candidate coming from the Congress would have an electoral advantage, a woman president would be no more constrained in this area than her male counterpart and might enjoy an advantage.

Women do tend to bring different priorities into the policymaking arena than their male counterparts, and women are also more likely to work across party lines to achieve their goals. . . . But because women legislators have tended to be slightly more liberal in their policy approach, should it be assumed that a woman president would be more liberal as well?[33]

Not necessarily, given the fact that the president serves as his or her party's de facto national leader. The role of political parties has diminished in recent decades, but the president is nonetheless the most visible spokesperson for the party and its legislative program. Therefore, a president's agenda can be shaped or even limited by the party he or she represents with Democrats pursuing a more moderate-to-liberal agenda than Republicans.[34] Partisan alignment, then, is probably a better predictor of political ideology than gender. A counterargument can also be made about the role of parties in presidential politics, since some recent presidents have moved away from their responsibilities as party leaders by exhibiting a more independent brand of governing. This trend is also consistent with the emergence of candidate-centered politics, which suggests a more middle-of-the-road, moderate ideology for a presidential candidate to get elected. Therefore, if presidents are elected based on the idea of candidate-centered politics, then a woman president from either party would probably be more centrist in her approach to the legislative agenda and would not focus solely on "women's issues."

POLITICAL COMMUNICATION: CONSTRUCTING A PRESIDENTIAL IMAGE

A president's communication strategy—public activities, speechwriting, and presidential and press relations—is an important base of power for presidents during the television age.[35] The rise of the rhetorical presidency and use of the presidential bully pulpit date back to Theodore Roosevelt, who advanced the president's role as the national leader of public opinion and used his rhetorical skills to increase the power of the presidency through popular support. Later presidents, though not all, would follow Roosevelt's strategy of relying on the bully pulpit in an attempt to lead democratically as the spokesperson for the American public. Use of the bully pulpit has become especially important since the start of the television age, where a president's overall success or failure as a leader can be determined by his rhetorical skills and public influence.[36]

Since the 1950s, three presidents stand out as successful in their use of the bully pulpit—Kennedy, Reagan, and Clinton. All were known for their frequent use of inspiring and eloquent speeches about public policy and their visions for the country. Other presidents during the twentieth century either abdicated the bully pulpit or used it ineffectively, which diminished presidential power during their terms and curtailed their leadership potential by allowing other political actors to shape the public debate. . . .

Can a woman president master the bully pulpit? Communication and linguist scholars have pointed to differences in how men and women communicate. In general, men view communication as negotiations in which they must maintain power, an "individual in a hierarchical social order in which he [is] either one-up or one-down." Women view communication as an opportunity for confirmation, support, and consensus, "an individual in a network of connections."[38] This difference has benefited women politicians in recent years. Television as a medium demands intimacy and the ability to express the private self, a skill that most presidents, with the exception of Reagan and Clinton, have had difficulty perfecting. Male politicians discuss goals, whereas women politicians reveal themselves through an intimate, conversational, and narrative style of speech. Presidents now govern extensively through the mass media, and "because the mass media are fixated on differences between the private and public self of public figures, a comfort with expressing instead of camouflaging self . . . is useful for a politician. The utility benefits females."[39]

The news media are also an important political actor for the president to consider, since the press can keep the president apprised of major concerns of the public, enable presidents to convey their messages to the public and political elites, and allow the president to remain in full public view on the political stage.[40] The president makes news simply by virtue of being the "ideological symbol of American democracy and nationhood" to both the press and the public. The president's relationship with the press is a combination of both strengths and weaknesses. Since the president is under constant scrutiny by the press, presidential leadership can be undermined both by a failure of the administration to effectively manage the news and by newsgathering norms within the journalism industry and the skepticism of the press.[41]

Women politicians have traditionally been viewed by the press as an anomaly—a unique occurrence that deserves attention because it is outside the norm.[42] Trivialization of women in the news media has also continued, through portrayals on television and in the movies that can lead to "symbolic annihilation" of women in general,[43] as well as the stereotyping that occurs in news coverage of women candidates and politicians.[44] In many campaigns, news media coverage has added to the negative stereotyping of women candidates, thus hurting their efforts to win an elected office, since the news media pay more attention to style over substance when covering female candidates. Since many voters may doubt the policy qualifications of women candidates, news coverage that downplays issues and highlights personal traits develops less favorable images for female candidates.[45]

* * * * *

CONCLUSION

In their discussion on women as national leaders, Michael Genovese and Seth Thompson point out that while the effects may be subtle, the role of gender cannot be overlooked.

> Anyone who rises to the top of a political system will have developed a set of strategies and a repertoire of behaviors for dealing with both challenges and opportunities. For the successful woman, the strategies she has developed and her style will inevitably be shaped and influenced by her society's definitions and expectations of gender. She will have learned, consciously or not, how to cope effectively with, and even turn to her advantage, the fact that she is a woman in a "man's world."[47]

There is little doubt that the first woman president will face significant challenges, especially in the accomplishment of reaching the White House. It may be difficult to predict how the nation will react to this historic first—although we know that she will be a woman, we cannot predict what style of leadership she will employ. It is known, however, that the presidency is an office, by constitutional design, of shared powers and limitations on presidential leadership. The style of leadership and governing may be fluid from administration to administration, and some presidents have overcome the constitutional barriers to achieve success, but the institutional features of the office remain static.

For a woman who has achieved the ultimate political prize of winning her party's nomination and the presidency, several gender questions will have already been addressed. Therefore, from an institutional standpoint, a woman president will face similar challenges as her male predecessors upon taking office. To achieve success in the current political environment, presidents must master the bully pulpit and employ an effective strategy of going public, develop an effective working relationship with Congress, and provide strong leadership at the international level. If even strong leaders are limited in their potential for greatness because of the potential for divided government or an uncooperative Congress, as well as the unpredictability of economic factors and international events, then issues of gender for a woman president, once elected, may be secondary. Or they may actually work to her advantage. If leadership, personality, and character can make a difference in the potential for presidential success, then perhaps the first successful woman president will embody certain characteristics and skills, gender-specific or not, that are similar to those of her more successful male predecessors. Women leaders must be judged as individuals, not merely as women. In the final analysis, it is important to remember that many men have also failed at the job of president, whereas only a handful have been considered successful or strong leaders. Some presidents are destined for greatness and some for obscurity, regardless of whether they are addressed as "mister" or "madam" president.

Notes

1. Duerst-Lahti and Kelly, "On Governance, Leadership, and Gender," p. 12.

2. Northouse, *Leadership*, p. 3.

3. Duerst-Lahti and Kelly, "On Governance, Leadership, and Gender," p. 13.

4. Neustadt, *Presidential Power*.

5. See Skowronek, *The Politics Presidents Make*; Rose, *The Postmodern President*.

6. See, for example, Kessel, *Presidents*; Cronin and Genovese, *The Paradoxes of the American Presidency*.

7. See, for example, Burke, *The Institutional Presidency*; Weko, *The Politicizing Presidency*; Warshaw, *The Keys to Power*.

8. See, for example, Jones, *Separate but Equal Branches*; Lammers and Genovese, *The Presidency and Domestic Policy*.

9. See, for example, Kernell, *Going Public*; Tulis, *The Rhetorical Presidency*; Hart, *The Sound of Leadership*; Stuckey, *The President as Interpreter-in-Chief*; Maltese, *Spin Control*; Han, *Governing from Center Stage*.

12. [Cronin and Genovese, *The Paradoxes of the American Presidency*,] pp. 118–127.

13. Greenstein, *The Presidential Difference*, pp. 194–200.

15. [Wayne, *The Road to the White House 2000*,] pp. 187–189.

16. For a discussion on this trend in the news coverage, see Patterson, *Out of Order*; and Sabato, *Feeding Frenzy*.

19. "Women in Elected Office, 2001, Fact Sheet Summaries," Center for the American Woman and Politics, Eagleton Institute of Politics, Rutgers University, 2001.

20. For a discussion of potential women candidates, see Han, "The Next Contender."

21. Huddy and Terkildsen, "Gender Stereotypes."

22. Kahn, *The Political Consequences of Being a Woman.*

24. Conway, Steuernagel, and Ahern, *Women and Political Participation*, p. 100.

27. Stapleton, "Introduction," p. 33.

28. Genovese, "Women as National Leaders," pp. 214–215.

33. Genovese, "Women as National Leaders," p. 215.

34. Cronin and Genovese, *The Paradoxes of the American Presidency*, pp. 207–209.

35. Han, *Governing from Center Stage*, pp. 2–3.

36. See Tulis, *The Rhetorical Presidency;* see also Milkis and Nelson, *The American Presidency.*

38. Tannen, *You Just Don't Understand*, pp. 24–25.

39. Jamieson, *Beyond the Double Bind*, pp. 94–95.

40. Graber, *Mass Media and American Politics*, pp. 272–273.

41. Paletz and Entman, *Media Power Politics.*

42. Rice, "Women Out of the Myths and into Focus," pp. 45–49.

43. See Tuchman, *Hearth and Home*, pp. 7–8; Paletz, *The Media in American Politics*, pp. 135–139.

44. See Braden, *Women Politicians.*

45. Kahn, *The Political Consequences of Being a Woman*, pp. 134–136.

47. Genovese and Thompson, "Women as Chief Executives," p. 7.

References

Braden, Maria. *Women Politicians and the Media.* Lexington: University of Kentucky Press, 1996.

Burke, John. *The Institutional Presidency.* Baltimore: Johns Hopkins University Press, 1992.

Conway, M. Margaret, Gertrude A. Steuernagel, and David W. Ahern. *Women and Political Participation: Cultural Change in the Political Arena.* Washington DC: Congressional Quarterly Press, 1997.

Cronin, Thomas E. and Michael A. Genovese. *The Paradoxes of the American Presidency.* New York: Oxford University Press, 1998.

Duerst-Lahti, Georgia and Rita Mae Kelly. "On Governance, Leadership, and Gender." In Georgia Duerst-Lahti and Rita Mae Kelly, eds., *Gender, Power, Leadership and Governance.* Ann Arbor: University of Michigan Press, 1995.

Genovese, Michael A. "Women as National Leaders: What Do We Know?" In Michael A. Genovese ed., *Women as National Leaders.* Newbury Park, CA: Sage, 1993.

Genovese Michael A., and Seth Thompson, "Women as Chief Executives: Does Gender Matter?" In Michael A. Genovese ed., *Women as National Leaders.* Newbury Park, CA: Sage, 1993.

Graber, Doris. *Mass Media and American Politics*. Washington, DC: CQ Press, 1997.

Greenstein, Fred I. *The Presidential Difference: Leadership Style from FDR to Clinton*. Princeton, NJ: Princeton University Press, 2000.

Han, Lori Cox. *Governing from Center Stage: White House Communications Strategies During the Television Age of Politics*. Cresskill, NJ: Hampton Press, 2001.

_____. "The Next Contender: Assessing the Pool of Women Candidates for President." *White House Studies* 1, no. 3 (2001).

Hart, Roderick P. *The Sound of Leadership Presidential Communication in the Modern Age*. Chicago: University of Chicago Press, 1987.

Huddy Leonie, and Nayda Terkildsen. "The Consequences of Gender Stereotypes for Women Candidates at Different Levels and Types of Office." *Political Science Quarterly* (Fall 1993).

Jamieson, Kathleen Hall. *Beyond the Double Bind: Women and Leadership*. New York: Oxford University Press, 1995.

Jones, Charles O. *Separate but Equal Branches: Congress and the Presidency*. New York: Chatham House, 1999.

Kahn, Kim Fridkin. *The Political Consequences of Being a Woman*. New York: Columbia University Press.

Kernell, Samuel. *Going Public: New Strategies of Presidential Leadership*. Washington, DC: Congressional Quarterly Press, 1997.

Kessel, John H. *Presidents, the Presidency, and the Political Environment*. Washington, DC: Congressional Quarterly Press, 2001.

Lammers William W., and Michael A. Genovese. *The Presidency and Domestic Policy: Comparing Leadership Styles, FDR to Clinton*. Washington, DC: Congressional Quarterly Press, 2000.

Maltese, John Anthony. *Spin Control: The White House Office of Communications and the Management of Presidential News*. Chapel Hill: University of North Carolina Press, 1994.

Milkis, Sidney M., and Michael Nelson. *The American Presidency: Origins and Development*. Washington, DC: Congressional Quarterly Press, 1999.

Neustadt, Richard. *Presidential Power*. New York: Wiley, 1960.

Northouse, Peter G. *Leadership: Theory and Practice*. Thousand Oaks, CA: Sage, 1997.

Paletz, David L. *The Media in American Politics: Contents and Consequences*. New York: Longman, 2002.

Paletz, David L. and Robert M. Entman. *Media Power Politics*. New York: Macmillan, 1981.

Patterson, Thomas E. *Out of Order*. New York: Vintage Books, 1994.

Rose, Richard. *The Postmodern President*. Chatham, NJ: Chatham House, 1991.

Sabato, Larry J. *Feeding Frenzy: Attack Journalism and American Politics*. Baltimore: Lanahan Publishers, 2000.

Skowronek, Stephen. *The Politics Presidents Make: Leadership from John Adams to George Bush*. Cambridge: Belknap/Harvard University Press, 1993.

Stuckey, Mary E. *The President as Interpreter-in-Chief*. Chatham, NJ: Chatham House, 1991.

Tannen, Deborah. *You Just Don't Understand: Women and Men in Conversation*. New York: Ballantine, 1990.

Tuchman, Gaye. *Hearth and Home: Images of Women in the News*. New York: Oxford University Press, 1978.

Tulis, Jeffrey K. *The Rhetorical Presidency*. Princeton, NJ: Princeton University Press, 1987.

Warshaw, Shirley Anne. *The Keys to Power: Managing the Presidency.* New York: Longman, 2000.

Wayne, Stephen J. *The Road to the White House 2000: The Politics of Presidential Elections.* New York: Bedford St. Martin's, 2001.

Weko, Thomas J. *The Politicizing Presidency: The White House Personnel Office, 1948–1994.* Lawrence: Kansas University Press, 1995.

*W*hile it is easy to overlook, the executive branch is made up of more than just the president, vice president, and the others close to the Oval Office. Certainly, the president is the head of this branch of government, as outlined by the Framers, but he (and potentially she) is only one of literally thousands of individuals who make up the entire executive branch. The most visible individuals under the president are the Cabinet secretaries—the Secretaries of State, Treasury, Defense, Commerce, the Attorney General, etc.—but it extends to the thousands of political appointees and career civil servants who also serve in the executive branch and make up the bureaucracy.

Again questions of representation come up in this aspect of our government. How diverse and representative is the executive branch as a whole? Do we need to have a bureaucracy that looks like America? Political scientists have asked these questions since Donald Kingsley, in 1944, first used the term "representative bureaucracy." We can examine these questions much like we did in the Congress section, although they fall under a different set of circumstances—bureaucrats are not elected and do not have constituents to represent.

In her piece, Susan Page reports that the executive branch under the leadership of George W. Bush has been the most demographically diverse administration in history, as it contains more women and people of color generally, and in the highest levels of the government. Bush also made diverse appointments that Page describes as "historic."

However, as we did in Section 10, we must wonder what impact these diverse individuals are having. Are they approaching their job differently? Are a wider range of opinions being heard and influencing governance? Does this lead to policy change? Page addresses these questions with anecdotal evidence from some in the Bush administration as well as its critics.

Bush Is Opening Doors with a Diverse Cabinet

SUSAN PAGE

With little fanfare and not much credit, President Bush has appointed a more diverse set of top advisers than any president in history.

In his first term, Bush matched the record that President Clinton set in his first term for appointing women and people of color to the Cabinet, and Bush had a more diverse inner circle at the White House. Since his re-election last month, the president has made a series of groundbreaking nominations.

Bush has named his White House lawyer, Alberto Gonzales, to be the first Hispanic to hold one of the powerful "big four" Cabinet jobs, attorney general.

He named his national security adviser, Condoleezza Rice, to be the first female African-American secretary of State, the Cabinet's senior position.

He also nominated Margaret Spellings, his domestic policy adviser, to lead the Education Department and Cuban-born business executive Carlos Gutierrez to head Commerce.

Some political analysts argue that Bush's appointments and his matter-of-fact approach to them signal a new stage in the racial history of the nation, one in which diversity in the top ranks is taken as a matter of course. Bush and Clinton, who don't agree on much, together may have set a new standard that future presidents in both parties will be expected to meet.

"Bush did not go out and say, 'I'm going to create an administration that looks like America,' which is how Clinton led off," says Paul Light, a political scientist at New York University who has studied presidential appointments. "He has just gone about recruiting a diverse Cabinet as an ordinary act. That's remarkable in the sense it sends to future administrations: 'This is just the way we're going to do business.'"

* * * * *

Among Washington insiders, what's more significant is the demographics of a more amorphous group: the aides and advisers whose counsel Bush trusts most. He is the first president whose innermost circle—the people he relies on in a crunch—includes a woman other than his wife.

Among Bush's closest aides are Karen Hughes and Rice. Hughes, a veteran of his Texas campaigns and a onetime White House aide who is now an outside adviser, is one of the few willing and able to tell Bush when she thinks he has erred. Rice, a foreign policy aide in the 2000 campaign who worked in the White House for Bush's father, has become like a member of the Bush family.

Even some Democrats grumbled during the presidential campaign that Bush had more African-Americans and Hispanics among his closest advisers than did Democratic challenger John Kerry, who won a majority of black and Hispanic votes.

"On the Democratic side, we see that and we say, 'Hmmm,'" says Donna Brazile, who was Al Gore's campaign manager in 2000 and is African-American. She credits Bush with instinctively believing that surrounding himself with able women and people of color helps him make better decisions—a lesson she says some Democratic officeholders and candidates have yet to absorb.

But some don't think Bush deserves much credit. His appointments below the Cabinet level have included a lower proportion of blacks and women than in Clinton's administration. Detractors fault his policies on affirmative action, civil rights and taxes for failing to help many minorities. His relations with civil rights groups are rocky; he is the first sitting president since Warren Harding (1921–23) who hasn't addressed the NAACP.

Critics also say there's a shortage of diversity on at least one measure: diversity of opinion. Bush's appointments, especially for his second term, have put a premium on loyalists who are more likely to endorse and carry out his policies than to press alternatives. Three of the seven Cabinet nominees he has announced since the election are White House staffers.

* * * * *

A RECORD OVERLOOKED?

Bush's defenders and some other analysts say his record on diversity deserves more notice than it has received. Dan Bartlett, the White House communications director, calls it "a strong governing management trait that has been under-reported."

One reason it has gotten little attention is because Bush himself rarely talks about it. At a convention of minority journalists in August, Bush declared, "If you look at my administration, it's diverse, and I'm proud of that." But he doesn't cite numbers. Bartlett and other Bush aides sounded surprised when told that Bush's record on diversity in top jobs matched that of Clinton, who was praised for expanding opportunities for women, blacks and Hispanics.

Another reason Bush hasn't gotten as much credit as Clinton: The interest groups most likely to praise diversity of personnel generally disagree with Bush on policy. Leaders of the NAACP and NOW opposed Bush's re-election and criticize him for curtailing affirmative action and other programs designed to help women and minorities.

"There's diversity of color, but it's the policies that one would be more interested in," says New York Rep. Charles Rangel, a Democrat who is one of the senior black members of Congress.

* * * * *

Until Clinton, presidential Cabinets were overwhelmingly the province of white Anglo men. They made up 85% of the appointments by President Reagan, who over eight years had only one African-American and one Hispanic in his Cabinet. White Anglo men made up 71% of the first President Bush's Cabinet. (The Cabinet statistics in this story reflect those offices designated by law as Cabinet posts. Some presidents have chosen to give other officials comparable Cabinet-level status.)

* * * * *

Before Bush, no person of color had been named to any of the four most prestigious Cabinet jobs—at the departments of State, Treasury, Defense and Justice. Now he has named two blacks as secretary of State and a Mexican-American as attorney general.

Also notable is the ease and familiarity of Bush with his appointees. Clinton named the first woman to one of the "big four" posts, but only after a bumpy nationwide search for a prospective female attorney general settled on Janet Reno, the district attorney in Dade County, Fla. The two didn't know each other until she went to the White House to discuss the job.

In contrast, Gonzales has worked for Bush since his days as the Texas governor. Rice has been by his side since the 2000 campaign.

*****

Bartlett said Bush's comfort level with powerful women might reflect the influence of his strong-minded mother, Barbara Bush.

"It's so clear that these people weren't picked so they would be the first Latino something or the first black woman something else," says Stephen Hess, a scholar at the Brookings Institution who has studied White House operations. "He picked them because they are, in his mind, the best people for these jobs."

Only after a moment do you "blink and look and say, 'Oh, my goodness, it's a black woman,'" Hess says.

CULTIVATING HISPANICS

Some of Bush's appointments reflect traditional moves to balance the Cabinet and score political points, of course. "There has been an effort by the president to reach out and ensure that his staff and his team reflect the diversity of our country," Bartlett says.

For instance, Bush and the Republican Party determinedly have cultivated the support of Hispanics, the nation's fastest-growing ethnic group. In his first term, he named Cuban-American Mel Martinez secretary of Housing and Urban Development. Within a year after Martinez resigned to run what turned out to be a successful campaign for a U.S. Senate seat in Florida, Bush had chosen the Cuban-born Gutierrez for the Commerce Department.

*****

AND THE POLITICAL PAYOFF?

In the short term, Bush modestly improved his standing among women and people of color in this year's election over 2000, although issues other than his record on appointments are seen as the key factors behind the changes.

Among women, he lost to Kerry, but his gap of 11 percentage points between him and Gore four years ago narrowed to 3 points this time, according to a media-sponsored survey of voters as they left polling places on Election Day. His proportion of the black vote inched up from 9% to 11%. The exit poll showed that his share of the Hispanic vote jumped from 35% to 44% . . .

Over the long term, Republicans and Democrats agree that the impact could be considerable. The presence of minorities in high-profile jobs could destigmatize the Republican Party among young African-Americans, who remain the most loyal

Democratic voting bloc, and could encourage young Hispanics to move toward the GOP.

"It shows respect" to name Latinos to such powerful positions, says New Mexico Gov. Bill Richardson, the nation's senior elected Hispanic official and a former member of Clinton's Cabinet.

"The president has done more than diversify his Cabinet," Brazile says. "President Bush has opened new doors for minorities and women to consider the benefits of joining the ranks of the Republican Party."

*I*n this section's final article, Julie Dolan takes up questions of representation in the executive branch that are similar to those examined in the previous piece, but does so in a more empirical manner and examines the bureaucracy in more depth. Dolan considers the backgrounds as well as the qualifications of political appointees in the executive branch and summarizes the argument that a representative bureaucracy—at least in terms of political appointees—does in fact have an impact on government and policy.

Political Appointees in the United States: Does Gender Make a Difference?

JULIE DOLAN

Information about women who hold appointive office is a neglected area.
—EILEEN SHANAHAN, FORMER ASSISTANT SECRETARY, HEW[1]

With every new presidential administration in the United States, the incoming president is in charge of appointing thousands of individuals to work throughout the executive branch of government and assist him in fulfilling his constitutional responsibility to "faithfully execute the laws of the Nation" (Pfiffner 1996). When the Center for American Women and Politics (CAWP) first began studying female political appointees in the early 1980s, very few women had ever served in Cabinet positions or other high-ranking executive positions within the federal government. In fact, in 1977, almost two hundred years after the founding of the United States, President Carter appointed only the fourth and fifth women ever to serve as Cabinet Secretaries (CAWP 1998). As Carroll and Geiger-Parker note in the introduction to the very first study of female political appointees, "for the first time in history, women had been appointed in large enough numbers to survey and to compare with other appointees" (1983a, ix).

Julie Dolan, "Political Appointees in the United States: Does Gender Make a Difference?" *PS: Political Science and Politics*, vol. 34, no. 2 (June 2001), pp. 213–216. Copyright © 2001 American Political Science Association. Reprinted with the permission of Cambridge University Press.

Since then, the number of women in high-ranking executive branch positions in the federal government has expanded greatly. During the eight years of the Reagan administration, 277 women were appointed to high-ranking positions requiring Senate confirmation. Following Reagan, George Bush appointed 181 women, while President Clinton surpassed both of his predecessors combined, appointing 592 women throughout his tenure, including the first women ever to serve as Secretary of State (Madeleine Albright) and as Attorney General (Janet Reno), positions considered part of the president's inner cabinet (Garcia 1997; Women's Appointments Project 2001). Although George W. Bush's administration is only a few months old as of this writing, he has thus far appointed six women to high ranking administrative positions, making history by appointing the first female Secretaries of Agriculture and Interior (Ann Veneman and Gail Norton), the first female National Security Adviser (Condoleezza Rice), and the first Asian-American woman to serve as a cabinet Secretary, Elaine Chao (at the Department of Labor) (Dewar 2001; Vargas 2000; Washington Post 2001; Women's Appointments Project 2001).[2] [Editors' Note: As an earlier reading suggests, this has changed.]

Despite the recent increases for women into high-ranking, high-profile administrative positions in the federal government, we still know very little about these women. Since Eileen Shanahan long ago lamented the lack of knowledge about female appointees, very little research has systematically explored the careers, policy contributions, or perspectives of these high-ranking executive women. This essay reviews the existing research on female appointees in the executive branch, reflecting on what we know thus far about women's experiences in reaching the top of the federal government and the impact they have upon arrival. The essay focuses primarily upon those women serving in the federal government, but also includes findings from state governments, where appropriate.[3]

RECRUITMENT OF FEMALE APPOINTEES

Although President Clinton appointed women to nearly a third of all executive positions requiring Senate confirmation, women remain far from equal with men in the ranks of the president's lieutenants (Women's Appointments Project 2001). How do they arrive in their positions? Do they bring different qualifications to their jobs than their male colleagues?

Most early research on women appointed to presidential and gubernatorial administrations examines their backgrounds, finding that female appointees are as well-educated and distinguished as their male counterparts (Borrelli 1997b; Bullard and Wright 1993; Carroll 1986; Carroll 1987; Carroll and Geiger-Parker 1983a; Carroll and Geiger-Parker 1983b; Fisher 1987; Martin 1989; Martin 1991; Martin 1997; McGlen and Sarkees 1993). In fact, there are remarkably few differences in background qualifications between the women and men called to serve. Men are slightly more likely to have an advanced degree while women are more likely to have attended private colleges and universities; women are also likely to come from more advantaged backgrounds than do their male colleagues, at least as evidenced by their father's and mother's occupations (Bullard and Wright 1993; Carroll 1986; Carroll and Geiger-Parker 1983a; Carroll and Geiger-Parker 1983b; McGlen and Sarkees 1993; Martin 1997). Among previous Republican appointees, women arrived with greater federal administrative experience than do their male colleagues (Martin 1997), while women tapped for the Carter administration brought greater state government experience than did their male counterparts (Carroll 1986; Carroll and Geiger-Parker 1983a). Female presidential appointees are more often recruited from the Washington, D.C. area than are male appointees (Martin 1991, 1997), but even so Borrelli (1997b) argues that female "insiders" (those with previous government experience in Washington) receive more skeptical treatment during Senate committee hearings than do male insiders.[4] Lastly, the agencies and departments in which appointees are chosen to serve vary by gender, with female political appointees more often selected for posts in agencies and departments dealing with stereotypically female concerns (health, education and social services) (Carroll and Geiger-Parker 1983a; CAWP 1998; Kleeman 1987).

GENDER AND POLITICAL IMPACT

Does it matter if women are presidential appointees? Representative bureaucracy scholars would answer yes, that the demographic makeup of the executive branch of government does indeed affect the substantive outputs of government (Kranz 1976; Krislov and Rosenbloom 1981). According to theory, a diverse public sector is important not only for symbolic reasons, but because governmental decisions are expected to be more responsive to the public when the workforce "looks like America." Individuals from different social backgrounds bring different attitudes, priorities, and perspectives to their jobs. With a diverse federal executive, "the wide range of concerns generally voiced in a highly pluralistic nation is more likely to be heard . . . than in one drawn disproportionately from a single social group" (Shafritz et al. 1992, 230). Reagan appointee Amorette Hoeber nicely illustrates this point:

> [Y]ou have to have a wide variety of people in the building in order to get the decisions made well, because it is that sort of a consensus process where you get all different points of view expressed, and women's backgrounds tend to be different than men's backgrounds. Therefore, they bring something to the table, in addition to the image sorts of things (quoted in McGlen and Sarkees 1993, 219).

As legislative scholars have repeatedly shown, female politicians bring different perspectives to government, often being more attuned than men to policy problems and issues that concern women (Burrell 1994; Dodson et al., 1995; Dolan 1997; Gertzog 1995; Swers 1998; Thomas 1994).

As presidential appointees, women have likewise used their positions to speak out for and draw attention to problems commonly affecting women in society. Serving as President Carter's Secretary of Commerce from 1977 to 1979, Juanita Kreps encouraged the formation of the President's Interagency Task Force on Women Business Owners, a major initiative to help women increase their numbers in the private sector (Lamson 1979, 58). Appointed as the first woman to head the National Institutes of Health, Bernadine Healy advocated women's health issues from the beginning of her tenure and proposed a $625 million NIH study involving 150,000 women and studying breast cancer, osteoporosis, and heart disease (Schroeder and Snowe 1994). Two months after taking office as the first female Secretary of State, Madeleine Albright instructed U.S. diplomats to make "the furtherance of women's rights a central priority of American foreign policy" (Lippman 1997).[5]

Beyond these anecdotes, systematic research examines executive women's attitudes, reasoning that attitudes provide legitimate clues about likely behavior. Women who are attentive to women's concerns on paper are expected to be more responsive to women's policy concerns when opportunity for action arises. Numerous studies confirm that female appointees, both at the state and federal level, are more feminist, liberal and Democratic than their male colleagues (Bullard and Wright 1993; Carroll 1986; Carroll 1987; Carroll and Geiger-Parker 1983a; Carroll and Geiger-Parker 1983b; Havens and Healy 1991; Stanwick and Kleeman 1983).[6] Surveys of presidential and guberna-torial appointees indicate that female Republican and Democratic appointees are more supportive of childcare, abortion rights, and the Equal Rights Amendment than their male colleagues (Carroll 1987; Carroll and Geiger-Parker 1983a; Carroll and Geiger-Parker 1983b; Havens and Healy 1991; Stanwick and Kleeman 1983).[7] Thus, the existing attitudinal evidence suggests that female appointees, as a group, respond to the distinct concerns and preferences of the female citizenry.

However, attitudes may not translate directly into policy output that benefits women as a group. For instance, a female appointee may work in a position that offers few opportunities to voice a distinctly feminine perspective. Thus, scholars try to determine how female appointees affect policymaking and the nature and sub-stance of government outputs. To date, most studies focus on women's managerial responsibilities and talents. Within both federal and state administrations, a majority of female appointees indicate that they frequently hire women as staff members, doing their part to facilitate the entry of even greater numbers of women into governmental positions (Carroll and Geiger-Parker 1983a; Carroll and Geiger-Parker 1983b).[8] Conducting personal interviews with male and female appointees in the Departments of State and Defense, McGlen and Sarkees (1991, 1993) find that males and females exercise slightly different leadership styles, with female appointees more often express-ing greater satisfaction in dealing with subordinates and managing their staffs. Further, when asked to identify their major accomplishments, female appointees more often listed management accomplishments as well as accomplishments that affected women (McGlen and Sarkees 1991, 1993). Although research regarding the impact of female appointees is still preliminary, the influx of women into federal government over the past eight years provides ample opportunities for further study.

DIRECTIONS FOR FUTURE RESEARCH

As this brief review demonstrates, the literature on women in the executive branch has certainly grown since the CAWP first began conducting research in the early 1980s, but opportunities for additional research remain. We know a great deal about women's recruitment patterns and qualifications, but considerably less regarding whether policy outputs differ because of women's presence. Scholars studying presidential appointees could draw from legislative studies (i.e., Kathlene 1994; Rosenthal 1997; Thomas 1994) to identify creative approaches for assessing women's impact in the fourth branch of gov-ernment. However, much more of legislators' words and actions are preserved on public record (votes, floor speeches, committee membership, etc.) than are political appointees', making it more difficult to isolate and interpret political appointees' behavior.

Another open line of research concerns the salience of race. We know almost nothing about women of color in the executive branch, even though a number of women of color have served in highly visible posts (e.g., Hazel O'Leary, Alexis Herman, Aida Alvarez, Condoleezza Rice and Elaine Chao). Small sample sizes have made it difficult to explore women from different racial backgrounds, but ongoing changes provide us with additional opportunities to ascertain the political responsiveness and career patterns for these women. Doing so will provide a much more comprehensive understanding of gender at the top of the executive branch.

Notes

1. Eileen Shanahan, former Assistant Secretary for Public Affairs at HEW, quoted in Carroll and Geiger-Parker, 1983.

2. The other two Bush appointees are Christine Todd Whitman, head of the Environmental Protection Agency, and Karen Hughes, White House Counselor (Hughes 2000).

3. For general reviews of women in the bureaucracy, see Dolan (2001), Lepper and Farrell (1980), and Stewart (1990).

4. For a case study of Roberta Achtenberg's journey through Senate confirmation proceedings, see Schroedel, Spray and Snyder (1997). For details about the confirmation hearings of other Clinton appointees, see Borrelli (1997a).

5. For biographical sketches of numerous federal executive women, see Stineman (1980), Lamson (1979), Center for American Women and Politics (1998), and Cooper and Wright (1992).

6. See also McGlen and Sarkees (1991, 1993) who find female appointees within the Departments of State and Defense are more conservative than their male colleagues.

7. Research uncovers attitudinal differences among women and men employed within the career ranks of both state and federal governments, too. See Dolan (2000), Guy and Duke (1992), Hale and Branch (1992), Hale, Kelly and Burgess (1989), Hale, Kelly, Burgess and Shapiro (1987), Kawar (1989), Kelly and Newman (2000), Naff (1998), and Stanley (1989).

8. These findings are consistent with research from municipal governments, where female mayors likewise appear to make government employment more accessible to women (Riccucci 1986; Saltzstein 1986).

References

Borrelli, MaryAnne. 1997a. "Campaign Promises, Transition Dilemmas: Cabinet Building and Executive Representation." In *The Other Elites: Women, Politics, and Power in the Executive Branch*, eds. MaryAnne Borrelli and Janet M. Martin. Boulder, CO: Lynne Rienner Publishers, Inc.

_____. 1997b. "Gender, Credibility, and Politics: The Senate Nomination Hearings of Cabinet Secretaries-Designate, 1975 to 1993." *Political Research Quarterly* 50:171–97.

_____, and Janet M. Martin, eds. 1997. *The Other Elites: Women, Politics, and Power in the Executive Branch*. Boulder, CO: Lynne Rienner Publishers, Inc.

Bullard, Angela M., and Deil S. Wright. 1993. "Circumventing the Glass Ceiling: Women Executives in American State Governments." *Public Administration Review* 53:189–202.

Burrell, Barbara C. 1994. *A Woman's Place is in the House: Campaigning for Congress in the Feminist Era*. Ann Arbor: University of Michigan Press.

Carroll, Susan J. 1986. "Women Appointed to the Carter Administration: More or Less Qualified?" *Polity* 18:696–706.

_____. 1987. "Women in State Cabinets: Status and Prospects." *The Journal of State Government* 60:204–208.

_____, and Barbara Geiger-Parker. 1983a. *Women Appointed to the Carter Administration: A Comparison with Men.* New Brunswick: Center for American Women and Politics, Rutgers, The State University of New Jersey.

_____. 1983b. *Women Appointed to State Government: A Comparison with All State Appointees.* New Brunswick: Center for American Women and Politics, Rutgers, The State University of New Jersey.

Center for American Women and Politics. 1998. *Women Appointed to Presidential Cabinets: Fact Sheet.* New Brunswick: National Information Bank on Women in Public Office, Eagleton Institute of Politics, Rutgers, The State University of New Jersey.

Cooper, Terry L., and N. Dale Wright, eds. 1992. *Exemplary Public Administrators: Character and Leadership in Government.* San Francisco: Jossey-Bass Publishers.

Dewar, Helen. 2001. "Senate, in Voice Vote, Confirms 7 for Cabinet." *The Washington Post,* January 21, A-28.

Dodson, Debra L., ed. 1991. *Gender and Policymaking: Studies of Women in Office.* New Brunswick: Center for American Women and Politics, Rutgers, The State University of New Jersey.

_____, et al. 1995. *Voices, Views, Votes: The Impact of Women in the 103rd Congress.* New Brunswick: Center for American Women and Politics, Rutgers, The State University of New Jersey.

Dolan, Julie. 1997. "Support for Women's Interests in the 103rd Congress: The Distinct Impact of Congressional Women." *Women & Politics* 18(4):81–94.

Dolan, Julie. 2000. "The Senior Executive Service: Gender, Attitudes and Representative Bureaucracy." *Journal of Public Administration Research and Theory* 10:513–29.

Dolan, Julie. 2001. "Women in the Executive Branch: A Review Essay of their Political Impact and Career Opportunities." 2001. *Women & Politics.* Forthcoming.

Fisher, Linda L. 1987. "Fifty Years of Presidential Appointments:" In *The In-and-Outers: Presidential Appointees and Transient Government in Washington,* ed. G. Calvin Mackenzie. Baltimore: Johns Hopkins University Press.

Garcia, Rogelin. 1997. *Women Appointed by President Clinton to Full-Time Positions Requiring Senate Confirmation, 1993–1996.* Washington, DC: Congressional Research Service.

Gertzog, Irwin. 1995. *Congressional Women: Their Recruitment, Integration, and Behavior.* Second edition. Westport, CT: Praeger Publishers.

Guy, Mary E., and Lois Lovelace Duke. 1992. "Personal and Social Backgrounds as Determinants of Position." In *Women and Men of the States: Public Administrators at the State Level,* ed. Mary E. Guy. Armonk, NY: M.E. Sharpe.

Hale, Mary M., and M. Frances Branch. 1992. "Policy Preferences on Workplace Reform." In *Women and Men of the States: Public Administrators at the State Level,* ed. Mary E. Guy. Armonk, NY: M.E. Sharpe.

_____, and Rita Mae Kelly. 1989. *Gender, Bureaucracy, and Democracy.* Westport, CT: Greenwood Press.

_____, and Jayne Burgess. 1989. "Women in the Arizona Executive Branch of Government." In *Gender, Bureaucracy, and Democracy: Careers and Opportunity in the Public Sector,* eds. Mary M. Hale and Rita Mae Kelly. Westport, CT: Greenwood Press, Inc.

_____, and Rhonda Shapiro. 1987. "Women in the Executive Branch of Government." In *Women and the Arizona Political Process,* ed. Rita Mae Kelly. Lanham, MD: University Press of America.

Havens, Catherine M., and Lynne M. Healy. 1991. "Cabinet-Level Appointees in Connecticut: Women Making a Difference." In *Gender and Policymaking: Studies of Women in Office*, ed. Debra L. Dodson. New Brunswick: Center for American Women and Politics, Rutgers, The State University of New Jersey.

Hughes, Polly Ross. 2000. "Bush Picks ALCOA Exec for Treasury; Taps 3 More for Cabinet." *The Houston Chronicle*, December 21, A-1.

Kathlene, Lyn. 1994. "Power and Influence in State Legislative Policymaking: The Interaction of Gender and Position in Committee Hearing Debates," *American Political Science Review* 88:560–76.

Kawar, Ama1. 1989. "Women in the Utah Executive Branch." In *Gender, Bureaucracy, and Democracy: Careers and Opportunity in the Public Sector*, eds. Mary M. Hale and Rita Mae Kelly. Westport, CT: Greenwood Press, Inc.

Kelly, Rita Mae, and Meredith A. Newman. 2000. "The Gendered Bureaucracy: Agency Mission, Equality of Opportunity, and Representative Bureaucracy." *Women and Politics.* Forthcoming.

Kleeman, Katherine E. 1987. "Women in State Government: Looking Back, Looking Ahead." *Journal of State Government* 60:199–203.

Kranz, Harry. 1976. *The Participatory Bureaucracy: Women and Minorities in a More Representative Public Service*. Lexington, MA: D.C. Heath and Company.

Krislov, Samuel, and David H. Rosenbloom. 1981. *Representative Bureaucracy and the American Political System*. New York: Praeger Publishers.

Lamson, Peggy. 1979. *In the Vanguard: Six American Women in Public Life*. Boston: Houghton Mifflin Company.

Lepper, Mary M., and Sarah Farrell. 1980. "Bibliography: Women in Bureaucracy." *Women & Politics* 1(4):65–75.

Lippman, Thomas W. 1997. "State Department Seeks Gains for Women: Albright Is Stressing Rights Concerns in Foreign Policy Agenda." *The Washington Post*, March 25, A-1.

Martin, Janet M. 1989. "The Recruitment of Women to Cabinet and Subcabinet Posts." *Western Political Quarterly* 42(1): 161–72.

_____. 1991. "An Examination of Executive Branch Appointments in the Reagan Administration by Background and Gender." *Western Political Quarterly* 44:173–84.

_____. 1997. "Women Who Govern: The President's Appointments." In *The Other Elites: Women, Politics, and Power in the Executive Branch*, eds. MaryAnne Borrelli and Janet M. Martin. Boulder: Lynne Rienner Publishers, Inc.

McGlen, Nancy E., and Meredith Reid Sarkees. 1991. "The Unseen Influence of Women in the State and Defense Departments." In *Gender and Policymaking: Studies of Women in Office*, ed. Debra L. Dodson. New Brunswick: Center for American Women and Politics, Rutgers, The State University of New Jersey.

_____. 1993. *Women in Foreign Policy: The Insiders*. New York: Routledge.

_____. 1997. "Style Does Matter: The Impact of Presidential Leadership on Women in Foreign Policy." In *The Other Elites: Women, Politics, and Power in the Executive Branch*, eds. MaryAnne Borrelli and Janet M. Martin. Boulder: Lynne Rienner Publishers, Inc.

Naff, Katherine C. 1998. "Progress Toward Achieving a Representative Federal Bureaucracy: The Impact of Supervisors and their Beliefs." *Public Personnel Management* 27:135–50.

Pfiffner, James P. 1996. *The Strategic Presidency: Hitting the Ground Running*. Second edition. Lawrence, KS: University Press of Kansas.

Riccucci, Norma M.1986. "Female and Minority Employment in City Government: The Role of Unions." *Policy Studies Journal* 15:315.

Rosenthal, Cindy Simon. 1997. *When Women Lead: Integrative Leadership Styles in State Legislatures*. New York: Oxford University Press.

Saltzstein, Grace Hall. 1986. "Female Mayors and Women in Municipal Jobs." *American Journal of Political Science* 30:140–64.

Schroedel, Jean Reith, Sharon Spray, and Bruce D. Snyder. 1997. "Diversity and Politicization of Presidential Appointments: A Case Study of the Achtenberg Nomination." In *The Other Elites: Women, Politics, and Power in the Executive Branch*, eds. MaryAnne Borrelli and Janet M. Martin. Boulder, CO: Lynne Rienner Publishers, Inc.

Schroeder, Patricia, and Olympia Snowe. 1994. "The Politics of Women's Health." In *The American Woman: 1994–95*, eds. Cynthia Costello and Anne J. Stone. New York: W.W. Norton & Company.

Shafritz, Jay M., Norma M. Riccucci, David H. Rosenbloom, and Albert C. Hyde. 1992. *Personnel Management in Government*. Fourth edition. New York: Marcel Dekker, Inc.

Stanley, Jeanie R. 1989. "Women in the Texas Executive Branch of Government." In *Gender, Bureaucracy, and Democracy: Careers and Opportunity in the Public Sector*, eds. Mary M. Hale and Rita Mae Kelly. Westport, CT: Greenwood Press, Inc.

Stanwick, Kathy A., and Katherine E. Kleeman. 1983. *Women Make a Difference*. New Brunswick: Center for American Women and Politics, Rutgers, The State University of New Jersey.

Stewart, Debra W. 1990. "Women in Public Administration." In *Public Administration: The State of the Discipline*, eds. Naomi B. Lynn and Aaron Wildavsky. Chatham, NJ: Chatham House Publishers, Inc.

Stineman, Esther. 1980. *American Political Women: Contemporary and Historical Profiles*. Littleton, CO: Libraries Unlimited, Inc.

Swers, Michele. 1998. "Are Congresswomen More Likely to Vote for Women's Issue Bills Than Their Male Colleagues?" *Legislative Studies Quarterly* 23:435–48.

Thomas, Sue. 1994. *How Women Legislate*. New York: Oxford University Press.

Vargas, Daniel J. 2000. "Condoleezza Rice Is New National Security Adviser." *The Houston Chronicle*, December 28. YO-7.

"Senate Unanimously Confirms Chao as Secretary of Labor." 2001. *The Washington Post*, January 30. A-2.

Women's Appointments Project. 2001. "History of Women's Appointees." Washington, DC: 2001 Women's Appointments Project. <www.appointwomen.com/history.html>. Accessed 29 January 2001.

DISCUSSION QUESTIONS

1. Is America ready for a female president, or a president who comes from a minority group? If so, which has a greater likelihood of getting elected? Why? Would it make a difference if a minority candidate was a man or a woman? Does the candidate's political party affiliation matter?
2. What does it say about the United States that so many other nations have put a woman into their top governmental position—Margaret Thatcher in Great

Britain, Michelle Bachelet in Chile, Golda Meir in Israel, Corazon Aquino in the Philippines, or Helen Clark in New Zealand—but has yet to do so itself?

3. How does the "war on terror" affect the chances of a woman getting to the Oval Office, given the gender stereotypes Cox Han identifies?

4. Considering the criteria Cox Han lays out for leadership and governing, can a woman be successful as president?

5. How do the concepts of symbolic (or descriptive) and substantive representation, which were first laid out in the Congress section, apply to those who serve in the White House, the president's administration, *and* the bureaucracy? Where is it more important to have descriptive representation (if at all)? Where is it more important to have substantive representation (if at all)?

Additional Resources

http://www.npr.org
National Public Radio's web site includes a commentary by Michael Goodwin, the Pulitzer Prize–winning executive editor of *The New York Daily News*, on the diversity in the Executive Branch under George W. Bush (http://www.npr.org/templates/story/story.php?storyId=4176540).

http://thewhitehouseproject.com
The White House Project is an organization that strives to advance women's leadership in all areas and offices, up to the presidency. Their web site includes information on their activities, events, research, and media appearnaces.

http://pdba.georgetown.edu
The Political Database of the Americas (PDBA) at Georgetown University offers information about institutions and political processes, branches of government, elections, political constitutional studies, and other subjects on nations in North, Central, and South America, including information on individuals who hold executive offices in nations in those countries (http://pdba.georgetown.edu/Executive/executive.html).

Chisholm '72: Unbought and Unbossed (2005) is the first historical examination of Brooklyn Congresswoman Shirley Chisholm's campaign to become the Democratic Party's presidential nominee in 1972. The documentary follows Chisholm from the announcement of her candidacy to the Democratic National Convention (http://www.chisholm72.net).

12

THE COURTS: SYMBOLIC AND SUBSTANTIVE REPRESENTATION

The U.S. Supreme Court. A number of groups have advocated that, as a matter of democratic theory and practice, the Court should become more diverse by adding more females and minorities.

Some of the most dramatic and hard fought political battles in the United States have occurred over the nomination and confirmation of U.S. Supreme Court justices. After all, the Supreme Court is in the position of rendering decisions regarding civil rights, equal opportunity, justice, discrimination, and equal access—the entire range of diversity issues detailed in the Introduction. In many respects, the Court has become the linchpin governmental institution regarding diversity-related issues, since it is the final legal arbiter over many of the cleavages and conflicts associated with diversity.

Consequently, the struggle over who becomes a Supreme Court Justice can reveal many of the diversity-related cleavages and conflicts that exist in U.S. politics. In 1987, President Ronald Reagan's nomination of Robert Bork was defeated by the U.S. Senate. In 1991, President George H. W. Bush's nomination of Clarence Thomas was eventually approved by the thin margin of 52–48, and after a spirited and hotly debated nomination process. Justice Thomas encountered considerable opposition to his nomination from some in the U.S. Senate—in part because his politics were much more conservative than Justice Marshall's (and therefore seen by many as an inappropriate successor to the seat) and because of a controversy that emerged over allegations by a former employee (Anita Hill) that Thomas sexually harassed her while both worked at the federal Equal Employment Opportunity Commission. At the same time, it appeared that those on both sides of the Thomas nomination agreed or assumed that, because of Marshall's ground-breaking appointment by President Johnson, this was considered to be an "African-American seat" on the Court.

In 2005 George W. Bush found himself in a unique position when he had to nominate two individuals to fill vacancies on the high court in the wake of Justice Sandra Day O'Connor's resignation and Chief Justice William Rehnquist's death. This certainly put Washington, D.C. in an uproar since O'Connor was the first woman appointed to the Court and there was great interest in who would replace her. The two individuals who filled these two slots on the Supreme Court (John Roberts eventually took Rehnquist's place and Samuel Alito replaced O'Connor) created a stir in several circles, in part because both were white males. Many people felt that O'Connor's seat should be considered a "woman's seat," and that not nominating a woman or minority group member to that seat would be taking a step back in matters of racial and gender equality or representativeness.

The ferocity surrounding these and other nominations, in addition to the fact that they are chosen by a president who is likely to pick a nominee who reflects his own ideology, often has to do with competing philosophies of judicial styles—some advocate either for an "activist court," others for judicial restraint. Potential justices can be seen to interpret the Constitution in an expansive or "liberal" way, or adopt a more conservative "strict constructionist" approach, in which the language of the Constitution is interpreted more literally.

Issues of demography add yet another layer to the highly contested nomination process. Here, the rationale was that purveyors of justice in a democratic political system should reflect the heterogeneity of the U.S. population as a whole. Such *symbolic representation* (the concept introduced in Sections 10 and 11) was considered to be an important value in and of itself, since a democracy's governmental institutions should include individuals representing the country's major social groups. Moreover, and similar to the ideas discussed in Section 10, it was assumed that demographic representativeness (race and gender especially) on the bench would influence legal opinion and increase the legitimacy of the courts.

Each of the following readings addresses the often competing values of symbolic versus substantive representation on the Supreme Court. Taken together, they challenge the reader to decide whether demographic diversity is by itself an important value in our democratic system.

*J*ohn Roberts originally was nominated to replace retired Justice Sandra Day O'Connor (although Roberts was later nominated to replace Chief Justice William Rehnquist who died not long after O'Connor had announced her retirement). To some observers, it would be most appropriate for President Bush to select another *woman to replace Justice O'Connor. Some even called it a "woman's seat." After Roberts was nominated by the president, O'Connor was quoted by a newspaper as saying, "He's good in every way, except he's not a woman." (Spokane Spokesman-Review, July 20, 2005). This controversy encourages us to think about what qualifications a nominee must have and to what degree, if any, these qualifications include membership in particular demographic groups. The fact that so many groups (Latino/a, Asian-American, Native-American, openly gay, etc.) do not enjoy any physical representation among the justices adds yet another dimension of diversity politics as it relates to the Court.*

This importance is engaged directly by Washington Post *reporters Dan Balz and Darryl Fears. Their article summarizes many of the arguments made on behalf of those who support making demographic diversity on the court a determining factor for nomination. They consider the selection of women, as well as the possibility of a Latino or other minority member.*

This article identifies the arguments that are commonly made regarding the importance of demographic diversity as a symbol of a democratic government. Moreover, it gives an indication of the politics surrounding the nomination process and how diversity considerations have emerged as important elements of that process. Even though President Bush ultimately selected two white males to fill those seats, the energetic dialogue surrounding the nomination of both Chief Justice Roberts and Justice Alito included considerable discussion regarding the demographic diversity of the Court.

Some Disappointed Nominee Won't Add Diversity to Court

DAN BALZ AND DARRYL FEARS

Justice Sandra Day O'Connor offered a quick and pithy reaction to President Bush's nomination of federal appellate judge John G. Roberts Jr. as her successor on the Supreme Court. "That's fabulous," she told the *Spokane* (Wash.) *Spokesman-Review* after a day of fly-fishing. "He's good in every way, except he's not a woman."

O'Connor's reaction reflects the view of just one person, but as someone who gained a reputation for having an intuitive sense of public attitudes and mores during her two decades on the court, she put a spotlight on the obvious trade-off involved in Bush's decision.

Given the opportunity to maintain some modicum of gender balance on the court, or even make history by appointing the first Latino justice, as many Hispanics had openly advocated, the president selected a white male to fill the O'Connor vacancy. In doing so, he was following the precedent of most other presidents: In the history of the Supreme Court, only four of more than 130 nominees—Justices O'Connor, Ruth Bader Ginsburg and Clarence Thomas and former Justice Thurgood Marshall—were not white men.

Whether that presents a serious problem for a president who has made the expansion of the Republican Party's coalition central to his political and governing strategy was a matter of debate yesterday. But there was widespread agreement that the selection of Roberts will put more pressure on Bush to name a woman or minority to the court should another vacancy occur during his presidency.

"I think it raises the stakes significantly for the next one, whoever that might be," said Democratic strategist Anita Dunn. "I think right now there's disappointment. If there were another vacancy [filled by a white man], there would be anger."

Hispanic leaders were most vocal in expressing their disappointment that Bush had not made history with his selection. "We're disappointed, to say the least," Hector M. Flores, national president of the League of United Latin American Citizens, said while attending the National Council of La Raza convention in Philadelphia. Flores had lobbied hard in behalf of Attorney General Alberto R. Gonzales.

Manuel Mirabal, president of the National Puerto Rican Coalition, attending the same convention, agreed, saying there might be political consequences for Republicans who had hoped to cut deeper into the Democrats' 60 percent share of the Hispanic vote in the last presidential election.

Others questioned how much long-term fallout Bush faces. Even some Democrats pointed out that he has put together diverse Cabinets in both terms and has put women in positions of power in the White House and elsewhere.

But the choice not to fill the O'Connor seat with a woman or minority was not lost on Bush's allies yesterday as they sought to rally behind Roberts while addressing the deficiency on the diversity front.

"Some people have asked me, 'Well, didn't you want a woman?' Well, yes, of course I did," said Sen. Kay Bailey Hutchison (R-Tex.). "Of course I think diversity is important on the Supreme Court. I would like to see another woman. I would like to see a Hispanic American on the Supreme Court. But I believe first and foremost what we want is the very best person. And, for this time, the president has chosen John Roberts."

Sen. Ken Salazar (D-Colo.) released a letter addressed to the president lamenting what he said was a missed opportunity to assure the inclusion of women at all levels of government. "You and I both have two daughters," Salazar wrote. "The profound message we should be giving to them is that their gender creates no limitations for them to live up to their God-given potential. Yet, I fear that with the loss of Justice Sandra Day O'Connor from the United States Supreme Court, we are sending the opposite message."

Hispanic leaders might have been more vocal in their disappointment were it not for the fact that many worried that Bush would appoint a conservative Latino whose views conflict with their own agendas. "My greatest fear was that President Bush would choose someone who will not be sensitive to our demands," and that fear has not abated, said Cesar A. Perales, president of the Puerto Rican Legal Defense and Education Fund.

Gonzales was viewed by Hispanics as a Republican centrist, the best they could hope for among the available candidates, Rodolfo de la Garza, a Columbia University political science professor who specializes in Latino politics, and other experts said. But supporting him outright would have been awkward, because human rights groups with whom they are allied opposed Gonzales for his role in providing legal authority that led to the torture of prisoners in Iraq.

Democratic strategist Jim Jordan said that by not appointing a woman or Latino, Bush has "highlighted a negative stereotype of the party—a party that truly only welcomes conservative white males. That's an unflattering view of the party and one frankly we thought they were trying to ameliorate."

But Republican National Committee spokesman Brian Jones said that the committee's vigorous outreach to minorities would continue. "I don't think this is something that's going to derail the efforts underway at this point," he said.

Republicans said yesterday they are confident the O'Connor vacancy will not be the last Bush will be asked to fill, given the health of Chief Justice William Rehnquist. But the Spokesman-Review reported that O'Connor said she doubted the president would name a woman as chief justice. "So that almost assures," she said, "there won't be a woman appointed to the court at this time."

Research editor Lucy Shackelford contributed to this report.

*I*n this next piece, Kevin Johnson picks up the Latino theme and encourages readers to assess the relative value of (1) physical and (2) ideological representation on the Court. Johnson indicates he personally holds more liberal views and concedes that any nominee of President George W. Bush's (Latino or otherwise) likely would be politically conservative. In this terrain, he nonetheless argues that Bush should have nominated a Latino to the Court. Yes, that individual would be politically conservative, but he sees considerable value in diversifying the court so that a Latino is present. Johnson uses the (ultimately failed) federal circuit court nomination of Miguel Estrada as an illustrative example throughout, as well as the importance to African-Americans of Justice Thurgood Marshall's appointment to the Court. Of course, Marshall's record as a civil rights attorney suggested that his selection would provide both symbolic and substantive representation to an under-represented group. In his overall argument, Johnson appears to take the position that symbolic representation is an important component of a democratic government, even if substantive representation would not likely be achieved.

The First Latino Supreme Court Justice?

KEVIN R. JOHNSON

Recently, President George W. Bush nominated conservative, Honduran-born attorney Miguel Estrada to the U.S. Court of Appeals for the D.C. Circuit. The nomination has provoked controversy.

A graduate of Harvard Law School and a former law clerk to Associate Justice Anthony Kennedy, Estrada would be the first Latino on the D.C. Circuit, often a stepping-stone to the U.S. Supreme Court. After a stint in the prestigious Solicitor General's office, Estrada currently is with the prominent law firm of Gibson, Dunn & Crutcher, which represented President Bush in the contentious 2000 litigation over the voting in Florida. Although he meets the educational and professional qualifications for the job, Estrada's conservative politics, temperament, and connection to the Latino community have become issues for many.

Indeed, Latino advocacy groups are deeply divided about Estrada's nomination. The Hispanic National Bar Association endorses the nomination. But the Puerto Rican Legal Defense and Education Fund strongly opposes Estrada's confirmation.

That person might or might not be Estrada, but whoever it might be, it would literally make history.

THE POSSIBLE IMPACT OF THE NOMINATION OF THE FIRST LATINO SUPREME COURT JUSTICE

The possible appointment of a Latino Justice to the Supreme Court has been on the table for well over a decade. The much-publicized Census 2000 revealed that Hispanics currently comprise more than 12.5 percent of the total U.S. population, or almost 35 million people, roughly approximating the number of African Americans in the country.

In light of the demographics, we should expect—some might say demand—to see a Latino on the Supreme Court in the twenty-first century. If and when it does happen, what will be the impact of the historic appointment?

By way of comparison, consider President Lyndon Johnson's landmark nomination of Thurgood Marshall to the Supreme Court in 1967. Justice Marshall, of course, was the first African American to serve on the high Court.

JUSTICE THURGOOD MARSHALL AS A BEACON OF HOPE

Marshall's appointment undisputedly meant a great deal to African Americans, to the Court as an institution, and to the nation. In announcing Marshall's nomination, President Johnson remarked that the appointment was "the right thing to do, the right time to do it, the right man and the right place."

Kevin R. Johnson, "The First Latino Supreme Court Justice?" *FindLaw's Writ*, October 17, 2002. Reprinted by permission of Findlaw, a Thomson Reuters business. writ.news.findlaw.com

Marshall, of course, was a revered African American civil rights lawyer and the architect of *Brown v. Board of Education*, the major civil rights decision of the twentieth century. The meaning of his appointment thus could not have been clearer—and its meaning for African Americans was especially important.

The appointment provided a touchstone for African Americans, as the nation's racial sensibilities underwent a radical, at times violent, transformation during the civil rights movement of the 1960s. And the mere presence of an African American on the nation's highest court—almost unthinkable just a few years before—forever changed the United States.

During Justice Marshall's tenure on the Supreme Court, it moved in a more conservative direction, away from his intellectual leanings. As a result, Justice Marshall wrote increasing numbers of dissents. In the role of "the Great Dissenter," or "our Supreme conscience," Justice Marshall again gave voice to the sentiments of many African Americans.

Thurgood Marshall also had an impact on his fellow Justices and the Supreme Court as an institution. His rich career as a civil rights lawyer allowed him to spin tales that gave real-life meaning to many of the cases that came before the Court. Justices Kennedy, O'Connor, and White—all moderate or conservative Justices—each wrote about how much they gained from Justice Marshall's experiences.

HOW A LATINO JUSTICE'S PERSPECTIVE MIGHT CHANGE THE SUPREME COURT

As Thurgood Marshall's appointment was for African Americans, the addition of the first Latina/o to the Supreme Court would be a historic "first." Importantly, a Latina/o would likely bring new and different perspectives to the Court and its decision-making process. Consider one decision by way of example.

In the 1975 case of *United States v. Brignoni-Ponce*, the Supreme Court stated that Border Patrol officers on roving patrols could consider the race of the occupant of an automobile in making an immigration stop. In the Court's words, "[t]he likelihood that any given person of Mexican ancestry is an alien is high enough to make Mexican appearance a relevant factor" in deciding to stop a vehicle. A form of racial profiling in immigration enforcement thus was declared constitutional.

A Latino Justice might well approach the reliance on race and physical appearance in immigration stops in a wholly different way. For one thing, a Latino would more likely understand why "Mexican appearance" is a deeply flawed criterion on which to base an immigration stop. He or she would understand, for instance, that there is no single "Mexican appearance." Rather, Latinos come in all shapes, sizes, and appearances, not just the stereotypical ones.

A Latino Justice would also likely understand another fallacy in the Court's reasoning in *Brignoni-Ponce*: if merely having apparent Mexican ancestry made one likely to be an "illegal alien," hundreds of thousands, if not millions, of Latino citizens and lawful immigrants could be subject to vehicle stops. In fact, Mexican ancestry hardly makes one especially likely to be an "alien"—as a Latino Justice could not help but know.

Many non-Latino citizens nevertheless assume that Latinos—native born citizens in this country or not—are "foreigners," and treat them as outsiders to the national community. A Latino Justice would be in a position to correct these beliefs, and could as a result have a strong, positive effect on the Court's immigration and immigration enforcement decisions.

Similarly, a Latino also might look differently than others at various civil rights issues, including those implicated by English-only rules, bilingual education, and criminal law enforcement. To this point, no Supreme Court Justice has emphasized, as Justice Marshall consistently did for African Americans, the long history of discrimination Latinos have faced.

A LATINO CLARENCE THOMAS?

Some observers might suggest that this analysis is politically and otherwise naive and that a Latino appointment by President Bush will more likely resemble Justice Clarence Thomas than Justice Thurgood Marshall. It is not a coincidence, they might point out, that Bush's first Latino federal appeals court nominee, Estrada, is quite conservative; a Supreme Court nominee would likely be very conservative, too.

But even so, the appointment of a Latino to the Supreme Court would signal a movement toward full membership for Latinos in American social life, just as Thurgood Marshall's appointment did for African Americans. For one thing, the naming of a Latino Justice in and of itself would symbolize the growing inclusion of Latinos in the "respectable" mainstream—rather than simply in the entertainment industry where one cannot miss Jennifer Lopez and Ricky Martin. Such a first would mark the true arrival of Latinos.

The debate about Miguel Estrada's confirmation gives us an idea of what to expect in the future when a President—perhaps President Bush—nominates the first Latino to the U.S. Supreme Court. Controversy will surround the nomination and the stakes will be high, especially for the Latino community. Consequently, this is the time to pay attention—for the Estrada confirmation process may be a harbinger of things to come.

*A*s has been common in Supreme Court nominations over the past 30 to 40 years, a recent dialogue (if not debate) emerged over who should be nominated to fill Justice Sandra Day O'Connor's seat once she retired. In this selection, Cass Sunstein downplays the perceived importance of demographic characteristics when considering a U.S. Supreme Court nominee. Rather, he argues that intellectual differences among Supreme Court members will produce the overall best decisions—and this is the diversity that we should endorse, rather than diversity based on symbolic representation. Sunstein suggests that the best arguments, counter-arguments—and ultimately, decisions—come from a range of perspectives on the Court. While Sunstein agrees that there is important symbolic value in demographic diversity, he argues that " . . . it's not all that important to ensure that the court 'looks like America.'" Because this article makes a different argument than many others about representation on the Court, it begs for important debate on what type(s) of diversity should be prioritized in the nomination and selection of Supreme Court justices.*

A Diversity of Minds, Not Biology

Cass R. Sunstein

Judge John G. Roberts Jr. fits the standard profile of a Supreme Court nominee: a middle-aged white man, appointed after serving on a federal appellate court.

Whatever they think of Roberts' merits, many people had hoped for something different—something other than the standard profile. First Lady Laura Bush, for instance, said, "I would really like for him to name another woman." While describing Roberts as "first-rate," Justice Sandra Day O'Connor said she was "disappointed . . . to see the percentage of women on our court drop by 50%." Others have hoped, and continue to hope, for a Latino justice, or perhaps for another African American. Still others, including Senate Minority Leader Harry Reid, argue that the president should be considering people "outside the box," including candidates from state government, the executive branch or even Congress, rather than taking the now-usual route of elevating someone from the federal Court of Appeals.

The question of diversity on the Supreme Court has been with us for a long time. In the past, there was a de facto "Jewish seat" on the Supreme Court, first filled by Louis Brandeis and then for many years by Felix Frankfurter, who was succeeded by Arthur Goldberg, followed in turn by Abe Fortas. (Justices Ruth Bader Ginsburg and Stephen Breyer are both Jewish.) There is, in effect, an African American seat today. Thurgood Marshall was replaced by Clarence Thomas and, unless another African American is named to the court first, when Thomas leaves he will almost surely be replaced by an African American. President Bush will be under intense and possibly irresistible pressure to ensure that his next nominee is a woman.

Unfortunately, all this focus on demographics misses the most important point. What the court most needs is intellectual diversity. It should have people with a range of perspectives, different kinds of knowledge and different points of view. For many questions that come before the court, expertise is important, and it is impossible for anyone to be an expert in everything. The court has greatly benefited from having Breyer, a specialist in copyright law, and Justice Antonin Scalia, a specialist in separation of powers. And for the most important questions, internal differences are crucial because they sharpen arguments and increase the likelihood that the court will get it right.

On lower courts, the evidence shows that intellectual diversity makes a big difference. On three-judge panels, Republican appointees show far more extremism when they are sitting only with other Republican appointees. The same is true of Democratic appointees, who shift to the left on panels made up solely of Democratic appointees. The evidence also suggests that the increased moderation reflects greater attention to competing arguments—and even a closer attention to the law itself.

Cass R. Sunstein, "A Diversity of Minds, Not Biology," *The Los Angeles Times*, July 23, 2005, p. B19. Reprinted by permission of the author. © 2005 Cass R. Sunstein.

The Supreme Court is similar. If the nine justices share the same basic orientation and background, their views and inclinations will not be tested. They are likely to miss important counter-arguments and alternative points of view. If Sen. Reid is right to contend that the president should think "outside the box," it is because people with different experiences add a valuable perspective. Those who have served in the Legislature or in state government are likely to know things that appellate court judges haven't been able to learn.

None of this means that demographic considerations should be entirely irrelevant. It would be certainly disturbing if the court was made up solely of white men. For symbolic reasons, demographic diversity is valuable. Children of all kinds should be able to see people of all kinds on the court. What's more, women and African Americans can bring perspectives to the court's deliberations simply because of their background. Recent evidence suggests, for example, that female judges are likely to be more attentive than male judges to the claims of sexual harassment victims, in part because of their own experiences.

But the most valuable kind of diversity involves ideas, not biology. Bush may have an opportunity to make several more appointments to the Supreme Court. No one should complain if he selects a woman or an African American—or, for the first time, a Latino or Asian American. But it's not all that important to ensure that the court "looks like America." For the highest court in the land, what matters most is the range of arguments and perspectives.

*T*he next article attempts to systematically measure whether symbolic representation translates into substantive representation in the courts. Jennifer Segal conducts a scholarly investigation into this issue by examining the federal district court decisions made by appointees of President Bill Clinton. Some previous studies have argued that female or minority judges are more politically liberal and more likely to be activist. Moreover, a common assumption is that female and minority judges may be more sensitive to the needs of disadvantaged groups in society. Segal's analysis suggests that having females and minorities on the bench does make a difference. Compared to white men (who are still, by far, the majority of federal district court judges), women and minority judges are more likely to render different decisions than their white male counterparts on cases involving race, gender, and some economic issues. Segal's work thus indicates that the debate over symbolic representation that defines the first three pieces is about more than just whether the court should look like America. The degree to which the court does, or does not, approximate America has direct ramifications for judicial decision making. It is important not to overstate the differences between judges but, on some issues, demography matters for judicial outcomes.

Representative Decision Making on the Federal Bench: Clinton's District Court Appointees

JENNIFER A. SEGAL

REPRESENTATION AND PRESIDENTIAL APPOINTMENTS

The concept of representation has at least two dimensions (Krislov 1974; Perry 1991; Pitkin 1967). One is symbolic, provided by the similarity of personal characteristics between the representative and the constituents he/she serves; representatives who "look" like their constituents deliver symbolic representation. Another dimension is substantive, provided by policies that are made in the interest of particular constituents; representatives who pursue the interests of their constituents deliver substantive representation.

In the context of the federal courts, symbolic representation has been readily apparent with the appointment of non-Protestant, nonwhite, and nonmale judges to the federal bench (Goldman 1997; Gryski, Zuk, and Barrow 1994; Marshall 1993; O'Brien 1996; Perry 1991). The 1970s marked a distinct move away from the historically white and male federal bench. President Carter initiated earnest attempts to populate the courts with less "traditional" judges, including Hispanics, Asians, and Native Americans, but most notably, blacks and women (Goldman and Saronson 1994; Goldman and Slotnick 1997). . . . [D]uring his single term in the White House, 37 blacks were appointed to the district and circuit courts. After Carter, Clinton has made the second largest contribution by matching Carter's 37 black judges during his first term in office, and appointing 14 more thus far in his second term. In contrast, Reagan appointed seven blacks during his two terms in office and Bush appointed 13, including Clarence Thomas, during his one term as President.[1]

Reagan and Bush had better records for appointing female federal judges, but were still outdone by Carter and now Clinton. While Reagan appointed 29 women and Bush appointed 36, Carter paved the way by increasing the number of female judges by 40. The 1992 election of Clinton marked the next influx; by the end of his first term in office, Clinton had appointed 61 women to the district and circuit benches, and he has added 19 more during his second term.

Such diversity, however, does not necessarily lead to substantive representation on the federal bench. While any judge might deliver rulings that specifically favor the interests of various societal groups, it is reasonable to expect that judges who are also members of those groups would exhibit greater support (Goldman 1979; Martin 1982). And, as was true for the Reagan administration's judicial selection,[2] the last two Democratic presidents have at least tried to create a judiciary that would promote their positions on civil liberties and rights issues (Davis 1989; Goldman 1997;

Jennifer A. Segal, "Representative Decision Making on the Federal Bench: Clinton's District Court Appointees," *Political Research Quarterly*, vol. 53, no. 1 (March 2000), pp. 137–150, copyright © 2000 by University of Utah. Reprinted by permission of SAGE Publications.

Rowland, Carp, and Stidham 1984). Indeed, both Carter and Clinton have made public statements suggesting that diverse appointees would bring with them different experiences and perspectives that would positively influence their decision making (for example, Clinton 1996; Davis 1989: 21).

IS THERE A DIFFERENCE BETWEEN TRADITIONAL AND NONTRADITIONAL JUDGES?

The research on this question is relatively limited as a result of the historically low number of black and female (and other minority) judges on the bench. Nevertheless, a number of studies have introduced theoretical expectations and provide an empirical basis from which to work.

The expectation that symbolic leads to substantive representation is based generally on the belief that nontraditional judges are more liberal than their liberal, traditional colleagues. It has been posited that women may be more activist (Martin 1982: 313) and that both female and black judges may be more sensitive to the needs of disadvantaged groups in society (Goldman 1979). Thus, in cases dealing with issues that are particularly sensitive to ideology, such as race and gender, criminal justice, and some economic issues, female and black judges may make different decisions than their colleagues (Walker and Barrow 1985).

More specifically, female and black judges may rule differently in specific types of cases for which they may have special empathy as members of particular societal groups (Songer, Davis, and Haire 1994). Goldman (1979: 494) has argued that nontraditional appointees have "certain qualities of the heart and mind" that may facilitate their policymaking. And, Marshall (1993: 149) suggests that this may be especially true for blacks on civil rights issues because black attitudes tend to be one-sided and quite distinct from whites.

In contrast, there are equally compelling arguments about the absence of meaningful differences between traditional and nontraditional judges. One stems from the attitudinal model which posits that the explanatory power of background characteristics derives from their contribution to the formation of political attitudes and values, the most proximate influences on judicial decision making (Segal and Spaeth 1993: 231–33). Indeed, the Supreme Court clearly illustrates that jurists with similar background characteristics often vote differently; Justices O'Connor and Ginsburg do not always agree, Marshall and Thomas have very different voting records, as do two of the Catholic justices, Brennan and Scalia. This may indicate that symbolic representation does not necessarily lead to substantive representation from the federal bench.

A related argument is that heterogeneity within societal groups may limit the possibility of substantive representation. For example, the difference between Marshall and Thomas on nearly every constitutional issue and principle demonstrates the opposing views that American blacks can have. Additionally, the recent affirmative action debates suggest that the black community is divided over how to deal with race discrimination. Women also disagree on issues like health care, abortion, family leave, and crime. And, importantly, many issues that relate to blacks and women have affected others—many whites are supportive of affirmative action policies, and many men are concerned with issues related to childbirth and child-rearing, equal pay, and other gender discrimination. Therefore, treating groups as homogenous and expecting that political officials can accurately identify and make policy in the interests of those groups may be inappropriate.

The empirical tests of substantive representation have provided support for both sets of expectations. Some studies have found little gender difference at all. Davis (1992) found no clear difference in the "voices" (as defined by Carol Gilligan 1982) used by male and female judges in cases involving discrimination and government's duty to protect. These results were buttressed by an examination of Justice O'Connor's voting behavior (Davis 1993).

Additionally, Walker and Barrow (1985) discovered unexpected differences between Carter's traditional and nontraditional district court judges. For example, in personal liberties cases, where greater support was expected from female and black judges, male judges were more supportive of the claims, and there was no significant race difference. Similarly, there were no significant differences in criminal rights cases either. Most interesting, women were no more sensitive to gender issues than were their male colleagues, and black judges were only marginally more supportive than whites in cases involving black issues.

Moreover, black federal judges do not appear either to advocate black interests in racial discrimination cases or actively to promote other interests of the black community (Davis 1989). And a recent report on Justice Thomas's voting record suggests that, "the civil rights community was correct in predicting that Thomas would often oppose its interests" (Perry and Abraham 1998: 161).

Finally, these findings have been supported by examinations of state court judges. There appears to be little difference between male and female trial judges in their conviction and sentencing decisions (Gruhl, Spohn, and Welch 1981) as well as little difference in sentencing by black and white trial court judges (Welch, Combs, and Gruhl 1988).

Nevertheless, there is also support for the expectation that symbolic representation does indeed translate into substantive representation from the bench. Several studies demonstrate that the connection is issue specific. For instance, gender was important in circuit court decision making in employment discrimination cases (Davis, Haire, and Songer 1993; Songer, Davis, and Haire 1994), but not in obscenity and search and seizure cases (Songer, Davis, and Haire 1994). Additionally, interviews with members of the National Association of Women Judges (NAWJ) revealed that the judiciary would not reflect "the total fabric of society" if women were not on the bench. Women do have different perspectives and life experiences that should be represented on the bench and they are likely to be more sensitive than men to issues like sexual discrimination (Martin 1993: 169). Additionally, female state supreme court justices appear to have Representative role orientations insofar as they cast pro-woman votes more often than their male colleagues (of the same party) in cases involving women's issues (such as sex discrimination, child support, and property settlement) (Allen and Wall 1993).

These mixed findings may be a consequence of analyses based on different courts, different issues, and different methodologies. Certainly, more research in this area is warranted. With the election (and reelection) of President Clinton and his appointment of additional nontraditional judges, this is the perfect time to consider further the question of substantive representation on the federal bench.

*****

THE REPRESENTATIVE NATURE OF CLINTON'S DISTRICT COURT APPOINTEES

Like Walker and Barrow, who found that there were no significant race differences among Carter's appointees (1985: 606), these data indicate that, for all intents and purposes, black judges are not significantly different from their white counterparts in their support of a variety of issues before their benches. Most notable is the absence of any race differences for black issues; black judges are clearly no more supportive of black claims than white judges. And, while the odds ratios suggest that black judges are more likely than white judges to support the policy positions of women, other minorities, and federal economic regulation,[10] the only statistically significant race difference exists for personal liberties claims, for which black judges have less support than their white colleagues.

The gender analysis also presented results similar to those found by Walker and Barrow, which suggested that Carter's female judges did not fulfill their representative role (1985: 605). . . . Women are significantly less likely to support the claims of members of the societal group to which they are expected to have the greatest affinity. And, despite the odds ratios that suggest they are more likely to support the government, and criminal, black, and personal liberties claims than their male colleagues, female judges are significantly more supportive only in cases involving black and personal liberties issues. . . .

These results suggest that, despite their symbolic representation of specific societal groups, the behavior of Clinton's black and female appointees does not support the expectations that they actively promote the interests of those groups as they perform the duties of their office.[11] Rather, the results appear to speak to a number of competing hypotheses about the absence of race and gender differences, discussed previously. One is made by attitudinalists, that ideology and policy preferences provide the most meaningful explanation of judicial decision making. Thus, the explanation for the lack of variation between Clinton's traditional and nontraditional appointees may be explained by their similar ideology and partisanship, such that they are more likely to vote similarly than differently on many issues. Despite their position as symbolic representatives, their ideological orientation has a greater impact on their policymaking, even when they are confronted with issues that are important to their own group.

Another argument that finds some support in these results emphasizes the impact of heterogeneity among the black and female communities on substantive representation. As noted previously, diversity within these groups may present representatives with difficulties. For instance, Clinton's judges may be unable to identify particularly black and female issues. If blacks have varying ideas about their interests and the issues that are important to them, and women experience similar variation, then substantive representation from the bench will be increasingly difficult. Similarly, if the issues have become increasingly complicated and less group-specific, then it may be difficult to represent particular group interests. As a consequence, judges who may indeed be sensitive to and inclined to rule in support of certain group interests, may find themselves unable to do so.

While these arguments may explain the absence of race and gender differences, they do not explain as well the inverse relationships that are evident among black judges who are less supportive of personal liberties claims and female judges who rule against women's claims more often than their colleagues. Such unexpected results may best be understood in the context of judicial socialization. For instance, it may be that female and black judges are aware of the expectations associated with their appointments, but are compelled to perform in the opposite manner to counterbalance internal or external criticism of their job performance. With continued attention to the question of substantive representation on the federal courts as Clinton's appointees spend more time on the bench, we will be in a better position to evaluate the impact of socialization on their decision making.

CONCLUSION

These results support those of Walker and Barrow (1985), and clearly indicate that despite his apparent intentions, President Clinton's black and female district court appointees are no more likely to serve the policy interests of their own communities than are his white and male appointees. Indeed, it is equally clear from the data on Clinton's appointees that these judges, regardless of their race or gender, are not inclined to support a judicial role that is particularly sensitive to the claims of various out-groups in American society.

These results speak to the Republican outcry over Clinton's nominees of the last several years. Despite evidence that his federal judges tend to be noncontroversial and politically moderate (Goldman and Slotnick 1997; Stidham, Carp, and Songer 1996), conservatives both in and out of the Senate have waged ideological battle with the White House over the alleged activism of Clinton's judges (Carney 1997). Republicans' continued dissatisfaction with many of Clinton's moderate nominees suggests that their vehement response is based less on the nominees' general ideology and more on the perceived notion that they will vote in particular ways on issues of import to conservatives.

The data presented here, however, suggest that this notion is inaccurate and that the political hoopla that has surrounded Clinton's nominations to the federal bench is unwarranted. While his partisanship and domestic agenda legitimately may cause his political opponents concern about his choices for the federal judiciary, it appears that Clinton's call for diversity on the district court bench has been largely symbolic in its effect. Any Democratic hopes or Republican worries about substantive representation from Clinton's nontraditional (or traditional, for that matter) judges—any concern about their ideological extremism and judicial activism—is, simply, unfounded.

Notes

1. Statistics on the Reagan and Bush appointees are from Goldman and Saronson (1994). Statistics on Clinton appointees, valid as of June 8, 1999, were provided by the Office of the Counsel to the President and the Office of Policy Development at the United States Department of Justice.

2. According to Goldman (1997: chapter 8) and others (e.g., Craig and O'Brien 1993: 174), a primary part of Reagan's conservative agenda was the selection of federal judges who would overturn judicial decisions about issues like affirmative action and abortion, and return the judiciary to one of self-restraint rather than activism.

10. An odds ratio represents a conditional odds, which is the chance of falling into one category of a variable, compared to falling into the other categories of that variable, from within a particular category of another variable. An odds ratio of 1.0 indicates the absence of a relationship or difference between the two variables; a ratio greater than 1.0 indicates a positive relationship and a ratio less than 1.0 indicates a negative relationship. See Bohrnstedt and Knoke (1994) for a general explanation of odds ratios, and Rowland and Carp (1996: 180–81) for a concise description of their application to the analysis of federal district court decision making.

11. Individual pairs of judges were also examined in an effort to determine whether the aggregate data . . . were masking any gender or race differences. Judicial pairs were analyzed if each of the judges had made rulings in five or more cases in each issue area (Walker and Barrow 1985: 604). There were insufficient cases for an analysis of the race pairs in cases involving black and women's issues. There was one gender pair with enough cases to examine these issues, but for neither set of issues were there significant gender differences. For the other issue areas and for both sets of paired judges, there were few significant gender or race differences— and they provided mixed support for the aggregate results about the differences, or rather lack thereof, between Clinton's traditional and nontraditional federal district court judges.

References

Allen, David W., and Diane E. Wall. 1993. "Role Orientations and Women State Supreme Court Justices." *Judicature* 77: 156–65.

Bohrnstedt, George W., and David Knoke. 1994. *Statistics for Social Data Analysis*. 3rd ed. Itasca, IL: F. E. Peacock.

Carney, Dan. 1997. "Vote to Limit Judges' Powers Indicates Rocky Path Ahead." *Congressional Quarterly*, June 14, 1997, p. 1379.

Clinton, William J. 1996. Remarks by the President to the Colorado Democratic Coordinated Campaign and the African American Initiative of Colorado Democrats. Red Lion, Denver, CO. October 30, 1996. White House Electronic Publications, www.pub.whitehouse.gov/WH/Publications/html/.

Craig, Barbara Hinkson, and David M. O'Brien. 1993. *Abortion and American Politics*. Chatham, NJ: Chatham House.

Davis, Abraham L. 1989. *Blacks in the Federal Judiciary*. Bristol, IN: Wyndham Hall.

Davis, Sue. 1992. "Do Women Judges Speak 'in A Different Voice'?: Carol Gilligan, Feminist Legal Theory, and the Ninth Circuit." *Wisconsin Women's Law Journal* 8: 143–73.

Davis, Sue. 1993. "The Voice of Sandra Day O'Connor." *Judicature* 77: 134–39.

Davis, Sue, Susan Haire, and Donald R. Songer. 1993. "Voting Behavior and Gender on the U.S. Courts of Appeals." *Judicature* 77: 129–33.

Gilligan, Carol. 1982. *In a Different Voice: Psychological Theory and Women's Development*. Cambridge, MA: Harvard University Press.

Goldman, Sheldon. 1979. "Should There Be Affirmative Action for the Judiciary?" *Judicature* 62: 488–94.

Goldman, Sheldon. 1997. *Picking Federal Judges: Lower Court Selection From Roosevelt Through Reagan.* New Haven, CT: Yale University Press.

Goldman, Sheldon, and Matthew D. Saronson. 1994. "Clinton's Nontraditional Judges: Creating a More Representative Bench." *Judicature* 78: 68–73.

Goldman, Sheldon, and Elliot Slotnick. 1997. "Clinton's First Term Judiciary: Many Bridges to Cross." *Judicature* 80: 254–73.

Gruhl, John, Cassia Spohn, and Susan Welch. 1981. "Women as Policymakers: The Case of Trial Judges." *American Journal of Political Science* 25: 309–22.

Gryski, Gerard S., Gary Zuk, and Deborah J. Barrow. 1994. "A Bench That Looks Like America? Representation of African Americans and Latinos on the Federal Courts." *Journal of Politics* 56: 1076–86.

Krislov, Samuel. 1974. *Representative Bureaucracy.* Englewood Cliffs, NJ: Prentice-Hall.

Marshall, Thomas R. 1993. "Symbolic Versus Policy Representation on the U.S. Supreme Court." *Journal of Politics* 55: 140–50.

Martin, Elaine. 1982. "Women on the Federal Bench: A Comparative Profile." *Judicature* 65: 306–13.

Martin, Elaine. 1993. "The Representative Role of Women Judges." *Judicature* 77: 166–73.

Perry, Barbara A. 1991. *A "Representative" Supreme Court?: The Impact of Race, Religion, and Gender on Appointments.* New York: Greenwood Press.

Perry, Barbara A., and Henry J. Abraham. 1998. "A 'Representative' Supreme Court? The Thomas, Ginsburg, and Breyer Appointments." *Judicature* 81: 158–65.

Pitkin, Hanna F. 1967. *The Concept of Representation.* Berkeley: University of California Press.

Rowland, C. K., Robert A., Carp, and Ronald Stidham. 1984. "Judges' Policy Choices and the Value Basis of Judicial Appointments: A Comparison of Support for Criminal Defendants among Nixon, Johnson and Kennedy Appointees to the Federal District Courts." *Journal of Politics* 46: 886–902.

Rowland, C. K. and Robert A. Carp. 1996. *Politics and Judgment in Federal District Courts.* Lawrence: University Press of Kansas.

Segal, Jeffrey A., and Harold J. Spaeth. 1993. *The Supreme Court and the Attitudinal Model.* New York: Cambridge University Press.

Songer, Donald R., Sue Davis, and Susan Haire. 1994. "A Reappraisal of Diversification in the Federal Courts: Gender Effects in the Courts of Appeals." *Journal of Politics* 56: 425–39.

Stidham, Ronald, Robert A. Carp, and Donald R. Songer. 1996. "The Voting Behavior of President Clinton's Judicial Appointees." *Judicature* 80: 16–20.

Walker, Thomas G., and Deborah J. Barrow. 1985. "The Diversification of the Federal Bench: Policy and Process Ramifications." *Journal of Politics* 47: 596–617.

Welch, Susan, Michael Combs, and John Gruhl. 1988. "Do Black Judges Make a Difference?" *American Journal of Political Science* 32: 126–36.

1. In your view, what method of selecting judges produces the most representative result—appointments (as in the federal court system) or election (as in the state court systems)? Why? Which method is better in your opinion?

2. How does the importance of having a demographically diverse Supreme Court compare with the importance of other considerations (such as ideology) for having someone on the bench? In other words, doesn't the appointment of Clarence Thomas (at least on matters of civil rights) make the issue of demographic representation exclusively symbolic and not substantive? Does this matter to Kevin Johnson, who wrote "The First Latino Supreme Court Justice?"?

3. Some observers have argued that with the passage of anti-gender discrimination laws during the 1970s and the increase of females into the legal profession, women may be more fully integrated into the federal court system than either Congress or the Executive branch. Do you agree or disagree? Why? How would you go about measuring or addressing this?

4. If there are different "perspectives" that come from demographic differences, does that mean that there is a "politics" of the U.S. Supreme Court based on diversity? Explain.

5. Do you agree with Cass Sunstein that "it's not all that important that the Court 'looks like America'"? Said differently, is there a positive value to our country to have a demographically diverse U.S. Supreme Court? Explain your answer.

Additional Resources

http://www.supremecourtus.gov
The official site of the U.S. Supreme Court provides information on the Court's calendar, summaries of court opinions, and information on how to locate amicus briefs.

http://www.oyez.org
This site provides biographical information (including financial disclosure statements) for the Justices, as well as court cases and decisions.

http://www.naacpldf.org
The legal defense arm of the National Association for the Advancement of Colored People (NAACP), this organization takes legal action to protect the rights of minorities in a wide variety of areas, including education, employment, housing, voting rights, and environmental justice.

http://www.maldef.org
The Mexican-American Legal Defense and Education Fund (MALDEF) brings legal complaints and provides legal representation to Latinos in a wide variety of areas, including immigration, employment discrimination, K–12 and higher education, and voting rights. The organization also provides information and education on issues such as domestic violence, hate crimes, school desegregation, and policy-community relations.

12 Angry Men (1957; remade in 1997) is an examination of racial/ethnic prejudice and the jury system, as jurors deliberate the fate of a poor Latino youth accused of murder.

13 CIVIL RIGHTS AND CIVIL LIBERTIES: PROTECTING *EVERYONE'S* RIGHTS IN A DEMOCRACY

Racial and ethnic profiling is an important civil rights issue in the United States. African-Americans have been profiled ("Driving While Black"), and since 9/11, those who appear to be of Middle Eastern heritage also have been profiled ("Flying While Arab").

Visualize a white male driving within the speed limit on an interstate highway somewhere in the United States. A highway patrol officer pulls him over and frisks the driver and asks to inspect the trunk. The driver asks, "What did I do?" The officer says, "we are on the lookout for white males who may be terrorists. We know that Timothy McVeigh and Terry Nichols—two white males—were involved in the Oklahoma City bombing." Such racial profiling is unlikely for white males, but it happens frequently for African-Americans and Latinos, and since September 11, 2001, has happened regularly for those traveling by airplane that are of Middle Eastern nationality or heritage.

In a democracy, civil rights and civil liberties are fundamental components to an open and free society. Civil rights (equal protection of the law, freedom from discrimination) are embodied in the Declaration of Independence, the U.S. Constitution and Amendments, in many federal statutes, and in numerous U.S. Supreme Court decisions. Civil rights are a continuing source of political debate, but often are resolved in the federal court system. Many of these debates and court decisions involve the protection of political minority group members (which often—but not always—includes women, gays and lesbians, and particular racial and ethnic groups) within a system of majority rule. This prevention of "tyranny of the majority" is a basic principle of democratic theory and practice.

Civil liberties are considered to be freedoms that individuals in a democracy enjoy from governmental interference or intrusion. Civil liberties also were central to the Framers' ideas of government and democracy. These liberties are contained largely in the Bill of Rights of the U.S. Constitution, and include freedom of speech and the press, religion, and assembly. They also protect individuals dealing with the criminal justice system, by providing for due process of law guarantees (that includes standards of obtaining evidence, the right to legal representation and a speedy trial, freedom from self-incrimination, and others).

Many of this country's most enduring and deeply felt political cleavages and conflicts involve civil rights and civil liberties. Affirmative action stands out in this regard. This civil rights policy attempts to create opportunities (in higher education and employment, for example) for groups historically denied equal opportunity in those areas. For instance, the factor of race as it relates to admissions decisions by colleges and universities has been controversial at least since the Supreme Court's decision in *Regents of the University of California v. Bakke* (1978). In the years after the *Bakke* decision, universities have eliminated racial quotas but continued to use race as one factor in their admissions decisions (which was upheld as constitutional in the *Bakke* decision). Partly in reaction to these decisions, voters in some states have passed state constitutional amendments prohibiting the use of race in government hiring or university admissions decisions.

All the readings in this section point in one shared direction: The political debate over civil rights and civil liberties will likely remain heated in the future. While the particular civil rights issue—or affected minority group—may change over time, finding the appropriate balance between majority rule and protection of minority rights will continue to challenge to the U.S. political system, our legal system, and our individual attitudes.

*T*he year 2005 saw continued attention to affirmative action by the courts. Two university admissions court cases involved the University of Michigan. These cases included complaints involving the school's college of literature, science, and the arts (Gratz v. Bollinger) and its law school (Grutter v. Bollinger). James E. Coleman's article summarizes the two U.S. Supreme Court opinions that rejected the undergraduate admissions policy that included a "point system," where African-Americans (and members of other minority groups) were given extra points toward their admission score simply because of their race, but upheld the law school's more flexible set of decision rules on admission. Coleman's article thus explains the current law of the land as it relates to affirmative action and college admissions.

As the article indicates, proponents of the policy tend to see affirmative action as a way to amend current and past inequities. They also stress the value of a diverse learning environment. Opponents typically see affirmative action as discriminatory in its own right and wonder how the policy encourages equity. As students of politics, it is important to both understand what affirmative action is, and is not, and to engage the debates surrounding it.

An Ode to Justice Lewis F. Powell, Jr.: The Supreme Court Approves the Consideration of Race as a Factor in Admissions by Public Institutions of Higher Education

JAMES E. COLEMAN, JR.

In a 5–4 decision involving the University of Michigan School of Law, the United States Supreme Court upheld the "flexible" consideration of race as one factor among many for admissions to public institutions of higher education. *Grutter v. Bollinger*, No. 02-241. The decision was announced by Justice Sandra Day O'Connor; joining her in the majority were Justices Stephen G. Breyer, Ruth Bader Ginsburg, David H. Souter, and John Paul Stevens. Chief Justice William H. Rehnquist and Justices Antonin Scalia, Anthony M. Kennedy, and Clarence Thomas dissented. In a related case, the Court in an anti-climatic 6–3 decision rejected a formalistic point-system plan used by the University of Michigan to admit undergraduates. *Gratz v. Bollinger*, No. 02-516. The decision in the undergraduate case was announced by the Chief Justice; he was joined in the judgment by Justices O'Connor, Thomas, Kennedy, Scalia, and Breyer. Justices Stevens, Souter, and Ginsburg dissented.

Although some have portrayed the Court's action as a "split decision," in fact, as far as 5–4 decisions go, it is a definitive and decisive victory for race-conscious affirmative action. For the first time, a majority of the Court has held unequivocally that "student body diversity is a compelling state interest that can justify the use of race in university admissions." This explicitly adopts the diversity rationale of Justice Lewis Powell's opinion in *Regents of the University of California v. Bakke*, 438 U. S. 265 (1978), which the Court in *Grutter* described as the touchstone for constitutional analysis of race-conscious admissions policies.

In deciding that a diverse student body was a compelling state interest, the Court was persuaded that the benefits of such diversity "are substantial." Relying upon an

James E. Coleman, Jr., "An Ode to Justice Lewis F. Powell, Jr.: The Supreme Court Approves The Consideration of Race as a Factor in Admissions by Public Institutions of Higher Education: *Gratz v. Bollinger*; *Grutter v. Bollinger*." Reprinted by permission of Duke University School of Law, Program in Public Law, Supreme Court Online. www.law.duke.edu/publiclaw/supremecourtonline/index

impressive and diverse line-up of *amici* supporting the Law School's admissions policies, the Court identified promotion of cross-racial understanding and the breakdown
of racial stereotypes among the benefits of diversity. The Court deferred to the Law
School's judgment of the importance of diversity to its educational mission. This was
consistent with the Court's prior recognition that education is pivotal to "sustaining
our political and cultural heritage," and is "the very foundation of good citizenship.
Brown v. Board of Education, 347 U. S. 483, 493 (1954). For this reason, the diffusion of knowledge and opportunity through public institutions of higher education
must be accessible to all individuals regardless of race or ethnicity. . . ."

The Court explicitly endorsed the Law School's goal of using race and ethnicity to
achieve a "critical mass" of otherwise underrepresented minority students, who will
not feel isolated on campus or reticent in discourse to express their individual views,
freed of the sense that their presence was intended to be representative. What distinguishes this "critical mass" from an unconstitutional quota is the flexibility with
which it is pursued. As opposed to the rigid race-conscious formula struck down in
Gratz, the Law School's pursuit of diversity involved an individualized review of
"each and every applicant," based upon all of the information contained in the file. In
contrast, the undergraduate program relied upon a mechanical, predetermined formula that automatically awarded points toward admission based solely upon race and
ethnicity, without regard to the individual contribution the applicant would make to
the goals of diversity.

Although race or ethnicity might be the deciding factor for the admission of a particular individual, the flexibility that the Court found in the Law School's holistic
approach was that in practice it also valued other forms of diversity, and no single
form of diversity trumped any other form. In time, the public's embrace of the Court's
decision in *Grutter* likely will be influenced by the extent to which the holistic
approach to admissions required by the decision also opens opportunities at highly
selective institutions for non-minority applicants.

Finally, the Court emphasized that all race-conscious programs eventually must
end. Justice O'Connor expressed the hope that twenty-five years from now race-conscious admissions will not be necessary. That places the burden on universities to
review periodically their admissions policies, to adopt race-neutral policies when they
will serve the goals of meaningful diversity and selectivity, and to eliminate the consideration of race when race-neutral policies can achieve the compelling interest of a
diverse student body. Actually achieving an end to race-conscious admissions in
twenty-five years belongs in the same category of aspirations as achieving a color-blind
society. But, what undoubtedly will be important in twenty-five years is the record
established by selective universities and the states that support them to show that
they have made a good faith effort to move in that direction.

Perhaps the most important thing that can be said about the Court's decision in the
short-term is that it provides a roadmap for navigating the hazards of race-conscious
admissions. First, universities must start with a clear written statement of the goals of
its admissions policies, against which the good faith implementation of those policies
can be judged. Although the Court does not explicitly identify this as a constitutional
requirement, it is clear from Justice O'Connor's opinion that the Law School's written
admissions policy was critically important to the Court's willingness to presume that

the Law School had acted in good faith in implementing it. Second, the policies must require the university to review conscientiously each applicant for admissions, based upon all the information in his or her file. Although the university may establish a threshold level of minimum qualification, it may not automatically admit or reject any applicant who meets that minimum threshold, without an individualized evaluation of his or her application.

Finally, although the university may set goals for attaining a critical mass of underrepresented minority students, it cannot pursue such goals in an inflexible mechanical way that makes race and ethnicity shields that effectively exempt some applicants from competing for admissions. It is the implementation of this aspect of the Law School's policies that caused Justices Kennedy to conclude that, after all was said and done, those policies ultimately operated like a quota. Justice O'Connor does not provide an easy answer to this conundrum. Instead, she looks to how the policies actually operate in other areas of diversity to see if race and ethnicity were being used flexibly. Thus, it was important to Justice O'Connor that the Law School's diversity goal was not merely to ensure some specified percentage of a particular racial or ethnic group, but rather to achieve the broader "educational benefits that diversity is designed to produce." In part, this was reflected in the fact that the Law School also gave serious consideration to other factors beside race and ethnicity that contribute to the benefits of a diverse student body. The Law School's good faith in considering such other factors was reflected in the finding that it "frequently accepts nonminority applicants with grades and test scores lower than underrepresented minority applicants (and other nonminority applicants) who are rejected." Although the Court undoubtedly will defer to a university's judgment about what constitutes a broadly diverse student body, this likely will be an area of heated if not fruitful litigation in the future.

Opponents of race-conscious admissions already have made clear that the Court's decision in *Grutter* will not end the contentious debate that affirmative action has spawned. But, the decision provides an understandable and realistic approach that universities committed to true diversity can take constitutionally to stay on the high road in that debate.

This selection takes up another controversial civil rights and civil liberties issue: gender discrimination. Public opinion polling results have indicated that both men and women agree that gender discrimination should not take place. The difficulty, or point of controversy, has been in determining what constitutes gender discrimination. Liza Featherstone's article summarizes the Dukes v. Wal-Mart *court case that alleges sex discrimination by Wal-Mart in its personnel practices, especially in promotions, wages, training, and work assignments. The litigants in this case qualified to file a class action suit—which is very cumbersome and difficult to do in the U.S. legal system. As a result, Wal-Mart is now facing the largest class action suit ever by current and former female employees over alleged gender discrimination. In consid-*

ering the arguments surrounding this case, you might also discuss the civil liberties and civil rights issues presented by major retailers like Wal-Mart. On the one hand, these stores offer low prices that many enjoy—especially those on limited incomes. For instance, Wal-Mart has become a phenomenon of low prices, and it is now the country's largest retailer. But a company's focus on low prices may have its own set of costs. The company typically does not pay for its employees' health insurance premiums, and Wal-Mart has been criticized for employing (and under-paying) illegal aliens, for forsaking U.S.-made products for cheaper products made in other countries such as China, and for aggressively pressuring its suppliers to lower prices that they charge to the company. Do these actions lead to violations of civil rights and liberties?

Wal-Mart Values

LIZA FEATHERSTONE

Wal-Mart is an unadorned eyesore surrounded by a parking lot, even its logo aggressively devoid of flourish. Proving that looks don't matter, however, the retail giant has a way with women: Four out of ten American women visit one of Wal-Mart's stores weekly. They like the low prices, convenience and overall ease of the shopping experience. Even snobbish elites are discovering its delights: A few months ago, *New York Times* fashion writer Cathy Horyn revealed, to the astonishment of fellow urban fashionistas, that much of her wardrobe comes from Wal-Mart ("Marc Jacobs?" "No, it's Wal-Mart"). Retail consultant Wendy Liebmann ecstatically dubs Wal-Mart the "benchmark by which American women rate all shopping."

Would that $15 runway knockoffs were Wal-Mart's primary contribution to women's lives. But Wal-Mart is not only America's favorite shopping destination; it's also the nation's largest private employer. The majority of Wal-Mart's "associates" (the company's treacly euphemism for employees) are women. Their average wage is $7.50 an hour, out of which they must pay for their own health insurance, which is so costly that only two in five workers buy it.

Yet Wal-Mart is not only a horrifyingly stingy employer: Many workers say it is also a sexist one. From the Third World factories in which its cheap products are made, to the floor of your local Wal-Mart, where they're displayed and sold, it is women who bear the brunt of the company's relentless cost-cutting. Ellen Rosen, a resident scholar in Brandeis University's Women's Studies Research Program, recently observed that around the world, Wal-Mart's business practices "may be leading to a new kind of globally sanctioned gender discrimination."

Liza Featherstone, "Wal-Mart Values." Reprinted with permission from the December 16, 2002 issue of *The Nation*. For subscription information, call 1-800-333-8536. Portions of each week's *Nation* magazine can be accessed at www.thenation.com.

Gretchen Adams worked for Wal-Mart for ten years, in five different states. As a co-manager, she opened twenty-seven "Supercenters" (gargantuan, twenty-four-hour grocery/general merchandise hybrids). "There were so many inequities," she sighs with amazement, reflecting on her time at Wal-Mart. She saw men with little to no relevant experience earning starting salaries of $3,500 a year more than her own. "I had the title but not the pay," she says. "They take us for idiots."

Adams is now a witness in *Dukes v. Wal-Mart*, in which seven California women—current and former Wal-Mart employees—are charging the company with systematic sex discrimination in promotions, assignments, training and pay. Betty Dukes, for whom the suit is named, is a 52-year-old African-American woman who still works at Wal-Mart. First hired by the company in 1994 as a part-time cashier in Pittsburg, California, she was an eager employee with a sincere admiration for founder Sam Walton's "visionary spirit." A year later, with excellent performance reviews, she was given a merit pay raise and a full-time job. Two years later, after being promoted to the position of customer service manager, she began encountering harsh discrimination from her superiors; she says she was denied the training she needed in order to advance further, while that same training was given to male employees. She was also denied the opportunity to work in "male" departments like hardware, and was made to sell baby clothes instead. "I can mix a can of paint," she told reporters just after filing the suit. "I want the chance to do it."

When Dukes complained about the discrimination, managers got back at her by writing her up for minor offenses like returning late from breaks, offenses routinely committed by her white and male co-workers, who were never punished, she says. When she kept complaining, she was denied a promotion and finally demoted back to her cashier job. She went to the Wal-Mart district office to complain, but the company did nothing. Being demoted was not just humiliating: It deprived Dukes of other promotions, and her cashier job offered fewer hours and a lower hourly wage. When she was once again eligible for promotion, four new management positions, none of which had even been posted, were filled by men.

Along with more than seventy witnesses, the other named plaintiffs in *Dukes v. Wal-Mart* tell similar stories:

In August 1997, Patricia Surgeson, then a single mother of two, began working evenings as a part-time cashier in a Wal-Mart tire and lube department while attending community college. Within two weeks, while she was stocking shelves, she says, a male co-worker began grabbing and propositioning her. He was allowed to remain in his job, while she was transferred to the health and beauty aids department. Over the next four years, Surgeson held more responsible jobs at Wal-Mart, but these promotions weren't accompanied by raises. Many of her male co-workers were paid better than she was, she charges, even though they had less responsibility and were newer to the company.

Hired to work in the returns department in the Livermore, California, store in fall 1998, Cleo Page, who had already worked in two other Wal-Mart stores, was quickly promoted to a customer service manager position. Interviewing a little over a year later for a promotion, she charges, she was told that it was a man's world, and that men controlled management positions at Wal-Mart. She was repeatedly passed over for promotions, which were given to male employees, and to white women. (Page, who is African-American, also has a race discrimination claim against Wal-Mart, as does Betty Dukes, but these charges are not part of the class-action suit.) At one point, her store manager discouraged her from applying for the sporting-goods department manager position, she says, because "customers would feel comfortable" buying sporting goods from a man. She heard male co-workers complain that "women were taking over" the store, and she heard them ask each other if they knew other men who would be interested in working at Wal-Mart.

* * * * *

Women make up 72 percent of Wal-Mart's sales work force but only 33 percent of its managers. A study conducted for the *Dukes* plaintiffs by economist Marc Bendick found such discrepancies to be far less pronounced among Wal-Mart's competitors, which could boast of more than 50 percent female management. Even more striking, comparing Wal-Mart stores to competitors in the same location, Bendick's study found little geographic variation in these ratios, and little change over time. In fact, the percentage of women among Wal-Mart's 1999 management lagged behind that of its competitors in 1975. (Wal-Mart spokesman Bill Wertz says it's "too soon" to say how the company will defend itself against these charges.)

Depending on the outcome of a class-certification hearing next July before a San Francisco federal judge, *Dukes v. Wal-Mart* could be the largest civil rights class-action suit in history, affecting more than 700,000 women. Though a California judge ruled recently that the case must be limited to California plaintiffs, discovery is nation-wide, as is the proposed class. If the plaintiffs have their way, any woman employed by the company from 1999 on would win damages. But even more important, says Brad Seligman, Betty Dukes's lawyer, "The idea is to change Wal-Mart. We will not have done our job unless we transform the personnel system at Wal-Mart and make sure there are additional opportunities for women."

Dukes is the culmination of a long history of individual sex-discrimination suits—including sexual harassment and pregnancy discrimination—against Wal-Mart, going back at least to 1981. Courts have often, though of course not always, ruled for the plaintiffs in these cases; in several sexual-harassment suits juries have awarded employees millions of dollars in punitive damages. Wal-Mart recently settled an EEOC sexual-harassment suit on behalf of a group of Wal-Mart employees in Mobile, Alabama, and several women unconnected to *Dukes* have discrimination suits under way.

Some of the lawsuits against Wal-Mart reflect common grievances cited by working women, inequities hardly unique to Wal-Mart, but that women's advocates rightly find particularly outrageous in the world's largest corporation. For example, a suit filed in Georgia by Lisa Smith Mauldin, a Wal-Mart customer service manager and a 22-year-old divorced mother of two, charges the company with sex discrimination because its health plan does not cover prescription contraceptives (it does cover other prescription drugs, but as the complaint spells out in painstaking legalese, only women get pregnant). Mauldin works thirty-two hours a week and makes $12.14 an hour, so the $30 monthly cost of the Pill is a significant burden for her (and certainly a pro-hibitive one for many fellow employees, who earn significantly lower wages). In September Mauldin's suit was certified as a class action, demanding reimbursement for all female Wal-Mart employees who have been paying for birth control out of pocket since March 2001, and demanding that Wal-Mart's insurance cover FDA-approved prescription contraceptives in the future.

Wal-Mart is also criticized for indifference to the workers, mostly young women, who make the products sold in its stores. While most major-clothing stores traffic in sweated labor, Wal-Mart's record on this issue is unusually bad. Much of the clothing sold at Wal-Mart is made in China, where workers have no freedom of association. Unlike many companies, Wal-Mart has adamantly refused to tell labor rights advocates where its factories are, rejecting even the pretense of transparency. Last year, Wal-Mart was removed from the Domini 400 Social Index, an influential socially responsible investment fund, for its failure to make sufficient efforts to uphold labor rights and for its "unresponsiveness to calls for change." Other than Nike, Wal-Mart is the only company that has been booted from the fund for this reason.

Last June, citing all of the above issues, the National Organization for Women named Wal-Mart its fifth "Merchant of Shame" and launched a public education campaign against the retailer. "It's part of our emphasis on economic justice. We don't think Wal-Mart is a woman-friendly workplace," says Olga Vives, NOW's vice president for action. NOW has asked Wal-Mart for a meeting to discuss its complaints, but since the company has not responded, Vives says, "we are getting their attention in other ways." On September 28, 600 NOW chapters demonstrated at Wal-Mart stores across the country, from Tallahassee to Salt Lake City.

NOW has been cooperating closely with the United Food and Commercial Workers, who have been trying for several years to organize Wal-Mart workers [see John Dicker, "Union Blues at Wal-Mart," *The Nation*, July 8, 2002], an effort ruthlessly resisted by the company. Gretchen Adams, who quit Wal-Mart in December 2001, now works as an organizer with the UFCW. She's angry, not only about the way she was treated, but also about the plight of the hourly workers she supervised. "They were not paid enough to live on. There were a whole lot of single mothers," she says. "They would come in crying because they had hard decisions: whether to take their child to the doctor or pay their rent." Many hourly workers were on public assistance because their pay was so low, she recalls.

Not a single Wal-Mart store is unionized yet, but there's substantial evidence that many of the problems suffered by Wal-Mart's female employees would be alleviated by a union. A study on women in the retail food industry, published in February by the Institute for Women's Policy Research and funded by the UFCW, found that women workers in unions faced smaller gender and racial wage gaps, and earned 31 percent higher wages than women who were not in unions. In addition, the study showed that two-thirds of women in unionized retail jobs had health insurance, while only one-third of their nonunion counterparts did. Such advantages were even more dramatic for part-time workers, who are even more likely to be women.

At a November 18 press conference in Washington, DC, to announce a UFCW-initiated National Day of Action on November 21—rallies were held in more than 100 cities and towns, supported by a broad coalition of religious, environmental, student and labor groups—NOW president Kim Gandy said Wal-Mart should know that "continuing their greedy, abusive ways will cost them the business of thinking consumers." This seems unlikely, though it's probably important to make the threat. In any case, the UFCW is not calling for a nationwide Wal-Mart boycott. "We are calling for a boycott in Las Vegas," says Doug Dority, president of the UFCW. In Las Vegas, where a vigorous organizing campaign is under way, Wal-Mart has committed numerous violations of the right to organize. Las Vegas is also the most heavily unionized city in the United States. Elsewhere, however, the UFCW is not ready to take that step. "It's hard to boycott and organize at the same time," says Dority. "Because Wal-Mart uses that against you: 'Hey, the union is trying to take away your job.'"

Still, it makes sense for activists to appeal to the possible solidarity between Wal-Mart's female customers and its female work force. UFCW vice president Susan Phillips said in a recent speech, "As women, we have tremendous power. We control both sides of the cash register. We are the cashiers on one side and we are the customers on the other side. If we join hands across the cash register, we can change the economic future for women in America." Far from telling consumers not to shop at the "Big Box," on the November 21 Day of Action many UFCW locals dramatized consumer power through "shop-ins," urging protesters to go into the store, buy something while wearing a T-shirt with the UFCW's phone number on it, and tell employees they supported their right to join a union. In Seekonk, Massachusetts, a UFCW local even gave each November 21 protester a $20 bill to spend at Wal-Mart, donating the purchases to a nearby women's shelter.

In fact, Wal-Mart customers and workers have much in common: They are increasingly likely to be anybody in America. The working poor are even more likely than other Americans to shop at Wal-Mart, not necessarily because they find it a shopper's paradise—though of course some do—but because they need the discounts, or live in a remote area with few other options. (Many Wal-Mart workers say they began working at their local Wal-Mart because they shopped there; when they needed a job, they filled out its application, because Wal-Mart was already such a familiar part of their lives.) Through shoppers and "associates" alike, Wal-Mart is making billions from female poverty.

In addition to court mandates and worker organizing, changing Wal-Mart is going to take massive pressure from many constituencies; union locals will need an approach to coalition-building that is highly community-specific, yet networked nationwide, similar to that used by the progressive labor organization Jobs With Justice. The range of groups that turned out on November 21 was promising, and they have vowed to stay committed to a "People's Campaign for Justice at Wal-Mart."

Asked how long it will take to unionize Wal-Mart, Gretchen Adams, who is 56, answers without hesitation: "The rest of my life." But she's determined. As a manager opening a new store in Las Vegas, Adams says, "I was not allowed to hire any experienced help, because they might be union." Now, she deadpans, "I'm trying to get Wal-Mart the help it needs."

In this selection, we turn to the issues of driving a car and flying in a domestic airplane mentioned at the beginning of this section, and how the lenses of diversity and civil rights and liberties are relevant. The issue of racial profiling emerges on the

roads and in the air. Racial profiling can be defined as using a person's race as a primary factor in stopping, arresting, or interrogating individuals. Before 9/11 most cases involving profiling concerned race and the criminal justice system. Typically, profiling debates centered on police use of race as a (or the) factor in deciding whether to stop and interrogate drivers of vehicles. This has become known as "driving while black." It has been argued by some that the higher percentages of African-Americans arrested or in prison are due, at least in part, to the discriminatory behavior by the police in performing their law enforcement duties, while many law enforcement officials claim that it is a necessary tool in fighting crime.

Since 9/11, much of the public focus on profiling has centered on a number of cases where those who appear to be of Middle Eastern descent (even if they are American citizens) have been denied boarding, or who have been taken off airplanes even after clearing all checkpoints. This has become known as "Flying While Arab," and is the subject of the article by David Harris, a professor of law at the University of Toledo. In this piece Harris makes clear that, even without raising the issue of its constitutionality, racial profiling is a relatively ineffective tool for law enforcement. This has been demonstrated in the 'war on drugs' and the use of profiling of Latinos and African-Americans. As Harris points out, "race and ethnic appearance are very poor predictors of behavior." In addition, profiling by police alienates minority communities, thus further reducing police effectiveness in prevention and apprehension. Added to that are the civil rights and civil liberties issues surrounding profiling. Does the Constitution allow profiling based on race or ethnic appearance if it is the only factor? What if race or ethnicity is one of several factors? Even if race and ethnicity is one of several factors, how well does a demographic characteristic of an individual translate to behavior?

Flying while Arab: Lessons from the Racial Profiling Controversy

DAVID HARRIS

In the aftermath of the September 11 tragedies in New York and Washington DC we Americans have heard countless times that our country has "changed forever." In many ways, especially in terms of national and personal security, this is quite true. Americans have always assumed that terrorism and other violent manifestations of the world's problems did not and would never happen here, that our geographic isolation

---

David Harris, "Flying while Arab: Lessons from the Racial Profiling Controversy," *Civil Rights Journal*, vol. 6, no. 1 (Winter 2002), pp. 8–13. Reprinted by permission of the author. © 2002 David Harris.

by the Atlantic and Pacific Oceans protected us. Indeed, since the Civil War, the United States has experienced no sustained violence or war on its own soil. Sadly, we know now that we are vulnerable, and that like countries all over the world, we must take steps to protect ourselves.

This is the new reality that Americans find themselves adjusting to: searches and inspections of ourselves and our belongings when we enter public buildings and areas, such as government offices, sports stadiums, and airport concourses; increased presence of law enforcement and even military personnel; enhanced police powers and curtailed civil liberties; and new powers and tactics our government will use to deal more strictly with foreigners and immigrants. While some of these changes amount to little more than inconveniences, others—particularly changes in the law that limit individual freedom while expanding government power—are in fact major changes in our way of life and the core values and meaning of American society. The U.S. Congress has already passed a sweeping piece of legislation, increasing government power over everything from wiretaps, e-mail, formerly secret grand jury information, to the detention and trial of noncitizens.

We know that the United States is a nation of immigrants—that, in many ways, immigrants built our great nation. We know that the immigrant experience has, in many ways, been at the core of the American experience, along with the experiences of African Americans liberated from slavery. The diversity and energy that immigrants have brought to our country has been, and continues to be, one of our greatest strengths. But, we also know that we have sometimes dealt harshly and unfairly with immigrants and noncitizen residents, especially in times of national emergency and crisis. Thus, it is critical that we try to understand the implications of the changes that have taken place and will continue because of the events of September 11—changes in the very idea of what America is, and in what it will be in the future.

One of these changes has been particularly noticeable—both because it represents a radical shift in what we did prior to September 11, and because it also continues a public discussion that was taking place in our country before that terrible day. Racial profiling—the use of race or ethnic appearance as a factor in deciding who merits police attention as a suspicious person—has undergone a sudden and almost complete rehabilitation. Prior to September 11, many Americans had recognized racial profiling for what it is—a form of institutional discrimination that had gone unquestioned for too long. Thirteen states had passed anti-profiling bills of one type or another, and hundreds of police departments around the country had begun to collect data on all traffic stops, in order to facilitate better, unbiased practices. On the federal level, Congressman John Conyers, Jr., of Michigan and Senator Russell Feingold of Wisconsin had introduced the End Racial Profiling Act of 2001, a bill aimed at directly confronting and reducing racially biased traffic stops through a comprehensive, management-based, carrot-and-stick approach.

September 11 dramatically recast the issue of racial profiling. Suddenly, racial profiling was not a discredited law enforcement tactic that alienated and injured citizens while it did little to combat crime and drugs; instead, it became a vital tool to assure national security, especially in airports. The public discussion regarding the targets of profiling changed too—from African Americans, Latinos, and other minorities suspected of domestic crime, especially drug crime, to Arab Americans, Muslims, and others of Middle Eastern origin, who looked like the suicidal hijackers of September 11. In some respects, this was not hard to understand. The September 11 attacks had caused catastrophic damage and loss of life among innocent civilians; people were shocked, stunned, and afraid. And they knew that all of the hijackers were Arab or Middle Eastern men carrying out the deadly threats of Osama bin Laden's al Qaeda terrorist network based in the Middle East, which of course claims Islam as its justification for the attacks and many others around the world. Therefore, many said that it just makes sense to profile people who looked Arab, Muslim, or Middle Eastern. After all, "they" were the ones who'd carried out the attacks and continued to threaten us; ignoring these facts amounted to some kind of political correctness run amok in a time of great danger.

* * * * *

CATEGORICAL THINKING

We must hope that we have learned the lessons of . . . history—that the emotions of the moment, when we feel threatened, can cause us to damage our civil liberties and our fellow citizens, particularly our immigrant populations. And it is this legacy that should make us think now, even as we engage in a long and detailed investigation of the September 11 terror attacks. As we listen to accounts of that investigation, reports indicate that the investigation has been strongly focused on Arab Americans and Muslims. What's more, private citizens have made Middle Eastern appearance an important criterion in deciding how to react to those who look different around them. Many of these reports have involved treatment of persons of Middle Eastern descent in airports.

In itself, this is not really surprising. We face a situation in which there has been a terrorist attack by a small group of suicidal hijackers, and as far as we know, all of those involved were Arabs and Muslims and had Arabic surnames. Some or all had entered the country recently. Given the incredibly high stakes, some Americans have reacted to Middle Easterners as a group, based on their appearance. In a way, this is understandable. We seldom have much information on any of the strangers around us, so we tend to think in broad categories like race and gender. When human beings experience fear, it is a natural reaction to make judgments concerning our safety based on these broad categories, and to avoid those who arouse fear in us. This may translate easily into a type of racial and ethnic profiling, in which—as has been reported—passengers on airliners refuse to fly with other passengers who have a Middle Eastern appearance.

USE OF RACE AND ETHNIC APPEARANCE IN LAW ENFORCEMENT

The far more worrying development, however, is the possibility that profiling of Arabs and Muslims will become standard procedure in law enforcement. Again, it is not hard to understand the impulse; we want to catch and stop these suicidal hijackers, every one of whom fits the description of Arab or Muslim. So we stop, question, and search more of these people because we believe it's a way to play the odds. If all the September 11 terrorists were Middle Easterners, then we get the biggest bang for the enforcement buck by questioning, searching, and screening as many Middle Easterners as possible. This should, we think, give us the best chance of finding those who helped the terrorists or those bent on creating further havoc.

*****

As we think about the possible profiling of Arabs and Muslims, recall the arguments made for years about domestic efforts against drugs and crime. African Americans and Latinos are disproportionately involved in drug crime, proponents of profiling said; therefore concentrate on them. Many state and local police agencies, led by the federal Drug Enforcement Administration, did exactly that from the late 1980s on. We now know that police departments in many jurisdictions used racial profiling, especially in efforts to get drugs and guns off the highways and out of the cities. For example, state police in Maryland used a profile on Interstate 95 during the 1990s in an effort to apprehend drug couriers. According to data from the state police themselves, while only 17 percent of the drivers on the highway were African American, over 70 percent of those stopped and searched were black. Statistics from New Jersey, New York, and other jurisdictions showed similar patterns: the only factor that predicted who police stopped and searched was race or ethnicity. (2) No other factor—not driving behavior, not the crime rate of an area or neighborhood, and not reported crimes that involved persons of particular racial or ethnic groups—explained the outcomes that showed great racial or ethnic disproportionalities among those stopped and searched.

But as we look back, what really stands out is how ineffective this profile-based law enforcement was. If proponents of profiling were right—that police should concentrate on minorities because criminals were disproportionately minorities—focusing on "those people" should yield better returns on the investment of law enforcement resources in crime fighting than traditional policing does. In other words, using profiles that include racial and ethnic appearance should succeed more often than enforcement based on other, less sophisticated techniques. In any event, it should not succeed less often than traditional policing. But in fact, in departments that focused on African Americans, Latinos, and other minorities, the "hit rates"—the rates of searches that succeeded in finding contraband like drugs or guns—were actually lower for minorities than were the hit rates for whites, who of course were not apprehended by using a racial or ethnic profile. That's right: when police agencies used race or ethnic appearance as a factor—not as the only factor but one factor among many—they did not get the higher returns on their enforcement efforts that they were expecting. Instead, they did not do as well; their use of traditional police methods against whites did a better job than racial profiling, and did not sweep a high number of innocent people into law enforcement's net.

The reason that this happened is subtle but important: race and ethnic appearance are very poor predictors of behavior. Race and ethnicity describe people well, and there is absolutely nothing wrong with using skin color or other features to describe known suspects. But since only a very small percentage of African Americans and Latinos participate in the drug trade, race and ethnic appearance do a bad job identifying the particular African Americans and Latinos in whom police should be interested. Racial and ethnic profiling caused police to spread their enforcement activities far too widely and indiscriminately. The results of this misguided effort have been disastrous for law enforcement. This treatment has alienated African Americans, Latinos, and other minorities from the police—a critical strategic loss in the fight against crime, since police can only win this fight if they have the full cooperation and support of those they serve. And it is precisely this lesson we ought to think about now, as the cry goes up to use profiling and intensive searches against people who look Arab, Middle Eastern, or Muslim.

PROFILING TO CATCH TERRORISTS

Using race, ethnic appearance, or religion as a way to decide who to regard as a potential terrorist will almost surely produce the same kinds of results: no effect on terrorist activity; many innocent people treated like suspects; damage to our enforcement and prevention efforts.

Even if the suicide hijackers of September 11 shared a particular ethnic appearance or background, subjecting all Middle Easterners to intrusive questioning, stops, or searches will have a perverse and unexpected effect: it will spread our enforcement and detection efforts over a huge pool of people who police would not otherwise think worthy of attention. The vast majority of people who look like Mohammed Atta and the other hijackers will never have anything to do with any kind of ethnic or religious extremism. Yet a profile that includes race, ethnicity, or religion may well include them, drawing them into the universe of people who law enforcement will stop, question, and search. Almost all of them will be people who would not otherwise have attracted police attention, because no other aspect of their behavior would have drawn scrutiny. Profiling will thus drain enforcement efforts and resources away from more worthy investigative efforts and tactics that focus on the close observation of behavior—like the buying of expensive one-way tickets with cash just a short time before takeoff, as some of the World Trade Center hijackers did.

This has several important implications. First, just as happened with African Americans and Latinos in the war on drags, profiling of Arabs and Muslims will be overinclusive—it will put many more under police suspicion of terrorist activity than would otherwise be warranted. Almost all of these people will be hard-working, tax-paying, law-abiding individuals. While they might understand one such stop to be a mere inconvenience that they must put up with for the sake of national security, repetition of these experiences for large numbers of people within the same ethnic groups will lead to resentment, alienation, and anger at the authorities.

Second, and perhaps more important, focusing on race and ethnicity keeps police attention on a set of surface details that tells us very little and draws officers' attention away from what is much more important and concrete: behavior. The two most important tools law enforcement agents have in preventing crime and catching criminals are observation of behavior and intelligence. As any experienced police officer knows, what's important in understanding who's up to no good is not what people look like, but what they do. Investigating people who "look suspicious" will often lead officers down the wrong path; the key to success is to observe behavior. Anyone who simply looks different may seem strange or suspicious to the untrained eye; the veteran law enforcement officer knows that suspicious behavior is what really should attract attention and investigation. Thus focusing on those who "look suspicious" will necessarily take police attention away from those who act suspicious. Even in the current climate, in which we want to do everything possible to prevent another attack and to apprehend those who destroyed the World Trade Center and damaged the Pentagon, law enforcement resources are not infinite. We Americans must make decisions on how we run our criminal investigation and prevention efforts that move us away from doing just anything, and toward doing what is most effective.

Third, if observation of suspicious behavior is one of law enforcement's two important tools, using profiles of Arabs, Muslims, and other Middle Easterners can damage our capacity to make use of the other tool: the gathering, analysis, and use of intelligence. There is nothing exotic about intelligence; it simply means information that can be useful in crime fighting. If we are concerned about terrorists of Middle Eastern origin, among the most fertile places from which to gather intelligence will be the Arab American and Muslim communities. If we adopt a security policy that stigmatizes every member of these groups in airports and other public places with intrusive stops, questioning, and searches, we will alienate them from the enforcement efforts at precisely the time we need them most. And the larger the population we subject to this treatment, the greater the total amount of damage we inflict on law-abiding persons.

And of course the profiling of Arabs and Muslims assumes that we need worry about only one type of terrorist. We must not forget that, prior to the attacks on September 11, the most deadly terrorist attack on American soil was carried out not by Middle Easterners with Arabic names and accents, but by two very average American white men: Timothy McVeigh, a U.S. Army veteran from upstate New York, and Terry Nichols, a farmer from Michigan. Yet we were smart enough in the wake of McVeigh and Nichols' crime not to call for a profile emphasizing the fact that the perpetrators were white males. The unhappy truth is that we just don't know what the next group of terrorists might look like.

* * * * *

CONCLUSION

The terrorist attacks in New York and Washington, DC, present us with many difficult choices that will test us. We will have to ask ourselves deep questions: Who are we, as a nation? What is important to us? What values lay at the core of our Constitution and our democracy? How will we find effective ways to secure ourselves without giving up what is best about our country? The proper balance between safety and civil rights will sometimes be difficult to see. But we should not simply repeat the mistakes of the past as we take on this new challenge. Only our adversaries would gain from that.

Notes

2. For Maryland numbers, see John Lamberth, testimony before the Congressional Black Caucus, 1998, accessed at www.lamberthconsulting.com/downloads/cbc_presentation.doc; see also Wilkins v. Maryland State Police, No. CCB-93-468 (order of Apr. 22, 1997) and Maryland State Conference of NAACP Branches, et al. v. Maryland Department of State Polic, et al., 72 F.Supp 2d 560 (September 1999). For New Jersey, see John Lamberth, "Revised Statistical Analysis of the Incidence of Police Stops and Arrests of Black Drivers/Travelers on the New Jersey Turnpike Between Exits or Interchanges 1 and 3 from the Years 1988 through 1991." November 1994, accessed at www.lamberthconsulting.com/research_articles.asp. For New York,

see Eliot Spitzer, Attorney General of the State of New York, "The New York Police Department's 'Stop and Frisk' Practices: A Report to the People of the State of New York," 1999, accessed at www.oag.state.ny.us/press/reports/stop_frisk/stp_frsk.pdf.

The final piece in this section shifts our analysis to the rights of gay, lesbian, or transgender Americans—groups that have not enjoyed the same sort of legal protections as those of African-Americans or women when it comes to issues of civil rights and liberties. Indeed, questions of gay marriage and same-sex partner health benefits, military service by gays, and adoption rights by gays have seen considerable opposition in the United States, with less legal recourse available to challenge such opposition.

In the context of a discussion on civil rights, the Eric Deggans reading points out a certain irony regarding the issue of gay rights. As described in the St. Petersburg Times *newspaper article, Deggans notes that many African-Americans, in large part because of their religious beliefs, take a fairly conservative attitude toward gay rights. There is less tolerance for gays (who are, or are not, African-American) and, in general, no sense of a bond or a feeling of a common struggle that might be expected, given the civil rights struggles experienced by African-Americans. This reading thus challenges an assumption of many diversity debates: that minority groups "naturally" align or feel an affinity for one another. Readers may ask themselves whether it is fair to think solidarity "should" develop between particular groups, why it does or does not, and if, ultimately, this solidarity furthers or undermines American democracy.*

Similar Struggles: Gay Rights and Civil Rights

ERIC DEGGANS

* * * * *

Ask Nadine Smith whether the struggle for gay rights can be compared to black people's classic civil rights struggle, and she chuckles a little before responding.

As executive director of the Tampa-based advocacy group Equality Florida, she's at the center of the fight for gay marriage rights, gay adoption rights and more. And

Eric Deggans, "Similar Struggles: Gay Rights and Civil Rights," *St. Petersburg Times,* January 18, 2004, p. 1P. Reprinted by permission of the St. Petersburg Times.

as a black lesbian, Smith admits she "sort of lives in the intersection" of all those questions.

Comparing the struggles to conquer homophobia, sexism and racism aren't academic exercises for her; it's the story of her life.

"Sometimes this question is phrased in a way that plays into the hands of bigots by asking people to rank oppression . . . asking people "Who has it worse?'" Smith said. "I've experienced racism, sexism and homophobia. And the worst one is whatever one you're dealing with right now."

The Rev. Walter Fauntroy offers a similarly pensive response to the same question. Now age 70, Fauntroy was the Washington, D.C., coordinator for the historic March on Washington in 1963 that produced Martin Luther King's renowned "I Have a Dream" speech. As a former delegate for Washington in the U.S. House and former head of the Congressional Black Caucus, he spearheaded countless civil rights initiatives in the community and in the legislature.

But when a proposal surfaced to include a gay speaker on the 20th anniversary celebration of the March in 1983, Fauntroy chaired the group of organizers who turned it down (he said gay speakers have appeared at anniversary celebrations since 1993).

And though he believes black and gay people's struggle for rights are "exactly" the same when it comes to five key areas—access to income, education, health care, housing and criminal justice—he draws the line at the most visible issue now before the courts and community: gay marriage.

"My religious tradition says (homosexuality) is an abomination," said Fauntroy, who serves as pastor of the New Bethel Baptist Church in Washington and has publicly supported a constitutional amendment defining marriage as "the union of a man and a woman."

"Don't come to me asking society to attribute to a same-sex union the term "marriage.' It's a misnomer," the pastor added. "Have your same-sex union; have your contracts. But don't confuse my young people into thinking they don't need one another. Don't tell my young women they don't need a man."

As the country prepares to celebrate the birthday of one of the country's greatest civil rights leaders Monday, the question resurfaces: Is the fight to expand gay rights comparable to the civil rights struggle for black people that remains Martin Luther King's greatest legacy?

If so, will those opposing gay marriage laws, gay adoption rights and openly gay military service wind up on the same side of history as segregationists and alarmists who once opposed so-called "race-mixing"?

And if not, why not?

One component clouding the issue on all sides is emotion. Black people, who may or may not agree with homosexuality itself, remain wary of associating other struggles with the effort to end America's centuries-long legacy of racism and segregation. Gay people suspect that much of the resistance to comparing the two struggles stems from homophobia.

"A lot of people have a visceral reaction to the thought of gay sex," said Matt Foreman of the National Gay and Lesbian Task Force in Washington. "It's been called in our movement, the "Ick Factor.' But if you have an opportunity to sit down and talk with someone about the issues, many times they come around."

Put the question to Henry Louis Gates Jr.—one of the country's leading scholars on race and civil rights as chair of African and African American Studies at Harvard University—and he reacts as if you've asked him whether rain is wet.

"The black community has traditionally been homophobic . . . (it's) deeply rooted in our culture, and I don't understand why," said Gates, now launching a PBS series and companion book on the current state of black America called America: Beyond the Color Line.

"I don't understand why the movement to legitimize gay marriage would bother people so much," added Gates, while noting that, outside issues of civil rights and social justice, black people often hold conservative political viewpoints. "We have to fight to educate people and transform that visceral response . . . (because) one of the strengths of the black civil rights movement is that it's served as a model for so many other movements. We who have suffered so much should also be the most compassionate."

And Gates isn't the only prominent black voice to take this point of view. Both black presidential candidates, Carol Mosley Braun, who dropped out Thursday, and Al Sharpton, have called the gay marriage fight a civil rights issue in the traditional sense—along with luminaries such as Julian Bond, Martin Luther King III and his mother, Coretta Scott King.

Staffers at the King Center in Atlanta declined to schedule an interview with Mrs. King, saying they preferred to focus on community service at the celebration of Dr. King's birthday. But she has spoken out on the subject in the past, equating homophobia to racism.

"I still hear people say that I should not be talking about the rights of lesbian and gay people and I should stick to the issue of racial justice," Mrs. King said in 1998, according to Reuters news service. "But I hasten to remind them that Martin Luther King Jr. said, "Injustice anywhere is a threat to justice everywhere. 'I appeal to everyone who believes in Martin Luther King Jr.'s dream to make room at the table of brother- and sisterhood for lesbian and gay people."

Indeed, plans for a nationwide series of rallies during Valentine's Day week to protest a constitutional gay marriage ban—including a Feb. 14 rally at Lowry Park in Tampa—bear all the hallmarks of classic, grass-roots civil rights actions. the rallies are sponsored by Metropolitan Community Churches, the Equality Campaign and DontAmend.com.

But those who say homosexuality is immoral and unhealthy charge that gay activists are "hijacking" the nation's civil rights movement; using hard-fought gains for racial minorities and women to justify an orientation many find morally repugnant.

"Skin color or ethnicity involves no moral choices . . . but how you conduct yourself sexually does," said Robert Knight, a former Los Angeles Times staffer who now serves as director of the Culture & Family Institute, an affiliate of Concerned Women for America, which advocates the promotion of biblical values among citizens.

"They are trying to hijack the moral capital of the black civil rights movement and use it to force society to affirm their behavior, regardless of other people's moral beliefs about it," added Knight, who can quote reams of medical studies and surveys backing his religion-based belief that homosexuality is a dysfunctional choice, not a born trait.

Fauntroy expressed fears that infighting among black people and gay people over such questions may distract progressive voters at a time when the focus should be elsewhere: namely, on breaking conservatives' hold on the White House and Congress during an important election year.

"Right wing racists . . . use these one-sided issues to divert attention from the fundamental issues of how you spread income around," he said. "I am still smarting from the use of prayer in the schools and abortion . . . to foster voting on sideshow issues. I resent having to spend my valuable time discussing another sideshow issue."

* * * * *

When organizers of the 40th anniversary of the March on Washington officially invited gay and lesbian advocacy groups to help plan last year's celebration—a first in the history of the event—Matt Foreman joined in, helping draw an estimated 1,500 gay and lesbian supporters to the celebration.

And on some issues—the way religion is used to justify persecution, the way unpopular court cases are paving the way for mainstream acceptance—he sees the parallels between his struggle for civil rights and the struggle to eradicate racism. But even Foreman thinks some gay rights advocates go too far.

"The problem is that . . . people in the gay and lesbian movement have frequently tried to cloak themselves in the civil rights movement for African Americans without recognizing the differences . . . and that has quite rightly been seen as offensive," said Foreman, who pointed out a recent press release from one advocacy group calling marriage bureaus "the new lunch counters" for gay people, evoking the sit-in protests at segregated restaurants in the '60s.

"We don't have separate restrooms, we are not being met by dogs and truncheons (and) that is a huge, profound difference," he added, noting that people of color may be even more offended in hearing such comparisons come from a group the media often portrays as affluent, male and white.

"Gay people have been persecuted throughout history, but there is nothing to compare to state-sanctioned centuries of oppression," Foreman said. "And many gay and lesbian people are able to or are forced to hide their orientation and avoid discrimination." The key, for some, may lie in separating the history of each group's persecution from their struggles to overcome it. Trying to draw similarities between racism and homophobia seems a losing proposition. But looking at the progress both groups have made in fighting to earn new rights may be instructive.

For example, when the Supreme Court struck down laws against interracial marriage in the 1968 Loving vs. Virginia case, a Gallup Poll showed 72 percent of respondents disapproved of such unions. It would take 23 years of regular surveys before the percentage of those approving interracial marriage would outnumber the percentage of those who disapproved.

The lesson: Polls showing widespread current opposition to gay marriage (at 60 percent among both white and black people, according to a November poll by the Pew Research Center), may change with time.

In his 1996 book One More River to Cross: Black and Gay in America, author Keith Boykin devoted an entire chapter to "The Common Language of Racism and

Homophobia," noting that arguments once used to justify segregation and racial oppression now surface in antigay discussions.

Indeed, the position gay rights activists find themselves in now—victory in several key court decisions that has sparked a backlash in the mainstream; sympathetic media coverage that is changing some minds—could be comparable to the position black civil rights activists found themselves after the Loving case or the Brown vs. Board of Education decision striking down school segregation in 1954.

"It's amazing to me how we don't learn from our past experiences," said Boykin, a former writer for the Clearwater Times. "(Pulitzer Prize-winning historian) Barbara Tuchman once said every successful revolution eventually puts on the robes of its oppressor. I'm afraid in the case of black people, we've seen that happen again."

But for some who oppose homosexuality, no amount of historical comparison will change their minds.

"Just because I don't want a gay man to teach my son in school, that is not discrimination," said Rev. Richard Bennett Jr., whose African American Council of Christian Clergy in 2002 circulated fliers to Miami-area black churches saying Dr. King would be "outraged" at efforts to link gay rights advocacy with the black civil rights struggle."

"If my daughter plays with a little girl who says I have two mommies or two daddies, that's affecting my children," he added. "For them to compare the civil rights with gay rights—it should be offensive to every African-American in the whole United States."

DISCUSSION QUESTIONS

1. Should colleges and universities use a student's race as a factor in determining who will be admitted to their institution? What are the reasons for using race as a factor; what are the reasons against using race?

2. Should it be permissible for the police or for airline security officers to "target" minorities or those who look like they are from the Middle East? Is the public's safety more important than the inconvenience of a few individuals, especially when it comes to something as important (and fatal, if the wrong decisions are made) as air travel? Alternatively, does racial profiling threaten the very values Americans hold dear and want to protect from attack? Is it even fair to assume that those of Middle Eastern heritage are more apt than other groups to want to harm the United States?

3. What's so wrong with Wal-Mart, if anything? Why is it a problem if the company aggressively seeks to cut costs? Don't we as consumers want the lowest possible prices? Is it possible that products can be "too cheap" (that is, are inexpensive, but at costs not reflected in the price of the product)? If Wal-Mart is found guilty of gender discrimination will you still shop there? Should others? Who is most apt to have that choice?

4. Should U.S. citizens who are gay have all of the same rights as heterosexual citizens (including the right to marriage, to adopt, and serve in the military)? Why or

why not? Are some of our prevailing attitudes about public policy based on religious beliefs that might not be accommodating to modern society?

5. Why is U.S. politics and society seemingly so focused on race and gender? Would the polity be more effective if all policies were "race neutral"? Wouldn't that be the most fair? Alternatively, would "race or gender neutral" undermine the guarantee that minority rights are protected in a land of majority rule? How, if at all, can we strike the right balance?

Additional Resources

http://www.aclu.org
The American Civil Liberties Union engages in legal action, advocacy, and education on a wide range of civil rights and civil liberties issues. The web site includes information on racial profiling, through its Racial Justice Program.

http://civilrightsproject.ucla.edu
This web site provides research information on topics relating to civil rights issues, including higher education admissions, affirmative action, K–12 desegregation, immigration, segregated living patterns in metropolitan areas, and criminal justice.

http://www.now.org
The web site for the National Organization for Women (NOW) includes information on matters related to gender discrimination and advocacy for women's rights.

http://www.naacp.org
The web site for the National Association for the Advancement of Colored People (NAACP), covering a wide range of civil rights and civil liberties issues.

http://www.glaad.org
The Gay and Lesbian Alliance Against Defamation advocates for gay and lesbian rights, tracks portrayal of gays in the media, and provides opportunities to mobilize supporters on a variety of policy issues.

http://pdba.georgetown.edu/IndigenousPeoples/introduction.html
The Center for Latin American Studies Program at Georgetown University has established a "Political Database of the Americas" that provides information on civil rights and civil liberties, constitutions, political participation, and demographic trends related to indigenous people.

http://www.nifi.org/
The National Issues Forums Institute is a non-partisan organization that seeks to promote deliberation of public policy issues. Among the topics covered include affirmative action, immigration policy, and civil justice.

To Kill a Mockingbird (1962) is based on Harper Lee's Pulitzer–Prize winning book, this film traces the attempt by a white attorney, Atticus Finch, to defend an African-American man accused of raping a white woman in Alabama during the 1930s.

Mississippi Burning (1988) is a fictionalized account of the murder of three civil rights workers by the Ku Klux Klan in the 1960s.

Eyes on the Prize (Part I, 1987; Part II, 1990) is a 14-hour PBS documentary covering the U.S. Civil Rights Movement and divided into two parts: *America's Civil Rights Years* (1954–1965) and *America at the Racial Crossroads* (1965–1985). Considered by many to be an important record of the civil rights movement, using primary sources and tracking the impact of the civil rights movement on average people.

Director Spike Lee explores race relations in the United States through such films as *Do the Right Thing* (1989), *Jungle Fever* (1991), and *Malcolm X* (1992).

PHOTO CREDITS

SECTION 1 – PAGE 7
Image Bank/Getty

SECTION 2 – PAGE 27
James Nielsen/AFP/Getty

SECTION 3 – PAGE 48
NBC Archive

SECTION 4 – PAGE 74
Steve Miller/AP

SECTION 5 – PAGE 108
Chris Stewart/Dayton Daily News/AP

SECTION 6 – PAGE 138
Joe Raedle/Getty

SECTION 7 – PAGE 169
Joshua Roberts/Reuters/Landov

SECTION 8 – PAGE 195
John Paul Filo/CBS/Landov

SECTION 9 – PAGE 228
Brennan Linsley/AP

SECTION 10 – PAGE 249
Roger L. Wollenberg/UPI/Landov

SECTION 11 – PAGE 275
Jason DeCrow/AP

SECTION 12 – PAGE 304
Larry Downing/Reuters/Landov

SECTION 13 – PAGE 323
Peter Marshall